P9-DNI-442

CONCORD FREE
CONCORD
MA
PUBLIC LIBRARY

SEP 2 5 2013

Drinking History

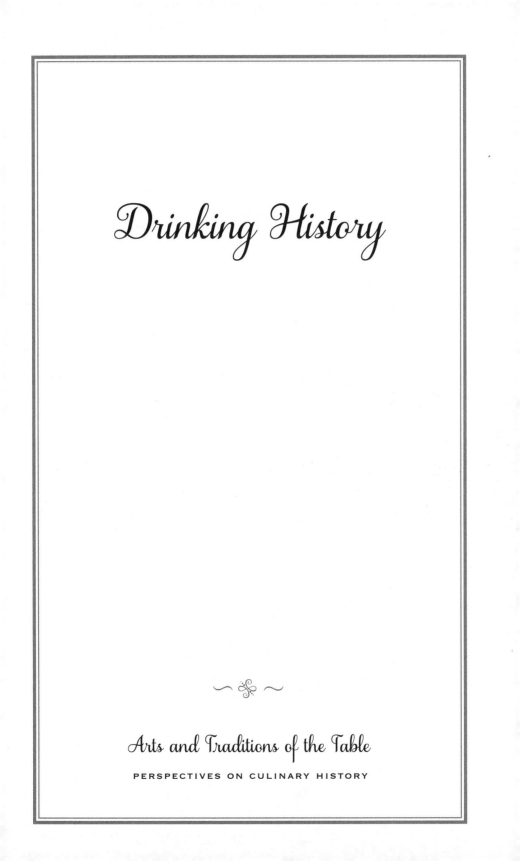

Arts and Traditions of the Table

PERSPECTIVES ON CULINARY HISTORY

ANDREW F. SMITH

Drinking History

Fifteen Turning Points in the
MAKING OF AMERICAN BEVERAGES

COLUMBIA UNIVERSITY PRESS / NEW YORK

6 41. 2
Smith

Columbia University Press
Publishers Since 1893
New York   Chichester, West Sussex
cup.columbia.edu

Copyright © 2013 Andrew F. Smith
All rights reserved

Library of Congress Cataloging-in-Publication Data

Smith, Andrew F., 1946–
   Drinking history : fifteen turning points in the making
of American beverages / Andrew F. Smith.
      p. cm. — (Arts and traditions of the table)
   Includes bibliographical references and index.
   ISBN 978-0-231-15116-0 (cloth : alk. paper)
   ISBN 978-0-231-53099-6 (e-book)
   1. Beverages—United States—History. I. Title.
TP527.S65 2013
641.2—dc23

                                                           2012010134

∞

Columbia University Press books are printed on permanent and durable
acid-free paper.

This book is printed on paper with recycled content.
Printed in the United States of America

c 10 9 8 7 6 5 4 3 2 1

Cover image: Courtesy of The Advertising Archives / Cover design: Lisa Hamm

References to Internet Web sites (URLs) were accurate at the time of
writing. Neither the author nor Columbia University Press is responsible for
URLs that may have expired or changed since the manuscript was prepared.

Contents

Contents

Preface

HUMANKIND'S most basic physical need is water, which for most Americans is readily available and cheap. However, not content to just replenish our bodies with plain water, we have devised ingenious ways to flavor and process it into all sorts of palatable drinks, which are sometimes nutritious and health enhancing but other times not. We have added natural and artificial substances—bark, leaves, seeds, spices, beans, nuts, honey, herbs, fruit, flowers, grasses, grains, sugars, vitamins, minerals, and all sorts of chemicals—to water and processed it in ingenious ways, creating a great cornucopia of beverages that are alcoholic and nonalcoholic, carbonated and caffeinated, heated and room temperature, cool and frozen, watery and thick, spicy and plain.

I am particularly intrigued by the wild assortment of beverages Americans drink. Today alone, the total number of domestic and imported beers, wines, spirits, coffees, teas, sodas, bottled waters, sports drinks, energy drinks, and dairy drinks consumed in America surely run into the tens of thousands. These beverages are sold in several forms—bottled, boxed, canned, frozen, powdered—and sipped, sniffed, savored, guzzled, quaffed, or chugged from glasses, mugs, cups, bottles, cartons, or straight from a tap or fountain. They can be bought in all sorts of places—supermarkets, convenience stores, vending machines, bars, lounges, fast food chains, restaurants, saloons, cafes, cafeterias, ordered online, and even made in the home.

As a culinary historian, I am curious about how Americans created this diverse and complex beverage scene and why beverages have shifted over time. American beverage history is complex, and numerous books and articles have been written about particular drinks; even more have been written about major historical events, such as the Revolutionary War, the Whiskey Rebellion, and Prohibition, in which particular beverages played key roles. It would be impossible to condense a complete discussion of American beverage history into a single book.

For the past few years, I have grappled with two related questions: Why do Americans drink the beverages that we do? And how can the evolution of American beverages be presented in the most understandable fashion? My answer has been to focus on fifteen events or turning points that introduce threads of American beverage history. Thirteen of these events focus on beverage categories that often intersect, and two focus on historical periods—colonial beverages and the temperance and prohibition movements, which have affected American beverages for 400 years. American drinking habits are embedded in broader societal trends, such as those related to industrialization, transportation systems, internal migrations, external immigrations, political reform efforts, advertising and promotion, scientific discoveries and new technologies, governmental regulation and taxation, corporate centralization, and globalization. The relationships between American beverages and these broader trends are significant, but I touch upon them only tangentially in this book.

This book introduces American beverage history—its significant events, creators, celebrities, promoters, and controversies. It is also introduces the vast literature on American beverage history. In this work, I have tried to present the entire history of American beverages, both alcoholic and non-alcoholic, simply because of the tremendous interconnections among them. An increase in sales of one beverage usually results in a decrease in sales of other beverages. Focusing just on one beverage or a beverage category often fails to illuminate these connections.

My approach is mainly explanatory and descriptive rather than normative. Although this is primarily a book about America's past, it is also about how we think about beverages today. For those who believe that American beverages are on the right track, this book offers a partial history of how we arrived at a system that has emphasized convenience, massive diversity, corporate concentration, and consumer choice. For those interested in changing the current system, this book offers insight into how we ended up where we are today—and perhaps even provides inspiration for alternative approaches for the future.

Acknowledgments

I WOULD LIKE TO THANK Linda Civitello, Janet Clark, Lynne Olver, and Barry Popik for uncovering significant sources; Frank Clark for his comments on early versions of the colonial chapter; Alice Ross for her comments on beverages consumed by American Indians; Mark Pendergrast for his comments on coffee and soda; Erika Janik for her comments on cider; Peter LaFrance for his comments on beer; Joseph Carlin for his comments on cocktails; Ian Williams for his interview and comments on rum and tequila; Tyler Colman for his comments on wine; Alissa Hamilton for her interview and comments on orange juice; Kevin Kosar for his comments on whiskey and distilled spirits; Elizabeth Rojak for her comments on bottled water; Clarissa Dillon for her information about gin in colonial America; and Anne Mendelson for her comments and reviews of the milk chapter. I would also like to thank those on the 19th Century Foodways, SavoryFare 2, and Association for the Study of Food and Society listservs who responded to my queries.

I warmly thank Charles Roebuck, Bonnie Slotnick, and Tatiana Kling, who read, edited, and commented on the manuscript, and my agent, Giles Anderson, for his comments on the book proposal and constant encouragement.

Finally, I would like to thank my students at the New School, especially those in my Drinking History class, who have listened, considered, and argued with me about these past turning points and current implications. I have enjoyed every moment of our formal and informal dialogues and I thank you all for your thoughtful disagreements and kind encouragements over the years.

Although all comments and responses have been appreciated, not all have been accepted or incorporated. I accept all responsibility for any errors that may appear in this work.

Drinking History

Prologue

IN THE BEGINNING was water. Life on Earth began in the oceans, and when life forms emerged on dry land 400 million years ago, water remained quintessential to life. The body weight of all animals is mostly water. Humans, for instance, consist of approximately 55 to 75 percent water, depending on body composition and age.[1] Without water, life on Earth (as we know it) would not exist.

In its purest form, water has no calories, proteins, fats, carbohydrates, vitamins, or minerals, yet it is the most important nutrient for humans. It is the universal solvent, and many substances, such as minerals (calcium, sodium), gases (oxygen, carbon dioxide), and nutrients (B vitamins and vitamin C), are easily dissolved in it; water is an essential part of the human metabolic process. Water performs a variety of functions in the body. It helps carry nutrients to cells, removes waste, and is vital to maintaining the body's temperature. Without regular infusions of water—which for humans should not exceed three days—life ends.

For most of human history, people took water directly from rivers, streams, lakes, and springs. When humans settled down into communities, they dug wells, collected rainwater, and constructed aqueducts to ensure an adequate supply for their personal needs and to support agriculture. Along with settlement also came water polluted with poisonous substances and pathogenic microorganisms, which can cause diseases such as typhoid fever, dysentery, hepatitis, cholera, and many more.

Historically, groups in particular areas developed preferences for beverages with specific flavorings and characteristics: coffee berries in East Africa and the Arabian Peninsula; grapes and grains from the Middle East; tea leaves, citrus, and rice from China; hops and herbs from Europe; sugarcane and spices from South and Southeast Asia; apples from inner Asia; sassafras, cactus, and berries from North America; kola nuts from Africa; and maize, cocoa, and vanilla from Central America. Then there were the domesticated mammals—sheep, donkeys, camels, llamas, horses, and cows—that humans have milked for thousands of years. These things and many more have influenced American beverage history.

Precisely when humans first arrived in North America is unknown. The traditional view is that indigenous peoples from Asia crossed the Bering Strait at least 16,000 years ago and moved down the west coast of the continent.[2] As glaciers receded after the last Ice Age and the North American climate stabilized about 8000 B.C.E., American Indians moved into the present-day Midwest, finally arriving in northeastern America about 1,000 to 2,000 years ago.

Inhabitants of the Americas in prehistoric times mainly drank water, but like those in the Old World, they also flavored their water with a diversity of plants, roots, barks, leaves, herbs, fruit, and cacti. People of pre-Columbian Central America, for instance, enjoyed *atole* (a thick drink made from cornmeal) and *pulque*, a mildly alcoholic beverage made by fermenting sap from the maguey (*Agave americana*) cactus. Chocolate frothed with chili peppers was a favorite beverage of the Aztec elite in Mexico.

Indigenous peoples in what is today the American Southwest were influenced by beverage developments in Mexico. Native Americans groups in Arizona and New Mexico made mildly fermented beverages from corn (*tizwin* or *tulpi*), mesquite pods, agave, and other others. These indigenous peoples may have been the only American Indian groups who made and drank fermented liquids prior to the arrival of Europeans.[3]

Farther north, American Indians created flavored water from such sources as sumac and other berries, indigenous fruit, tree blossoms, mesquite pods, pine needles, saguaro and other cacti, bee balm (*Monarda didyma*), roasted acorns, manzanita fruit (*Arctostaphylos manzanita*), and honey locust beans (*Gleditsia triacanthos*), to name a few.[4] They also drank the broth of boiled meat, according to George H. Loskiel, an eighteenth-century missionary in Pennsylvania. For other occasions, Loskiel observed that the American Indians ground roasted chestnuts, added hot water, and served the drink like coffee. Yet another beverage was made from dried berries, which were ground and combined with water and a sweetener, creating a beverage that was "very agreeable to them."[5]

American Indians drank beverages made from *miko hoyanidja* (pounded roots of a species of willow tree), *pasa* (pounded roots of button snake-root), and *hilis hatki* (ginseng).[6] The most notorious beverage downed by a wide range of the East Coast and Gulf Coast groups was a caffeinated black tea brewed from the stems of yaupon holly (*Ilex vomitoria*), which was employed in specific medicines and ceremonies; as its Latin name suggests, it induces vomiting.[7] These beverages were widely consumed, but they were usually reserved for special occasions.

Although some of these beverages continued to be consumed into the nineteenth century, few survived for long after the arrival of Europeans.[8] The exceptions were a few flavorings, such as sassafras, wintergreen, sarsaparilla, and some tree saps, needles, and buds that were appreciated by European colonists.

Some have survived as flavorings in American beverages.[9] Sassafras (*Sassafras albidum*), an aromatic deciduous tree that is native to eastern North America, was used by American Indians to make a medicinal tea. The roots of sassafras were used by European colonists to flavor beer and to make a medicinal aromatic beverage that was sold on the streets; it was often served with milk and sugar.[10] Sassafras was a popular beverage in the South, particularly during the Civil War.[11] Historically, the sassafras root was an ingredient in root beer, but its use was banned in 1960 by the U.S. Food and Drug Administration.[12] Today, sassafras is used by homebrewers as a beer flavoring.

Wintergreen (for example, *Gaultheria procumbens*) was employed by American Indians as a medicinal tea; it too was an early ingredient in root beer. Today, it is typically used in products such as gum, mints, and mouthwash. Sarsaparilla (*Smilax regelii*) was also consumed as a tea and was used with sassafras in making root beer. In 1819, the U.S. Patent Office issued one of the first patents for a soft drink, which was flavored with sarsaparilla and mead.[13] Today, boutique bottlers continue to use sarsaparilla in carbonated soft drinks.

The sap of the sweet birch (*Betula lenta*) was also made into a medicinal tea in pre-Columbian times. Birch beer, a carbonated boutique soft drink that is usually made from birch bark, is commercially produced today. The sap, buds, and needles of the spruce tree (members of the genus *Picea*) were employed by European Americans in the colonies to make spruce beer, and they have continued to be used as flavorings in some commercial beers and soft drinks.[14] Likewise, American Indians employed the sap of the sugar maple (*Acer saccharum*) as a medicinal "precious remedy."[15] Maple syrup became an important sweetener in America and it continues to be employed in some boutique beers and soft drinks today.

Maize was the most important domesticated plant in pre-Columbian North America. Southwestern Indians made a lightly fermented beverage from corn, and other groups may have done so as well. Some American Indians squeezed juice from corn canes to use as a sweetener to flavor water and other beverages. Maize was readily adopted by most early European colonists as a food and it became an important component in a variety of colonial beverages, including beer and whiskey. Maize has remained America's most important agricultural commodity. It is used in the making of spirits, and corn syrup and other corn products are important components of many beverages that Americans consume today.

Despite diverse pre-Columbian potables, the beverages made from leaves, berries, grapes, grains, grasses, and animals imported from the Old World dominated what most Americans drank then—and still drink. These imports began arriving en masse in 1607.

Clark's Inn, also known as the State House Tavern, built in 1693, was located across the street from the Pennsylvania State House (Independence Hall) in Philadelphia and was a meeting place for colonial and state officials. (Library of Congress, Prints and Photographs Division)

1
Colonial Diversity

O N APRIL 26, 1607, three ships—the *Susan Constant*, the *Godspeed*, and the *Discovery*—sailed into the Chesapeake Bay with approximately 100 colonists onboard. These colonists founded a small settlement along the James River, which became the first successful English colony in North America.

From the beginning, the Jamestown settlement was none too promising, and one serious problem that the colonists faced concerned the issue of beverages. They had brought beer and malt with them, but eventually their supplies ran out and they were reduced to drinking water, which did not please them at all. Although soon after his arrival the colonist George Percy wrote that he was "almost ravished" at the sight of "fresh-waters running through the woods,"[1] he later complained bitterly that there was "neither taverne, beere-house, nor place of relife" in Jamestown.[2] As the colonists dumped refuse into the river and polluted their shallow wells, Percy's views of Virginia water changed: the "cold water taken out of the River; which was, at a floud, verie salt; at a low tide, full of slime and filth, which was the destruction of many of our men."[3]

Six years after the colony's founding, life was still difficult there. A Spanish spy reported the following: "There are about three hundred men there more or less; and the majority sick and badly treated, because they have nothing to eat but bread of maize, with fish; nor do they drink anything but water—all of which is contrary to the nature of the English—on which account they all wish to return and would have done so if they had been at liberty."[4]

Despite these massive hardships, however, Jamestown had turned a corner. More colonists arrived, and things improved. Even without their preferred beverages, the early colonists at Jamestown set in motion a series of events that would change American drinking habits forever.

Background

The first English attempt to establish a colony in North America began on Roanoke Island in 1585. Unfortunately, much of the food supply—including beer—was lost when the boat carrying provisions capsized in the surf while trying to land. Once the fledgling colony was established, the ships left, taking much of the remaining beer with them. The colonists were resourceful, however. Thomas Harriot, an astronomer and ethnographer who learned the Algonquin language before arriving in Roanoke in 1585, later wrote that the colonists took corn and made "some mault, whereof was brued as good ale as was to be desired. So likewise by the help of hops thereof may bee made as good Beere."[5] The colonists' interest in beer was understandable: it was the most important beverage in England, so much so that English families expended an estimated one-third of their budgets on malt for brewing.[6] By the time Harriot's account was published in 1590, however, the Roanoke colony had disappeared, forever leaving unanswered the question of what had happened to the settlers. Almost twenty years passed before the English tried again to establish a colony in North America.

The second English attempt to establish a colony in North America was Jamestown. It was enough of a success a decade after its founding that it encouraged the English to establish more settlements, the next of which was in Massachusetts. In 1620, English settlers stocked the *Mayflower* with both water and beer for the trip to America; these supplies were carefully rationed on the voyage and continued to be rationed in the new settlement that the colonists established at Plymouth. When the *Mayflower* first arrived off Cape Cod, a landing party was sent to reconnoiter the area. The colonists sampled their first "New England water with as much delight as ever we drunke drink in all our lives."[7] Their delight likely resulted from the contrast between the fresh, cold springwater they found and the foul-tasting barreled water they had been drinking on the *Mayflower*. The sailors on the ship were more concerned with the other beverage onboard. They calculated how much beer would be needed for their return voyage, and when their reserves dropped to that amount, the *Mayflower* weighed anchor and left Plymouth.

Although the Plymouth colonists would have appreciated plentiful stores of beer, they "supplied themselves with water," as one resident later put it.[8] William Bradford, the longtime governor of the settlement, wrote that eventually water became as "pleasant unto them as wine or beer had been in foretimes." He was quick to add that "water was not as wholesome as the beer and wine" but concluded that the available water was as good as any in the world and "wholesome enough to us that can be content therewith."[9]

Compared with Jamestown and later southern settlements, New England was well endowed with lakes, springs, streams, and rivers. William Wood, an early resident of Plymouth, proclaimed in 1634 that New England was as

well watered as any land under the Sunne, [with] every family or every two families having a spring of sweet waters betwixt them, which is farre different from the waters of England, being not so sharp, but of a fatter substance and of a jetty color; it is thought there can be no better water in the world, yet dare I not preferre it before good Beere, as some have done, but any man will choose it before bad Beare, Wheay or Buttermilke. Those that drinke it, be as healthfull, fresh and lustie as they that drinke beere.[10]

Even when beer and other beverages were available, water remained America's most commonly consumed beverage; the poor, of course, could not afford to drink much else. But all colonists drank water—either straight or mixed with other beverages, such as cider, wine, beer, and milk. They sometimes sweetened or flavored water with molasses or ginger. As small cities developed in the eighteenth century, their residents usually obtained water from public pumps placed at intervals along the streets. However, contamination of the water supply by sewage became a problem as urban areas grew. This problem was well understood by colonists, who learned to collect rainwater instead of using groundwater, boil water before drinking it, mix water with alcoholic beverages, or just drink something else entirely. In 1724, a Virginian reported that "good springs of excellent water abound everywhere almost, which is very cooling and pleasant in summer, and the general drink of abundance, not so much out of necessity as choice."[11] This was no exaggeration, and European visitors agreed. A German traveler concluded that of all the beverages consumed in Philadelphia, the best was "delicious and healthy water."[12] On the western frontier, where alcohol was less available, water was much more important. As one surveyor on the frontier reported in the 1720s, "All we drink here is water and sometimes rum, but that is very dear and [we have] very little money to buy it."[13]

Throughout the colonial period, water was an essential component in traditional medical potions. For dealing with various diseases, one source recommended drinking warm water, water gruel, barley water, sage or balm tea, or flaxseeds or mullein leaves in water.[14] However, some of the drinking water in the colonies was far from salubrious. One observer credited the ladies of Charlestown, South Carolina, with being "extremely temperate," even to the point of drinking the city's water, which contained sand and dirt.[15] According to a Swedish visitor to New York in the mid-eighteenth century, Albany's water was acidic and "not very agreeable."[16] New York City water was not much better. Wells were dug in the settlement early on; however, because the relationship between drinking water, waste disposal, and disease was only dimly understood, epidemics of typhoid and other diseases ran regularly through the city. More wells were dug, but the water was brackish and not good for drinking. Many residents were fearful of getting sick from impure water and visited springs just north of the settlement, which was then only on the southern tip of Manhattan Island, seeking a fresh and safe supply of drinking water.[17]

Colonial Alcoholic Beverages

It was not just polluted water that drove colonists to drink. Alcohol had been an integral part of social life in Europe for hundreds of years. As one British historian put it, alcohol played a role "in nearly every public ceremony, every commercial bargain, every private occasion of mourning and rejoicing." It was "an essential narcotic which anaesthetised men against the strains of contemporary life."[18]

English colonists brought these drinking traditions with them to America. As American society evolved, alcohol was imbibed when waking in the morning and before retiring at night. It was served before, during, and after meals, social gatherings, weddings, funerals, ordinations, auctions, dances, barbecues, quilting bees, barn raisings, husking bees, land clearings, militia musters, church services, horse races, courtroom proceedings, legislative sessions, royal holidays, and political rallies. Many events included drinking toasts to a wide variety of individuals, including the king, governors, visiting dignitaries, and other prominent personages, or to each other; indeed, it was considered impolite and occasionally unpatriotic not to drink to someone's health. At election time, candidates commonly purchased alcohol for their supporters. When a political leader called a meeting or dined with other officials, the usual venue was a tavern, where alcohol flowed freely. When a sick or an injured person needed something to dull the pain or medication for a specific disease, alcohol was usually part of the answer. Drink also was used to pay laborers, especially at the autumn harvest when alcohol was mandated by contract. As there was little specie in the American colonies, alcohol also served as currency and a means of trade. Not only were alcoholic beverages considered healthful and nutritious, but they also imparted pleasure and provided sustenance because they contained calories.[19]

The alcoholic drinks served during the early colonial years were the same as those commonly found in England. The most important of these beverages was beer. English colonists brought beer and malt with them, and both were imported from England throughout the colonial period. When the *Arabella* and a small fleet of ships arrived in Massachusetts to found the settlement of Boston in 1630, they brought with them "10,000 gallons of beer, 120 hogs heads of malt for brewing and 12 gallons of distilled spirits; in addition, each family brought their own stores."[20]

Wealthy colonists imported beer—the Virginia planters buying from both England and Holland. They also imported malt, which most colonists could not afford. The varieties of barley initially introduced into North America did not fare well, so colonists tried virtually anything to brew and flavor their beer, including wheat, cornstalks, maple sap, elderberries, gooseberries, nuts, bark, various roots, pine chips, hemlock, and assorted leaves. A French immigrant to America was delighted with the strange variety of ingredients, including "pine chips, pine buds, hemlock, fir leaves, roasted corn, dried apple-skins, sassafras roots, and bran. With these, to which we add some hops and a little malt, we compose a sort of beverage which is very pleasant."[21]

Perhaps the most American beers were those made with berries from the persimmon (*Diospyros virginiana*), a small tree that originated in eastern North America. British writer Samuel Morewood, an admirer of persimmon beer, disclosed just how it was made: "The ripe fruit is braised and mixed with wheat or other flour, and formed into cakes which are baked in an oven. These are afterwards placed over the fire in a pot full of water, and when they become blended with the fluid, malt is added, and the brewing completed in the usual manner: thus is produced a beer preferable to most others."[22]

By far the most common beer brewed in colonial America was made from molasses. William Penn, the founder of Pennsylvania, wrote in 1685 that "our Beer was made mostly of Molasses, which well boyled with Sassafras or Pine infused into it, makes a very tolerable Drink: but now they make Mault and Mault begines to be common."[23] In Maine, molasses beer was flavored with sassafras root, wormwood, and bran.[24] In Virginia, molasses beer was brewed by "the poorer sort" with bran and "*Indian* Corn Malted with drying in a Stove; with Persimmons dried in Cakes and baked; with potatoes and with the green stalks of Indian Corn cut small and bruised; with Pompions [pumpkins], with the Jerusalem artichoke which some people plant purposely for that use, but this is the least esteemed."[25] However, it was not just "the poorer sort" who enjoyed molasses beer but the wealthy planters as well. In fact, it was a favorite drink of George Washington, whose recipe has survived:

TO MAKE SMALL BEER

Take a large Sifter full of Bran Hops to your Taste. —Boil these 3 hours. Then strain out 30 Gallons into a Cooler, put in 3 Gallons Molasses while the Beer is scalding hot or rather drain the molasses into the Cooler & strain the Beer on it while boiling Hot. Let this stand till it is little more than Blood warm. Then put in a quart of Yeast if the weather is very cold, cover it over with a Blanket & let it work in the Cooler 24 hours. Then put it into the Cask—leave the Bung[hole] open till it is almost done working—Bottle it that day Week it was Brewed.[26]

Home brewing continued well into the eighteenth century, especially in rural areas, but commercial breweries quickly became the primary source of beer in the cities. Virginia had two breweries by 1629, and Massachusetts licensed its first in 1637.[27] The Dutch, who settled the region around present-day New York beginning in 1624, loved beer even more than did the English settlers. New Amsterdam had its first brewery in 1632, and although taverns were licensed and regulated in the colony, illegal establishments were common.[28]

Colonists planted apple trees shortly after their arrival in America. As their orchards bore fruit, hard cider became a popular beverage in New England and the Middle Colonies. Apples also grew in some areas of the

Carolinas and Virginia, where historian Robert Beverley wrote in 1702 that apple orchards were "wonderfully quick of growth; so that in six or seven years time from the planting, a man may bring an orchard to bear in great plenty, from which he may make store of good cider, or distill great quantities of brandy; for the cider is very st[r]ong, and yields abundance of spirit." Horse-powered cider mills were constructed, and hard cider became so cheap that virtually everyone drank it, including children. Mulled cider—a festive drink enriched with sugar, egg yolks, and spices—was sometimes spiked with a tot of rum for an extra kick. By the mid-seventeenth century, cider had eclipsed beer as the beverage of choice in New England, and it maintained this position throughout the colonial period. Jean Anthelme Brillat-Savarin, the French culinary philosopher and author of *The Physiology of Taste* (1825), was a great admirer of American cider. After dining at a Connecticut farmhouse in the 1790s, Brillat-Savarin noted that "at either end of the table [were] two vast jugs of cider so excellent that I could have gone on drinking it for ever."[29] In areas where apples were not grown, cider-filled barrels were acquired from apple-growing regions.

Native New World grapes were abundant, and some colonists, including Thomas Jefferson, took a stab at winemaking. Although the wild grapes lacked the qualities needed for making a palatable beverage that was competitive with imported wine, they came to be added to other beverages as flavoring and a source of sugar. Some colonists imported grape plants from Europe, but they did not thrive in America.

Undaunted, Americans experimented with perry (pear cider), mobby (peach wine), and other fruit wines and brandies made from cherries, currants, black raspberries, plums, and quinces. Peach brandy, according to the American political economist Tench Coxe, was "the most exquisite spirit in the world."[30] Perhaps the most unusual American brandy was made from persimmons. A British writer noted that it was made "by putting a quantity of the fruit into a vessel for a week, until it becomes quite soft. Water is then poured in and left for fermentation, without the addition of any other ingredient to promote it. The brandy is then made in the common way, and it is said to be much improved when mixed with sweet grapes, that are found wild in the woods."[31]

Colonists also imported wines and brandies. Fortified wines, such as port and Madeira, traveled well, and Americans, like their British cousins, preferred such sweet wines. Wines imported from Europe were taxed, whereas wines imported from European possessions were not. As a result, wines from the Portuguese Azores or Spanish Canary Islands were less expensive than those from Continental Europe, and these wines became popular in colonial America. A Virginia minister opined that "the common wine comes from Madeira or Fayal, which, moderately drunk, is fittest to cheer the fainting spirits in the heat of summer, and to warm the chilled blood in the bitter colds of winter, and seems most peculiarly adapted for this climate."[32] Added to the colonial wine list were claret (i.e., Bordeaux), Canary, port, sherry, and muscadine. Sack (fortified white wines from Spain and the Canary Islands) and hock (German white wines) were also common by the late eighteenth century. Wine was widely available in taverns, but many colonists eschewed it, considering it pretentious. For the most part, wines were favored by the upper class.

Well-to-do colonists did not limit themselves to just one or two favorite beverages, however. Wait Winthrop, son of the Connecticut governor John Winthrop, enjoyed balm tea, beer, Canary wine, palm wine (made from coconuts), sage tea, and regular wine.[33] Massachusetts judge Samuel Sewall—notorious throughout history as a judge involved in the Salem witch trials—drank ale, beer, Canary wine, "chockelat," cider, "Madera," sack, sack posset, sage tea, "sillibub," tea, and wine, as well as water; in fact, he often quaffed several different beverages at the same occasion.[34] Every colonist who could afford them drank a similarly diverse menu of beverages.

Alcoholic beverages were also an important item of trade with the American Indians. Although pre-Columbian peoples in Mexico made alcoholic beverages, most North American Indians did not. When Europeans wanted to obtain furs from the Indians, they found that hard liquor was ideal for the exchange: it was easy to transport and did not spoil easily. The Indians used the liquor medicinally, employed it in ceremonies as a means of gaining transcendence, and offered it as a gesture of hospitality and sociability.[35] Because Indians lacked the technology to distill their own alcoholic beverages, liquor was highly prized, and European colonists used it to great advantage in trade for fur, land, and many other items. Alcohol killed and impoverished many Indians during and after the colonial period; it harmed even those who did not drink it by creating tensions within families and communities.

Nonalcoholic Beverages

Despite the almost universal popularity of alcoholic beverages, many colonists drank nonalcoholic beverages as well. Goats and cows were imported into America shortly after colonization began, and both provided milk. As the number of cows increased, milk became a very important beverage, drunk by young and old alike. Milk was often diluted with water and was also added to coffee, tea, chocolate, and some alcoholic concoctions.[36]

Stimulating hot beverages—coffee, tea, and chocolate—arrived in North America almost simultaneously in the mid-seventeenth century. All three were fashionable in Europe at the time. Coffee, the first of these beverages to arrive in the colonies, was adopted by many immigrant groups, such as the Pennsylvania Germans. Tea quickly became America's favorite hot beverage, appearing at breakfast and supper as well as on the afternoon tea table. Colonists who could not afford imported tea sometimes imbibed native North American substitutes, such as sage tea and black tea. Hot chocolate lagged behind tea and coffee, but it too became popular in the colonial period, especially for breakfast.[37]

By the 1680s, coffeehouses modeled on those in Europe emerged in Boston, New York, and Philadelphia, and shortly thereafter in other cities. These establishments usually served coffee, tea, and chocolate, and they provided colonial newspapers and English magazines for customers to peruse while engaging in conversations with their compatriots. Large coffeehouses occasionally provided rooms for holding trials, city council meetings, and other public events. Taverns (also called public houses, ordinaries, and inns) that catered to the wealthy also offered coffee, tea, and chocolate.

By the mid-eighteenth century, coffee, tea, and chocolate were readily available in all the colonies. Shops sold coffee beans, tea leaves, and chocolate beans for drinking. Home consumption of these beverages increased throughout the eighteenth century, at least among the well-to-do colonists.[38] Because coffee, tea, and chocolate were unaffordable or unavailable on the western frontier (then just a few hundred miles from the Eastern Seaboard), colonists there made do with substitutes such as burned rye, parched beets, peas, potatoes, and a variety of herbs, roots, barks, and leaves.[39]

Coffee and chocolate were imported directly from the French colonies on Martinique and Santo Domingo, as well as from the Dutch colony in what is present-day Suriname, which were all free of the import taxes required by England for goods shipped from European nations. Tea, which could legally come only from England, was more expensive. However, as one colonist gleefully proclaimed, tea was "as cheap [as] or cheaper than in England."[40] This was because much of the tea shipped to colonial America was smuggled in by the Dutch and abetted by the colonists, especially those in New England.

Ardent Spirits

Most traditional English beverages—beers and ciders—had relatively low alcohol contents. The exceptions were brandies (many of which were imported) and gin, which originated in Holland but became a British main-stay.[41] In America, apple and other fruit brandies were quite popular.

The most common distilled spirit in colonial times was rum, which had been introduced into the North American colonies from Barbados in the mid-sixteenth century. However, rather than pay for expensive West Indian rum, New Englanders imported cheap molasses and distilled the liquor themselves. The first Boston rum distillery was founded in 1657. Because rum produced in America was inexpensive and highly alcoholic compared with beer, ale, and cider, its use quickly spread, especially among the less affluent. It was typically drunk in taverns, where people of all levels dined and drank. Sailors favored grog, which was rum mixed with water, and grog shops were common in port cities.

Many colonists favored mixed drinks, which appeared in many guises. Flips (beer sweetened with sugar, molasses, dried pumpkin, or honey and strengthened with rum) had become popular by 1690. Possets, made from spiced hot milk and ale or beer, evolved into eggnog and other beverages. Syllabub—spiced milk or cream whipped to a froth with sweet wine or cider and sugar—was a spirituous drink for festive occasions. Shrubs—composed of citrus juice from imported oranges, lemons, and limes mixed with vari-ous spirits—were popular drinks before the Revolutionary War, as were hot toddies (made of liquor, water, sugar, and spices) and cherry bounces (made from cherry juice and rum). The most popular mixed drink was punch, which was usually composed of rum, citrus juice, sugar, and water and had myriad variations. Milk punches made with egg yolks, sugar, rum, and grated nut-meg were common for parties and balls. There were iced punches for sum-mer and hot punches for winter. Sangaree—a mixture of wine, water, sugar, and spices—evolved into what is now called sangria.[42]

Alcoholic beverages even made it into newspapers of the day and occa-sionally inspired poetry of sorts. On February 13, 1744, the *New York Gazette* published the following recipe, which likely originated in England but was widely reprinted in America:

A RECEIPT FOR ALL YOUNG LADIES THAT ARE GOING TO BE MARRIED, TO MAKE A SACK POSSET

From famed Barbados, on the Western Main,
Fetch sugar half a pound: fetch sack from Spain,
A pint; and from the Eastern Indian coast
Nutmeg, the glory of our Northern toast;
O'er flaming coals together let them heat,
Till the all-conquering sack dissolves the sweet;
O'er such another fire let eggs, twice ten,
New born from foot of cock and rump of hen;
Stir them with steady hand, and conscience pricking
To see the untimely fate of twenty chicken;
From shining shelf take down your brazen skillet;
A quart of milk from gentle cow will fill it;
When boiled and cooled, put milk and sack to egg,
Unite them firmly, like the triple League;
Then covered close, together let them dwell
Till Miss twice sings, *You must not kiss and tell.*
Each lad and lass snatch up their murdering spoon,
And fall on fiercely, like a starved dragoon.[43]

Colonists also made distilled spirits from corn and other available grains. At first, these distilled spirits were made for home consumption. As grain harvests increased, however, farmers realized that it was more profitable to sell part of their crop in the form of alcohol, which was less bulky and easier to transport over the poor colonial roads than were wagonloads of grain. This was particularly important for those farming in isolated rural areas, such as western Pennsylvania. By the mid-eighteenth century, a new spirit called whiskey emerged; it became especially popular among the Scots-Irish who lived in isolated rural areas, such as western Pennsylvania, Maryland, Virginia, and the Carolinas.

Distilled from grains (mainly wheat, rye, and corn), whiskey was of minor importance in colonial America before the influx of large numbers of Scots-Irish immigrants beginning in the late seventeenth century. After that, whiskey production and consumption in America increased slowly.[44] However, by 1770, whiskey making was a common practice throughout the colonies. It had the distinct advantage of being cheap; in addition, unlike rum, which was dependent on imported molasses, whiskey could be made with American-grown grains. This was particularly important for colonists on the frontier. These colonists did not have easy access to molasses but did have plenty of grain, much of which was converted into whiskey that could then be traded. Because whiskey could be made by anyone with a still, its popularity burgeoned in the years before the Revolutionary War.

At the 1785 ordination of Joseph McKean, a minister in Beverly, Massachusetts, eighty people drank "30 Bowles of Punch" before the ceremony. At the dinner that followed and afterward, six of the guests drank tea while another sixty-two downed eight bottles of brandy, twenty-eight bottles of wine, forty-four bowls of punch, and a large quantity of cherry rum.[45] A Frenchman who moved to Philadelphia in 1794 reported that the Americans drank throughout the meal until dessert; after the women withdrew, more bottles went around continuously, with "each man pouring for himself. Toasts are drunk, cigars are lighted, diners run to the corners of the room hunting night tables and vases which will enable them to hold a greater amount of liquor."[46]

According to modern estimates, the annual consumption of absolute alcohol (pure ethanol containing less than 1 percent by weight of water) in 1770 was 3.5 gallons per person, which is equivalent to 7 shots of hard liquor per day.[47] Another modern estimate, for the year 1790, puts annual consumption by those older than age fifteen at 6 gallons of alcohol per person, which is equal to 34 gallons of beer and cider, more than 5 gallons of distilled liquor, and 1 gallon of wine.[48] These numbers are just averages, of course. Because some colonists, especially women, did not drink, others obviously downed much more than average—and many were chronic drunks.[49]

Concerns arose about alcohol consumption in colonial America. One visitor to Maryland reported that the colonists there drank "so abominably together" that when ships arrived bearing wine and brandy, many colonists used their money for drinking and were short of funds to purchase necessities for the remainder of the year.[50] The clergy and political leaders frequently sought to reduce alcohol production and sales. Manufacturing was licensed, and the hours of operation for liquor stores and taverns were regulated by law.

Taverns

Men went to taverns to drink, but taverns also played important social, political, and economic roles in colonial times. Taverns were places where men met to drink, socialize, discuss events of the day, engage in business transactions, and occasionally participate in political processes—all of which were ratified with drink. Taverns were centers for the transmission of information, as they commonly made newspapers available, and they were also places where travelers would bring news from other communities. News would be passed along, discussed, and analyzed over brimming glasses of drink.

Because few rural communities had large public buildings, taverns frequently hosted civic functions, such as court sessions and official gatherings.[51] As taverns increasingly functioned as community centers, they competed with churches and local governments for the loyalties of citizens. Tavern owners played important roles as well; they were generally well informed about current happenings, and they shared what they knew. Many owners were upset when royal governors attempted to control liquor consumption, as were distillers; in fact, many of them became revolutionary leaders. Meetings of groups such as the Sons of Liberty and militiamen were frequently convened at taverns and public houses, and revolutionary activities were often planned and launched from those establishments. One Boston tavern, the Green Dragon, was a hotbed of political activity. The Massachusetts royal governor purportedly called it "a nest of sedition," while Daniel Webster, a leading statesman during the antebellum period, characterized the Green Dragon in 1821 as the "headquarters of the Revolution."[52]

Diversity

Colonists brought their own drink preferences with them. However, once they arrived in the New World, these beverages were Americanized. Colonial beer, for instance, was often made from different ingredients than traditional English beer. Because colonists came from different social classes and many came from different countries, no single beverage dominated the American scene.

Few of the specific beverages preferred by the colonists—sweet wines, dark bitter beers and ales, fermented fruit wines, morning bitters, and the mixed punches of the period—survived much beyond independence. Yet European colonists set America on a path to beverage diversity with a wide variety of beers, wines, spirits, mixed drinks, and nonalcoholic beverages such as coffee, tea, and chocolate. One of these beverages—rum—was actually what set the English North American colonies on the path to revolution.

Postscript

🍺 Plymouth Plantation resident William Wood returned to England in 1633, where he wrote *New-Englands Prospect* (1634). He died the following year.

🍺 After founding the colony of Pennsylvania, William Penn spent most of his life in England, where he died in 1718.

🍺 Joseph McKean served several years as a pastor in Beverly before becoming president of Bowdoin College in 1802. He died five years later.

🍺 Daniel Webster served in the U.S. House of Representatives and the Senate, and he was secretary of state under President Millard Fillmore. He ran unsuccessfully for president of the United States and died in 1852.

The sugar factory and distillery at Estate Clifton Hill, Christiansted, St. Croix. (Library of Congress, Prints and Photographs Division)

2

An Essential Ingredient in American Independence

GEORGE GRENVILLE became Great Britain's first lord of the treasury in April 1763, shortly after the country emerged from the Seven Years' War. The war had pitted the alliance of Britain, Prussia, and Portugal against France, Russia, Austria, Sweden, and Spain. By the war's end in February 1763, the British had captured French factories in India, slave stations in Africa, and several sugar islands in the Caribbean. In North America, British and colonial forces defeated the French in Canada. The Treaty of Paris, which ended the war, mandated that most of the captured territories be returned to the original mother countries, but the British kept Canada and several Caribbean islands. Great Britain was the world's greatest colonial power.

To pay for the war, the British government raised taxes on its well-to-do citizens and doubled the country's national debt. Maintaining the vast new empire that Britain acquired in North America required an additional 10,000 soldiers to garrison forts and monitor the American Indians, which had an annual cost of approximately £300,000.[1] Grenville did not believe that England's wealthiest citizens would tolerate more taxes, nor did he believe that Britain could go further into debt to protect its newly acquired empire. He concluded that the prime beneficiaries of these expenditures—particularly the British colonies in North America—should shoulder some of the burden of "defending, protecting, and securing the said colonies and plantations."[2]

The North American colonies had indeed reaped tremendous benefits from the war. New England merchants provisioned the British Army in North America. Merchants also profited by trading with French islands, including Martinique and Guadeloupe, after their capture by the British. New England began legally importing molasses from these former French possessions. By 1764, Rhode Island alone had imported 14,000 hogsheads of molasses, of which about 11,500 came from the French West Indies.[3] Profits were made and businesses flourished during the Seven Years' War.[4] The most valuable boon to the colonies, however, was the elimination of their greatest and only real military threat—the French in Canada and the lands west of the Allegheny Mountains to the Mississippi, which after the war were potentially open for settlement.

Lord Grenville proposed that Parliament of Great Britain levy a tax on North American imports of five products, the most important of which was molasses (from which New Englanders made rum). A British tax on molasses had already been on the books for thirty years, but colonists had simply subverted the law by smuggling in molasses or bribing customs officials. Grenville's proposed Sugar Act would actually lower the existing import duties from 6 pence to 3 pence on "every gallon of molasses or syrups, being the growth, product, or manufacture, of any colony or plantation in America, not under the dominion of his Majesty."[5] The tax would not pay for all of the added expenses of the British military in North America, but it would cover some expenses, which members of Parliament thought was only fair.

The passage of the Sugar Act generated minimal discussion in Parliament. Because it lowered the tax on molasses to be paid by American colonies, most members believed that the colonists would be happy with the law and reduced tax. No one in colonial America, however, had voted on the tax or for the representatives who established the tax. This fact provided the basis for the catchphrase "no taxation without representation" that reverberated throughout the colonies and subsequently into American history textbooks.

Colonial protests caused such a furor that the British Parliament repealed the law the following year. But the Sugar Act was only the first salvo of the tax war that would ignite the Revolutionary War in 1775. As John Adams, the future president of the United States, later wrote, "I know not why we should blush to confess that molasses was an essential ingredient in American independence. Many great events have proceeded from much smaller causes."[6] A historian later noted, "Commerce and politics were so inextricably mingled that rum and liberty were but different liquors from the same still."[7]

Although rum would continue to be made in America for decades, its production and consumption would soon decline and almost disappear.

Background

Sugarcane (*Saccharum officinarum*) was domesticated somewhere between New Guinea and Southeast Asia thousands of years ago. In prehistoric times, sugarcane was disseminated to India, then from India to China and eventually to the Mediterranean via Arab middlemen. Europeans first encountered sugar while on the Crusades. When European explorers arrived in the Caribbean in the sixteenth century, they brought sugarcane with them, and the plant thrived in the New World. Sugarcane cultivation is labor intensive, and European colonizers imported Africans to work the sugarcane fields as slaves. Estimates vary, but it is thought that at least 7 million Africans were eventually brought to the New World to work in sugarcane fields.

Sugarcane, which has the highest sugar content of any plant, was cultivated mainly for the production of table sugar. Once cane is cut, however, it begins to ferment, and people who lived near and worked in cane fields drank mildly alcoholic cane-based beverages. In the seventeenth century, cane juice was subjected to distillation, a process that increases its alcohol content exponentially. By this processing of sugarcane, rum was born.

The first steps in sugar manufacturing were to crush the cane to release its juice and boil the juice down to a thick syrup. The syrup was then transferred to a new pan and boiled again to remove impurities; this process was repeated several times. With each boiling, the syrup became thicker until finally the sugar crystallized, leaving behind a thick and dark byproduct called molasses. Molasses has a relatively high sugar content, and it can be used as a preservative because it does not ferment. When molasses is diluted with water, however, it ferments and turns into a type of beer, which was avidly enjoyed by slaves and laborers. By using a still and other equipment, molasses can be transformed into a very strong alcoholic beverage, estimated at 67 percent alcohol (134 proof).

European colonies in the New World produced different types of alcoholic beverages from sugar and its byproducts. In Portuguese Brazil, the beverage was *cachaça*. In the French West Indies, it was *rhum*—a word most likely originating from Barbados, where the beverage was variously called kill-devil, rumme, and rumbullion. Eventually, these terms were shortened simply to "rum."

The Dutch immigrants introduced sugarcane to Barbados and other Caribbean islands. They also taught the plantation owners how to convert the cane into sugar. Slaves were imported from Africa to grow the sugarcane and operate the mills that produced sugar. These islands quickly converted to sugar production, as did the Leeward Islands and Jamaica (after its conquest by the British in 1655). Sugarcane growers bought out many of the original settlers of Barbados, who moved on to other British colonies, especially the Carolinas in North America.

Large sugarcane plantations thus emerged on the British and French West Indian islands. Growers paid their expenses by selling molasses and rum to England or the English colonies in North America. The sale of these byproducts meant that the islands' prodigious sugar production was pure profit, according to Adam Smith. Growers made huge fortunes in sugar production; many owners left overseers to run their plantations and returned to England, where they purchased estates. These sugar growers and their merchant allies emerged as a powerful political force that influenced the English Parliament throughout the eighteenth century, and often their self-interest diverged from the interests of those in the British colonies in North America.[8]

To sustain the rapidly expanding slave populations in the West Indies, food and other essentials had to be imported, much of it from British North America. Some sugar and rum were shipped from the West Indies to the North American colonies, but the primary export item was molasses, which was used as a sweetener.[9] (Molasses remained the primary sweetener used in America until the early twentieth century.) Molasses also was used to make mildly alcoholic beverages. The early-eighteenth-century historian Robert Beverley recorded that colonists in Virginia used molasses to make a type of beer for the "poorer sort." It was often flavored with bran, corn, persimmons, potatoes, pumpkins, and even Jerusalem artichokes.[10]

In New England, molasses imported from the West Indies was used to make rum, which quickly became the distilled beverage of choice in the North America. New England was ideally suited for rum production: the region had access to the metal and skilled workers needed to make the stills, an abundance of ships to transport the bulky molasses from the Caribbean, and plenty of wood for fueling the stills and making barrels for the rum.

From its beginnings, rum was condemned by religious leaders. Reverend Increase Mather, president of Harvard College, noted in 1686 that rum was "an unhappy thing that of later years a kind of *Strong* Drink hath been *common* amongst us, which the poorer sort of people, both in Town & Country, can make themselves drunk with, at cheap & easy rates. They that are poor and wicked too (Ah most miserable creatures), can for a penny or two make themselves *drunk*." He elaborated on the "*Strong* Drink," reporting that "Reverent Mr. Wilson once said in a Sermon, there is a sort of drink come into the country, which is called Kill-Devil, but it should be call'd Kill-men for the Devil." Increase's son, Cotton Mather, a highly influential Puritan minister, also cautioned about the dangers of rum: "There is a Hazard lest a Flood of RUM, do Overwhelm all good *Order* among us."[11]

Despite concerns, the number of New England distilleries multiplied. By 1737, Boston had 177 taverns and retail shops that sold alcoholic beverages;[12] by 1763, the region had 159 distilleries making rum.[13] Massachusetts, Rhode Island, and Connecticut became the centers of rum manufacturing in the eighteenth century. Rum was sold throughout the colonies. By the 1760s, kegs of rum were carried on horseback over the Appalachian Mountains to the western parts of Maryland, Pennsylvania, and Virginia, where the spirits served two functions—to buck up soldiers in widely scattered forts and to supply American Indians with the alcohol that would contribute to the destruction of their societies.

As New England ramped up rum production, its price declined. In Boston, for instance, rum dropped from 3 shillings, 6 pence per gallon in 1722 to 2 shillings in 1738.[14] As rum became more affordable, it also became America's ardent spirit of choice. By 1748, Massachusetts distilleries alone produced 2.7 million gallons of rum annually.

Most colonial rum stayed in North America; some was exported to England, but the English preferred rum made in Barbados, which was stronger and better tasting. Some rum was sold, given, traded, or exchanged with American Indians, who had had no previous exposure to distilled alcohol. One result was that drunkenness contributed to the social and economic collapse of many Indian tribes from the Appalachians to the Mississippi. Indian spokesmen regularly complained to colonial legislatures about the harm caused by rum. As one Iroquois leader lamented to officials in Albany, New York, "You may find graves upon graves along the Lake, all which misfortunes are occasioned by Selling Rum to Our Brethren."[15]

Colonial legislatures passed laws against giving or selling rum to Indians, but these statutes were habitually ignored. The offer of a few barrels of rum was a cheap way to get Indians to sign a peace treaty or sign away their land. Benjamin Franklin wrote of one case in which he refused to hand over the rum until after the Indians had signed the treaty; this way, the Indians could not claim that they were drunk when they signed it. After the signing, Franklin gave the rum to the Indians, and almost immediately they became inebriated. Franklin wrote:

> At midnight a number of them came thundering at our door, demanding more rum, of which we took no notice. The next day, sensible they had misbehaved in giving us that disturbance, they sent three of their old counsellors to make their apology. The orator acknowledged the fault, but laid it upon the rum; and then endeavored to excuse the rum, by saying, *"The Great Spirit who made all things, made every thing for some use, and whatever use he designed any thing for, that use it should always be put to. Now, when he made rum, he said, 'let This Be For The Indians To Get Drunk With'* and it must be so."[16]

Rum and Slavery

Barbados was uninhabited when the English colonized the island in 1627. The island was settled by English and Scots-Irish farmers who tried to grow tobacco and other saleable crops on small farms. Plantations needed labor—preferably cheap labor—and there was little available in the Caribbean, so plantation owners purchased and shipped slaves from West Africa. However, the mainland North American colonies had a better climate for growing tobacco, and the colonists in Barbados could not compete. When sugarcane was introduced into the island beginning in 1642, large sugar plantations dominated the island. Many more slaves were needed to plant and harvest sugarcane and convert it into sugar and rum. What would later be called "triangular trade" developed: ships acquired sugar and rum in Barbados and other British West Indian islands and transported them to England, where finished goods were acquired. The ships then took these goods and part of their rum cargo to West Africa, where they were exchanged for slaves. Once the slaves were procured in Africa, the slavers then proceeded to the West Indies, where the human cargo was exchanged for sugar and rum.

Rum played such an important role in the slave trade that it became a medium of exchange in Africa. To save space on the voyage from Barbados, rum was concentrated by running it through a still a few additional times, which markedly raised its alcohol content. When the barrels of concentrated rum were unloaded in Africa, water was added to bring the liquor down to a standard proof; this reconstituted rum was traded for slaves. In 1759, slavers could purchase a male slave for 90 gallons of rum; by 1774, the price had jumped to 230 gallons. A female slave cost 66 gallons of rum in 1768/1769, but that price almost tripled to 180 gallons in 1773/1774.[17]

Textbook discussions of "American" triangular trade state that ships from New England picked up molasses in the Caribbean and brought it to New England, where it was converted to rum. The rum was then shipped to Africa and traded for slaves, who were transported to the Caribbean. Some American ships participated in all legs of the triangular trade.[18] The best estimate is that North American ships carried 145,000 slaves to the New World prior to 1808—slightly less than 5 percent of the total number of slaves transported on British ships. Although American rum was traded, it was inferior to rum made in the Caribbean or England. The average amount of alcohol on American ships engaged in this slave trade was approximately 3 to 7 percent of a ship's total cargo, meaning that many other goods were also exchanged.[19] Although American ships were engaged in the slave trade, American rum was a minor part of this exchange.

Consuming Rum

Historically, expensive imported brandy and Madeira (a fortified wine from the Portuguese archipelago of the same name) were the alcoholic beverages of choice for the American elite. Hard cider, beer, and ale—which were cheaper and lower in alcohol content—were traditionally drunk by members of the middle and lower classes. Rum was in a class by itself—cheap but strong. During the eighteenth century, rum was very popular in the British North American colonies; some colonists drank it straight, but it was usually diluted with water. Rum mixed with water—a drink called grog—was the mainstay of sailors. It was also favored by the pirates who plundered throughout the Caribbean during the seventeenth and eighteenth centuries. In the harbor towns of North America, unsavory "grog shops" were frequented by sailors of all stripes.

Rum was quaffed in quantity by the less affluent and even slaves, when they could get it. However, people in the higher echelons of society looked down on the consumption of rum; they considered rum drinkers to have "vulgar taste."[20] This is not to say that wealthier and more sophisticated Americans did not also drink rum; but rather than drinking rum straight or watered down in the form of low-class grog, they served it in more "refined" ways, such as in punches that combined rum with citrus juices (orange, lemon, and lime). Dozens of rum drinks with amusing and memorable names were popular. Hard cider mixed with rum was called stonewall. Cherry bounce, a potent combination of cherry juice and rum, was made by soaking cherries in a cask of rum for a year. A calibogus (or just bogus) was a combination of rum and spruce beer; molasses was sometimes added. Switchel (stitchel or swizzle), a refreshing summer beverage, was a combination of rum, vinegar, molasses, and ginger or some other aromatic flavoring. A manhattan (unrelated to today's cocktail of that name) consisted of rum, beer, and sugar. A bombo was rum, sugar, water, and nutmeg; without the nutmeg, such a drink was called a mimbo or mamm. A flip was a combination of rum, milk, eggs, and sugar. Rum combined with bilberries was called a bilberry dram; mixed with warmed cider, it was called a Sampson. A doctor was fresh milk mixed with rum, whereas a toddy was rum with egg yolks and sugar and usually served hot. A sling consisted of two parts water for each part of rum. A julep, usually made with brandy (or later with bourbon), was also made with rum. Tafia, a low-grade rum and water drink, became popular in New Orleans in the nineteenth century. In addition to being served as a beverage, rum was used for medicinal purposes. In the South, rum combined with bitter bark was called morning bitters. A mintwater, made from rum and mint, was considered to be soothing to upset stomachs.[21]

Rum also was consumed by children. Dr. Johann David Schöpf came to America as a physician for a Hessian regiment fighting alongside the British during the American Revolution. When the war ended in 1783, he toured the new nation, noting that "spirituous drinks being so universally in use, nobody thinks it harm to give them to children as well." American women often gave rum and other ardent spirits to their children to stop their crying. On one occasion, Schöpf observed that "our host's five-year-old child seeks to get hold of rum or grog wherever he can, and steals furtively to the flask; we saw him almost every day staggering and drunken; he was besides weak and thin as a skeleton, just as another very young child of a neighbor, addicted to the same vice. The parents observed this but were at no pains to prevent it; and the servants and other people appeared even to be amused at the drunken children and to egg them on."[22]

Molasses and Sugar Acts

The British approach to trade, called mercantilism, required that all the sugar produced in their colonies be shipped first to England or other English colonies, and from there sold and transported to other countries. Because the West Indian sugarcane growers had a monopoly on selling sugar to England and English colonies, they could raise the price as much as they pleased, guaranteeing themselves the maximum profit.

Plantation owners and merchants in the British West Indies used most of the molasses from their sugar production to make high-quality rum, which they exported to England or sent to Africa to be traded for slaves. Little molasses remained for export to British colonies, and what was available was marked up considerably to generate even more profits. The French government, however, did not want Caribbean rum imported into metropolitan France, where brandy producers objected to the competition. Because the French did not use molasses as a sweetener, the French West Indies ended up with massive surpluses of the sweet syrup. Rather than toss it in the ocean, the French government permitted its colonies to sell molasses to anyone who would buy it, and the obvious market was the British North American colonies. In the French West Indies, molasses cost 60 to 70 percent less than the molasses from the British West Indies, so New England colonial ships acquired it in bulk from the French Caribbean islands of Martinique and Guadeloupe.[23] By 1700, the New England was buying more molasses from the French colonies than from British colonies.

In exchange for the molasses, New England merchants sent lumber, fish (mainly salt cod), and other provisions. In addition, shipyards built large and fast ships, which were occasionally armed with cannons, and sold them to sugarcane growers in the French West Indian colonies so they could safely and easily transport their sugar, molasses, and rum to New England or Europe.[24] Because of this trade, the British West Indian sugar growers lost much of their business; as a result, in 1716 they urged the British Parliament to pass a law that would greatly restrict New England from importing sugar, molasses, and rum from the French and other European colonies in the Caribbean. This would give the British West Indies a monopoly on the sugar, molasses, and rum trade, thus allowing the sugarcane growers to charge whatever they wanted for those products. Parliament did not pass the law that year, but sugar growers kept up the pressure and the Molasses Act was finally passed in 1733. The law placed a duty of 6 pence per pound on sugar, molasses, rum, and spirits imported to the North American colonies from non-British islands.[25]

The intent of the Molasses Act was to force New Englanders to trade only with the British colonies in the West Indies; the goal of the large West Indian sugar growers was to end rum manufacturing in New England, which competed with their own rum production. Had the Molasses Act been enforced, it likely would have crippled New England's fishing and lumber businesses, which produced the products sold to the French and Dutch West Indian islands in exchange for their excess molasses. Enforcement also would have greatly handicapped the slave trade, in which some New Englanders were also involved. But passing the Molasses Act and enforcing it were two different things. The only enforcement provision of the law was for customs officials to collect the tax, but there were thousands of coves where goods could be landed that could not be patrolled by the few custom officials; therefore, New Englanders began massive smuggling operations for the heavily taxed products. It was a major misstep to pass the Molasses Act but not enforce it—a blunder that would have serious repercussions thirty years later.[26]

When Parliament permitted growers in the British West Indies to trade sugar directly with any country in Europe, the growers' fortunes changed and they stopped pressing for enforcement of the Molasses Act. Even so, the law remained on the books for the next thirty years, and molasses was openly smuggled into North America by respectable merchants—including John Hancock—who would later become leaders of the American Revolution.

The Sugar Act, passed by the British in 1764, was intended to help defray the cost of the French and Indian War. It was less onerous than the Molasses Act passed thirty years earlier because it levied only 3 pence per gallon on imported molasses. However, the law provided for stronger enforcement, including sending British warships to American ports to enforce the collection of the import duty. American colonials, especially those in New England, took great exception to the Sugar Act. As a committee in the Massachusetts colonial House of Representatives reported:

> Our pickled fish wholly, and a great part of the cod fish, are fit only for the West India market. The British Islands cannot take off one third of the quantity caught; the other two thirds must be lost, or sent to the foreign

plantations, where molasses are given in exchange. The duty on this article will greatly diminish its importation hither; and being the only article allowed to be given in exchange for our fish, a less quantity of the latter will of course be exported. The obvious effect of which must be the diminution of the fish trade not only to the West Indies, but to Europe; fish suitable for both those markets being the produce of the same voyage. If, therefore, one of these markets be shut, the other cannot be supplied. The loss of one is the loss of both, as the fishery must fail with the loss of either.[27]

By the time the act was passed, New Englanders had been smuggling molasses and other contraband for thirty years, but stricter enforcement of the Sugar Act made smuggling more risky.

New England's legislatures, merchants, and distillers believed that an enforced molasses tax would destroy the rum-making business, which was the region's second most important industry after shipbuilding. What distinguished this law from previous legislation was the inclusion of forty-one provisions for enforcement. Customs officers were sent from England, and the Royal Navy was directed to implement the law and prevent smuggling. Previously, apprehended smugglers were tried in colonial courts before juries of their peers, who routinely exonerated the smugglers. Under the new laws, smugglers were to be tried in British vice admiralty courts, which had no juries.[28]

Twenty-seven British warships were assigned to enforce the Sugar Act, and the presence of these ships sharply curtailed smuggling. Because this was a major colonial economic activity, particularly in New England, enforcement harmed merchants, depressed the distilling business, irritated colonial assemblies, and significantly reduced New England's imports and exports of all goods. Colonists held protest meetings, merchants boycotted imported British goods, and colonial assemblies vigorously protested the Sugar Act. Because it was not easy to defend smuggling, the target of the colonial protest was the tax levied by the British Parliament, which at the time was solely elected by men (mainly property owners) in Great Britain.

Colonial protests against the Sugar Act, which was repealed, set the stage for even bigger protests against the next bill approved by Parliament—the Stamp Act, passed in 1765. This new law included "certain Stamp Duties, and other Duties, in the British Colonies and Plantations in America, towards further defraying the expenses of defending, protecting, and securing the same."[29] In response to this law, large numbers of colonials vigorously opposed it.

Parliament heeded the colonial protests and repealed the Stamp Act in 1766. Parliament also reduced the tax on molasses to 1 penny per gallon on imports from either British or foreign colonies. This lower tax could easily have been paid without any disruption to New England's economy, and many merchants did comply. However, old smuggling patterns continued, and roughly one-third of the molasses coming into New England continued to be smuggled in from French, Dutch, and Spanish colonies in the Caribbean.

Although the British Parliament repealed the Stamp Act, it still asserted its right to tax the North American colonies, which caused continual friction with many colonial leaders. In 1767, Parliament passed the Townshend Acts, which imposed duties on certain goods, such as paint, lead, glass, and tea. The taxes were minor, but from both the British and American standpoints they set a precedent. The revenues were intended, in part, to pay the expenses of Royal governors so that they would not be dependent on or beholden to colonial legislatures. Agitation against the Townshend Acts led to the Boston Massacre on March 5, 1770, in which three men were shot and killed by British soldiers. Parliament responded by rescinding all the taxes except for the tax on tea; colonial opposition to this led to the Boston Tea Party in 1773—and, subsequently, to the American Revolution.

The Founding Beverage and Its Decline

Virtually all of America's founding fathers had some connection with rum. Nineteen-year-old George Washington had traveled to Barbados in 1751 and toyed with the idea of remaining there; Washington enjoyed his rum, and on at least one occasion he used his supply of the beverage to influence his election to the Virginia House of Burgesses. Another time, Washington sent an unruly runaway slave on a ship bound for the Caribbean, with a note requesting that the captain of the ship trade the man at any Caribbean port for a hogshead of the best rum and another of molasses, plus other goods.[30] Washington requested allotments of rum for his Continental Army during the Revolutionary War; sufficient quantities could not be secured, however, so the soldiers had to find other forms of alcohol with which to warm, embolden, and divert themselves.

Thomas Jefferson also drank rum, and his plantation was kept well stocked with it. John Hancock, the Boston merchant who signed the Declaration of Independence with the boldest signature, smuggled in molasses from the Caribbean to make rum. Although Benjamin Franklin preferred other alcoholic beverages, he frequently drank rum. Paul Revere enthusiastically enjoyed his rum. Moreover, rum was the prevailing drink in taverns where colonials upset with British policies congregated, and it was in these taverns that the Revolution began.[31]

During the American War of Independence (1775–1783), trade between the North American colonies and the Caribbean was disrupted, and rum became scarce. At the end of the war, Great Britain initially refused to permit direct trade between the British West Indies and the newly independent nation; imports of molasses from the British Caribbean declined, but French, Dutch, and Spanish Caribbean possessions made up for the loss. When the United States was formed in 1788, one of the provisions in the new Constitution was that all states agreed to end the international slave trade in twenty years. American rum exports to Africa escalated as the deadline neared. In 1806, Rhode Island alone sent 831,588 gallons of rum to Africa.[32] In 1808, it became illegal to import slaves into the United States. Great Britain had outlawed the slave trade the previous year, and Britain and the United States stationed warships off the West African coast to suppress the slave trade. The outlawing of the international slave trade ended rum's connection with slavery and its role as a medium of exchange in Africa. When the international slave trade ceased, rum production in the United States tanked.

It was not just the end of the slave trade that slowed rum production: Great Britain and France were at war intermittently from 1789 to 1815, and the War of 1812 between the United States and Britain made it difficult for Americans to acquire rum, sugar, or molasses. American rum makers substituted maple sugar for imported molasses. By the early nineteenth century, according to a British writer, maple sugar was "the basis of a large proportion of the rums at present manufactured by the Americans, to the great injury of the British colonies, as is manifest from the great decrease in the exports of these articles from thence to the States."[33] But maple sugar was also used as a sweetener, and it was much more expensive than molasses. The price of rum escalated while at the same time the price of whiskey declined. Whiskey became the ardent spirit of choice by most Americans. Rum continued to be imported and manufactured in the United States, but its market share dropped precipitously.

Demon Rum

Yet another reason for rum's decline was the rise of the temperance movement. Dr. Benjamin Rush of Philadelphia is credited with founding the

American temperance movement. Rush was a late-eighteenth-century renaissance man; he was a signer of the Declaration of Independence, a member of the Continental Congress, and surgeon-general to the Continental Army. He also was a professor of medical theory and clinical practice at the University of Pennsylvania in Philadelphia. Rush was strongly opposed to the consumption of rum, whiskey, and brandy on medical grounds, and he published several pamphlets on the medical problems associated with the consumption of "ardent" spirits. To illustrate his concerns, Rush wrote the pamphlet *A Moral and Physical Thermometer, or, a Scale of the Progress of Temperance and Intemperance*, which was first published in 1783 and was reprinted many times during the next fifty years. At the bottom of Rush's "thermometer," the most dangerous drink was "pepper rum." Pepper rum was made from Jamaica spirits—the rum with the highest alcoholic content in colonial days—combined with a spoonful of ground pepper; this concoction was used by the ailing "to take off their coldness."

Rush believed that hard liquor and drunkenness gave rise to such vices as lying, swearing, fraud, anarchy, murder, and suicide. He declared that drinking strong alcohol would bring on various diseases, including tremors, epilepsy, dropsy, jaundice, apoplexy, and madness—and that excess consumption of alcohol was invariably fatal. He believed that the repercussions of rum drinking included debt, hunger, black eyes, and death on the gallows, to name a few.[34] Rush also expressed concern about the consumption of even small amounts of spirits. He described a man who might start out with a taste for a toddy—a combination of a little rum, water, and sugar—and then progress inevitably to grog, with a greater proportion of rum to water: "After a while nothing would satisfy him but slings made of equal parts of rum and water, with a little sugar. From slings he advanced to raw rum, and from common rum to Jamaica spirits." The drinker, Rush predicted, "soon afterwards died a martyr to his intemperance."[35]

Rum became less and less a part of American life in the nineteenth century, but it continued to be served at many functions. In writing about Vermont in the 1820s, Horace Greeley, founder of the *New York Tribune*, recalled the following:

> In my childhood . . . there was scarcely a casual gathering . . . without strong drink. Cider, always . . . Rum at all seasons and on all occasions, were required and provided. No house or barn was raised without

a bountiful supply of the latter. . . . A wedding without "toddy," "flip," "sling," or "punch," with rum undisguised in abundance, would have been deemed a poor, mean affair.

Dances, militia trainings, election days, and even funerals, wrote Greeley, were inadequately celebrated absent "the dispensing of spirituous consolation.[36] This atmosphere, and the effects of his own father's drinking, convinced Greeley to abstain from alcohol. He joined tens of thousands of other abstainers and became a strong temperance advocate.

As the temperance movement picked up steam, rum remained a symbolic target even as it faded from favor in America. The phrase "demon rum" gained currency during the late 1840s, when it became a rallying cry of the temperance advocates. In this case, however, "rum" was used generically to represent ardent spirits. Rum again surfaced in the election of 1884, which pitted Grover Cleveland, governor of New York, against James G. Blaine, a former congressman and senator from Maine who was the incumbent secretary of state. A week before the election, Blaine decided to wind up his campaign in New York, which appeared likely to support him in the election. One of the functions Blaine attended was a public meeting of the Religious Bureau of the Republican National Committee, where he was welcomed by the eighty-two-year-old Reverend Samuel D. Burchard. Speaking on behalf of a group of Protestant clergy, Burchard proclaimed that the antecedents of the Democratic Party were "rum, Romanism, and rebellion"—a nice alliteration that branded Democrats as opponents of temperance who were pro-Catholic and disloyal to the Union. The Catholic vote had been leaning toward Blaine, but when the candidate did not immediately disavow Burchard's statement, Democrats reprinted it and circulated it to Catholic precincts in New York and other cities. Although Blaine subsequently distanced himself from Burchard's statement, the damage had been done. Blaine lost New York and three other states by slightly more than 1,000 votes each, and he lost the election, making Grover Cleveland the first Democrat elected to the presidency since before the Civil War.[37]

Rum Revival

Rum eventually reemerged as an important beverage in America. This was partly due to Caribbean immigrants who began arriving in the twentieth century. During Prohibition, speakeasies served "rum" of questionable provenance and content. As the taste of this rum left much to be desired, bartenders doctored it up with other ingredients to disguise its unpleasant flavor. In this way, rum became the basis for some of America's favorite cocktails, and these remained popular—and became tastier—once Prohibition ended. American rum distillers reemerged after repeal in 1933. During World War II, American soldiers were stationed in the Caribbean and many enjoyed the locally produced rum. After the war, inexpensive rum was imported from the Caribbean, especially Puerto Rico and Cuba.

Beginning in the late 1940s and 1950s, Americans began to vacation in the Caribbean, Latin America, and the South Pacific, where they too became acquainted with rum. For those unable to vacation in these tropical paradises, theme restaurants serving rum-based tiki or boat drinks emerged. Polynesian-themed establishments such as Trader Vic's, Don the Beachcomber, and myriad "tiki bars" nationwide popularized rum drinks such as the daiquiri, pink flamingo, mai tai, planter's punch, and zombie. With the introduction of jet air travel and modern air conditioning, American tourists flocked to the Caribbean and returned to the United States with an increased appreciation for rum. Latin American cocktails, such as the piña colada, Cuba libre, and mojito, became very popular, and rum manufacturers, such as Bacardi, Captain Morgan, Don Q, and Ron Rico, have vastly expanded their operations and sales in the United States. Aged rums have gained adherents; flavored rums, such as raspberry, vanilla, banana, spice, and coconut, have gained the attention of younger drinkers. This renewed interest encouraged the construction of boutique rum distilleries once again in New England. Rum aficionados now talk of single malts, aged rum, and "upmarket mixologists specify premium brands for their cocktails where the flavours are important," reports Ian Williams.[38]

Rum enabled the colonists to destroy many American Indian societies, permitting a rapid expansion westward beyond the Appalachian Mountains. The British tax on molasses contributed to the American Revolution. Rum was a key element in the slave trade, which enslaved millions of men, women, and children; slavery, in turn, was a major cause of the Civil War, in which hundreds of thousands of Americans died. Finally, drunkenness associated with rum was a precipitating factor in the rise of the temperance movement, which led to Prohibition in the twentieth century.

Postscript

Rum's major selling point for most of American history was its low cost, and the rum was usually mixed with other ingredients. Beginning in the 1980s, Americans began drinking premium aged rums that are enjoyed neat.

After his tour of America after the American Revolution, Johann David Schöpf returned to Germany, where he died in 1800.

Samuel D. Burchard was roundly chastised for his comments at the time of the 1884 presidential election, and he was blamed for Blaine's defeat. Burchard lived on until 1891.

In 1872, Horace Greeley ran for the presidency on the Liberal Republican Party line, and the Democratic Party supported him as well. He lost the election in a landslide to Ulysses S. Grant. Greeley died in New York a few weeks after the election.

After his defeat in the 1884 presidential election, James G. Blaine continued working on his memoirs, *Twenty Years in Congress*, the second volume of which was published in 1886. He remained in Washington, D.C., where he died in 1892.

Grover Cleveland was defeated in the 1888 presidential election, but was reelected in 1892, making him the only president to serve two nonconsecutive terms. Cleveland died in 1908.

No other beverage affected early American history more than rum, but it would be tea that sparked the American War for Independence.

Nathaniel Currier, *The Destruction of Tea at Boston Harbor* (1846). (Museum of the City of New York; Scala/Art Resource, NY)

3

Tea Parties

O N DECEMBER 16, 1773, Bostonians and representatives from surrounding communities assembled at the Old South Meeting House in Boston. Not only was the meeting house filled, but a crowd of several thousand milled around outside. New England citizens had been assembling at town meetings like this for the past several weeks, but this was by far the largest gathering. Most of those assembled had come from Boston and the surrounding communities, but one group had come from as far away as Maine, which was then part of the Massachusetts Bay Colony. The topic of discussion at these meetings was a single question: What should be done about the tea that arrived on three ships at Griffin's Wharf in Boston Harbor a few weeks earlier? Tea was one of America's most popular beverages and all of the meeting attendees drank it, but this tea had been taxed by the British Parliament. Although the tax was negligible, the colonists were unwilling to pay it. For the colonists, as well as for the British Parliament, the tax was a matter of principle. Parliament maintained that it had the right to tax its colonies, but many North America colonists believed that only their own legislatures could levy a tax; in this case, the Massachusetts colonial assembly had not done so. The North American colonists' view became popularized by James Otis, a Boston lawyer, who said in a speech that "taxation without representation was tyranny."[1]

Many citizens attended the December 16 meeting because the tea onboard one ship would likely be landed under British military escort the next day. Colonial law required that any tax on goods brought into port must be paid within twenty days of a ship's arrival; if the tax was not paid, the customs collector of the port was authorized to impound the goods. Bostonians had already tried several different solutions to prevent this, including asking the consignees (the local merchants who had ordered the tea) to disavow their commissions, which would mean that there would be no one to pay the tax and no reason to unload the tea. The consignees, however, had refused; when pressured by the Sons of Liberty and others opposed to paying the tax, the merchants fled to the Castle William, the fort in Boston harbor controlled by the British military.

Colonists had also asked one ship's captain to simply take the tea back to England. The captain had agreed to do so, but he needed clearance papers from British port authorities to depart. The captain requested clearance, but the port authorities refused to grant permission until the tea was landed. To prevent the ship from just leaving the port without official clearance, the royal governor, Thomas Hutchinson, an American-born lawyer and former judge who had attended Harvard, ordered British warships to patrol the mouth of the harbor. The assemblage at the Old South Meeting House had previously requested that the ship's captain ask Hutchinson directly for permission for his ship to return to England with the tea, and the request had been turned down. It was not likely that Hutchinson would agree to permit the ship to leave without unloading the tea this time either. Hutchinson had ordered some of the tea himself through his son, and the assembly had censured him for doing so. On several previous occasions, in fact, the Massachusetts assembly had requested that Hutchinson be removed as governor, but these requests had been ignored by the British government.

On the afternoon of December 16, the citizens assembled at the Old South Meeting House were waiting for Hutchinson's decision. Little is known about the decisions made during the meeting because the attendees intentionally kept minimal records. At dusk, the ship's captain arrived at the church and informed the attendees that Governor Hutchinson had refused permission for the ship to leave once again. Samuel Adams, a brewer and political leader who had advocated for independence from Great Britain as early as 1769, announced that "this meeting can do no more to save the country."[2] John Hancock, a merchant and leader of the assemblage, proclaimed, "Let every man do what is right in his own eyes!" The meeting was interrupted by calls for "Boston Harbor a tea-pot this night!" and "Hurra for Griffin's Wharf!"[3]

A short time later, fifteen to twenty men appeared at the meeting, cheered on by the attendees. The men's faces were smeared with grease and lamp black; they were dressed in blankets and wore large woolen caps, supposedly to look like Mohawk Indians. Armed with tomahawks, hatchets, pistols, and rifles, the men marched from Old South Meeting House to Boston Harbor; other men, who wore even clumsier garb acquired from a store on Fort Hill, joined the original group. When they arrived at Griffin's Wharf, a crowd of about a thousand people watched the proceedings and cheered on the men. The boarding parties were well organized; they divided into three groups—one for each ship that carried tea—and boarded each vessel simultaneously.

To avoid damage to the ships and harm to the crews, the raiders politely asked the few crew members onboard for access to the tea consignment. The crews willingly obliged; in some cases, they even assisted by hoisting tea chests from the ships' holds. The raiders then staved the chests and threw them into the harbor. As the destruction progressed, onlookers without disguises joined in. British sailors on men-of-war a short distance away in the harbor, as well as British Army troops at the castle, did nothing to intervene.

Three hours later, all 342 tea chests (about forty-three tons valued at £18,000) were destroyed, and the raiders and spectators departed. As the crowd left the wharf, British Admiral John Montagu, who was staying with a loyalist family a few blocks from the port, told some participants: "Well, boys, you have had a fine pleasant evening for your Indian caper—haven't you? But mind, you have got to pay the fiddler yet!" The participants and onlookers then went to a tavern where they proceeded to have dinner and drink. The following day, some tea was still afloat in the harbor, so several colonists rowed out and dispersed it to prevent tea-hungry Bostonians from absconding with it.[4]

On the day after the Boston Tea Party, as the event would inevitably be called, John Adams, the future second president of the United States, wrote in his diary: "This Destruction of the Tea is so bold, so daring, so firm, so intrepid and inflexible, and it must have so important Consequences, and so lasting, that I cannot but consider it as an epocha [*sic*] in history. The question is: Whether the destruction of this tea was necessary? I apprehend it was absolutely and indispensably so."[5] This simple act of defiance set in motion events that culminated sixteen months later in the beginning of the Revolutionary War.

Background

The consumption of tea (an infusion of cured leafs and buds of the *Camellia sinensis* plant) is thought to have originated in southwestern China at least 5,000 years ago. In the succeeding millennia, tea drinking expanded slowly to other parts of Asia, and finally to Europe in the early seventeenth century. Tea drinking was adopted in England in the mid-seventeenth century, and colonists brought the custom to British North America soon afterward.

The mercantilist economic policy of the British government dictated that tea be imported from China to England; from there, it was exported to British colonies. English merchants made a profit in the transaction, and the policy upped the price of the beverage in the colonies. Hence, until the early eighteenth century, tea was a luxury that only the well-to-do could afford. By 1720, however, tea production in China shot up to meet demand. Tea became widely available; as the price dropped, tea drinking became increasingly popular. In fact, tea became the most common libation in the British North American colonies, second only to water.

Tea was more than just a beverage; social functions emerged around tea drinking. As Massachusetts historian Alonzo Lewis reported about life in the 1730s, "When ladies went to visiting parties, each one carried her tea-cup, saucer and spoon. The tea-cups were of the best china, very small, containing as much as a common wine-glass."[6] By 1737, a traveler in New England reported that tea had become "the darling of our women. Almost every little tradesman's wife must set sipping tea for an hour or more in the morning, and it may be again in the afternoon if they can get it. They talk of bestowing thirty or forty shillings upon a tea equipage."[7] Tea parties, usually composed of women, were commonly held throughout the colonies. By the mid-eighteenth century, drinking tea had expanded to the lower classes. Peter Kalm, a Swedish scientist who visited America in 1750, noted that "there is hardly a farmer's wife or a poor woman who does not drink tea in the morning."[8]

Not everyone knew how to prepare tea properly at first. When a woman in Haverhill, Massachusetts, first acquired tea, she purportedly boiled a whole pound of it in water and added a large piece of beef. It was so strong that the family could not consume it—or so the story goes.[9] In western Pennsylvania, another colonist boiled ham with a mess of tea leaves rather than typical greens.[10] Some women in Connecticut boiled the tea in a kettle and served it with the leaves for thickening.[11] Long Island resident Mrs. Miller told a number of stories about the awkward manner of consuming tea: one person boiled it in a pot and ate it like samp porridge. Another spread the tea on his bread and butter; after he bragged about eating half a pound at a meal, a neighbor informed him how long a time a pound of tea should last. Miller remembered:

> The first teakettle that was in East-Hampton . . . came ashore at Montauk in a ship (the *Captain Bell*). The farmers came down there on business with their cattle, and could not find out the use of the tea-kettle, which was then brought up to old "Governor Hedges." Some said it was for one thing, and some said it was for another. At length one, more knowing than his neighbors, affirmed it to be the ship's lamp, to which they all assented.[12]

Such popularity did not mean that everyone liked tea imports. In 1734, a New York writer reported: "I am credibly informed that tea and china ware cost the province, yearly, near the sum of £10,000; and people that are least able to go to the expence, must have their tea tho' their families want bread. Nay, I am told, often pawn their rings and plate to gratifie themselves in that piece of extravagance."[13]

Benjamin Franklin reported in the *Pennsylvania Gazette* in 1742 that a Quaker, Benjamin Lay, went to the marketplace with his late wife's tea china and began breaking the cups and saucers as a protest against tea drinking. Evidently, Lay believed that tea "was a luxury, causing the expenditure of much money, and producing little good." Boys in the market pushed him away and grabbed as much of the china as they could and ran off with it, saving some of it from destruction.[14] In 1762, William Smith, writing in his history of New York, noted bitterly that "our people both in town and country are shamefully gone into the habit of tea-drinking."[15] Pennsylvania Germans did not consume tea, and neither did many settlers in the back country or frontier—but these people were the minority.[16] Everyone else drank tea, especially women.

Taxing Tea

Tea may well have remained one of America's most important beverages had the British Parliament not needed money after the Seven Years' War (1756–1763). However, Parliament began passing revenue bills that required the British North American colonies to help foot some of the bill for the war and the cost of defending the vast new territory acquired in the war.

One bill was the Townshend Act, passed in 1767, which taxed a number of products—including paper, paint, and tea—imported into the colonies from Great Britain. The colonists objected strenuously to the taxes because their own colonial legislatures had not given their consent.

Colonial resistance to the British tax acts included refusals to import the taxed products and boycotts of products that managed to arrive. It was at this time that the Sons of Liberty were first organized in New York (later expanding to Massachusetts and other colonies). Women began making homemade "liberty tea," consisting of herbs and leaves of common plants steeped in hot water.[17] The *Boston Gazette* reported in 1768 that tea was made from a shrub grown near Portland, Maine. It was served to

> a circle of Ladies and Gentlemen in Newbury Port, who pronounced it nearly, if not quite, equal in Flavor to genuine Bohea tea. . . . So important a Discovery claims, especially at this Crisis, the Attention of every Friend of America. If we have the Plant nothing is wanting but the Process of curing it, to have Tea of our own Manufacture. If a Receipt cannot be obtained, Gentlemen of Curiosity and Chymical Skill would render their Country eminent Service, if by Experiments they would investigate the best method of preparing it for use.[18]

Resistance to the tax acts was strong in Boston. British troops were sent to the city in 1768; two years later, their presence led to the Boston Massacre, which killed three Bostonians and wounded others. In 1770, the British Parliament extended a peace offering to the colonists by rescinding all the Townshend taxes—except for the tax on tea. That tax caused the price of tea in Britain and the colonies to be at least 80 percent higher than the price for tea on the world market. As a result, an estimated 4 to 6 million pounds of tea were smuggled into Great Britain alone.[19] The price of tea was even higher in the British colonies because tea could be legally shipped into the colonies only from England, which involved extra shipping costs, warehousing, and even more taxes. In British North America, the East India Company even had a harder sell because tea had been boycotted on and off by many merchants since 1767 when the British Parliament had first levied the tea tax. When any ship arrived in Boston carrying tea from England, extensive discussion ensued among the populace about what should be done. John Hancock, a wealthy merchant and supporter of the colonial cause, agreed to return the "detestable weed" back to the consignees in London without charge.[20]

Colonial anger grew. Delegations of citizens visited merchants to discourage them from selling tea, women pledged to not to buy tea, and colonial assemblies expressed their dissatisfaction over British policies. Tea continued to be imported, but it was put in storage because few merchants would sell it. As the *Boston Gazette* reported in April 1770, "There is not above one seller of tea in town who has not signed an agreement not to dispose of any tea until the late revenue acts are repealed."[21]

Americans continued to consume tea, but most of it was smuggled in from Dutch sources. Perhaps as much as 3 million pounds of smuggled tea arrived in the colonies, and smuggling cost the British East India Company an estimated £40,000 annually in lost revenue. So as not to offend those organizing the boycott of taxed tea, American colonists made the smuggled tea in coffee pots and drank it in back rooms.[22] But was the tea really smuggled in? Colonists did not know for sure. John Adams confessed in his diary in 1771 that, while dining with John Hancock, he "drank green tea, from Holland, I hope, but don't know."[23] Although the boycott continued, tea as a topic of discussion subsided.

The issue might have quietly died had the East India Company, which imported tea from China, not begun to suffer financial reverses due to the boycott and smuggling. By 1773, the East India Company had 17 million pounds of tea sitting in chests in warehouses that it could not sell in England or North America. The company was teetering on the verge of bankruptcy, so much so that the British government had to lend it money. Parliament wanted the company to thrive so that the government would have a revenue stream and the East India Company would be able to pay off its loan.

Officials of the East India Company had a good idea to solve their problem. They approached Parliament with the idea of lowering the tax even more so that English tea would be more competitive with smuggled Dutch tea. Parliament responded by passing the Tea Act, which lowered taxes on tea shipped from England to the North American colonies. Colonists would have to pay only 1 penny per pound. To take advantage of this change, which the East India Company believed would be well received in North America, the company rushed 600,000 pounds of tea to North America. Seven ships loaded with tea were sent to ports from Charleston to Boston.[24] From Parliament's perspective, this had the advantage of establishing the principle that Parliament could tax British colonies.

This strategy might have worked in 1766. However, by 1773, the colonists were united in their opposition, in principle, to any tax Parliament levied that had not been approved by their own colonial legislatures. Even if the tax on tea was lower, it was still a tax levied by Parliament, not by their own assemblies. Therefore, the leaders in the North American colonies banded together to oppose the landing of any taxed tea.

It was Boston where the first tea ships arrived in late November 1773. After numerous attempts to send the ships back to England failed, colonists tossed the tea into the harbor on December 16. The ship destined for Charleston, South Carolina, arrived on December 3. Opponents of the tea tax convinced local consignees who had ordered the tea to refuse its delivery. The law required all duties on the tea to be paid by the twenty-first day after the ship arrived; if the duties were not paid, the tea could be confiscated. This is precisely what happened in Charleston: all 257 chests of tea were confiscated by the port's customs collector. Leaders in other colonies were disappointed because Charleston was the only city in which the tea was unloaded. But the tea remained in storage for more than two years, until July 1776, when it was sold by local officials to help support the revolution.[25]

America's largest city, Philadelphia, had been astir for weeks before the *Polly*, another of the ships laden with tea, arrived at the city's waterfront on December 25, 1773. The harbor pilots who escorted ships into Philadelphia's shallow harbor were warned not to bring this ship near the port, so it anchored four miles away. Meanwhile, an estimated 5,000 men gathered in the city, and many more were on the way from surrounding communities. These colonists decided that the ship would not land and the tea would not be unloaded. The consignee for the tea denounced the contract he had made, and the leaders of the meeting convinced the ship's captain to leave the harbor within twenty-four hours, which he did. His departure may have been hastened by a threat that his ship would be burned if it did not leave.[26] In New York, the consignees withdrew their orders for tea based on threats to them if they did not. Thus the ship bound for New York returned to England.[27] It was only in Boston—where the British had a strong military presence—that the matter came to a head when neither the loyalist colonial governor nor those opposed to paying the tax on tea would back down when the ships carrying the tea arrived in the harbor.

When word of the Boston Tea Party reached England, the news astonished and angered most leaders there. They considered the action an act of defiance (which it was) and concluded that Parliament must respond forcefully if it were to retain its authority over the colonies. In their view, Parliament had "to make such provisions as should secure the just dependence of the Colonies, and a due obedience to the laws, throughout all the British dominions." Parliament thus decided to punish Boston, which had been a hotbed of resistance to royal policies for the previous eight years. In March 1774, Parliament passed the Boston Port Bill, "interdicting all commercial intercourse with the port of Boston, and prohibiting the landing and shipping of any goods at that place" until Bostonians paid the East India Company for the tea that had been destroyed and complied with Parliament's tax on imported tea.[28] In addition, the new law disbanded the Massachusetts colonial assembly and prohibited all public meetings in Boston. To enforce these measures, Great Britain sent more warships and troops to the city.

These actions might well have forced Boston's compliance with the British law, but surrounding communities came to the city's relief by sending food and supplies. The British actions alienated other colonies, and they too sent money and supplies to help those in Boston who suffered as a result of British policies. A number of colonial leaders established committees of correspondence to improve communications among the colonies. What emerged from these efforts was the First Continental Congress, which met in Philadelphia in September 1774 and consisted of representatives from twelve colonies. One of the first things this Congress did was pass a nonimportation agreement, by which those colonies represented at the meeting agreed not to import or export any goods to Great Britain, Ireland, or the West Indies.

Attempts to unload shipments of taxed tea continued but faced major opposition. A tea ship destined for Boston arrived on March 7, 1774; it too was boarded by men in disguise and its tea destroyed.[29] In April 1774, two tea ships—the *Nancy* and the *London*—entered New York harbor at about the same time. The tea consignee to the *Nancy* sent a note to the captain, reporting that the populace of the city was "violently opposed" to the landing or vending of the tea and "that any attempts in us, either to effect one or the other would not only be fruitless, but expose so considerable a property to inevitable destruction." The *Nancy* returned to England without unloading its tea. The captain of the *London* claimed that there was no tea onboard, but when the ship was searched, it was found to contain eighteen chests of tea. The Sons of Liberty, dressed like American Indians, threw the chests into New York harbor and threatened the captain, who hid to avoid bodily harm. He left New York at the earliest opportunity.[30]

In August 1774, the brig *Mary and Jane* arrived at the St. Mary's River in Maryland with several packages of tea on board, consigned to merchants in the towns of Georgetown and Bladensburg. The merchants who had ordered the tea were called before the Charles County Committee, whose members supported the boycott of tea. After it became clear that the duty on the tea had not been paid, the consignees agreed to send the tea back to England.[31] The *Peggy Stewart*, a ship owned by a merchant named Anthony Stewart, arrived in Annapolis, Maryland, on October 15, 1774. Thomas William, a merchant in the city, had contracted for the tea while in London and, according to the commander of the brig, brought back seventeen chests (about 2,320 pounds) of that "detestable plant" with him without the commander's knowledge. Stewart paid the duty on the tea, but left it on the vessel. Subsequently, Stewart and Williams were brought before the Committee of the County, composed of citizens of Anne Arundel County who supported the tea boycott. When threatened with tarring and feathering and hanging, Stewart agreed to burn his ship with the tea onboard. The committee also required Stewart and Williams to acknowledge their misdeeds in the *Maryland Gazette*. Both Williams and Stewart wisely headed off to London with their families shortly after the incident.[32] Six months after the burning of the *Peggy Stewart*, the American War of Independence broke out.

When the Party Was Over

Although tea was available sporadically in North America during the Revolutionary War, it was considered unpatriotic to drink it. John Adams particularly loved tea and tried to acquire some in Falmouth shortly after the Boston Tea Party. But in a letter to his wife, he wrote that he asked the proprietress of the house where he was staying in Falmouth, "Is it lawfull for a weary Traveller to refresh himself with a Dish of Tea provided it has been honestly smuggled, or paid no Duties?" The proprietress replied, "No sir, . . . we have renounced all Tea in this Place." Adams thereafter drank coffee, but he added in the letter to his wife the rousing comment, "Tea must be universally renounced, and I must be weaned, and the sooner the better."[33] As historian Benjamin W. Labaree wrote, an "anti-tea hysteria" swept the colonies.[34]

On April 13, 1776, the Continental Congress lifted the ban on selling tea while keeping the ban on buying tea from the East India Company. All East India tea then warehoused in America was sold.[35] Although the consumption of tea was limited by the British blockade, it appears to have been regularly available throughout the American Revolution. George Washington tried to acquire as much tea as possible for the Continental Army, and Swedish military officer Jean Axel, Comte de Fersen, reported that tea was available to the troops at Valley Forge, even though many necessities were not.[36]

French military officers in America during the Revolution commented freely on the custom of drinking tea. Claude Victor Marie, Prince de Broglie, who visited Philadelphia in 1782, drank twelve cups at the home of Mrs. Robert Morris. Of this experience, he wrote:

I partook of most excellent tea and I should be even now still drinking it, I believe, if the Ambassador had not charitably notified me at the twelfth cup, that I must put my spoon across it when I wished to finish with this sort of warm water. He said to me: it is almost as ill-bred to refuse a cup of tea when it is offered to you, as it would be indiscreet for the mistress of the house to propose a fresh one, when the ceremony of the spoon has notified her that we no longer wish to partake of it.[37]

Claude C. Robin, a Catholic abbot serving as the "chaplain-in-chief" of the French Army in America, took delight in tea drinking while in Newport, Rhode Island: "[T]he greatest mark of civility and welcome they can show you, is to invite you to drink it with them"[38] Louis Philippe, Comte de Ségur, another aristocrat who served in the French Army in America, recounted that he was in good health despite the "quantity of tea one must drink with the ladies out of gallantry, and of Madeira all day long with the men out of politeness."[39]

Others purportedly suffered due to tea's absence. When the Frenchman J. P. Brissot de Warville visited America after the war, he reported on "several persons whom the deprivation of tea had made ill for a long time, although they had tried illusive means, by substituting the infusion of agreeable simples for that of the tea-leaf."[40]

When the American Revolution ended in 1783, tea drinking again became fashionable among America's well-to-do. Tea parties and tea balls regained their former glory.[41] In 1791, a visiting Prussian military officer, Dietrich Heinrich, Freiherr Von Bülow, reported that in Philadelphia a guest was expected to consume two cups of tea.[42] Médéric Moreau de Saint-Méry, a French Creole from Martinique, was an early leader of the French Revolution; he ran afoul of other radicals in France and took his family to America during the 1790s. Moreau de Saint-Méry reported that Americans "passionately loved" their tea, which was served at the first and second meals of the day;

tea constituted the entire third meal, when "the whole family is united at tea, to which friends, acquaintances and even strangers are invited. . . . Evening tea is a boring and monotonous ceremony. The mistress of the house serves it and passes it around, and as long as a person has not turned his cup upside down and placed his spoon upon it, just so often will he be brought another cup."[43] Tea remained an important beverage in America after the War of Independence—especially among the well-to-do—but the price remained high because it could be acquired only from China.

All the Tea in China

Prior to the Revolutionary War, all legally sold tea had been shipped from China to England and then to North America. Tea smuggled into the colonies came from China via Holland, as American vessels could not trade directly with China. As the war was ending, Robert Morris, a Philadelphia merchant and a signer of the Declaration of Independence, saw a great opportunity: it was time to cut out the middlemen and trade directly with China. Morris joined with others to outfit a ship, the *Empress of China*, which sailed out of New York on February 22, 1784, and returned fifteen months later with a cargo mainly of tea. When this tea was sold, each investor netted $30,000. Other ships made the journey to China as well, and soon a thriving business between the two countries was under way. By 1789, more American ships were sailing to Canton, China, than to any country other than Great Britain. During the following decade, American consumption of tea remained constant.[44]

During the last year of the American Revolution, a German flute maker named John Jacob Astor immigrated to America. Starting from scratch, Astor built a business based on the fur trade and made a fortune. When he saw the profits in the tea trade with China, Astor jumped in, shipping furs to China and bringing back tea in return. Astor's trade with China began in 1800 and ended in 1826, earning him another fortune. Astor invested this money in Manhattan real estate and then farm land, making himself a third fortune.[45]

During the War of 1812, a new type of sailing ship was launched in Baltimore—fast sailing ships that could outrun the blockade that Great Britain maintained during the war. After the war ended in 1815, even larger versions of these clipper ships began sailing to China to acquire tea; this trade that continued to generate good sales in the United States up until the Civil War.

Despite increased sales, however, tea slipped in favor; during the 1830s, coffee consumption overtook that of tea.

Poisonous Tea

During the eighteenth century, some medical professionals questioned the benefits of tea drinking. A physician from Edinburgh, Scotland, for instance, demonstrated in 1707 that green tea "had the same effect as henbane, tobacco, cicuta, etc., on the living tissues of the animal body; in all cases first diminishing and finally destroying their vital properties." In 1730, a writer in the *New York Gazette* proclaimed that tea produced fatal effects on health and mind. A scientist from Sweden who visited the colonies in 1750 believed that American women lost their teeth because of the amount of tea they were drinking—although after more careful consideration, he concluded that probably was not accurate. In 1803, an English doctor named Thomas Beddoes demonstrated that tea was "as powerfully destructive to life as laurel water, opium, or digitalis." Indeed, the doctor claimed that even "a small quantity of a strong decoction of tea or coffee will destroy human life."[46]

Beginning in the 1830s, a number of American health professionals also opposed the consumption of tea. The food reformer Sylvester Graham, for example, believed that tea was "stimulating food" and therefore should be banned. The medical professional William Alcott maintained that tea was not only useless, but positively hurtful. He concluded that it was a narcotic and therefore poisonous.[47] Many health professionals throughout the nineteenth century agreed. As Dio Lewis, a Harvard-trained physician who campaigned around the country against the use of tea, noted in one of his books:

> I frequently met three or four middle-aged or old women, and during several hours had opportunity to observe them closely. If some time had passed since they had partaken of tea, they were unsocial and irritable. Their eyes would not sparkle, except on hearing the question, "I wonder when tea will be ready?" When they had drank their two cups "that would hold up an egg," what a loosening of tongues! Each would talk straight on, for an hour, without a comma; but when its influence was over, they fell into weariness and irritability again, only to be revived by another dose. When we witness the same phenomenon among opium eaters, we are sure they are ruining their health. That tea-drinking seriously impairs the health of many women, I know. How exactly alike all strong tea-drinkers

are—the same black teeth and dry, yellow skin; the same expression of eye; the same nervousness and periodical headache.[48]

It wasn't health concerns, however, that dethroned tea as America's most important hot beverage. It was the introduction of lower-cost and higher-caffeinated coffee from Central and South America beginning in the 1830s. Coffee gave a greater jolt to consumers and had none of the feminine associations as tea did.

Tea Revival

Despite medical concerns about tea and coffee's rise to ascendency, tea continued to be consumed in large quantities, especially by women.[49] Afternoon teas became common in restaurants and homes, particularly in the South. Tea drinking was buttressed by the arrival of immigrants from tea-drinking countries. It was first the Irish who arrived en masse due to the potato famine that began in the late 1840s, and later immigrants from Russia who began arriving later in the century. During the 1850s, articles appeared in American magazines extolling "tea for the ladies," and tea was romanticized in other articles about plantations in Ceylon, China, and India. Tea wagons prowled city streets offering tea, coffee, and other specialty items.

The most unusual innovation in tea drinking began in the 1850s, when many Americans started drinking tea as an iced beverage in the summer. By that time, ice was widely available throughout the United States, and it chilled other beverages.[50] Serving iced tea with lemon was fashionable; it was called "à la Russe." Iced tea became extremely popular in the United States after the Civil War, especially in the South.[51]

Despite the decline in per capita tea consumption, fortunes were still to be had in importing and retailing tea. New Yorkers enjoyed tea. By 1860, there were sixty-five retail tea shops in the city.[52] J. Stiner & Company, for instance, made good money importing and selling tea. It diversified the products that it sold; by 1871, it was New York's largest chain store operation.[53]

Another tea shop was launched by George F. Gilman and George H. Hartford. They imported teas, coffees, and other products. Gilman and Hartford opened a retail tea store in New York City and also began selling tea through the mail. Three years later, they named their business the Great American Tea Company. Sales were good enough that Gilman and Hartford started buying tea in bulk, which enabled them to lower their expenses even further and undersell other grocers. Like J. Stiner & Company, Gilman and Hartford expanded their line of goods to include coffee and other luxury products. By 1865, the partners had five small stores in New York City. The completion of the transcontinental railroad in 1869 made it possible for the Great American Tea Company to receive shipments of tea and other specialty goods from Asia via San Francisco, and then transport them by train throughout the United States. Hartford and Gilman opened stores across the nation, and they changed the name of the new bicoastal company to the Great Atlantic and Pacific Tea Company, subsequently shortened to A&P. In the 1870s, A&P was the largest distributor of tea in America. Over the next few decades, the A&P stores gradually augmented their inventory to include a full range of groceries.[54]

Other companies that started out as tea distributors followed similar paths. In 1876, Bernard H. Kroger, for instance, began selling tea and coffee door to door in Cincinnati. Eight years later, he and a friend formed the Great Western Tea Company. By 1885, the company had four stores. The company expanded its offerings and, in 1902, the company's name was changed to Kroger Grocery and Baking Company. Tea was readily available in specialty stores as well as grocery stores, which expanded throughout the nation in the late nineteenth century.

Tea consumption was not just boosted by its availability in grocery stores and specialty shops. Tea companies promoted their products, as did plantation owners in India. The Indian Tea Association sent Richard Blechynden to the United States to promote its tea. In 1893, Blechynden invested $15,000 to build and staff the East India Pavilion at the World's Columbian Exposition in Chicago. The pavilion included exhibitions demonstrating how tea was grown and manufactured. Tea was served at the pavilion and throughout the exposition by vendors. When the Louisiana Purchase Exposition was held in St. Louis in 1904, plantation owners in India and Ceylon thought it was worthwhile to increase their investment to $150,000 to lavishly promote their teas. At both fairs, iced tea was distributed; because the summers were hot, it received visibility among fairgoers.[55]

Per capita tea consumption hit a peak in 1897 with Americans consuming an average of 1.56 pounds of tea. The federal government then placed a 10-cent per pound tariff on imported tea. Tea consumption declined to a per capita consumption of 1 pound by 1907. To stop this decline, tea distributors created the National Tea Association to press for increased tea consumption. It was a losing battle, with per capita consumption continuing to decline thereafter.[56]

There were some positive developments. Tearooms became common in many large cities and rural areas in the United States during the late nineteenth century. These tearooms were largely owned, operated, and frequented by women, who saw the establishments as good alternatives to the saloons where men congregated. Although tearooms did not revolve around tea—they were more like lunchrooms—tea was an important item on their menus. Tearooms became particularly popular during Prohibition but went out of fashion after repeal in 1933.[57]

Until the early twentieth century, tea was purchased in bulk; loose tea had to be measured for each cup of tea. Hot water was then added, and the tea had to be steeped. The tea then had to be strained from the cup. This process was simplified by the invention of tea bags, eggs, and balls in the early twentieth century.[58] By the 1920s, restaurants began using tea bags as a more efficient way to make and serve tea. During the following decade, a diversity of tea bags were manufactured and home use increased.[59]

Tea drinking largely disappeared in America during World War II, when importation of tea from Asia was impossible. However, it reemerged as an important beverage after the war ended. Lipton introduced the four-sided tea bag in 1952, and Instant Tea came out five years later. In the 1960s, countercultural groups began marketing herbal teas. Celestial Seasonings, for instance, was established in 1969 in Boulder, Colorado. The company offered herbal teas that were additive free, organically grown, or gathered in the wild; some of the teas were suggested as remedies for ailments such as sore throat and insomnia. Erewhon, after acquiring the venerable cereal company U.S. Mills in 1986, is now one of largest retailers, manufacturers, and distributors of natural foods (including tea) in the United States. Celestial Seasonings, sold to Kraft in 1984, became independent again in 1988 and is now the country's largest purveyor of specialty teas.

Yet another recent development has been the rise of bottled and canned ready-to-drink teas in the late 1980s. These teas include a number of different product lines, including Ferolito Vultaggio and Sons (AriZona), Honest Tea, Thomas J. Lipton, Nestlé (Nestea), South Beach Beverages (SoBe), and Turkey Hill. The most successful bottled teas have been those released by the Snapple Beverage Company in 1987. Today, there are "an endless number of categories, types, blends and brands to chose from," notes Laura C. Martin.[60]

Tea was an unlikely beverage to set in motion a series of events that would lead to a revolution, but the Boston Tea Party was the spark that ignited the American War of Independence. Tea also became important in American trade with China during the early and mid-nineteenth century. Today, it is the most consumed hot beverage in the world, but in the United States it lags far behind coffee and soda.

Postscript

On April 15, 1775, General Thomas Gage, commander of the British forces in Boston, ordered the destruction of the arsenals and arms that the colonists had collected in Lexington and Concord, thus beginning the Revolutionary War. On June 17, 1775, he won a pyrrhic victory over the colonial forces on Breeds and Bunker Hill. As soon as word reached London of this engagement and its 1,000 British casualties, Gage was recalled to England, where he remained until his death in 1787.

Faced with death threats even after he burned his brig, Anthony Stewart took his family to London. When the British Army occupied New York in 1776, Stewart moved back to the city and joined an association of other Loyalists. When the war was over, Maryland confiscated Stewart's property, declared him a traitor, and sentenced him to death. Like many other Loyalists fleeing the American Revolution, Stewart fled to Nova Scotia.

After the American Revolution, Prince de Broglie returned to France, where he was guillotined during the French Revolution in 1794.

J. P. Brissot de Warville became a leader of the French Revolution, but he ran afoul of those who were even more radical, and he too was guillotined in October 1793.

Jean Axel, Comte de Fersen, the Swedish military officer, became a close friend of Marie Antoinette, France's queen, before the American Revolution and remained in contact with her after the war. After King Louis XVI was guillotined during the French Revolution, Fersen set up an escape plan for Marie Antoinette, but before it could be implemented, she too was guillotined. Fersen returned to Sweden, where in 1810 he was tortured and murdered by a mob who disagreed with his political views.

The aristocrat Louis Philippe, Comte de Ségur, survived the French Revolution and died in France in 1830.

🔖 Upon his return to Prussia, Dietrich Heinrich, Freiherr Von Bülow, wrote a number of works that were contemptuous of Prussia. Because of this, he was thrown into prison, where he died in 1807.

🔖 Robert Morris engaged in land speculation in Philadelphia and lost his fortune. He was thrown into debtors' prison, where he became ill. He died shortly after his release from prison in 1806.

🔖 When John Jacob Astor died in 1848, he was the wealthiest man in America.

🔖 George F. Gilman remained president of the Great Atlantic and Pacific Tea Company until 1879; he died in 1901. George H. Hartford became president of the company in 1879 and remained in that position until his death in 1915. At that time, there were more than 3,000 A&P grocery stores in the United States. Hartford's sons took control of the business and expanded the number of stores even further. The efforts of both Gilman and Hartford ensured that A&P would be the largest grocery store chain for more than fifty years.

🔖 Samuel Adams served as a delegate to the Continental Congress and also the Massachusetts ratifying convention for what became the U.S. Constitution. He was elected lieutenant governor of Massachusetts in 1789 and then governor in 1793. He died in Boston in 1803.

🔖 The 1773 Boston Tea Party has regularly served as an inspiration for disgruntled anti-tax advocates ever since. Its most recent reincarnation is the tea party movement, which emerged in 2009.

🔖 When refrigerators with freezer compartments became common in the mid-twentieth century, iced tea became one of America's favorite beverages. Today, most tea in the United States—about 85 percent—is consumed iced.

🔖 Although taxes on tea and rum contributed to the American War of Independence, a tax on whiskey would lead to a rebellion against the United States.

Capture of the Whiskey-Tax Collectors, depicting the
apprehension of tax collectors in Pennsylvania during
the Whiskey Rebellion of 1794. (From *Columbus and
Columbia: A Pictorial History of Man and the Nation*
[ca. 1893]. Private collection/© Look and Learn/The
Bridgeman Art Library)

4

Tarantula Juice

RUM WAS THE DOMINANT American spirit before the Revolutionary War. However, when the war broke out in 1775, the importation of molasses from the Caribbean almost ceased, and it remained difficult to acquire molasses during the following eight years. Whiskey, however, was the obvious alternative. Whiskey could be made from abundant locally grown grain, so its production and consumption skyrocketed during the war.

In 1778, distilleries in Virginia bought so much of the available grain for whiskey making that the state legislature prohibited the distilleries from using it to make spirits; legislators wanted to ensure there was enough grain for bread production. It is noteworthy that this law was in effect for only three months before it was repealed.[1] When the American Revolution ended in 1783, the British forbade molasses trading with their colonies in the Caribbean, but the other European colonies increased their exports of molasses to the new nation. Although rum distillers quickly regained some of their market share on the East Coast, many Americans had become fond of whiskey; in addition, it was less expensive than rum. Therefore, whiskey's popularity continued to grow after the war's end.[2]

The Revolutionary War caused another important change to American whiskey drinking. Prior to the war, the British had decreed that the lands west of the Appalachian Mountains were reserved for the

American Indians. Some settlers from the East Coast violated this decree, but when the peace treaty ending the American Revolution gave all British-controlled lands east of the Mississippi River to the fledgling nation, thousands of American settlers headed west. The population of western Pennsylvania increased from 33,000 at the war's end to 95,000 by 1800. Most settlers west of the Appalachians carved out subsistence farms and grew grains, including wheat, rye, and corn. Because transportation was difficult for bulky goods, grains could be more easily converted into whiskey, which was more compact, easier to transport, and valuable. Whiskey production increased, and it would soon become America's spirit of choice. But before this happened, a problem arose: Congress needed money to help pay the debts incurred during the American Revolution. An excise tax on distilled spirits, including whiskey, was the solution—and it would lead to a rebellion.

Background

Fermented beverages such as wine, cider, and beer were created in ancient times and commonly produced in prehistoric Europe. Consisting mainly of water, these ancient beverages were relatively low in alcoholic content—from 1 to 6 percent, depending on the product and the process by which it was made.

The concept of distilled spirits arrived in Europe from Muslim lands in approximately the twelfth century. Distillation is a relatively simple process in which alcohol is separated from a fermented liquid, such as wine or cider. Because water has a higher boiling point than alcohol, heating a fermented liquid to at least 172°F but less than 212°F will vaporize the alcohol but not the water. The gaseous ethanol then can be captured through a still; once cooled, the alcohol returns to a liquid state. This method is not perfect; some water also evaporates, but the alcoholic content can be intensified by repeating the distillation process several times. After the introduction of distillation, distilled spirits quickly spread throughout the continent of Europe, becoming an important part of daily life. Distilled spirits were used medicinally; they also were added to wine to increase its alcoholic content.

Making distilled spirits became quite popular in some places in Europe. In the Middle Ages, Europeans frequently called distilled spirits by the Latin name *aqua vitae*, which means "water of life." In the Gaelic language of Ireland, the phrase became *uisce beatha*, which may have been transformed into the English word "whiskey"—a distilled liquor made from grains (mainly wheat and rye).

During the colonial period, an estimated 250,000 Scots-Irish immigrants arrived in America, bringing their love of whiskey with them. By 1760, whiskey making was a common practice throughout the colonies.[3] Whiskey was frequently drunk in the morning, when it was combined with wild cherries (or other bitter fruit or bitter bark) to produce morning bitters. Workers at harvest time also devoured it in great quantities.[4]

Grain growers who were located west of the Appalachians, faced a challenge. Few mountain roads connected their lands to the East, and no navigable rivers or canals ran from the East Coast to the western areas. Moreover, the mouth of Mississippi River, then controlled by Spain, was often closed to American shipping. Shipping bulky grain over the mountains to eastern cities was thus too expensive to be profitable. The solution was to convert the grains, mainly rye, into a less bulky product—whiskey. Not only was whiskey a cheap substitute for rum, which had to be conveyed over the mountains from the East Coast, but it also was a liquid asset. Small quantities could be carried on horseback to local and regional markets, where it was bartered for commodities, such as salt or iron, that were not produced in the West.[5] Sharecroppers and tenant farmers could even pay their rent with whiskey, and employers could compensate their laborers with it as well.[6]

There was always plenty of whiskey to go around on the frontier—maybe even too much. Whiskey-loving frontiersmen were prone to violence when they overindulged, and their behavior exceeded anything that visiting easterners had previously witnessed.[7] Perhaps it was just snobbery; those who visited the frontier and wrote about their experiences were mainly from the upper class. To them, whiskey was the poor man's drink. The elite preferred imported wine or brandy, of which they drank copious quantities.[8]

Anti-Whiskey Movement

The rise of American whiskey production elicited some fervent opposition. During the Revolutionary War, Continental Army soldiers were given a daily ration of whiskey, rum, or cider when available. Soldiers could also buy alcohol from sulters and other local sources. Soldiers and officers drank considerable quantities of alcohol, and inebriation caused many problems during the war.[9]

One man who was deeply concerned with drinking in the Continental Army was Dr. Benjamin Rush of Philadelphia, the nation's first surgeon general. During the American War for Independence, Rush became concerned with alcoholism in the army, so he wrote a pamphlet, *Directions for Preserving the Health of Soldiers* (1777), arguing against the use of alcohol to diminish the effects of extreme cold or heat. The use of alcohol for this purpose, Rush pointed out, did not produce the desired effect; it was merely an excuse to drink. Rush also was concerned with the alcohol consumption of army officers. He urged his friend John Adams, the future president of the United States, to pass a resolution stating that "if any major or brigadier general drink more than a quart of whiskey . . . in twenty-four hours, he shall be publically reprimanded at the head of his division or brigade."[10] Rush and George Washington had a falling out, and Rush was removed from his position with the Continental Army; however, he remained an important political leader.

Rush wrote a letter to the *Pennsylvania Journal* in 1782 arguing against the then-common practice of providing workers with generous allotments of distilled beverages during harvest time; he suggested water, beer, and buttermilk as alternatives, but his advice was widely ignored. Rush believed the best way to discourage people from drinking was to educate them. In 1773, he helped establish Dickinson College in Carlisle, Pennsylvania, located in a region on the frontier settled initially by Scots-Irish immigrants and later by Germans. While visiting the college in 1784, Rush saw still houses on virtually every farm. "The Quantity of Rye destroyed & of Whisky drank in these places is immense," he wrote in his diary, and he feared "its effects upon their industry—health & morals are terrible. I was sorry to hear that the Germans in some places were beginning to be corrupted with it."[11] The Scots-Irish did indeed enjoy their whiskey, which was the national beverage in Ireland. They had brought their love of *uisce beatha* with them to western Pennsylvania.

Upon returning to Philadelphia after his visit to Carlisle, Rush launched an educational campaign against distilled spirits with the publication of a pamphlet, *An Enquiry into the Effects of Spirituous Liquors on the Human Body and Their Influence upon the Happiness of Society* (1784). In it, he concluded that "a people corrupted by strong drink cannot long be free people" and that Americans should give up ardent spirits "suddenly and entirely."[12]

Rush then encouraged the prestigious College of Physicians of Philadelphia to endorse temperance. It worked. The college proclaimed that distilled alcoholic beverages—rum, whiskey, and brandy—gave rise to serious and tragic illnesses, including "Dropsy, Epilepsy, Palsy, Apoplexy, Melancholy and Madness; which too seldom yield to the powers of medicine." The college further observed that "where distilled spirituous liquors do not produce these terrible and obstinate diseases they generally impair the strength of the body so as to lessen its ability to undergo that labour, either in degree or duration, which it is capable of without them." The College of Physicians requested that the Pennsylvania state legislature enact a law "for the checking the improper use of distilled spirituous liquors."[13]

Whiskey Tax

As a result of the American Revolution, the states that had borne the brunt of the conflict were left with heavy debts. Some states paid down their debts, but others did not. When the Constitution was ratified and Congress first met in 1789, one of the important questions for those attending was what to do with these debts. Secretary of the Treasury Alexander Hamilton and others wanted the federal government to assume responsibility. Virginians Thomas Jefferson, then the secretary of state, and James Madison, a leader in the House of Representatives, opposed this. They argued that since Virginia had already paid off half of its war debts, it was unfair that Virginians should now pick up part of the burden for other states that had not bothered to do so. However, Jefferson and Madison wanted the nation's capital (then in Philadelphia) to be moved south, so they reached a compromise: the federal government would take care of the states' unpaid war debts, and the nation's capital would be moved to a spot along the Potomac River, which ran between Virginia and Maryland.

A serious problem remained, however: How could the federal government pay off the debts? The nation's main source of revenue at the time was import duties. Hamilton informed Congress that import duties would not cover the costs of both the federal government and the servicing of the war debts. At the request of Congress, Hamilton submitted the "Report on Public Credit" in January 1790. In the report, Hamilton recommended a tax on distilled spirits:

> Some of them, in the excess in which they are used, [are] pernicious luxuries. And there is, perhaps, none of them which is not consumed in so great abundance as may justly denominate it a source of national extravagance and impoverishment. The consumption of ardent spirits, particularly, no doubt very much on account of their cheapness, is carried to an extreme which is truly to be regretted, as well in regard to the health and the morals, as to the economy of the community.[14]

Although his proposal for taxes included several other beverages, including tea and coffee, the others were imported and already part of the federal government's purview; these were not new taxes but only increases in previously established revenue sources. However, an excise tax on the domestic production of spirits, such as whiskey, was a new tax.

Pro-Tax

Excise taxes on spirits had been levied previously in other countries, such as England and Ireland, but these laws proved ineffective because distillers simply refused to pay and enforcement was weak. Since its founding as a colony, Pennsylvania itself had passed at least nineteen laws taxing distilled spirits; these laws had levied fees on the retail sale of distilled spirits rather than on the production of the alcohol.[15] In March 1783, the Pennsylvania legislature passed another excise tax on distilled liquor that evoked strong opposition, particularly from farmers in western Pennsylvania. The inhabitants of Westmoreland County, for instance, petitioned the state legislature to repeal the tax. They viewed the law with "general disapprobation" and "universal abhorrence and detestation." Farmers reported that spirits were absolutely necessary to attract the hordes of laborers required for harvest. Moreover, since distilleries supplied whiskey in the same way that mills supplied flour, they wondered why they "should be made subject to a duty for drinking our grain more than eating it."[16] The Pennsylvania legislature rescinded the excise tax on distilled spirits and directed its senators and congressmen to vote against the bill to levy an excise tax on whiskey production that was introduced into Congress in May 1790.

Nationally, strong arguments on both sides of the excise tax issue were presented. Its supporters saw the bill as a good solution to the issue of war debts; if passed, it also promised public health benefits because it was thought that increasing the price of hard liquor would discourage consumption.[17] On the anti-tax side, there was strong opposition because of concern about the ability of the federal government to tax citizens directly—a power that the Confederation did not have. Pennsylvania representatives opposed the bill as directed by their state legislature. Southern representatives opposed the bill because whiskey was more commonly manufactured in the western portions of their states. The tax opponents carried the day, and the bill was soundly defeated in Congress in June 1790. Over the next few months, Congress explored other possible revenue sources, but all were rejected. Many feared that if legislators could not agree on a solution, the compromise reached earlier that year might be in danger.

Congress thus requested that Alexander Hamilton write another report identifying potential revenue sources. Hamilton submitted the "Further Report on Public Credit" in December 1790. In the report, Hamilton again recommended a tax on whiskey, and a new bill was introduced. This time, however, the excise tax generated considerable public support. The main reason for this shift was that Benjamin Rush and other physicians came out for the bill, hoping that the tax would reduce alcohol use and alcoholism. The College of Physicians of Philadelphia passed a resolution requesting that Congress endorse the excise tax as a means of reforming the "morals and manners" of whiskey drinkers. The physicians proclaimed that the "pernicious effects" of distilled spirits caused "a great proportion of the most obstinate, painful and mortal disorders, which affect the human body" and that "they are not only destructive to health and life, but . . . they impair the faculties of the mind, and thereby tend equally to dishonor our character as a nation, and to degrade our species as intelligent beings." They ardently urged Congress to "impose such heavy duties upon all distilled spirits as shall be effectual to restrain their intemperate use in our country." This resolution was published in the *Gazette of the United States* in January 1791, as were letters supporting the measure. One reader wrote that if women had been able to vote on this measure, it would readily pass because women suffered more from men's excessive drinking of distilled spirits. If the writer had his way, a 100 percent tax would be leveled on whiskey.[18]

The new bill would impose three different levels of taxes on distilled spirits. The heaviest tax was on imported spirits, such as wine and brandy; prices for these goods would increase by about 50 percent as a result of the new taxes, but the elites who enjoyed these luxury items could well afford the additional cost. A middle tax rate was levied on domestically manufactured spirits made from imported products—mainly rum, which was distilled from imported molasses. Rum was produced almost entirely on the East Coast, and these added costs were also easily passed on to consumers. The lowest tax rate was placed on distilled spirits made from domestic ingredients. This tax was 4 pence (about 8 cents) for each gallon of liquor distilled. For whiskey producers in the East, this tax was again simply passed on to consumers, who did not make much of a fuss about the increase.

In frontier areas, however, this last provision of the tax bill caused an upheaval. At the time, a gallon of whiskey cost about 28 cents in western

Pennsylvania, so the 8-cent tax increased the price by almost 25 percent. This was a hefty increase for subsistence frontiersmen, who produced whiskey to barter for goods they needed. Even worse, in the eyes of the frontiersmen, was that the tax had to be paid in coin by the manufacturer: there was little specie on the frontier, and what was available went for absolute necessities that could not be acquired by barter.

Yet another point of contention was that the tax bill did not discriminate between whiskey made for personal use or for commercial sale. Both were taxed equally. This did not affect large distillers engaged in a commercial business because they did not drink up their profits or barter their goods. But for smaller distillers on the frontier who produced whiskey for their own use as well as for sale, this was a heavy burden to bear. In addition, because much of the whiskey on the frontier was bartered, small producers had to pay the tax and then figure out a way to recoup the expense when bartering their whiskey.

Most of all, westerners objected to the enforcement provisions of the tax bill. In light of the failures of past efforts to collect excise taxes on distilled spirits, Hamilton had insisted on strong enforcement provisions that included taxation districts, government agencies, and a cadre of federal officers to administer and collect the funds.[19] The Pennsylvania legislature again directed its representatives to vote against the law, and other state legislatures opposed it is as well. In fact, all congressmen representing frontier districts voted against the bill with the excise provisions when it was brought to a vote in Congress in March 1791.

James Madison, then a leader in the House of Representatives and an opponent of Alexander Hamilton, concluded that there were no other obvious sources of revenue to pay down the debts and believed that an excise tax on distilled spirits would increase "sobriety and thereby prevent disease and untimely deaths." Madison restrained opposition to the bill in the House, making it possible for the legislation to pass Congress.[20] Passage was one thing; implementation, another.

Anti-Tax

When the excise tax became law, the federal government had been in place only a few years, and many Americans did not yet understand its function or powers. This lack of knowledge was particularly common in frontier areas; the arrival of news on the frontier was often severely delayed, and the information was limited and often thoroughly garbled when it did arrive.

Frontiersmen had strongly supported the American Revolution, and they faced great difficulties fighting American Indians incited by the British during the war. According to the Treaty of Paris, which ended the war in 1783, the British agreed to surrender forts in the frontier areas, but they still had not completely done so in 1791. Virtually every male on the frontier was a member of a militia; most had engaged in fighting Indians who continued to be encouraged by the British well after the war's end.

Many settlers on the western frontier were immigrants from Scotland, Ireland, or Germany who had opposed and successfully evaded previous excise taxes. These independent frontiersmen were not of a mind to deal reasonably with the new governmental entity of the U.S. Congress, which was trying to impose an excise tax from the national level. They were ready to fight.

Rebellion

The initial and most vociferous opposition to the whiskey tax arose in western Pennsylvania counties: Fayette, Westmoreland, Washington, and Allegheny. The anti-tax movement there was led by moderates, such as Albert Gallatin, a Swiss-American immigrant who farmed in Fayette County; Hugh Henry Brackenridge, an immigrant from Scotland living in Pittsburgh who helped found the *Pittsburg Gazette*; Judge William Findley of Westmoreland County, a Scots-Irish immigrant who was elected to the U.S. House of Representatives; and Irish-born John Smilie, who was an assemblyman in the Pennsylvania legislature. The people in the movement held meetings, passed resolutions opposing the tax, and drew up petitions that were signed and sent to the U.S. Congress and the Pennsylvania legislature.

Then, in September 1791, events took a violent turn when tax collectors were tarred and feathered by rogue gangs. Federal judges issued warrants for the arrest of the perpetrators, but the process servers were whipped, tarred, and feathered themselves. One was stripped and branded in several places with a hot iron. People who spoke in favor of the whiskey tax, or who were thought to support it, were treated similarly. William Faulkner—a captain in the army—was threatened with scalping, tarring, and feathering and compelled to print a notice in the *Pittsburg Gazette* stating that he would not support the whiskey tax. Opponents of the tax also broke into the homes of tax supporters and threatened the families. Local sheriffs refused to serve warrants for those identified as responsible for these acts, and the sheriffs themselves were indicted by federal judges. Meanwhile, some distillers announced that they would not pay the tax, and the opposition became highly organized.

The difficulty of enforcing the excise tax in western Pennsylvania raised more questions in Congress about the wisdom of the law. Alexander Hamilton defended the equity of the tax in his "Report on the Difficulties in the Execution of the Act Laying Duties on Distilled Spirits," which he wrote on March 5, 1792, to educate Congress on the ins and outs of the law. Hamilton believed that the tax was equitable because distilled spirits were so widely devoured throughout the United States. Because the taxes would be passed on to the consumers, the amount individuals paid would depend on their "relative habits of sobriety or intemperance." Although Hamilton understood that small producers made whiskey for themselves, he encouraged them to consume less.[21]

As a sop to protestors, Congress lowered the tax rates, but these changes and an appeal from President George Washington seemed only to embolden the insurgents in their opposition to the law.[22] Harassment of federal tax collectors became more widespread and violent. As the incidents of violence accumulated, President Washington stepped in. On September 15, 1792, Washington issued a proclamation that admonished "all persons whom it may concern to refrain and desist from all unlawful combinations and proceedings whatsoever, having for object or tending to obstruct the operation of the laws aforesaid; inasmuch as all lawful ways and means will be strictly put in execution for bringing to justice the infractors thereof, and securing obedience thereto."[23]

Federal marshals, district attorneys, and tax inspectors enforced the law, prosecuting tax delinquents and seizing their distilled spirits on the way to market. As a result, by late 1793 some large whiskey distillers complied with the law, and others expressed their willingness to do so. It looked as if the worst anti-tax fervor was over, but in January 1794 some of those complying with the tax had their barns burned, their stills and equipment destroyed, and their families intimidated.

Congress modified the whiskey tax yet again to make it more equitable, but this further encouraged those who wanted the law repealed. John Neville, the excise inspector for western Pennsylvania, helped to serve warrants on individuals who intimidated tax collectors and warrant servers. On July 16, 1794, forty opponents of the excise tax approached Neville's fortified home; Neville and others inside the house fired at them, wounding several. Neville sent a messenger requesting assistance from nearby justices and soldiers at Fort Lafayette in Pittsburgh, and twelve soldiers were dispatched to help. The following morning, 500 armed men marched on Neville's home, which was defended by only those twelve soldiers from the fort. Several attackers were killed or wounded; a number of the soldiers were also wounded, and one later died of his injuries. The other soldiers escaped along with Neville and his family, but Neville's house and property were destroyed. Neville fled first to Pittsburgh and then to Philadelphia.

Several thousand armed insurgents, with representatives from western Virginia and Maryland, met to discuss the tax. Albert Gallatin (a Swiss immigrant who had been elected to the U.S. Senate in 1793, but was removed from office because he had not lived in America for the requisite nine years), Hugh Henry Brackenridge (a judge), and William Findley (a U.S. congressman) were all opponents of the tax and urged moderation. However, the radicals ignored their advice and marched on Pittsburgh. As the insurgents neared the city, the townspeople proclaimed their opposition to the tax and brought out whiskey for the ragtag army, who greatly appreciated the drink. When the army of insurgents thought more soberly about taking Fort Lafayette, they remembered that it was well armed with cannons and decided it would be more prudent to skirt around it. Only one house was burned in the city. Without a clear target, the group gradually broke up without staging the attack.

By this point, however, the insurrection had gone too far. President George Washington had a choice—either enforce the tax law or fail to do so, thereby weakening the ability of the federal government enforce laws and raise revenue in the future. Washington sided with Hamilton. On August 17, 1794, he issued a proclamation demanding that those who attacked federal officers be brought to justice. Washington called out 12,950 militia detachments from Virginia, Maryland, New Jersey, and eastern Pennsylvania to suppress the insurrection. The president assumed his constitutional power as "commander in chief" to lead federal troops to western Pennsylvania. He traveled to Bedford, Pennsylvania, to review the troops, and then traveled to Maryland to view another portion of the army. As the troops moved toward Pittsburgh, the insurgent army dispersed. Some leaders fled westward; the majority just returned to their homes.

The federal army arrived in Pittsburgh in November 1794, but there was no bloodshed. Agents took testimony from many individuals and identified the leaders of the insurrection. Dragoons were sent to arrest them. Some were nowhere to be found; others who were arrested were released immediately due to lack of evidence. Alexander Hamilton wanted some of the most influential and visible leaders of the insurrection—specifically Findley and Gallatin—to be convicted of treason, but there was not much evidence against them either. A few minor participants were bound and carted off to Philadelphia, where they were held in prison for several months and then released without trial. Only twelve participants in the insurrection were tried; of these, ten were acquitted. There were too few witnesses, and those who did speak up gave contradictory testimony. Only two fairly low-level participants in the insurrection were convicted of treason and sentenced to be hanged. With the crisis over, President Washington stepped in and pardoned these last two insurgents. Officials issued pardons to other participants of the insurrection, most of whom signed loyalty oaths.

An unexpected but welcome bonus resulted: the economy in western Pennsylvania boomed in the aftermath of the turmoil. Soldiers who had come to enforce the liquor tax spent money on food, lodging, and supplies. Among other things, the troops bought liquor from local distillers—as long as they could prove that they had paid the excise tax.[24] Meanwhile, distillers paid the whiskey taxes as long as the troops remained in western Pennsylvania. When they left, however, enforcement slackened, and distillers went back to their old ways.[25]

Western Pennsylvania was the flashpoint in the insurrection against the excise tax, but it was by no means the only place where opposition flared. Local distillers also rose up in portions of Kentucky, Maryland, Virginia, North Carolina, and Georgia.[26] In Kentucky, the men responsible for enforcing the tax were treated as roughly as those in western Pennsylvania.[27] In western Virginia, anti-tax forces assaulted excise officers, destroyed their property, and terrorized proponents of the excise tax. A year after the insurrection was put down, no excise taxes were collected in Kentucky, the Northwest Territory, or the western parts of Virginia and South Carolina.[28] However, tax revenues from the nation as a whole increased during the remainder of the 1790s.

When Thomas Jefferson became president in 1801, he urged Congress to repeal the whiskey tax, which it did. A visiting Frenchman who was on hand for the celebration of the repeal wrote that the lodges were

> filled with drinkers, who made a shocking tumult, and appeared excessively intoxicated. The chambers, the entries, and the stairs were strewed with men, that were dead drunk; and those, to whom utterance remained, expressed only grumblings of rage and horrid imprecations. The passion

for spiritous liquors is one of the traits, that characterizes the inhabitants of the interior. This passion is so strong, that they quit their homes from time to time to go and get drunk at the tavern; and it may be doubted, whether there are ten in a hundred, who can refrain, when they have the opportunity for indulgence.[29]

Whiskey Dominant

The suppression of the insurrection against excise taxes on distilled spirits—more commonly known as the Whiskey Rebellion—established the principle that the federal government could tax citizens directly without having to go through individual state legislatures. This principle strengthened the national government and helped ensure its initial viability. However, such federal-state issues would be raised often over the next six decades and would be among the causes of the Civil War.

Not everyone was pleased with the outcome of the rebellion. At least 2,000 residents of western Pennsylvania moved farther west—many of them to Kentucky.[30] Whiskey had been distilled in Kentucky before the Whiskey Rebellion, but several of the early distillers were from western Pennsylvania. Corn was easy to grow in Kentucky, and it became the most important basis for distilled spirits there. Corn yielded a sweeter whiskey than that made from rye or wheat. The apotheosis of "corn liquor" was Kentucky bourbon, a uniquely American beverage that emerged in the early nineteenth century.

The rebellion and the exodus to Kentucky had little effect on what frontiersmen drank. An English visitor in the early nineteenth century noted that they unquestionably drank "too much, spirituous liquors," but there were good reasons for it: there were "no apples, and consequently no cyder. Malt liquor will not keep." Spirituous liquors were easily prepared and were "in fact the only beverage to which the settlers have access."[31]

Whiskey was drunk by men of all classes in great quantities. Production skyrocketed, and the price dropped. By the 1820s, whiskey was the cheapest of all beverages. The sole exception was water, but in many places whiskey was actually a safer drink due to contaminated water supplies. Whiskey was enjoyed in all regions of the country, but it was the universal alcoholic beverage in the western frontier areas, where it was variously called "fighting whiskey," "chain-lightning," "mountain howitzer," "tarantula juice, strychnine, red-eye, corn juice, Jersey lightning, leg-stretcher, 'tangleleg,' and many other hard and grotesque names."[32]

Excise Taxes

Excise taxes on liquor were reimposed in 1814 due to financial pressures related to the War of 1812, but were repealed four years later. Excise taxes were again levied during the Civil War to help pay for the war; unlike the earlier taxes, these taxes were maintained after the war. By 1875, excise taxes became the second most important source of the federal government's revenue, generating an estimated one-fourth of the total federal income. Anti-Prohibition advocates frequently pointed to these taxes as important financial contributions to the United States.[33] It was not until the passage of income tax in 1913 that it became possible for the federal government to survive without the excise taxes on liquor. This shift contributed to the drive for national prohibition, which took effect in 1920. When many Americans became unemployed during the Great Depression, federal revenues from income taxes sharply declined. One argument for the repeal of Prohibition was the reinstatement of excise taxes on liquor. When Prohibition ended in 1933, excise taxes were reimposed, and they have remained a federal revenue source ever since.

Contrary to the predictions of Benjamin Rush and many subsequent temperance proponents, the price increase that accompanied the excises taxes on distilled spirits did not reduce the amount of spirits Americans drank. Americans were willing to pay more for their whiskey rather than give it up.[34] For those unwilling to pay the tax, homemade moonshine was always an option, particularly in rural areas, and it thrived.

Postscript

Benjamin Rush remained a strong opponent of distilled spirits for the rest of his life. His pamphlet *An Enquiry into the Effects of Spirituous Liquors* went through several editions and numerous reprints during the next fifty years, and it would be cited thereafter as America's first temperance work. By the time he died in 1813, the temperance movement was well under way in America, and Rush has frequently been credited as its founding father.

Alexander Hamilton, a proponent of the excise tax on whiskey, resigned as secretary of the treasury in 1795; he was killed in a duel with Aaron Burr in 1804.

● George Washington was pleased with the way everything turned out after the Whiskey Rebellion. Congress had passed a law and the law had been enforced. This was an important precedent for the future. He was also pleased with the new national interest in whiskey—so much so that he built two very profitable stills at his home in Mount Vernon. He left office in 1797 and died two years later.

● Thomas Jefferson served two terms as president and then retired to Monticello, his home in Virginia, where he died in 1825.

● James Madison, whose support of the excise tax in 1791 guaranteed its passage in Congress, was elected president in 1808. He served two terms and died in 1836.

● Albert Gallatin, an opponent of the excise tax (Alexander Hamilton wanted him hanged for his involvement in the Rebellion), ran for Congress and defeated Hugh Henry Brackenridge. In 1801, he became secretary of the treasury and supported efforts to repeal the act in 1802.

● Hugh Henry Brackenridge founded the Pittsburgh Academy, which was later renamed the University of Pittsburgh. He died in Carlisle, Pennsylvania, in 1816.

● William Findley, an opponent of the whiskey tax, became a strong supporter of Jefferson and Madison. He served for twenty-eight years in the U.S. House of Representatives and died in 1821.

● John Smilie was elected to the House of Representatives in 1794 and served two terms. He died in 1812.

● In 1964, the U.S. Senate passed a proclamation stating that bourbon was a "distinct product of the United States" and prohibited the importation into the United States of anything "designated as 'Bourbon Whiskey.'"[35]

William Sidney Mount, *Cider Making* (1840–1841).
(Oil on canvas, 27 × 38⅛ in. [68.6 × 86.7 cm].
Purchase, Bequest of Charles Allen Munn, by exchange, 1966. Image © The Metropolitan Museum
of Art; Art Resource, NY)

5
Cider's Last Hurrah

GENERAL WILLIAM HENRY HARRISON was a successful military leader who is credited with winning the Battle of Tippecanoe against the Shawnee in 1811 and subsequent engagements against the British during the War of 1812. After that war, Harrison served in several governmental positions, but when Andrew Jackson was elected president in 1828, he retired to Ohio and lived off the proceeds from his farm. In 1836, Harrison was nominated by the Whigs to be their candidate for president. After being soundly defeated by the Democratic candidate, Martin Van Buren, the sixty-three-year-old Harrison again retired to his farm, where he most likely would have remained had it not been for the financial panic of 1837, which was followed by a five-year depression. Many Americans blamed Van Buren.

Van Buren was vulnerable when he ran for reelection. In December 1839, the Whigs met in Harrisburg, Pennsylvania, and once again nominated Harrison to run for president against Martin Van Buren. The Whigs generally had the support of those favoring temperance. John de Ziska, a Baltimore newspaperman who supported Van Buren, decided to tar Harrison as an old drunkard, attempting to cause a breach with Harrison's temperance supporters. All Harrison needed, reported de Ziska in the *Baltimore Republican*, was a good pension and "a barrel of hard cider" and he would "sit the remainder of his days in his log cabin by the side of a 'sea coal' fire, and study moral philosophy."[1]

Two Pennsylvania Whigs saw a way to turn de Ziska's comments to their candidate's advantage. They labeled Harrison the "log cabin and hard cider candidate"[2] and portrayed him as a man of the people who drank cider, the "poor man's beverage," while Van Buren sipped champagne. A Philadelphia manufacturer began making bottles shaped like replicas of log cabins and sold them filled with hard cider. Another firm produced hip flasks with a portrait of Harrison on one side and an emblem showing a log cabin, a plow, and a cider barrel on the other. Harrison's supporters built log cabins in cities, and plenty of hard cider was kept on hand for any thirsty visitor who dropped by.

Verses such as Ephraim Hubbard Foster's *Hard Cider: A Poem, Descriptive of the Nashville Convention* were published,[3] and songs celebrating Harrison's "log cabin" roots and his supposed love of hard cider were sung throughout the campaign. Here is one:

> They say that he lived in a cabin
> And lived on old hard cider, too;
> Well, what if he did? I'm certain
> He's the hero of Tippecanoe![4]

In Baltimore, New York, and Philadelphia, the *Hard Cider and Log Cabin Almanac* was published to extol the virtues of Harrison and his running mate, John Tyler.[5] Graphics representing the log cabin and the barrel of cider were independently published and widely distributed. Van Buren supporters did their best to counter these symbols, but they had nothing as rousing as Harrison's cider barrel and log cabin.[6] Hard cider was proffered lavishly at Whig political rallies and parades. At one event, 25,000 people showed up and were liberally "entertained" with hard cider. Cartoonists also made good use of cider barrel images. In one cartoonist's drawing, Van Buren is shown running down a hill chased by a cider barrel, shouting, "Stop that barrel!"[7]

Until the 1830s, temperance advocates were ambivalent about the consumption of hard cider. The beverage had low alcohol content and was not as pernicious as rum, whiskey, or brandy. However, Van Buren's supporters still tried to tar Harrison as a lush, but their message just did not resonate with the general electorate.

Many temperance supporters actually campaigned for Harrison in the election.[8] The *Pittsburgh Intelligencer* proclaimed that Harrison had not, in fact, drunk a bit of hard cider for many years. The paper noted that Harrison's connection to the beverage was through his ancestors, "who have been famous for the excellent cider which they manufactured."[9] Harrison may not have been a big cider drinker, but his supporters were. One wrote: "As to the matter of 'hard cider,' no statistics were kept of the gallons of vinegar consumed, but they were probably enough to have pickled the cucumbers from a million-acre patch! We reveled in 'hard cider,' and I think its antibilious tendency may have sweetened our temper; for with all our virtuous indignation against the Democratic 'spoilsmen,' we surely had the most jolly time ever known in a season of party contest."[10]

The jolly time campaign paid off. On Election Day in November 1840, William Henry Harrison, the hard cider and log cabin candidate, won with an impressive popular vote (57 percent to 43 percent) and an even more impressive electoral vote (234 to 60). One would think that Harrison's large electoral victory—in which hard cider had played a key role—would have guaranteed the beverage a promising future, but this was not to be.

Background

When Governor John Winthrop sailed for North America in 1629, his ship, the *Arabella*, was stocked with cider to fortify crew and colonists on the trip across the Atlantic.[11] English colonists also brought apple seeds with them when they arrived on American shores in the early seventeenth century, and they planted the seeds in America. It took a few decades for the trees to acclimatize to North American conditions, but by 1650, orchards were producing bountiful supplies of apples, especially in New England.[12] Orchards had several advantages over field crops: they required relatively little maintenance, they produced prodigious quantities of fruit, and farmers could plant grain between the rows of trees.[13] Farmers also could feed any excess apples to their pigs, lending sweetness to the taste of the pork.

The colonists planted different varieties of apples for specific purposes. For instance, apples with high sugar content were eaten right off the tree, whereas sour apples were used for cooking. Whole apples kept well if stored in a cool place, such as a root cellar; alternatively, they could be sliced and sun-dried to preserve them for subsequent seasons. The fruit was exceptionally versatile, providing the basis for jams, jellies, preserves, butters, pickles, sauces, and ketchups; apples could also be used to make cakes, dumplings, pies, tarts, and puddings, as well as juice, cider, and vinegar.

Hard cider was the most important commercial product of apples during the colonial era and early days of the republic. It was cheap and easy to make; any farmer with access to apples could crank out barrels of cider and set them aside to ferment without any specialized equipment. Even decayed or unripe apples could be used to make cider, as long as the fermented juice was boiled (ginger and molasses were sometimes added to pep the insipid flavor).[14] After water, hard cider quickly became America's most important beverage, and it remained as such well into the nineteenth century.

At first, cider making was done by hand. Apples were crushed in wooden mortars and the pomace was pressed in baskets. More sophisticated cider mills, run by horsepower, were in operation by 1652. Cider mills often were built on hillsides: carts were driven up and apples unloaded at the uphill side of the building, while barrels of cider were rolled out of the downhill side directly onto carts. A cider mill was equipped with two wooden cylinders—one with knobs and the other with corresponding holes—that were turned by horsepower. After apples were loaded in from the top, the turning cylinders drew in the fruit and crushed it. When the holes clogged up with pomace, the mill was stopped and one of the workers—usually a young boy—climbed into the works and scraped out the blockage. The pomace fell into a large shallow vat, from which it was shoveled onto a grooved press board. The pomace was alternated with layers of clean straw to a depth of about three feet, and then a board was placed on top and screwed down to squeeze the pomace. The apple juice collected in the channels of the press board and ran into a pan below. The fresh juice was stored in wooden barrels, where it fermented almost immediately. When the cider ran clear from the barrel's tap, it was ready to drink.

After pressing, the pomace was removed from the press and brought to a gentle boil, and the scum could be skimmed off. This unfermented apple juice could then be barreled. The pulp could be pressed again in a day or two, producing ciderkin, a mildly alcoholic drink for children.[15]

Hard cider was typically about 6 percent alcohol. For a stronger drink, the cider was boiled (to drive off some of its water content) before fermentation or the barrels were left outside during freezing weather. In the morning, the ice that formed on top of the cider was removed, leaving behind a more concentrated drink with a heavier alcoholic content. This was variously called heart cider, apple brandy, or more commonly applejack.[16] Distillers also often added sweeteners, such as molasses, that increased the beverage's alcoholic content; others added rum, which produced a beverage with a much stronger kick, called a stonewall.

By the late seventeenth century, cider was very common in colonial America. According to John Josselyn, an explorer who traveled to New England and lived there for a while: "Syder is very plentiful in the Countrey, ordinarily sold for Ten shillings a Hogshead. At the Tap-houses in Boston I have had an Ale-quart spic'd and sweetened with Sugar for a groat." A Connecticut magistrate told Josselyn that he made 500 hogsheads (about 100 gallons each) of cider from his orchards in one year.[17]

Cider was an important export item for New England colonies. Within the colonies, cider barrels served as a unit of exchange when specie was scarce. By the mid-seventeenth century, cider had eclipsed beer as the favorite beverage of New England, where it was "served at every meal, carried to workers in the fields, and drunk by young and old on every social occasion."[18] New England cider was exported to other colonies and was important even in areas of southern colonies, where apples were not easily grown.

Different types of apples gave cider varied flavors; cider was also flavored with additives. Cider royal was made by adding an equal amount of mead to cider and then fermenting the mixture. The Pennsylvania Germans drank their cider hot and sweet. They also made cider soup by adding bread and milk or by thickening the cider with cream and flour.[19] Other colonists added brandy and muscovado sugar to fermenting cider, which increased its alcohol content and improved its flavor. Aged cider bottled with raisins was called apple wine. Mulled cider was made by adding sugar, egg yolks, allspice, and occasionally rum.[20] Mole cider, favored by the Pennsylvania Dutch, was a hot beverage fortified with milk and beaten eggs.[21] A similar beverage, egg cider, was a New England concoction commonly made by breaking an "egg or two into a quart of heated cider, with a little sugar or molasses."[22] For a summer drink, cider was diluted with cold water and flavored with nutmeg.

Because different varieties of apples were used and the apples were of different ripeness, the quality of the cider varied greatly from very sweet to very sour. Consumers did not want sour cider, so cider makers combined sweet cider with it to produce a palatable drink.[23] Cider could also be used to make nogs, flips, punches, and nectars based on different fruit. Syllabub (cream whipped to a froth with sweet wine and spices), a favorite dessert of colonial times, could also be made with cider. Samuel Sewall, a Puritan judge in Massachusetts, recorded his special recipe for a syllabub that blended cider, sugar, cream, and nutmeg. Cider also was used to flavor cakes, and ham was often baked in cider.[24]

Cider vinegar was an important byproduct of cider production, especially because grape vinegar was available only as an expensive import. Cider vinegar was also used as a beverage, usually mixed with water. Not everyone liked cider vinegar beverages, though. As one foreign observer reported, it was "usually unwholesome, [causing] ague when it is fresh, and colic when it is too old. The common people damask the drink, mix ground ginger with it, or heat it with a red-hot iron."[25]

Virtually every farm in New England had an apple orchard, and even a modest orchard could produce prodigious quantities of apples. Pressing apples into cider made it possible to preserve thousands of apples in a small space. It was estimated that upstate Vermont families polished off an average of a barrel of cider per week in colonial times.[26] By the time of the American Revolution, one in every ten farms in New England operated its own cider mill. Throughout the colonies, cider was more popular than beer or ale.

The typical New Englander made from twenty-five to fifty cider barrels per year. The well-to-do usually had a cider barrel on tap, which was available for themselves and any guests who might drop by. Many colonists began the day with a draft of cider. Farmers carried cider jugs into the fields, and in winter people took them on hunting trips. Cider was always offered to guests, and a pitcher of cider was served at every meal. When the day ended, more cider was downed. In the 1790s, the French gastronome and culinary philosopher Jean-Anthelme Brillat-Savarin visited a Connecticut farmhouse where he saw "huge jugs of cider so excellent that I could have gone on drinking it for ever."[27] Cider was shipped from the countryside to towns and cities, where it was consumed in great quantities in taverns. It was also exported to the other English colonies in North America and the West Indies. In 1767, it was estimated that Massachusetts farmers drank 1.14 barrels of cider per capita, about the same as in New York, where cider was served at breakfast and was always available both during and between meals.[28] In addition, vast quantities of cider also were converted into apple brandy.[29]

The quality of cider produced in the colonies varied greatly. One traveler in America reported that the cider in Maine was purified by frost, colored with corn, and had the appearance and taste of Madeira.[30] A British visitor remarked that the cider in Virginia was better than he ever had in England: "It is genuine and unadulterated, and will keep good to the age of twelve years and more."[31] Israel Acrelius, a Swedish Lutheran missionary who lived in colonial Delaware in the mid-eighteenth century, criticized American cider because it was "drunk too fresh and too soon; thus it has come into great disesteem, so that many persons refuse to taste it."[32] The French historian and politician Médéric Moreau de Saint-Méry, who lived in the United States from 1792 to 1799, reported that the cider he sampled in Philadelphia was good, but the cider from Newark, New Jersey, deserved its reputation as the best in the country. As good as the cider was, however, Moreau de Saint-Méry's French colleague still found it inferior to French cider.[33]

Like most Americans, the founding fathers drank their share of cider. When George Washington ran for the Virginia House of Burgesses in 1757, he gave away "treats" to potential voters totaling 160 gallons of beer, ale, cider, and other alcoholic beverages. Washington had an apple orchard on his Virginia plantation and made his own cider, but because tidewater Virginia is not ideal apple-growing country, Washington occasionally ordered cider from up north.[34] In November 1775, the Continental Congress recommended that all soldiers receive a daily beverage ration consisting of a quart of either cider or spruce beer.[35] John Adams drank a morning gill (about a half pint) of cider before breakfast for most of his life.[36] Jefferson, too, liked his cider: he reported in his *Garden Book* that one type of apple, the Taliaferro, produced "unquestionably the finest cyder we have ever known, and more like wine than any liquor I have ever tasted which was not wine."[37] General William Heath, who fought at the Battle of Bunker Hill in 1775, was "a true farmer," according to J. P. Brissot de Warville, a French political leader, who visited Heath's farm in 1788. Warville wrote that Heath presented a glass of cider "with frankness and good-humor painted on his countenance," and his guest found the cider "superior to the most exquisite wines."[38]

Land Speculation

The Treaty of Paris (1783), which ended the Revolutionary War, gave the new nation title to all lands west to the Mississippi River. During the next several years, Congress passed ordinances encouraging the sale and settlement of this land. In 1786, Congress gave the Ohio Company of Associates 100,000 acres of land in Ohio to sell to settlers; other land companies received similar parcels of land. The Ohio Company established a "donation tract" to encourage settlement in the largely unoccupied areas of their land. Land was given without charge provided that settlers planted apple or peach trees;

this encouraged real settlers and not just land speculators. Whether settlers were in the donation tract or bought their own land, planting apple orchards made sense. The problem was that apples, if planted from seed, take several years to mature and bear fruit.

This is where John Chapman stepped in. Born in Leominster, Massachusetts, in 1774, he headed to western Pennsylvania like many other Americans at the time. In 1797, Chapman became a convert to Swedenborgianism, a religion inspired by the Swedish scientist and theologian Emanuel Swedenborg.[39] Chapman spent the remainder of his life as a missionary for his new religion. In approximately 1801, Chapman headed west again—this time to southeastern Ohio. On the way, he picked up some apple seeds at a cider mill in southwestern Pennsylvania and planted apple orchards along the way westward. Apple orchards provided a plentiful food supply, and Chapman could sell the seedlings to settlers who were streaming into Ohio. Chapman was not the first nurseryman in Ohio, nor was he the most fastidious orchardist; he often left the orchards he planted and returned a year or more later to sell the seedlings.[40] To produce edible apples, nurserymen needed to graft on the variety that they wanted. Chapman strongly opposed grafting. Although he likely ate the sour and small apples produced by his trees, most settlers would not have done so. These settlers likely used the apples to make hard cider.

Temperate Cider

The American temperance movement began in the late eighteenth century as a response to the problems associated with alcohol overconsumption. One prominent temperance advocate, Dr. Benjamin Rush, opposed rum, whiskey, and brandy, but he believed that small (that is, weak) beer, wine, and cider did not cause the drunkenness commonly associated with stronger drink. Rush believed that cider was an "excellent liquor" that contained "a small quantity of spirit, but so diluted and blunted by being combined with a large quantity of saccharine matter, and water, as to be perfectly inoffensive and wholesome." Cider promoted "cheerfulness, strength, nourishment, when taken only at meals, and in moderate quantities," proclaimed Rush.[41]

The temperance movement gained momentum during the early nineteenth century. In addition to opposition from the medical profession, many members of religious groups jumped on the temperance bandwagon.

As a result, the focus of the movement shifted from serious medical issues to a moral crusade against all alcohol. The temperance movement was ambivalent about hard cider. Some temperance advocates saw hard cider as "good and useful taken in moderation." For others, however, no alcoholic beverages, including cider, were "necessary or beneficial to health."[42] Early temperance societies permitted the use of beer, wine, and cider as substitutes for "ardent spirits."

In the early 1830s, some temperance leaders embraced "total" abstinence. The Dutch Reformed Church supported this principle, as would many Quakers, Universalists, Presbyterians, Methodists, and Baptists. As one proponent of total abstinence sloganized, "Hard cider, too, will never do." But there was still strong opposition to including cider in the ban on alcohol. As one opponent of total abstinence argued, declaring cider drinking "as disreputable as the use of ardent spirits" would have the opposite effect, for it "would reduce the offence of dram-drinking to the level of cider-drinking."[43]

Dr. William Alcott, one of America's prominent temperance advocates (and a vegetarian), lined up against drinking cider. He was particularly opposed to egg cider: "I have seen a family of children brought up to relish this as one of the greatest treats. And yet it is, as it were, a parent of abominations. Cider is bad enough for the human stomach; but cider, eggs and molasses form a compound still worse, and one which deserves not to be named, except to expose its folly, in any decent circle or civilized society."[44]

Others agreed. Some New England farmers chopped down their apple orchards, reported Alcott in 1834, due to the conviction that "generally prevails that fermented drinks must not be continued."[45]

Despite the strong support for total prohibition, temperance advocates were mixed in their views. Many opposed William Henry Harrison because he did not condemn the distribution of free cider at Whig rallies. Others believed that Harrison, who did not drink cider, rose above the cider-infused campaign that his supporters conducted on his behalf. Those supporting Harrison "had high hopes that the President-elect would lend his moral authority to the cause [of temperance]."[46]

Cider helped elect William Henry Harrison president, but his campaign may have swayed temperance advocates to expand their prohibitions beyond ardent beverages to all alcohol—beer, wine, and cider included. Virtually every temperance organization specifically opposed cider in their pledges after 1840. This had an immediate effect: the American Temperance Union reported in 1841 that cider mills had "vanished from the premises of almost every reputable New England farmer."[47]

In addition to the evangelical religious groups that supported temperance, new religious groups joined the anti-cider bandwagon as well. The Mormons loved apples and soft cider, but hard cider was prohibited. An American seaman named Joseph Bates—a follower of William Miller, who believed that the second coming of Jesus Christ would be coming soon—gave up "ardent spirits" in 1821. Over the following few years, he came to abstain from other alcoholic beverages as well, including cider. Bates, along with Ellen G. White, later helped found the Seventh-Day Adventist Church. Bates may have influenced White on the subject of cider: "So gradually does Satan lead away from the strongholds of temperance, so insidiously do wine and cider exert their influence upon the taste, that the highway to drunkenness is entered upon all unsuspectingly." White was even opposed to sweet or nonalcoholic cider:

> I have often heard people say, "Oh! this is only sweet cider. It is perfectly harmless, and even healthful." Several quarts, perhaps gallons, are carried home. For a few days it is sweet; then fermentation begins. The sharp taste makes it all the more acceptable to many palates, and the lover of sweet wine and cider is loath to admit that his favorite beverage ever becomes hard and sour.[48]

Unfermented cider was manufactured by boiling down fresh apple juice to a concentrate and bottling the nonalcoholic beverage. Gail Borden, who developed the process for canning concentrated milk in 1858, had begun marketing apple juice by 1864.[49] But temperance advocates argued against its consumption and sale; although not intoxicating, unfermented apple juice was basically the raw material for hard cider, and as such its availability would lead America's youth astray.

Russell T. Hall, one of the leaders of the homeopathic movement, was none too happy with sweet cider either:

> The apple is intended for food and not drink. It was made to be eaten; and if one can succeed in expressing the juice and getting it into his stomach before it ferments, he has gained nothing and lost something. He has gained no beverage, for there is no beverage under the sun except water, and he has lost the food of the apple. He may, indeed, eat the pomace of the fruit;

but he will find it a very different article of food from the unground apple. Nature has provided the best machinery in the world, both for grinding the fruit and expressing the juice. The teeth, jaws, tongue, and surrounding muscles constitute the proper "cider-mill."[50]

Cider's Fall and Rise

Cider consumption had been declining well before the temperance movement called for its total prohibition. This was partly because of two insect pests—codling moths (*Cydia pomonella*) and apple scab insects (*Venturia inaequalis*)—which destroyed whole orchards throughout the country. Orchards were abandoned as New Englanders and New Yorkers moved to the Midwest, where other crops were more profitable.

Although cider remained somewhat popular throughout the United States, especially in apple-growing areas, its consumption waned as the nineteenth century progressed. It was not just the temperance movement, religious groups, and insect pests that contributed to this decline—the rise of other beverages, particularly beer, also undermined cider's position as America's favorite alcoholic beverage. The industrial revolution took its toll as well, as apple growers and cider makers flocked to the cities, leaving few in the countryside to maintain cider production.

In the first two decades of the twentieth century, cider production dropped dramatically. Much of the cider sold commercially was homemade; being unfiltered and unpasteurized, it was susceptible to developing molds and bacteria that often led to health problems, damaging the product's reputation. Homemade cider also was often adulterated with contaminated water. As cities and states began passing pure food laws, it became increasingly difficult for home cider-making operations to meet the new regulations, especially after the U.S. Congress passed the Pure Food and Drug Act in 1906. In addition, because of the temperance movement, some cities and states passed laws prohibiting the sale of alcohol, including cider. When national Prohibition went into effect in 1920, commercial hard cider production stopped, but several New York cider manufacturers shifted to making sweet apple juice. However, the federal prohibition commissioner in New York refused to give the companies licenses to make sweet cider because it could easily be converted into hard cider. The Hildick Apple Juice Company and the Duffy-Mott Company brought suit against the commissioner and others. In 1922, the United States District Court held that the sale of sweet cider was not a violation of the Volstead Act.[51] Sweet cider production increased throughout Prohibition—the main reason being that purchasers converted it into hard cider.

When Prohibition ended, the demand for alcoholic hard cider did not recover. Nonalcoholic cider, however, found a receptive market during Prohibition, and sales of this benign beverage continued to grow during the twentieth century. Pediatricians highly recommended it for infants and children as a healthy source of vitamins. During the 1950s, apple juice became the most common fruit juice given to infants and children younger than twelve years.

Hard cider was all but forgotten, except for a few orchardists who continued to make it. The home-brewing movement took off in the late 1970s, which encouraged those interested in making cider. Apple growers began investigating heirloom varieties and traditional uses for apples, and many new cideries opened on the East and West coasts and in the Upper Midwest. Hard cider reemerged as a gourmet drink, and consumption in the United States increased twenty-fold between 1987 and 1997. Today, the United States produces about 6.5 million gallons of cider annually, and the field is "experiencing rapid growth, especially among small, craft producers, who are producing such a diverse array of products, from hard ciders to applejack and apple brandy, that it feels a bit like a colonial American renaissance," according to Erika Janik, author of *Apple: A Global History*.[52]

Postscript

⊟ William Henry Harrison may have won the presidential election in 1840, but his victory was short lived. His inaugural address, one of the longest on record, was delivered on a cold, rainy day, and Harrison refused to wear an overcoat or a hat. A few weeks later, he came down with a cold, which turned into pneumonia. President Harrison died just thirty-one days after his inauguration.

⊟ John Chapman died around 1845. He has remained a popular figure in American history. Books have been written about him, and he is often included in school textbooks. Walt Disney produced an animated short film about him in 1948; in the film, Disney popularized the Swedenborgian hymn, "Oh, the Lord is Good to Me," which includes references to apples, apple seeds, and apple trees, but no mention of cider. Michael Pollan, however, anointed him with the title of "American Dionysus."[53]

Advertisement for Valentin Blatz's Premium Export,
Milwaukee Lager Beer (1879). (Library of Congress,
Prints and Photographs Division)

6
The Most Popular Drink of the Day

GERMAN IMMIGRANT Johann Wagner set sail on a clipper ship bound to America in 1840. Many other Germans had made the same trip, but Wagner carried with him something that would change the way Americans refreshed themselves: *Saccharomyces pastorianus*, a yeast commonly used to brew beer in Bavaria. Unlike the yeast used by American, English, Dutch, and most other German brewers, Bavarian yeast settled to the bottom of the vat during fermentation, thereby slowing the brewing process. Because the beer took weeks to ferment, it had to be stored, which was why the Germans called it *lagerbier* (stored beer)—a term that morphed into the English name of "lager beer." This was Wagner's favored brew, and he knew the basics of how to make it. After settling in Philadelphia, then the brewing capital of America, Wagner set up a "very primitive establishment," in which the "brewing kettle was suspended from a beam over an open fire, and this kettle contained barely eight barrels," as a later account described it. Before leaving the city a few years later, he gave some yeast to his friend George Manger. Manger then went into brewing with a Philadelphia sugar refiner named Charles C. Wolf, and they became the first lager-beer makers in America—or so the story goes.[1]

It seemed unlikely that lager brewing would have much impact. At the time, Americans did not drink much beer; those who did wanted stout, porter, and ale—strong, bitter, and hearty brews based on hundreds of years of English and American traditions. Lager beer was lighter bodied, less bitter, weaker, and fizzier. German immigrants did prefer the beers of their homeland, but the majority of German Americans were not from southern Germany, where lager was popular. Yet another impediment to lager beer was its cost: the longer fermentation process made it more expensive to make than other beers; in fact, it was even more expensive than whiskey, America's national beverage at the time. For the poor, many of whom frequented saloons, money mattered, as did alcoholic content. For men wanting to drown their sorrows, whiskey—with its higher alcohol content—was the way to go, not a low-alcohol lager. Despite these obstacles, however, in less than a decade lager beer would become America's most popular beverage. Light brews dominated American beer production for the next 150 years, and they continue to do so.

Background

People have been fermenting grains to make ales and beers for thousands of years. In Europe, beer became the main alcoholic beverage in several areas, including the British Isles, Germany, and Holland. Early English, Dutch, Swedish, and German colonists brought their love of beer with them when they immigrated to the United States, and many also brought their own brewing techniques and equipment. These European immigrants set up breweries in New Amsterdam, Virginia, and Massachusetts shortly after the colonies were established. Some colonists tried to make their own beer: they steeped and germinated barley seeds and then dried them. This process partially converted the starches into sugars, which could then be fermented. Brewing is somewhat complicated, however, and it requires skill and experience. Colonists who did not want to brew their own beer could take their crops of barley and hops to a malt house to be brewed and barreled by established brewers. Others bought or imported malt and made beer at home.[2]

Despite widespread interest in beer during colonial times, it was eclipsed by cider and then later by rum and whiskey. The main problem with beer was spoilage. Small (weak) beer had to be consumed quickly after it was brewed. Strong beer had to be drunk soon after the cask was opened; otherwise, it turned sour or stale. Tavern owners in small communities just did not have enough beer business to make it worthwhile. Only in towns with large populations was beer profitable.

The quality of American beers was also an issue. When compared with English beer, for instance, American beer was bitter, cloudy, and strong—or so said European visitors. A Swedish visitor was unimpressed with the beer he encountered in America; he said it was "brown, thick, and unpalatable and only used by the common people."[3] It is not clear why this was the case. Except in a few cities, such as Philadelphia, New York, and Boston, skilled brewmasters were hard to find, so perhaps the problem with American beer was lack of expertise. Others have pointed to the varieties of barley that thrived in North America, which were different from the varieties found in England. Therefore, American barley varieties produced a different tasting beer. Perhaps it was the New World hops, the water, or the American climate. Modern researchers suggest another possibility: it might have been the size of the barrels in which the beer was fermented. German barrels were larger, permitting more air and slowing down fermentation; perhaps this made a difference in the brewing process.[4]

Whatever the reason for the lack of quality, experienced brewers faced other serious problems. The barley crops in America were often insufficient to meet demand because there were frequent crop failures. There were also few malt houses in the colonies to convert the barley into malt, and this was the beginning of a downward spiral. Few malt houses meant that it was uneconomical for farmers to grow barley. As there was often little barley, there was often little incentive to construct malt houses. The result was that there was little domestic malt production. Colonists who lived in cities could usually buy English barley or malt, but imports were more costly, which meant beer was expensive.

Distributing beer was yet another obstacle. Colonial roads were unimproved and often impassable, especially during winter; even in good weather, it was difficult to transport beer far from where it was brewed. Beer was distributed mainly through taverns, which were numerous in cities but far less so in harder-to-reach rural areas. Then there were the lack of "procuring a supply of strong bottles, and a peculiar taste for lively or foaming beer, which our summers do not favor," which were additional reasons why there was "inconsiderable progress of malt liquors, compared with distilled spirits," claimed a report on American manufacturing.[5]

Finally, there were many alcoholic alternatives. Cider, perry (pear cider), and mobby (peach wine) were easier to make and less costly than beer; they also were more popular than beer. Beer consumption declined further after 1750; simultaneously, whiskey and rum consumption surged. This shift to "spirituous liquors" worried many. The Massachusetts General Court in June 1789 encouraged the manufacture of beer "as an important means of preserving the health of the citizens."[6] However, this appeal (and others) did not work. By 1810, beer consumption was down to less than one gallon per person annually.[7] Two-thirds of the beer brewed in the United States at that time was made in New York and Pennsylvania. During the early nineteenth century, beer production in New York City declined due to a shortage of pure potable water for use in brewing. New York's ground water was needed for drinking purposes, and as the population expanded so did pollution of city water. By the 1820s, one observer later wrote, "beer had ceased to be made, as well as malt," in various parts of New England. Per capita beer consumption declined elsewhere in the country because of the increasing popularity of other alcoholic beverages.[8]

Because of its large population of German immigrants, Philadelphia was the nation's premier brewing city by the 1840s, and beer remained an important beverage in other parts of Pennsylvania. It was the "common table drink of every family in easy circumstances," as one observer put it.[9] It is no surprise that enterprising German immigrant brewers came to Pennsylvania and launched new breweries. A brewer named George Lauer arrived from Gleissweiler, in western Germany, in 1823; three years later, he opened a brewery in Reading, Pennsylvania. Lauer brewed strong beer at first, and later added ale and porter. In 1835, he turned the brewery over to his son, Friedrich Lauer.[10]

David G. Jüngling, an immigrant from Württemberg, Germany, opened a brewery in Pottsville, Pennsylvania, in 1829. Because Americans had a problem pronouncing his last name, he changed the spelling to Yuengling; his brewery would eventually be called D. G. Yuengling and Son.[11] Other German brewers immigrated to the Midwest, part of a large wave of more than 120,000 German immigrants who flooded into America in the 1830s.

Immigrating Beer

About 600 years ago, the German city of Munich passed a law requiring that all beer be brewed with barley and hops. For reasons unknown at the time, this beer survived longer than that made from other grains. Around the same time, German brewers made an important discovery: some strains of yeast, such as *Saccharomyces pastorianus,* created a very different type of beer than other strains. Rather than rise to the top—as did other yeasts—*Saccharomyces pastorianus* settled at the bottom of the vats. Bottom-fermenting yeast took much longer: the initial fermentation required ten to twelve days, and then secondary fermentation took another few weeks, during which the beer had to be kept in a cool place. For this reason, it was brewed only in the winter.[12] The resulting beer, known as lager, had a distinct commercial advantage: it could be kept for a longer time without spoiling.

The process of making lager was improved by Bavarian and other brewers over hundreds of years, but during most of this time only locals and visitors ever tasted lager. The rest of Europe was content with darker, top-fermented brews. Bavarians reportedly drank a gallon of beer every day, "for and at breakfast, for and at dinner." It took "the place of coffee in the afternoon," and it was "poured down at supper."[13] Bavarian workers spent about half of their income on beer, and it was a significant source of calories for many Bavarians.[14]

During the 1830s, a series of agricultural failures hit southern and western Germany. As a result, many Germans, especially those from Baden, Württemberg, and Bavaria, chose to immigrate to the United States, where land was relatively cheap. When German grain crops repeatedly failed, beer prices increased. In the early 1840s, bad weather in Germany again destroyed crops and beer prices rose again. Bavarians grumbled about rising prices, and the grumbling eventually turned into widespread riots.[15] When the price of beer went up again in May 1844, a "beer war" broke out in Munich. Riots continued on and off for months, leading more and more Germans to immigrate to America.[16]

When revolutions broke out all over Europe in 1848, Munich was particularly hard hit. All revolutions failed, but the Bavarian revolt was brutally suppressed, which generated even more immigration to the United States. Yet another series of crop failures during the early 1850s led still more Germans to immigrate. By 1850, an estimated 435,000 German immigrants had arrived in the United States; five years later, the number of German immigrants totaled more than 1 million.[17] This was just the beginning, with millions of Germans following during succeeding decades.

These newcomers to America came from all social classes and walks of life. There were small farmers, wealthy farmers, artisans, merchants, professionals, political dissidents, tradesmen, and even some prisoners and vagabonds.[18] Many new arrivals went into food-related businesses. Some opened restaurants, grocery stores, and delicatessens. Because virtually all Germans drank beer, some immigrants set up breweries, saloons, beer halls, and beer gardens (traditional open-air gathering places that served food, beer, and other beverages).[19]

Newly arrived Bavarian immigrants demanded lager beer. Although Johann Wagner gets credit for bringing the first bottom-fermenting yeast to the United States, it is likely that many Bavarians did the same, setting up lager breweries wherever they settled—Chicago, Cincinnati, Milwaukee, New York, Pittsburgh, and St. Louis in the 1840s; by 1850, there were lager breweries in Albany, Baltimore, Boston, Buffalo, Detroit, and Erie. Even Placerville, in California's gold rush country, boasted a lager brewery, as did many other smaller cities.[20] One journalist from the *New York Tribune* estimated that there were 500 German breweries nationwide by 1854, with most making lager beer.[21] Continued German immigration during the next several decades ensured the success of these breweries.

Philadelphia was the epicenter for the lager tidal wave that swept America. Charles C. Wolf and Charles Engel launched a successful lager brewery in 1845; their public seemed to have an unquenchable thirst. According to Wolf, "More than once, they drank the brewery dry," and the brewers had to place a notice announcing when lager would again be available.[22] Other breweries opened, including one launched by Gustavus Bergner and Charles Engel, who formed Bergner & Engel.[23] By 1857, there were thirty lager breweries in Philadelphia alone, and more lager was brewed in them than all other American breweries that made traditional ale, porter, and stout combined.[24] Three years later, the city had more than twice as many breweries.[25]

From Philadelphia, lager made its way westward. In the early 1840s, the Yuengling brewery in Pottsville, Pennsylvania, began turning out barrels of lager.[26] George Lauer and his son Friedrich started brewing lager in Reading, Pennsylvania, in 1844.[27] Although his firm was not the first or the largest brewer of lager, Lauer was "a man noted for his remarkable industry and untiring energy." He was a strong advocate for the beer industry and quickly became the unofficial head of American lager brewing.[28]

Advocates for bottom-fermented beer promoted it as "a very healthful drink," and many observers agreed that drinking lager was better than drinking whiskey.[29] By 1850, the *Trenton State Gazette* hailed lager beer as "probably the most popular drink of the day."[30] Some chefs also devised recipes using lager beer. William Vollmer, the Steward of the Union Club in Philadelphia, made soup with it:

RECIPE FOR COLD BEER-SOUP

Half a gallon of good Lager-beer is sweetened with a sufficient quantity of loaf sugar, to which is added a piece of whole cinnamon, and some lemon-peel, all is well stirred and put in ice. Before dishing it, the cinnamon and the lemon peel are taken out, and the liquid poured over grated black rye bread.[31]

Lager beer also took off in New York during the 1840s. Brewing in the city had been in decline, mostly because of the poor quality of the city's water supply. As the city expanded, the need for an improved water system became acute. So, in 1837 the city embarked on a massive project to bring water to Manhattan via a forty-one-mile aqueduct. It was completed five years later—just as German brewers flooded into the city. Among those immigrants was a Bavarian brewer named George Gillig, who opened New York's first lager beer brewery in 1844.[32] Other breweries were opened by Frederick and Maximilian Schaefer, who purchased the Sebastian Sommers Brewery in New York City in 1842; they began marketing lager beer under their own name in 1847. Franz Ruppert, who had come from Göllheim, Germany, launched what would eventually become the Jacob Ruppert Brewing Company with his brother in Turtle Bay (an area of Manhattan near the East River) in 1851.

Initially, only German saloons and restaurants served lager beer and only Germans drank it, but this soon changed. As New Yorkers began flocking to these establishments, other city saloons jumped on the lager wagon. By 1854, New York had "twenty-seven breweries, and many of them, such as Turtle Bay, Gilley's, and Schaefer's, brew[ed] more than ten thousand barrels, of thirty gallons each, of lager beer in the course of the year," proclaimed an observer in the *New York Tribune*. These breweries produced 85,000 barrels, equivalent to 30 million gallons, which were distributed by 2,000 retail outlets, large hotels, and restaurants.[33]

Most of New York's bars, saloons, and taverns served lager on tap by 1855. In September 1855, the *New York Times* reported that "a very large portion of the inhabitants of the City of New York, who a few months since, were in the habit of drinking one or more glasses of rum, gin or brandy, every day, are now using about the same number of glasses of *lagerbier* instead."[34] By the 1860s, there were an estimated 3,000 to 4,000 lager beer establishments in Manhattan alone, with many more in surrounding communities, and it was estimated that more than half of the people who frequented them were mainstream Americans.[35]

Success

By the start of the Civil War, there were 1,269 American breweries churning out more than 1 million barrels of beer annually.[36] Virtually all were making lager beer. The American scientist and writer Lewis Feuchtwanger proclaimed lager beer to be "the most popular drink in the United States" and observed that "large fortunes have been realized since its introduction into this country."[37] Songs, poetry, cartoons, and jokes referencing lager soon graced American magazines and newspapers.[38]

As more German immigrants moved into the Midwest, lager brewing skyrocketed. By 1857, Pittsburgh had twenty-six lager beer breweries producing 28,000 barrels of beer annually.[39] By the late 1850s, Cincinnati had thirty-six breweries, all but three of which produced mainly or exclusively lager beer.[40] Although much of Cincinnati's beer was shipped downriver, an Indiana newspaper snidely claimed that "the principal business of Cincinnati is drinking Lager beer."[41]

Milwaukee had twenty-six breweries in 1856, which brewed 75,000 barrels of beer (mostly lager). One was owned by Jacob Best, who had been brewing lager beer since 1845. Jacob Best's daughter married a steamship captain, Frederick Pabst, in 1860. Four years later, Pabst joined Best and Company in the brewing business. Best retired in 1866 and died three years later. Pabst and partners took over the business, which by 1870 was the largest brewery in Milwaukee. The company's name was not changed to the Pabst Brewing Company until 1889.[42] Another brewing company in Milwaukee was owned by Frederick Müller, an immigrant who had come to America from Riedlingen, Germany, in 1854. His brewery would become the Miller Brewing Company. Joseph Schlitz, a bookkeeper in a small brewery owned by August Krug, eventually took over the brewery, which he renamed the Joseph Schlitz Brewing Company. In 1873, Milwaukee breweries produced 260,000 barrels of lager; much of the beer was shipped downriver.[43]

By 1854, St. Louis had twenty-four breweries producing 40,000 barrels of lager beer annually.[44] Five years later, the city had thirty-five breweries producing 115,000 barrels of lager annually.[45] An additional 50,000 barrels of lager were brought to St. Louis each year from Milwaukee, Pittsburgh, and other cities. It seemed that most people in St. Louis, not just men, loved their lager. An observer wrote in 1878 that men and "two-thirds of the women of the city, including all classes, orders and conditions, are beer drinkers. Very respectable people, not addicted to visiting saloons, will send for pitchers or buckets of beer."[46]

The Bavarian Brewery Company of St. Louis, founded in 1853, went heavily into debt; its major creditor was Eberhard Anheuser, a German immigrant who had arrived in St. Louis in 1842. He had established a business that manufactured soap, by which he made enough money to invest in others businesses. Rather than sell the assets of the Bavarian Brewing Company, Anheuser took over its management in 1860. The company struggled through the turbulent times during the Civil War.[47]

Anheuser's daughter married Adolphus Busch, a brewery supply salesman, in 1861, and Busch joined his father-in-law's brewery business in 1865, when the company produced a very modest 4,000 barrels of beer. Under Busch's guidance, the company expanded. By 1870, the company was producing 17,000 barrels of beer; five years later, it topped 26,000. To increase sales, Busch launched a pilsner beer, which he called Budweiser because it was originally made of imported materials similar to those used in a brewery at Budweis, a small city in Bohemia (today the Czech Republic). Like Bavarians, Bohemians developed the use of bottom-fermenting yeast, and they invented a special process to make a pale lager beer. Busch claimed to have used this Bohemian process to make Budweiser beer. However it was made, sales were good and they have continued to be so ever since. After Anheuser's death in 1879, the company was renamed Anheuser-Busch. Sales surged in the late nineteenth century, and by 1901 the company was producing more than 1 million barrels.[48]

Beer Riot

Chicago was another destination point for German immigrants. Two German immigrants, John Huck and John Schneider, are credited with starting one of the first lager breweries in that city in 1847. More breweries and saloons opened as German immigrants flooded into the city. By 1862, Chicago had about twenty lager breweries, producing 150,000 barrels of lager beer annually.[49] Around this time, the great influx of German and Irish immigrants aroused a backlash in the United States.[50] Many who objected to the immigrants joined the Know-Nothing Party, which also promoted temperance. A number of cities, including Chicago, had blue laws that prohibited the sale of liquor on Sundays, but immigrants generally ignored these laws because many people often spent Sundays at beer gardens or saloons in Germany. Temperance advocates pointed out that many German immigrants were going to saloons on Sundays rather than to church. When a new mayor, Levi Boone—who was opposed to immigrants and had temperance leanings—was elected on March 6, 1855, he enforced the Sunday closing laws. He also urged the city's Common Council to raise liquor license fees from $30 to $300 and to require more frequent license renewals. The mayor openly acknowledged that his goal was to drive immigrant saloon owners out of business. In response, an estimated 500 German immigrants gathered in downtown Chicago on April 21 to protest the Sunday enforcement, fees, and renewal schedule. The demonstrators were met with a phalanx of police, who broke up the demonstration. Newspapers called the incident the "Lager Beer Riot." The following year, Mayor Boone was defeated and the requirements were repealed.[51]

Other cities passed similar restrictive laws and regulations, but they were largely unenforced. New York City banned the sale of liquor on Sunday in 1866, causing some Germans—many of them political refugees from Germany's failed 1848 revolution—to rally, proclaiming "Liberty and *lagerbeir*!" Others just crossed the Hudson River to New Jersey, where there were plenty of breweries, beer gardens, and saloons open on Sundays.[52]

Despite its popularity among many Germans, lager beer would not have lasted in the United States had its popularity not spread beyond the immigrant community. But it did, in fact, find a mainstream market. Lager beer was not as bitter as porter or as sour as the ales of the time. Lager also had a more appealing look. Porter and ales were "muddy" and were typically drunk in porcelain or pewter mugs. Lager, though, was served in large glass mugs, which accentuated the beer's sparkling golden color and clarity. Unlike other beers, lager also could be stored for months; even after barrels were tapped, the beer lasted longer without spoiling.[53]

Ironically, another reason for the increasing popularity of lager beer was the temperance movement. Temperance advocates were uniformly opposed to hard liquor—particularly rum, whiskey and brandy—but many were ambivalent about wine and beer. Some temperance leaders even supported beer as a nutritious alternative to whiskey and rum. During the late eighteenth century, Benjamin Rush, America's foremost medical professional of the day, supported the consumption of beer. In the early nineteenth century, however, many temperance advocates turned against beer as well. When lager beer arrived in America, the temperance movement was ready to condemn it. Many lager drinkers asserted that lager was not as intoxicating as other alcoholic beverages and that it had considerable nutritional value. Medical professionals gladly hailed "its advent among us, even with the possibilities of its being used to excess."[54] A writer in the *New York Herald* wrote that the "increase in the use of lager beer will do more to overthrow drunkenness and rowdyism, and to establish good order on their ruins than all the labors and the efforts" of temperance advocates.[55]

Despite widespread medical support for drinking lager beer (particularly as an alternative to spirits), the Pennsylvania Sons of Temperance proclaimed in 1850 that lager beer was, like rum and whiskey, highly alcoholic, "and therefore it must exert the same deleterious influence upon the organs of life as they do." The Sons of Temperance passed a resolution that their members could not "without violation of their obligations, use it as a beverage."[56]

Temperance criticism had no effect on beer-guzzling immigrants, however; neither did it matter to most other Americans, who visited beer halls to find out what all the fuss was about. In 1840, Americans drank slightly more than 1 gallon of beer per person annually. By 1860, this figure had more than tripled to 3.8 gallons, and that was just the beginning of lager beer drinking in the United States. Prior to the Civil War, lager beer consumption had been largely restricted to cities with German immigrant populations. But the Civil War, which began in 1861, exposed soldiers and sailors to lager beer in cities far from their homes. Many Germans served in the Union Army, and they were often supplied with lager beer.[57] Lager was also sold by sulters who peddled provisions to soldiers; it also was sold to Confederate prisoners. When the war ended, lager beer had a host of new partisans as a result of exposure to it during the war.

One German immigrant who served in the U.S. Army during the Civil War was Jacob Schueler, who had arrived in the United States in 1850. After the Civil War, Schueler moved to Denver, Colorado, where he went into the confectionary business. In 1872, he met another immigrant, Adolph Kuhrs, who had served a three-year apprenticeship in a brewery in Germany before coming to the United States in 1868. Kuhrs changed the spelling of his last name to Coors and, together with Schueler, launched a brewery in Golden, Colorado, in 1873.

By 1875, beer consumption in the United States had increased to 6.2 gallons per person. In that same year, the Valentin Blatz Brewing Company of Milwaukee popularized bottled beer in America. Previously, beer was mainly barreled and sold only on tap in saloons and other drinking establishments. Bottled beer had a longer shelf life; moreover, the bottling of beer, along with refrigeration, made it possible for grocery stores and other retail outlets to sell beer and thus made it easier for people to drink beer at home. Other companies began promoting their bottled beer. In 1882, Pabst tied a blue ribbon around the neck of its bottles and called it "Select."[58] This name changed to "Best Select" and then "Pabst Select." When the beer purportedly won an award at the World's Columbian Exposition in 1893, the slogan changed to "Pabst Blue Ribbon Beer."

Centennial

In 1876, the United States celebrated its centennial with an international exposition in Philadelphia. A number of American breweries, such as Joseph Schlitz and Valentine Blatz of Milwaukee, submitted bottled beer to a competition at the Philadelphia exposition, and many lager beers received awards. Bottled imported German beer was exhibited as well, and Bavaria was hailed as "the land of lager." If a visitor to the exposition wanted to sample lager beer, that too was possible. Temperance advocates persuaded organizers to ban the sale of hard liquor at the Centennial Exposition, which upset many who concluded that Puritans were running the Centennial. But wine and beer were permitted, which annoyed temperance leaders who had concluded that lager beer was just as bad as hard liquor. As it turned out, the summer of 1876 was an extremely hot one, and the lager beer stands at the Centennial Exposition were thronged with customers.[59]

Lager beer also was served in restaurants at the exposition. Restaurateur Philip J. Lauber of Philadelphia paid the hefty sum of $6,000 for the right to open a German restaurant and beer garden at the exposition, and he then spent the astronomical sum of $56,000 to construct it. It was a good investment. The restaurant at the three-acre facility could seat 1,000 customers simultaneously. Thousands more could sit and drink lager in the beer garden, where a German band serenaded customers. As a writer in *Scribner's Magazine* put it, "The consumption of lager here is simply amazing."[60] Lauber served Erlanger beer, a Bohemian-style lager brewed by Bernhard Stroh, a German immigrant. In 1850, Stroh established what would become the Stroh Brewery Company in Detroit.

When the Philadelphia Centennial Exposition closed, more than 10 million visitors had passed through its gates, and many of them had sampled lager beer for the first time. When they returned home, they wanted to be able to buy lager locally. Thanks to the nation's expanding railroad system, it was possible for many communities to acquire lager beer. The invention of refrigerated railroad cars in the late 1870s further increased the availability of lager. Around the same time, the introduction of ice machines and refrigeration technology made it possible for breweries producing beer by bottom fermentation to operate year-round rather than just during the winter. This, in turn, meant that lager also could be made in the warmer climates of southern states. The advent of refrigeration increased both the production and profitability of lager beer.[61]

Beer Gardens

Beer gardens were particularly popular with those who immigrated from Bavaria. Unlike saloons and beer halls, beer gardens were intended for the entire family, thereby playing an important role in preserving the identity of German immigrants. Outdoor lager beer gardens sprang up around the United States. Friedrich Lauer's brewery in Reading, Pennsylvania, for instance, had an adjacent six-acre beer garden; the tree-shaded space included a fountain and a fish pond.[62] In St. Louis, Franz Joseph Uhrig, who founded a lager brewery in 1846, opened a beer garden in a large wooded tract with a 210-foot-long manmade cave to keep the beer cold. Uhrig's beer garden offered stage shows and music pavilions, and food was available to accompany the beer.[63] Breweries in New Jersey offered beer gardens complete with billiard tables, pianos, dancing parties, and swings and merry-go-rounds "for the young folks."[64]

Pius Dreher opened Milwaukee's first beer garden in 1850. In its heyday, it drew 10,000 to 15,000 visitors a day from as far away as Cincinnati, Chicago, and other German communities in the Midwest. Another Milwaukee establishment, Schlitz Garden, was established in 1879 by the Schlitz brewery; it featured a concert pavilion, a dance hall, a bowling alley, refreshment parlors, and a three-story pagoda-like structure that offered a panoramic view of the city.[65] Other beer parks in Milwaukee were established in the late nineteenth century by the Pabst and Miller brewing companies.

In New York City, where land prices were high and the weather unpredictable, brewers set up indoor beer gardens in large halls planted with trees and flowers; sometimes part of the ceiling or a wall could be opened to let in the sun in good weather. These beer gardens could hold as many as 3,000 to 4,000 people at a time. Some were family oriented; others catered to the lower classes.[66] The largest beer garden in New York was the Atlantic Garden, an "immense room with a lofty curved ceiling, handsomely frescoed, and lighted by numerous chandeliers and by brackets along the walls. It is lighted during the day from the roof. At one side is an open space planted with trees and flowers, the only mark of a garden visible." The Atlantic Garden contained a restaurant, "several bars, a shooting gallery, billiard tables, bowling alleys, and an orchestra." As one observer wrote, there were "dense clouds of tobacco-smoke, and hurry of waiters, and banging of glasses, and calling for beer, but no rowdyism."[67]

Beer gardens served a variety of functions other than drinking. They served as social centers, concert halls, and athletic fields; civic, religious, and organizational meetings were held in them as well. Beer gardens were not just for German Americans; mainstream Americans and other immigrants frequented them as well. Anheuser-Busch would later capitalize on this idea by creating a series of theme parks called Busch Gardens in several American cities.

After the Civil War, the brewing industry rapidly changed partly due to scientific discoveries. In 1857, a brewery in France discovered irregularities in its fermentation process, so it asked a local scientist, Louis Pasteur, to investigate. After three years of work, Pasteur published a book documenting that yeast was a living organism responsible for fermentation. When yeast was exposed to oxygen, they produced a fungus; when yeast was deprived of oxygen, it fermented. He also concluded that other microorganisms caused spoilage. He continued his studies and discovered that heating liquids to just below the boiling point killed the microorganisms, stopped fermentation, and prevented spoilage. He published his findings in a second book, *Études sur la vin* (1865), and this process (soon called pasteurization) brought about revolutionary changes in the brewing, winemaking, and milk-making industries.

Other scientists built on Pasteur's discoveries, and scientific brewing emerged; spoilage decreased, flavors improved, and production accelerated. Just as these changes were under way, two other technological shifts would have just as important impacts on the brewing industry: rapid railroad expansion into all geographical regions of the nation and improved refrigeration systems. These made it possible for breweries to ship their beer throughout the United States with little spoilage. The beer industry, which had been local and regional in scope, suddenly became national. These changes generated cutthroat competition between the large breweries for increased market share. To enhance sales, breweries such as Schlitz, Pabst, Miller and Anheuser-Busch began targeting saloons.

Saloons

Beer's rise to stardom was closely associated with the rise of the saloon. The American saloon emerged from English tavern and public house traditions.[68] The name derived from *salon*, a French term meaning an ornate spacious hall that was often used for large public gatherings. The first American saloons were established in swank hotels in approximately 1840; they catered mainly to the upper class. Saloons provided various entertainment and usually contained a bar, which served whatever alcoholic beverages were in vogue at the time. To cash in on the upper-class cachet, grog shops, taverns, public houses, and lower-class dives renamed themselves as saloons. The upper class then launched private clubs where they could socialize with their own kind and drink their own beverages.

In popular mythology, the classic American saloon is the western establishment popularized in Hollywood cowboy movies, complete with swinging doors, rampant fighting, gambling, gunfights, and prostitution. As George Ade, an American writer and newspaperman, wrote in 1931:

> The truth is that the average or typical saloon was not a savory resort. . . . Nine-tenths of all the places in which intoxicants were dished out affected a splendor which was palpably spurious and made a total failure of any attempt to seem respectable. The saloon business was furtive and ashamed of itself, hiding behind curtains, blinds and screens and providing alley entrances for those who wished to slip in without being observed.[69]

As immigrants flooded into American cities beginning in the late 1840s, saloons catered to their needs. Ethnic saloonkeepers were magnets for the newly arrived. Many saloons were closely connected with political power in cities and towns. This upset temperance advocates, who concluded that saloons fostered "an un-American spirit among the foreign-born population of our country."[70]

Breweries considered saloons as their main means for distributing their products. For promotional purposes, breweries distributed cheap gifts, such as playing cards, bottle openers, corkscrews, calendars, matches, pocket knives, stationery, and postcards. To gain market share, breweries made exclusive arrangements with saloonkeepers to sell only their beer. In other cases, breweries bought saloons outright and hired managers to run them. Beer sales surged.[71] Profits generated were enormous, and large breweries competed with each other for national market share.

Breweries began pumping funds into saloons to upgrade their appearances and attract customers. Massive mahogany bars became de rigueur, as did mirrors, large pictures on the walls, tables and chairs, and entertainment. Saloons had bars—long narrow solid counters that separated the patrons from the liquor. The counter usually had stools in front of it, with brass foot railings for the comfort of the customers. Reproductions of famous paintings of presidents, such as Abraham Lincoln and James Garfield, or dramatic scenes, such as *Custer's Last Fight*, *The Spirit of '76*, and *Washington Crossing the Delaware*, as well as pictures of nude women often graced the saloons' walls. Occasionally, saloons had tables and chairs where patrons could chat or gamble. As competition picked up among saloons, entertainment—including pool tables, pianos, and occasionally dancing girls—became part of the saloon scene. Saloons provided a place where working-class men could socialize and get assistance from their peers when needed. As a report in 1901 stated, the saloon was the workingman's club.[72] Brewers bought up more saloons. In St. Louis, brewers owned 65 percent of the city's saloons. Schlitz owned fifty retail outlets in Milwaukee in 1887.[73]

Often with brewery assistance, saloons began offering free lunch to attract even more customers and to encourage drinking more beer. As competition increased among brewers, the numbers of saloons in America shot up and so did the amount of beer Americans drank. By 1885, Americans drank more than eleven gallons per person annually, and this was just the beginning.[74] The invention of inexpensive commercial beer bottles in late nineteenth century also made it possible for grocery stores and small restaurants to sell or serve a wide variety of beers, rather than having just a few on tap, as at a saloon. Due to the increasing number of saloons and the available of beer bottles, beer consumption continued to rise; by 1916, Americans were drinking twenty gallons of beer per capita in 1916—virtually all of it lager.[75]

Laws were passed to control crime and restrict the influence of bar owners and their allies, but most proved inadequate. Support grew for Prohibition. Bar owners tried to protect their interests by bribing police, judges, and politicians, but sometimes this was hardly necessary because bars served as clubhouses for big-city political bosses. This state of affairs further inspired the Prohibition movement, which culminated in the passage of the Eighteenth

Amendment to the Constitution in 1919 and the passage of the Volstead Act, from which America's saloons never recovered.

Microbrewing

During Prohibition, beer consumption dropped precipitously. It was just too difficult to manufacture and transport large quantities of beer without easy discovery. Some breweries survived by making near beer with less than 0.5 percent alcohol, which was legally permissible. Other breweries shifted production to non-beer products. Many breweries declared bankruptcy and did not reopen them after repeal. The few large breweries that survived Prohibition reemerged in April 1933, after Congress modified the Volstead Act by approving the sale of 3.2 percent beer in the United States. By June 1933, 31 breweries were up and running; by 1934, this number reached 756. Americans slowly increased their consumption of beer; since 1985, per capita consumption has hovered around twenty-one gallons per person.[76]

Throughout the 1970s, the home brewing movement picked up speed. A major problem facing home brewers was that it was illegal at the time to brew beer without registering with U.S. Treasury Department. In February 1979, Congress passed a law permitting home brewers to make up to 200 gallons of beer annually without registering.[77] The American Homebrewers Association was created in 1978 and had 3,000 members by 1984. By 2011, its membership exceeded 19,000. Many successful home brewers opened microbreweries, which supplied beer to others, and brew pubs, which sold their beer directly to customers. Only 8 such establishments existed in 1980; by 2009, there were 1,595.[78] The proliferation and success of microbreweries did not particularly harm large brewers, which still controlled 98 percent of the market share.[79]

Consolidation and Globalization

In 1934, there were 756 breweries in America; by 1992, this had decreased to 58. The market share controlled by the five big breweries increased from 19 percent in 1947 to 88 percent in 1992. Throughout the remainder of the twentieth century, brewers merged and were acquired. Large brewers could produce beer at a lower cost due to economies of scale. In 1947, the ten largest breweries controlled 28 percent of the beer market; by 1981, they controlled almost 94 percent of the market.[80] Five beers—Busch, Miller, Pabst,

Schlitz, and Coors—dominated the national market. These beers appealed to the largest number of potential customers, and some critics claimed that they were tasteless. Some American brewed their own beer at home. Consolidation has continued unabated. The brewery in Golden, Colorado, owned by Jacob Schueler and Adolphus Coors was a tremendous success; Schueler sold his share of the operation in 1880, and the company was renamed the Adolphus Coors Brewing Company. In 2005, it merged with the Canadian company Molson to form the Molson Coors Brewing Company, which today is the world's fifth largest brewing company.

In 2002, the Miller Brewing Company was acquired by South African Breweries, and the American operation's name was changed to SAB-Miller. It is the second largest brewing company in the world.

In 2008, Anheuser-Busch was acquired by ImBev, a Brazilian-Belgian firm. Anheuser-Busch sold its Busch Gardens theme parks in 2009 to the Blackstone Group, a private equity firm. Today, Anheuser-Busch ImBev is the largest brewing company in the world. Its Budweiser brand is one of the best-selling beers in America.

The F. & M. Schaefer Brewing Company was acquired by Stroh Brewing Company in 1981. In 1999, Stroh was acquired by the Pabst Brewing Company. Pabst also acquired twenty more companies, including the Joseph Schlitz Brewing Company. In 2010, Pabst itself was acquired by businessman C. Dean Metropoulos. The Pabst Brewing Company, now headquartered in Los Angeles, remains the only American-owned large brewing company.

Postscript

🍺 When the Brewers' Congress first met in 1862, Friedrich Lauer was selected as chair, a position he held for many years. He helped organize the United States Brewers' Association.[80] A few after Lauer's death in 1883, the association erected a monument to his memory in a public square of Reading, Pennsylvania.

🍺 The Bergner & Engel Brewing Company in Philadelphia survived until Prohibition. It reopened after repeal, but its equipment was outmoded and its distribution system weak. The company folded shortly thereafter.

🍺 The Jacob Ruppert Brewing Company in New York thrived throughout the late nineteenth century. In 1914, Jacob Ruppert, Jr., acquired the New

York Yankees baseball team. During Prohibition, he helped construct Yankee Stadium. Ruppert, like all brewers, suffered during Prohibition. A major strike hobbled the company in 1948, but it survived until 1965.

🍺 The firm founded in 1829 by David Yuengling in Pottsville, Pennsylvania, has survived. Today, D. G. Yuengling & Son is America's oldest operating brewing company. Unlike most of its rivals, past and present, it remains a family-owned company.

Berenice Abbott, *Milk Wagon and Old Houses, Grove Street, No. 4–10, Manhattan* (June 18, 1936). (The New York Public Library/Art Resource, NY)

7
Nature's Perfect Food

INFANT MORTALITY was high throughout the United States, but the rates were most appalling in cities, particularly Philadelphia, Boston, and New York. Worse still, the mortality rate was rapidly increasing. In 1814, for example, 25 percent of the babies born in Philadelphia died before they reached the age of five years. By 1839, this mortality rate had increased to almost 51 percent. Over a similar time period, the infant mortality rate in Boston increased from 33 percent to 43 percent; in New York, it increased from 32 percent to 50 percent. By the 1850s, children younger than ten years accounted for 62 percent of all deaths in New York City; other northeastern cities were not far behind.[1] Medical professionals were unclear as to the cause of this spike in the mortality rate among young children. Many believed that it was something in city air, whereas others attributed the increased death rate to communicable diseases, such as cholera and tuberculosis.

Temperance advocate Robert M. Hartley, a successful New York City merchant with no medical background, came to the conclusion that the sharp increase in child mortality rates was caused by bad milk from dairies associated with urban brewing and distilling operations. Hartley believed that milk was nature's perfect food, for adults as well as children—but not the milk that came from these urban dairies, where cows were fed poorly and stabled in filthy sheds. He circulated tracts, published exposés, spoke to large audiences, and set down his opinions in America's first book on milk, published in 1842. The campaign that Hartley launched eventually succeeded in closing many dairies, which may or may not have affected child mortality rates.[2] Hartley's campaign did affect milk consumption, however: as soon as Americans believed that milk was safe to drink, consumption skyrocketed.

Background

From the beginning of European colonization, Americans drank milk. English colonists imported cows into Jamestown, Virginia, shortly after the colony was founded. Thomas West, Earl De La Warr (better known as Lord Delaware), an early governor and captain-general of the colony, proclaimed milk to be "a great nourishment and refreshing to our people, serving also (in occasion) as well for Physicke as for Food."[3] By 1634, all the "better sort" of plantations of Virginia, proclaimed a visitor to Jamestown, had "plentie of milk."[4] Virginia plantation owner Landon Carter enjoyed marshmallow root boiled in milk and sweetened with brown sugar.[5] The Virginia planter William Byrd reported in his diary that he "ate milk for breakfast" almost every day. He drank it between meals, frequently flavoring it with barley, tea, hot corn pone, strawberries, apples, and rhubarb. When he was ill, he drank warm milk.[6]

Milk was plentiful in colonial New England. Cows arrived at Plymouth Plantation in 1624.[7] In the Massachusetts Bay Colony, established around what would become Boston in 1630, the colonists drank milk on its own and also used it in maize-based dishes, such as hasty pudding, samp, and suppawn. A favorite dish of the colonial period was baked pumpkin filled with milk and eaten with a spoon.[8] A rich combination of "curds and cream" was rated a delicacy throughout the colonies.[9] Milk porridge was frequently served for breakfast and supper.[10]

The Dutch settlers of New Amsterdam (later New York) were strongly committed to dairy farming. Unfortunately, the growth of the human population outpaced that of the dairy herds, leading Reverend Jonas Michaëlius to complain that milk "cannot here be obtained" except at a "very high price." He urged the Dutch West India Company to send more farmers and dairymen to the colony. The Dutch did so, and milk, cream, butter, and cheese became staples—as they had been in the old country. Herds of dairy cattle flourished on the island of Manhattan and in the settlements that were established north of the city in the Hudson Valley.[11] When the Swedish botanist Peter Kalm visited the Hudson Valley in 1749, he found milk in abundance:

farmers added milk to their tea, drank buttermilk, and enjoyed bowls of bread moistened with milk for breakfast and supper.[12]

A Swedish minister, Israel Acrelius, found that milk with water was "the common drink of the people." Milk was also used as a base to make a summertime punch with rum, sugar, and nutmeg grated over the top. This punch was also used as a medicinal preparation for dysentery. Barley was often boiled in milk, and bread was added to the mixture for a dinner dish. For supper, milk was poured over broken bread. Milk was also sometimes added to chocolate and drunk with a spoon.[13]

Americans served milk at meals and between meals. During the summer, it was served with ice.[14] Milk was also combined with staples such as rice, potatoes, and corn pone; added to coffee, tea, and hot chocolate; and employed in numerous desserts, such as curds and cream, fools, trifles, and floating islands. Syllabubs were rich milk or cream desserts flavored with wine and spices.

Milk spoiled quickly in the South and commercial dairying was limited, but most plantations and farms had a cow for milk for the children. Excess milk was converted into butter. The liquid byproduct leftover after making butter was called buttermilk, which was used as a drink—especially by southerners, who preferred buttermilk or sour milk to regular milk.[15] Soured milk was also used to make milk biscuits, pancakes, and waffles. It could also be boiled, with molasses added to make the drink sweeter.[16]

In the countryside, almost every small farm had at least one cow that supplied milk for the family's needs. Dairies also were established in most cities, but as the urban population mushroomed in the early nineteenth century, the demand for milk increased beyond the capacity of city dairies. In New York, private individuals tied cows to stakes in city streets and fed them garbage. Property owners charged for the privilege of herding cows in their streets. According to dairy historian John Dillon, "the disposition of the manure was a provision of the lease contract," and at the time there was an unlimited demand for manure to fertilize Manhattan's farms and gardens.[17]

For those who did not want to bother keeping cows in Manhattan, milk was available from street vendors who dispensed it in uncovered wooden pails.[18] These vendors commonly carried several gallons of milk at a time by employing a wooden yoke

three feet long chiseled out and smoothed to fit over the shoulders and the back of the neck, with nicely rounded arms extending over the shoulders.

A light chain or rope was suspended from each arm with a hook at the end. With this yolk across his shoulders the carrier stood between two pails or other containers, and by stooping forward attached the hooks to the vessels; then straightening up, the weight of the vessels rested on his shoulders.[19]

Milking Brewers and Distillers

In colonial days, most of New York City's milk was produced in urban dairies. As the city's population grew, the demand for milk increased. The business of distributing milk became more profitable; dealers multiplied and competition became intense. In the 1820s, some ambitious New York City dairymen adopted a British system that exploited another popular beverage—beer—to support milk production. Eager for larger profits, they built large stables near breweries. Mash or slop—the watery byproducts of brewing with grain—was siphoned from the breweries directly to cows' mangers through wooden chutes. By the 1830s, an estimated 18,000 cows in New York City and Brooklyn were being fed almost exclusively on brewery mash.[20] Distillers and brewers saved money by not having to cart away the brewery waste, and they enjoyed substantial profits from the sale of milk (as well as manure). They also made money selling the meat when the cows died. Moreover, at the time, milk was in great demand in cities, in part because of efforts by the temperance movement to discourage the consumption of alcoholic beverages.

It was the connection between breweries and distilleries and dairies that interested that Robert M. Hartley. He had been born in England in 1796, but his family had immigrated to the United States in 1799 and settled in upstate New York, where evangelical churches flourished. Hartley was particularly influenced by temperance views. He became a wool merchant in the Mohawk Valley, and then moved to New York City, where he expanded his operation.

Although he was a successful businessman, Hartley never lost his devotion to temperance. In 1829, he founded the New York Temperance Society and was elected its corresponding secretary in 1833. At the time, the temperance movement encouraged parents to give their children milk—a wholesome alternative, or so everyone believed, to alcoholic beverages. When considering ways to reduce alcohol consumption, Hartley investigated the brewing and distilling operations in the city and decided to attack one of its main profit centers—milk production. The cows ate the mash that came from distilling and brewing, and therefore the companies did not have to pay to discard it. The cows produced milk, which was in great demand because breastfeeding was declining. Breweries and distilleries made additional profits by selling manure to farmers; when the cows died, they sold the meat to butchers. Hartley believed that the profits of the dairy operations were so substantial that New York's alcohol industry would collapse if they were eliminated.[21]

So Hartley investigated the dairies, and what he uncovered was shocking: the milk produced in the brewery and distillery dairies was not rich in butterfat. Instead, it was extremely thin with a pale bluish cast. Brewers and distillers, as well as other milk distributors, adulterated their milk to make it appear wholesome and make more money. They added water for increased volume; brightened it up with chalk, carrot juice, and annatto; sweetened it with molasses to make the kids happy; and occasionally broke in a raw egg for creaminess. The dairies also were poorly managed and badly kept. Cows were frequently diseased; some cows could not even stand and had to be winched up so they could be milked.

Hartley concluded that poor quality and adulterated milk was the major reason that New York City's infant mortality had increased so steeply during the 1830s. He wrote to the dairy owners, threatening them with exposure in the press if they did not clean up their operations. When they failed to comply, Hartley launched a campaign against "swill milk" and "slop milk," publishing a series of pamphlets and articles opposing its sale. In 1842, he compiled his views and published America's first book about milk, *An Historical, Scientific, and Practical Essay on Milk, as an Article of Human Sustenance.* In it, Hartley affirmed his beliefs that milk was nature's perfect food and that drinking milk was part of God's design, but that the slop milk was killing the city's babies and children. To support his arguments, Hartley quoted and cited scripture throughout his book.[22]

Scriptural references might have been helpful for religiously oriented New Yorkers, but the medical profession considered his campaign a temperance rant and evangelical propaganda. Despite the extensive statistical data also published in Hartley's book, medical professionals generally disregarded his views. City officials were financially rewarded by the breweries and distilleries to turn a deaf ear to protests, so they also ignored his campaign. This did not stop Hartley. He funded the publication of still more circulars signed by physicians attesting to the deleterious effects of slop milk. However, most medical professionals still failed to support his theory that the milk produced by the dairies was the cause of the increase in infant mortality.[23]

Despite Hartley's exposé, the number of breweries exploded in New York during the 1840s and 1850s, and so did the number of dairies. But Hartley's efforts had raised alarm and attracted the interest of newspapers, which began investigations of their own into the atrocious conditions in the dairies. In 1847, the *New York Tribune* reported on "one of the largest and filthiest swill milk stables and urged the city to act." The exposés pressured the New York Academy of Medicine to establish a committee to investigate the controversy in 1847, but that group attacked Hartley's credibility. Still, the committee proclaimed that the dairies were nuisances due to the effects of diseased and adulterated milk, but they had no evidence that these dairies caused the spike in child mortality. The *New York Tribune* published another exposé in 1849.[24] Yet another series of exposés ran in the *New-York Evening Post* during the early 1850s; newspaperman John Mullaly collected these articles in a book, which was published in 1853.[25] The newly launched *New York Times* began featuring articles on swill milk in 1854.[26]

Despite the barrage of exposés, lectures, pamphlets, books, newspaper articles, and magazine articles, the sale of swill milk continued unabated. The brewing and distilling industries were just too ingrained in New York City's political system to permit anything more than superficial modifications. This changed in 1858, when *Frank Leslie's Illustrated Newspaper* "declared war" on the brewery dairies of Manhattan and Brooklyn. The first article, "Startling Exposure of Milk Trade of New York and Brooklyn!" reported that the stables surrounding the distilleries were "disgusting," "dilapidated and wretchedly filthy." The article described crude wooden shanties, thickly hung with cobwebs in which the cows were "arranged in double rows, their heads to the swill troughs and their tails, or rather the remnants of their tails, towards each other: so close that sometimes one cow actually lies on the other." The swill rushed from the brewery through chutes, foaming and "boiling hot and reeking with subtle poison it splashes into the troughs." At first, the cows refused the swill, "but after a week or two they seem[ed] to have a taste for it and in a short time we [found] them consuming from one to two or even three barrels of swill a day."[27]

Leslie continued the series of articles, and the controversy heated up when one of the newspaper's reporters was murdered while developing a story.[28] This death prompted the New York Academy of Medicine to form another committee, which blandly acknowledged the "unwholesomeness of slop-fed milk" and recommended that it "not be used as a diet by the infant population." But the committee once again demurred when it came to stating why or how milk from these dairies would have caused the increase in child mortality rates.[29]

The press coverage and medical reports finally forced New York City's Common Council and its Board of Health to hold hearings on the controversy, but thanks to pressure from brewers and distillers, the impact of swill milk on public health was effectively whitewashed. Eventually, however, Frank Leslie and others convinced the New York State Legislature to pass the Act to Prevent the Adulteration and Traffic of Impure Milk, which was enacted in 1862. Massachusetts had passed similar legislation in 1859, and other states soon followed.[30] Although enforcement of these laws was deficient, escalating land prices in cities and increasing competition from rural dairies made urban dairies less economical; one by one, the sources of swill milk closed.

Industrial Milk

Swill dairies were not the only cause of high infant mortality rates. City water supplies, for instance, were also deficient, and urbanites were more exposed to contagious diseases. Health professionals slowly improved city water supplies and better understanding of contagious diseases decreased infant mortality rates. However, urban infant mortality rates remained high and many believed that milk remained a major cause. Milk from swill dairies had been fresh because it was usually distributed quickly and efficiently, but swill milk's replacement from rural areas was often less so.

During the early nineteenth century, rural dairies had played little part in supplying milk for fast-growing cities, primarily because of the cost and difficulties of transporting milk into the cities.[31] This changed, however, as a result of improved transportation. The steamboat in the early nineteenth century made it possible for dairy farmers along navigable rivers, such as the Hudson, to ship milk to cities at relatively low cost.[32]

Expanding railroad systems enabled rural dairy farmers to ship fresh milk into cities on a daily basis, even if their farms were far from rivers. By 1842, for instance, the Erie Railroad had been extended as far as Goshen in Orange County, New York, which is northwest of New York City. To undercut the city dairies, Robert Hartley had visited upstate farmers and encouraged them to send milk to New York City.[33] Two years later, farmers in Goshen and neighboring communities organized the Orange County Milk

Association to do just that. Unfortunately, the early operators of the Erie Railroad provided irregular service, and the Orange County farmers still had a lot to learn about shipping milk.[34] Milk trains often took as long as thirty-six hours to reach the city from Orange County, and then more hours were expended distributing the milk in the city.

Unrefrigerated milk was a problem during cold weather, but it was a disaster in hot weather. Initially, farmers would strain the milk and pour it into tall tin pails; these pails were then carted to the train station, where the milk was transferred to fifty-gallon cans. Later, creameries for handling milk were established within convenient distances along railroad routes. Farmers delivered milk to a creamery, received credit for their delivery, and then returned home. The creamery employees cooled the milk with ice and then shipped it to depots, from which trains carried it to cities.[35] By the 1850s, one-third of all New York City milk was brought in from surrounding counties. Although rural cows were not fed on swill, as in urban dairies, there was still no guarantee that the milk shipped into the city from upstate New York was pure and wholesome.

Diseased Milk

Hygiene was not a high priority during the milking process in either cities or rural areas. Cows' udders were often caked with mud, and dairymaids and dairymen were not always paragons of cleanliness. Milk cans, pails, and bottles were often unsanitary; when they were washed, it was often with dirty water. The cows themselves were often ill—some had tuberculosis, which could be passed on to those who drank the milk. The practice of adulteration was common. Because milk was sold in bulk and the supplier could not be easily identified, dairy farmers frequently skimmed off the cream and topped up the remaining milk with water. Middlemen also added water to the milk to increase profits; this water often was unsanitary, infected with cholera and other waterborne diseases. In addition, because refrigerators did not yet exist and domestic iceboxes were not yet common, milk often spoiled in the home.

By the late 1860s, medical professionals had a better understanding of nutrition and the importance of milk in the diets of infants and young children. Many acknowledged that the composition and quality of milk could indeed be related to child mortality. Physician Austin Flint's medical text, *A Treatise on the Principles and Practices of Medicine*, first published in 1866, concluded that adulterated or poor-quality milk was responsible for the increase in child mortality rates. In response, chemists developed tests to identify adulterated milk.[36]

Concern about the quality of milk encouraged lawmakers to pass laws against adulteration. Beginning in the 1880s, both cities and states passed ordinances against the sale of watered-down or adulterated milk. In 1888, Newark, New Jersey, became the first American city to require inspections of dairies. Subsequently, other cities began doing the same.[37] By 1905, most states had such laws. Milk dealers strongly opposed such legislation, however, and adulteration continued to be widespread. In 1896, New York City required milk purveyors to be licensed, established standards for milk, and hired inspectors to examine milk to make sure that dealers complied with the law. Large milk companies could easily comply with these requirements, but many of their smaller competitors were driven out of business.[38] Thus began the consolidation of the dairy industry in the United States.

Bacteriological Contamination

Although the enforcement of laws increasingly prevented milk adulteration, there was yet another problem to resolve before the safety of the milk supply could be ensured. By the mid-nineteenth century, milk was a suspected culprit in the increased child mortality rates—and not just because of adulteration. However, no one knew exactly what the problem was.

The work of Louis Pasteur, a French scientist, led to an understanding of bacterial contamination of foods, including milk. Cholera had swept through Europe and the United States beginning in the 1830s, but it was not until the 1850s that the water supply was suspected of spreading the disease. During the following decade, Louis Pasteur focused his scientific research on what is now called bacteriology. His experiments demonstrated that beer, wine, and milk soured or spoiled because of microscopic living organisms. His discovery led to the germ theory of disease, which posited that microbes caused illness. Beginning in the 1880s, researchers isolated and identified various microbes that caused disease. First water and then milk were identified as potential transmitters of various infectious diseases, such as typhoid, scarlet fever, diphtheria, and diarrhea.[39]

Pasteur developed a process to kill the bacteria in wine and beer by heating the beverages to temperatures exceeding 158°F. When this process was applied to milk, however, it changed the taste of the milk; pediatricians worried that it also changed the nutritional content. It was finally discovered that heating milk to 145°F degrees for thirty minutes killed microbes without greatly affecting the milk's flavor or nutritional content. This process (today called pasteurization) was introduced into commercial milk production in 1889. However, cities did not begin to require milk to be pasteurized until 1908, and it would be two decades before pasteurization was widely mandated and enforced. In fact, it was not until 1920 that milk was pasteurized in most large American cities. The adoption of pasteurized milk was accompanied by a steep decline in child mortality rates.[40]

Bovine tuberculosis can also be transmitted to humans through milk. In the 1890s, tests were introduced to determine which cows had the disease.[41] Cities and states soon passed regulations requiring regular testing of cows for tuberculosis and the destruction of animals that had the disease. Many dairy farmers, unexpectedly faced with the loss of a large proportion of their herds, were outraged. But the enforcement of these regulations greatly decreased the incidence of tuberculosis among infants and children.[42]

The dairy industry made great strides during the late nineteenth century. In 1899, Henry E. Alvord, chief of the dairy division of the U.S. Department of Agriculture, proclaimed, "No branch of agriculture has made greater progress than dairying during the nineteenth century. . . . It is now regarded as among the most progressive and highly developed forms of farming in the United States."[43] Despite such assurances, cookbook authors, such as Mary Ronald, warned mothers in 1899 that milk was "one of the most subtle of disease-carriers. Hence every careful mother, before giving it to her children, subjects it to the sterilizing process, which is simply raising it to the degree of heat which destroys the germs."[44]

America's Perfect Food

Despite the aforementioned problems, milk consumption continued to increase in the United States. When Walter Gore Marshall, an English traveler, visited America in the 1880s, he reported that milk was very popular, writing, "I have often been filled with wonder and admiration upon seeing the amount of milk an American will drink at one meal, without apparently getting bilious."[45]

Traditionally, milk was distributed in forty- to eighty-quart cans. Drivers would cart the cans along city streets and then dip the milk from the cans into small milk cans brought by customers. This was not ideal. On rainy days, water poured into the milk cans from the dippers. As a New York milk company executive pointed out, on a rainy day, water went into the milk cans from the drivers' hands and clothes and "on a dusty day, when all sorts of dust, and especially the dust of horse-dung—which is the principal dust that we have in New York—is flying, the milk is not in good condition, will not keep as well, and there is abundant evidence in the flavor."[46] Milk began to be bottled in the 1880s, and this improved cleanliness.

With the introduction of pasteurization, per capita consumption of milk surged.[47] Americans not only drank milk by the glass but also used it in other ways as well—adding cream to their coffee, moistening their breakfast cereal, guzzling milkshakes, and feeding babies commercial infant formula. Nutritionists praised milk as the "perfect food," and the dairy industry launched a series of advertising campaigns to promote the health benefits of milk. The robust, happy children pictured in milk advertisements fostered the belief that milk was essential, nutritious, and pure.[48]

Until the mid-twentieth century, milkmen delivered dairy products directly to homes, and children were offered milk during the school day. To encourage children to drink milk at home, sweetened syrups and powders in chocolate, vanilla, and strawberry flavors appeared on the market. Lectures, songs, and plays that extolled the virtues of milk were performed in schools in an attempt to urge children to drink more milk, and teaching units developed by dairy councils were employed in the curriculum. School superintendents also required teachers to talk with students about the importance of drinking milk. To promote sales of milk to mothers, dairy councils advised pediatricians to urge mothers to give their children more milk.[49] Philanthropists, such as Nathan Strauss, owner of Macy's department store, established "milk stations" where the poor could receive free milk. City governments considered this to be such a good idea that they set up similar operations in communities across America.[50]

As a result of these promotional efforts, per capita milk consumption skyrocketed during the early years of the twentieth century. Homogenized milk arrived in 1927, resulting from a process that prevents the cream for separating from the rest of the milk. Five years later, the milk industry fortified milk with vitamins A and D, which further increased public perception of the healthfulness of milk. By 1950, the average American drank the equivalent of 600 glasses of milk per year. Although this consumption gradually declined in the years that followed—largely because of fear of the fat, calories, and cholesterol in whole milk—low-fat and nonfat milk and dairy products more than made up for the decrease.[51] Milk has regularly been combined with other beverages and ingredients, such as cereal. It is often added to coffee, tea, and chocolate drinks. In the twentieth century, a number of products with milk, such as milkshakes and smoothies, were popularized.

Milk Today

Although the swill dairies closed more than a century ago, controversies have continued to swirl around milk. The most significant concern is with recombinant bovine growth hormone (rBGH), which is injected into dairy cattle to increase milk production by 5 to 15 percent. The genetically engineered rBGH is secreted into milk and also is found in meat products; some evidence has shown that rBGH may have a detrimental effect on the human body. Based on this evidence, twenty-five European nations have banned rBGH, as have Canada, Australia, New Zealand, and Japan. It is still used in the United States, and many milk brands and milk products contain rBGH.[52]

Others are concerned with the type of milk offered today. Anne Mendelson, author of *Milk: The Surprising Story of Milk Through the Ages* (2008), believes that

> taking plain milk and putting it through technological hoops to create an extraordinary diversity of products like fat-free, .5%, 1%, or 2% milk-fat, and supposedly "whole" homogenized milk, with or without other wrinkles like added skim milk solids or reduced lactose content, does nothing of the kind. It has left consumers with a barrage of gimmicky niche-market choices but no access to true (unhomogenized) whole milk.[53]

Despite concerns, the United States is the world's largest producer of milk.[54] Although America no longer ranks as the largest consumer of milk on a per capita basis, milk remains one of the country's most important and healthful beverages.

Postscript

In 1842, Robert Hartley founded the New York Association for Improving the Condition of the Poor, an organization that was subsequently duplicated in many other cities across America. For his efforts in closing the swill dairies and in improving the health of the poor, Hartley has been identified as one of the founders of the public health movement in America, and he is considered by many to be America's first consumer advocate.[55]

Jerry Thomas preparing a blue blazer, as depicted
in the series "Our Bartenders," in the comic weekly
Under the Gaslight (1878–1879).

8
The Most Delightful and Insinuating Potations

THE NEW YORK PUBLISHER Dick & Fitzgerald specialized in "how-to" guides and reference works. On June 4, 1859, it announced the publication of *The Bar-Tender's Guide: or, Complete Encyclopedia of Fancy Drinks*; a few weeks later, it copyrighted the work. As was typical for the time, the publisher advertised books ahead of publication; if few orders came in, it simply did not publish the title. This is likely the reason for the delayed release of this now-classic manual *The Bar-Tender's Guide; or How to Mix Drinks*. The author was identified as Jerry Thomas, formerly the "principal Bartender at the Metropolitan Hotel, New York, and the Planter's House, St. Louis." For a decade, Thomas had traveled around the United States, working on and off in bars. Like most bartenders, he had collected recipes for various drinks that customers ordered. Thomas considered these formulas to be professional secrets—if everyone had them, professional bartenders would be rendered superfluous. But Dick & Fitzgerald paid Thomas to write down his recipes. By the time the book was published, Thomas had left the Metropolitan Hotel and was headed to California.

It is likely that neither Thomas nor his publisher thought the book would earn much money. In general, mixed drinks were made and served only in upper-class bars, and there was no reason for anyone who did not work in one to buy a book of drink recipes. But it was also unlikely that professional barmen would be interested in it, either. Each bartender had his own collection of secret recipes and would probably not want Thomas's. But when *The Bar-Tender's Guide* was finally published in 1862, the United States was deeply embroiled in the Civil War. In the North, the economy was booming, and the consumption of alcohol skyrocketed. Temperance was forgotten, and serious drinking once again emerged as the national pastime. Some wealthy men paid surrogates to serve in the army in their stead and partied throughout the war. Bars were opened to take advantage of the economic boom. These new establishments required more bartenders, and how better to learn the trade than from Thomas's book? After the war, the book would be reprinted many times under various names, with revisions and amplifications. Its recipes became the national standard for mixed drinks served in American saloons, hotel bars, restaurants, and homes. This was only the first in a long line of American cocktail manuals, and American cocktails would soon dominate the mixed drink world.[1]

Background

From the earliest colonial days, Americans enjoyed combining other ingredients with their alcoholic beverages. Many mixtures were based on European—particularly English—traditions. The shrub, a sweetened fruit drink (often made with orange, lemon, or lime juice) spiked with rum or brandy, was an English favorite.[2] The julep was another traditional English beverage that was considered a medicine. The English poet John Milton mentions a "cordial julep" in his poem "Comus" (1634). In America, juleps were based on brandy, whiskey, or rum, with sugar and a flavoring. Mint was a favorite flavoring, particularly in the South; the mint julep, initially savored in the morning, became a popular American beverage. Punches, which probably originated on the Indian subcontinent, were also traditional in Great Britain and Europe. The typical punch was a mixture of wine, spirits, fruit juice, spices, and sugar. Variations emerged in the American colonies, with rum and molasses becoming characteristic components.

Israel Acrelius recorded fifty-one different types of beverages just from his visits to Philadelphia and Wilmington, Delaware. The drink of the common people, according to Acrelius, was watered-down milk. Sailors (and others) drank grog—watered-down rum. Equal parts rum and water, sweetened with sugar, was called a sling. Rum added to warm beer was a hotch pot. With sugar added, a hotch pot became a manatham. If pieces of buttered toast were added, the drink was called a tiff. Rum with cherry juice added was called a cherry bounce. The restorative egg dram was made by adding rum and sugar to a beaten egg yolk. Punches were served in great variety; a typical one was made with rum (or other liquor), sugar, and lemon or lime juice. A milk punch consisted of milk, egg yolks, rum, sugar, and grated nutmeg over it. By the late eighteenth century, beverages containing milk and raw eggs were called egg nogs.[3] A sillibub was made by frothing warm milk with wine and sugar. Mead (fermented honey) was a simple combination of honey and water. As for cordials, Acrelius reported that "anise-water, cinnamon-water, apples in-water, and others scarcely to be enumerated" were poured "into wine and brandy almost without end."[4] The drinks Acrelius took note of were only a small fraction of the mixed beverages served in America at the time.

Bitters

Bitters—the distillations of flavorful (and medicinal) herbs, barks, and roots—were used in Great Britain to promote good digestion. Highland "bitters" made by infusing spices and herbs into whiskey, for instance, were taken as a "stomachic" before meals, especially breakfast.[5] In America, they came to be called "morning bitters" because they were frequently imbibed before breakfast. Morning bitters consisted of liquors (brandy, wine, Madeira, or rum), bitter tree barks, occasionally bitter fruit (such as wild cherries), and medicinal extracts (such as quinine).[6] Some consumers used morning bitters to prevent or combat fevers and expel parasites. In the southern colonies, bitters were employed to ward off malaria. The French visitor Constantin-François de Volney reported in 1803 that bitters were "one of the most efficacious" treatments for fevers: "I have met with several instances in Virginia and Pennsylvania of farmer's families, every person in which, who drank beer or water, was subject to agues, while the master of the house, who used spirituous liquors, and this even to excess, was constantly exempt from them."[7]

Most Americans, however, drank morning bitters because they liked the alcohol. Variations acquired a variety of colorful names, such as the fog dispenser, whiskey skin, Connecticut eyeopener, Alabama fogcutter, lightning smash, thunderbolt cocktail, streak of lightning, rum salad, brandy smash, gin flip, stone fence, Lisbon bitters, timber doodle, phlegm dispenser, steadier, gum tickler, antifogmatic, phlegm cutter, or gall breaker—to name a few.[8] The Englishman Isaac Holmes, who visited America in the early nineteenth century, noted that his hosts drank brandy and bitters or gin and bitters in the morning, before breakfast.[9] Morning bitters were composed of "rum, brandy, whiskey, or Madeira wine was flavored with the bitter bark of certain shrubs or trees."[10]

As the nineteenth century progressed, a bewildering variety of new mixed drinks materialized. The apple toddy was made with roasted apples, brandy, water, and sugar, cooled with a lump of ice.[11] A cobbler was made of wine, sugar, and lemon; it also was iced and sipped through a straw. A sherry cobbler was the same, but made with sherry.[12] Other iced drinks were called hail-stone and snow-storm. The Tom and Jerry was a British import consisting of eggs, sugar, and rum. It was named by or for the British writer Pierce Egan.

Unusual drink names would regularly shock English visitors. An English writer, Frederick Marryat, who observed New York's Fourth of July celebration in 1837, proclaimed that Broadway, the city's main street, was filled for a mile with booths that "were loaded with porter, ale, cider, mead, brandy, wine, ginger-beer, pop, soda-water, whiskey, rum, punch, gin slings, cocktails, mint juleps, besides many other compounds, to name which nothing but the luxuriance of American-English could invent a word."[13]

An unusual ingredient that was often included in American mixed drinks was ice. New Englanders harvested and exported ice beginning in 1806. The horse-powered ice cutter, invented in 1825, made the process faster and cheaper. By the 1830s, cheap ice was widely available in most large American cities throughout the year. Marryat proclaimed ice to be a great luxury. It was used for many purposes, but one that attracted Marryat was to make juleps, which consisted of mint, brandy, fruit and "rasped or pounded ice" filled up the tumblers, which were "very often incrusted outside with stalactites of ice. As the ice melts, you drink." With the thermometer at 100 degrees, Marryat proclaimed, the mint julep was "one of the most delightful and insinuating potations that ever was invented."[14] The American writer Charles F. Hoffman agreed: he immortalized the ice as "hail" in his poem, "The Origin of the Mint Julep." As time went on, ice became an essential ingredient in cocktails.[15]

The Rise of the Cocktail

The word "cock-tail," describing a drink, first appeared in print in 1803. Several sources place its origins in the late eighteenth century. New York author and historian Washington Irving wrote in 1809 that this class of beverages had originated in Maryland, whose inhabitants "were prone to make merry and get fuddled with mint-julep and apple-toddy. They were, moreover, great horse-racers and cock-fighters; mighty wrestlers and jumpers, and enormous consumers of hoecake and bacon. They lay claim to be the first inventors of those recondite beverages, cock-tail, stone-fence, and sherry cobbler."[16] New York State novelist James Fenimore Cooper attributed the invention of the "cock-tail" to one Elizabeth "Betty" Flanagan, a war widow who lived on the road from Sleepy Hollow to today's North White Plains at the time of the American War of Independence. In his novel *The Spy* (1821), Cooper makes the real Flanagan a colorful character, listing some of dubious attributes as "a trifling love of liquor, excessive filthiness, and a total disregard of all the decencies of language." During the Revolutionary War, Betty Flanagan drove a cart around the area selling liquor and other necessities to troops quartered on nearby farms. She reportedly stuck a feather taken from a loyalist's turkey cock into a drink that she made for a French officer serving with the American army. This drink was thereafter called a "cocktail"—or so Cooper would have us believe.[17]

Many other tales have been offered as to how the cocktail acquired its name. The only common thread among them was that it was an American invention. Recipes for cocktails appeared in print starting in the early nineteenth century, although there were different views on the meaning of the word. The first definition appeared in 1806, when the editor of a New York magazine, *The Balance*, defined the cocktail as "a stimulating liquor, composed of spirits of any kind, sugar, water, and bitters."[18] Other observers who encountered cocktails elsewhere during the next few decades gave similar definitions, although some excluded bitters as a necessary ingredient.[19] Cocktails were served in homes, taverns, and even ice cream parlors, but—except for a few favorites—they were usually concocted by professional bartenders in bars.

The precise origin of the bar is obscure. Some historians have suggested that it emerged from the grog shops commonly found in seaports in the eighteenth century or taverns, which indeed served alcohol. Others believe that bars started in various stores, such groceries, barber shops, bakeries, and private homes, which sold liquor for consumption off premise as a side business. Over time, as other businesses declined, liquor became the main attraction, and alcohol was served and drunk on-site in small rooms with spare furnishings. Spirits were stored in barred cages to prevent unauthorized access. When customers arrived, the proprietor would open a small window above a counter and serve customers beverages from the few bottles of alcohol on hand. Early establishments had only a few mugs from which everyone drank. Counters initially were just small wooden planks; as time went on, they were enlarged to service more customers and were renamed "bars." From their humble beginnings, bars increased in size and attractiveness, the liquor they served was diversified, and their accouterments became more refined.[20]

By the late eighteenth century, bars were featured in luxury hotels, which were built in American cities beginning in the 1790s. The nation's first was New York's City Hotel, built in 1794. For almost half a century, the four-story block-long hostelry was New York's premier inn—the place where wealthy and celebrated visitors stayed when they visited the city. It had high-ceilinged public spaces, and off the lobby was a barroom with a "liquor cage" so that the alcohol could be locked up when the bar was closed.[21]

Bars, especially those in urban areas, were upgraded into much larger rooms with long hardwood (mahogany or oak) counters that were some-times ornately carved. Counters sported brass foot rails and sometimes handrails, designed to accommodate standup drinking. The early nineteenth century saw a proliferation of great hotels in which well-appointed bars were de rigueur. A British naval officer described the style of the 1830s:

> The bar of an American hotel is generally a very large room on the base-ment, fitted up very much like our gin palaces in London, not so elegant in its decorations indeed, but on the same system. A long counter runs across it, behind which stand two or three bar-keepers to wait upon the custom-ers, and distribute the various potations, compounded from the contents of several rows of bottles behind them. Here the eye reposes on masses of pure crystal ice, large bunches of mint, decanters of every sort of wine, every variety of spirits, lemons, sugar, bitters, segars and tobacco; it really makes one feel thirsty, even the going into a bar. Here you meet every body and every body meets you. Here the senator, the member of Congress, the merchant, the store-keeper, travellers from the Far West, and every other part of the country, who have come to purchase goods, all congregate.[22]

In the St. Charles Hotel in New Orleans, according to a minister who visited there in the 1850s, the "ground floor was its bar room, and at ten o'clock at night you beheld it in its glory. At least a thousand men, speak-ing all languages, habited in all costumes, representing all nationalities, were engaged in laughing, talking, betting, quarrelling, chewing, smoking and drinking."[23] An English visitor to New Orleans reported that men "drink a great deal—they say the climate makes it necessary—but they also drink magnificently." The barroom at the St. Louis Hotel, he observed in 1859, was "circular-domed room nearly as large as the reading-room of the British Museum." But bars were for more than just drinking:

> These great bar-rooms serve the purposes of commercial exchanges. They have news bulletins, and the latest telegrams, as well as the daily newspapers. Men meet here to do business, and cargoes of sugar and tobacco, corn and cotton, change owners over glasses of "Old Bourbon," or "Mononga-hela." Here, too, are held auctions for the sale of stocks, ships, steamboats, real estate, and negroes.[24]

By the late nineteenth century, bar accessory manufacturers proliferated. They provided specialized equipment, gilt mirrors, special lighting fixtures, and special glasses for particular drinks. Upper-class bars were well stocked with a wide variety of American and imported beverages, and bottles were prominently displayed. Many bars featured dance floors, pianos, musicians, billiard tables, and other entertainment. Furniture often included tables and chairs for patrons to sit, read, talk, eat, drink, and gamble. Back rooms permitted groups to assemble; many immigrant and working-class groups had their start in these rooms. As back rooms often had back doors, even women's groups held meetings in them.[25]

Mixologists

As bars became popular, a new profession emerged: the bartender. The first publicly acclaimed bartender was Orsamus Willard of the City Hotel in New York. According to a British naval officer who stayed at the hotel in 1826: "The entrance to the house is constantly obstructed by crowds of people passing to and from the bar-room, where a person presides at a buffet formed upon the plan of a cage. This individual is engaged, 'from morn to dewy eve,' in preparing and issuing forth punch and spirits to strange-looking men, who come to the house to read the newspapers and talk politics."[26]

Willard, who lived at the hotel, was identified by another British visitor as a man "who never forgets the face of a customer," a tradition maintained by many subsequent bartenders. Willard served traditional wines, brandies, and spirits; he also concocted an inventive assortment of mixed drinks. His most famous and popular beverage was the mint julep, which consisted of "four or five stalks of unbruised mint" that were placed into a tumbler with ice, brandy, water, and sugar. For his celebrated apple toddy, Willard rolled apples in wet brown paper and buried them "in live embers till they [were] thoroughly roasted and quite soft; then a fourth part of apples, a fourth part of brandy, a fourth part of water, a lump of ice, and the whole to be rich with a fourth part of sugar, [made] the agreeable compound." His slings had a ratio of one-third rum, gin, or brandy to two-thirds water, sweetened with sugar and spiced with nutmeg. As anecdotally reported by another English visitor, when Willard added bitters to the sling, it became a cocktail.[27]

New York's Metropolitan Hotel, which opened in 1852, also had a prominent bar. Its most prominent bartender was a man named Jerry Thomas, who was born on Long Island around 1830. At the age of sixteen, he started tending bar in New Haven, Connecticut, but then he left went to sea. He traveled at least as far as Cuba, and possibly all the way to Europe. Thomas ended up in San Francisco in 1849, where the gold rush was just beginning. He jumped ship and took up the dual occupations of prospecting and tending bar. By the time he left in 1851, Thomas claimed to have socked away $16,000—a small fortune at the time. (Whether he earned the money prospecting, bartending, or by other means is unknown.) Thomas left California and settled in New York, where opened the first of four of his own bars, which received wide acclaim. He left New York and tended bar in Charleston, South Carolina, and St. Louis, where he kept the bar at the Planter's House Hotel. He also may have worked in New Orleans, Chicago, and Iowa. He returned to New York in 1858, where he tended bar at the Metropolitan Hotel. He was particularly known for mixing drinks in a flamboyant manner—a style that would continue to be the model for future bartenders.[28]

Then Thomas did what no other bartender had done: he started writing down his recipes for publication. Commissioned by the New York publisher Dick & Fitzgerald, he assembled a collection that would be published in 1862 as *The Bar-Tender's Guide; or How to Mix Drinks*. Shortly after the book appeared, Thomas returned to San Francisco, where he presided over the bar at the Occidental Hotel. In 1863, an English visitor noted that Thomas was "an accomplished artist. In the manufacture of a 'cocktail,' a 'julep,' a 'smash,' or an 'eye-opener,' none can beat him."[29] Beginning in the 1870s, dozens of bartenders throughout America published their own books.[30]

Throughout the late nineteenth and early twentieth centuries, the cocktail rose in importance, and there seemed to be no limits to the creativity of the American bartender. In the first edition of his bartending guide, Jerry Thomas had said that the cocktail "is a modern invention, and is generally used on fishing and other sporting parties, although some patients insist that it is good in the morning as a tonic." His book included only seven formulas for "cocktails," including versions made with brandy, champagne, whiskey, soda, and gin, and these were interspersed throughout the book.[31] A year after Thomas's death in 1886, a revised edition was published in which the first twenty-three recipes in the book were identified as cocktails. By the early twentieth century, the term "cocktail" had expanded to include any drink with two or more components, with one of them being alcoholic. One great advantage of the cocktail, from the bar owner's standpoint, was that the harsh flavor of cheap liquor could be disguised by the other ingredients in these "candied drinks."[32]

Two of the most celebrated cocktails were the Manhattan and the martini. The first may have been invented at New York's Manhattan Club during the 1870s. It first appeared in a bartender's guide in 1884. The second edition of Jerry Thomas's *Bar-Tenders Guide* (1887) includes a recipe for one consisting of vermouth, rye whiskey, bitters, two dashes of curaçao or maraschino, and ice.[33]

Recipes for a drink called the Martinez also appeared beginning in 1884, and the second edition of Thomas's *Bar-Tenders Guide* includes one made with gin, vermouth, bitters, two dashes of maraschino liquor, and ice. The following year, Harry Johnson's *New and Improved Illustrated Bartenders' Manual* offered a martini cocktail recipe (gin, vermouth, bitters, curaçao, gum syrup, and ice) and illustrations of two different "martine" glasses. Who precisely invented the martini—and how to concoct a perfect one—has been a topic of discussion ever since.[34]

As time went on, "cocktails" became a generic term for all mixed drinks, and they grew to be highly popular globally. Not everyone appreciated the evolution, however. George Edwin Roberts, who wrote England's first bartenders' guide, *Cups and Their Customs* (1863), dismissed these American drinks:

For the "sensation-drinks" which have lately travelled across the Atlantic we have no friendly feeling; they are far too closely allied to the morning dram, with its thousand verbal mystifications, to please our taste; and the source from which "eye-openers" and "smashers" come, is one too notorious for un-English behaviour to be welcomed by any man who deserves well of his country.[35]

Other Englishmen were just as upset with the names of American refreshments, calling them "detestable" and "a defect in American manners."[36]

Such xenophobic sentiments, however, quickly disappeared. The craze for American mixed drinks spread overseas; an American bar was created at the Paris Exposition in 1867. According to the British author George Sala, there were "'Cobblers,' 'noggs,' 'smashes,' 'cocktails,' 'eye openers,' 'moustache twisters,' and 'corpse revivers'" on hand, as well as "the mystic 'tip and tic,' the exhilarating 'morning glory,' the mild but health-giving sarsaparilla punch, to say nothing of 'one of them things,' which is a recondite and almost inscrutable drink."[37] In 1869, British bartender William Terrington identified dozens of American drinks as "sensations" in his *Cooling Cups and Dainty Drinks*. Of these "transatlantic 'notions,'" he wrote in the preface, they "well deserve the celebrity that attaches to them; and, as an occasional relish, all may claim to be regarded as both wholesome and exhilarating."[38] In 1871, two British bartenders published *The Gentleman's Table Guide*, in which more than half of their 112 formulas were identified as "American drinks."

American cocktails were the rage in England, especially after World War I.[39] Impetus for this change can be attributed in part to a Scotsman, Harry MacElhone, who had tended bar at the legendary Oak Bar at New York's Palace Hotel and Ciro's Club in London. In 1919, he published *Harry's ABC of Mixing Cocktails*, which contained more than "300 famous cocktails."[40] It was translated into other languages, and subsequent editions included more than 400 formulas.[41] MacElhone gained popularity when he bought the New York Bar in Paris in 1923. The bar actually came from New York. It had been deconstructed by two entrepreneurs and reconstructed in Paris, where it opened on Thanksgiving in 1911. The place became popular with American and British soldiers during World War I. When Harry bought the bar, he renamed it Harry's New York Bar. He served many prominent American journalists, writers, and expatriates, including Sinclair Lewis, Ernest Hemingway, Jack Dempsey, Rita Hayworth, and Humphrey Bogart. Some claim that Harry's was the world's most famous bar during the years between the world wars. Prohibition undeniably contributed to its success: bars, taverns, and saloons in the United States were closed, and fine restaurants were unable to survive without serving cocktails and wine. Americans who could afford the trip flocked to Europe to enjoy good food—and to drink alcohol legally.

Speakeasies

Magnificent hotels with elegant bars emerged throughout America: the Sazerac and Ramos in New Orleans; the bars at the Waldorf, the Knickerbocker, and the Hoffman House (with its Maxfield Parrish painting *Old King Cole* staring down on customers) in New York; Righeimer's in Chicago; the Touraine in Boston; the Planter's House and Tony Faust's in St. Louis; the Antlers in San Antonio; and the Palace in San Francisco.[42] Professional bartenders tried to make their bars respectable places that catered to businessmen and other upstanding folk. They sold a wide variety of beverages and specialized in mixed drinks.

At the vast majority of American bars and saloons, however, beer and whiskey were the stock-in-trade—not the cocktail. The clientele tended toward lowlifes: fighting, gambling, and prostitution were endemic. As George Ade, an American writer and newspaperman, wrote in 1931, cocktails were not served in saloons because the working class considered them to be dandified, pretentious, and a sign of effeminacy.[43] When Prohibition went into effect in 1920, the urban saloon was quickly replaced by the speakeasy, where bootleg booze was served by those willing to risk arrest. Unlike the saloons, speakeasies mainly served mixed drinks. Beer was voluminous and hard to make during Prohibition; it also was less profitable than spirits, which could be made in bathtubs. The harsh taste of Prohibition spirits called for some doctoring, and cocktails were almost a necessity. As bootleg alcohol was expensive (and speakeasy owners also had to bribe the police, judges, and city officials), drinks were pricier than they had been before Prohibition. Therefore, the customer base was no longer down-and-outers, workers, or small-time criminals, but mainly members of the middle and upper classes and big-name organized crime figures. Yet another change was that women, who generally avoided saloons, frequented speakeasies.

Cocktails were also offered at social gatherings in homes; the well-to-do hired bartenders to mix them properly. The cocktail party, reputed to have started in 1917, became popular during Prohibition. It was a low-risk way that the middle and upper classes could entertain and demonstrate their opposition to Prohibition. Cocktail parties continued their popularity among the wealthy and fashionable during the Depression. Such gatherings were an easy way to entertain a crowd: as a hired barman stirred up pitchers of martinis, foods was passed on silver trays. In some cases, a dinner party followed, but often the cocktails, the canapés, and the crowd were enough for both host and guests.

Along with cocktail parties came new fashions, such as cocktail hats, cocktail aprons, and cocktail dresses. The cocktail hour was popularized after repeal by President Franklin Roosevelt, who hosted them in the White House. He preferred drinking martinis. Cocktail parties helped create the need for finger food—foods that could be eaten while standing up and while one hand held a glass. After repeal, cocktail parties thrived, mainly because of the Depression. They were much less expensive than inviting guests over for dinner. After the Depression, the cocktail party was enshrined in American social life and—at least for businessmen—it could be a tax write-off. Cocktail lounges with waitresses in skimpy cocktail dresses also became popular during the 1930s.[44]

Cocktail Expansion

Mixed drinks were easy to make, and their flavors disguised cheap spirits. Many new cocktails were invented or popularized, including the Cuba libre, pink lady, Texas fizz, stinger, grasshopper, rusty nail, and salty dog, to name a few. These cocktails were first served in bars, but they also became popular at home parties.[45] The drinks were popularized during Prohibition through cocktail books and magazine articles and maintained their popularity after repeal.[46] The more unusual the ingredients and the stranger the drink's name, the more the bar could charge.

As new spirits were introduced and caught on, new cocktails were created to take advantage of their novel flavors. Rum, which had gone out of fashion in the mid-nineteenth century, reemerged in the twentieth century and became a common cocktail ingredient in drinks such as the daiquiri, mai tai, and zombie. Tequila, not well known in the United States except among Mexican Americans, emerged in the 1960s. The tequila sunrise, a colorful cocktail made with crème de cassis, lime juice, and sparkling water, is said to have been created at the Wright Bar at the Arizona Biltmore Resort and Spa near Phoenix. It first appeared in the 1930s but did not become popular until the 1960s, when simpler variations became the norm.

The margarita, a tequila drink typically served in a salt-rimmed cocktail glass, was popularized by the creator of the Trader Vic's and Señor Pico bars and restaurants, Victor Bergeron. Bergeron went to Mexico to find a good tequila cocktail recipe. "While tequila is made in Mexico you just don't find many drinks made with it," he wrote, and concluded that "nowhere in Mexico do you find many tequila drinks worth drinking." The margarita was the exception, so Bergeron developed his own version, composed of tequila, triple sec or Cointreau, and lime juice. By 1973, the Señor Pico restaurant sold more tequila than any other restaurant in the world.[47] Although Bergeron popularized the margarita, he did not invent it. Whatever its origins, the margarita quickly spread across America during the 1960s, becoming a staple in Mexican restaurants. In Mexico, margaritas were adopted by restaurants that attracted the tourist trade. The original margarita gave rise to all sorts of adaptations. Restaurateur Mariano Martinez purportedly assembled the first frozen margarita with crushed ice in 1971 at Dallas's El Charro Bar. For people who really did not like the taste of tequila, flavorings such as peach, strawberry, and mango were soon sold.[48]

Vodka was not an ingredient in the American cocktail scene until the late 1930s. The Smirnoff family had been making vodka in Russia since the 1860s. The family fled Russia during its revolution in 1917. Vladimir Smirnoff eventually reestablished the family business by setting up vodka factories in Poland and France. Under his leadership, vodka was distributed to Europe—but not the United States, which then was in the throes of Prohibition. Rudolph P. Kunett, who immigrated from what is today the Ukraine to the United States in 1920, had connections with the Smirnoffs before the revolution. When Prohibition ended in the United States in 1933, Kunett approached Vladimir Smirnoff in Paris about acquiring the rights to Smirnoff vodka sales in the United States. The deal was consummated, and Kunett opened the first vodka factory in the United States in Connecticut in 1934. It was a hard sell, however; despite considerable promotion, Americans were unwilling to give up their traditional alcoholic beverages for a new Russian one.

On the verge of bankruptcy, in 1939 Kunett approached British-born John G. Martin, who was president of a small American company, G. F. Heublein & Bros., in Hartford, Connecticut. Heublein had started as a restaurant, but expanded into manufacturing food products, such as A-1 Steak Sauce, and distilling liquor. In 1893, Heublein began manufacturing quart bottles filled with premixed alcoholic cocktails, including martinis and Manhattans.[49] Like most liquor companies, Heublein barely survived Prohibition, but after repeal, it revived.[50] In 1934, Martin joined Heublein and later became its president. In 1939, Martin bought the Smirnoff factory and name for $14,000, and he began promoting vodka nationally. Heublein supplied vodka recipes to magazines and also published its own cocktail book with vodka recipes.[51] Sales took off, especially after the company began advertising its vodka as "Smirnoff White Whiskey—No Smell, No Taste." The advertisement was illegal because vodka could not be advertised as whiskey, but the message that vodka had no color or taste made it appealing: vodka could be easily mixed with other beverages and flavorings, and it did not leave a smell on one's breath. One of the drinks that Martin helped promote was the Moscow mule, consisting of ginger beer and Smirnoff vodka.[52]

Vodka became the base for many now-classic cocktails, such as the vodka Collins and the screwdriver. The Bloody Mary, a combination of tomato juice, vodka, and other flavorings, was purportedly developed at Harry's New York Bar in Paris by Ferdinand "Pete" Petiot, who moved to New York as Prohibition was ending. Today, the most consumed alcoholic spirit in America is vodka, and much of it ends up in cocktails.

As the twentieth century progressed, the number of cocktails continued to expand. *The Savoy Cocktail Book* (1930), from London's Savoy Hotel, included almost 700 formulas; *Trader Vic's Bartender's Guide* (1947) contained more than 1,600.[53] This led the American writer and linguist H. L. Mencken to conclude that cocktails were "so numerous that no bartender can remember how to make all of them."[54] But this was just the beginning. In the second half of the twentieth century, thousands more cocktails have been invented. The cocktail may well be America's single most influential contribution to the world of alcoholic beverages. Joseph Carlin, author of *Cocktail: A Global History* (2012), estimates that there are more than 50,000 different cocktail recipes.[55]

Postscript

The City Hotel, where Orsamus Willard created the bartending profession, was torn down in 1849. Little is known about Willard's life after his tending bar at the City Hotel.

The Metropolitan Hotel, where Jerry Thomas bartended, closed in 1895.

Jerry Thomas died in 1885 and is buried at Woodlawn Cemetery in the Bronx. He is remembered as the "father of American mixology."[56]

Harry MacElhone, owner of Harry's New York Bar, left Paris in 1940 as German troops marched in during World War II. He returned to Paris when it was liberated and reopened his bar. He died on June 3, 1958.

🍸 John G. Martin served as chair of Heublein from 1961 to 1966. He died in 1986 at the age of eighty.

🍸 Heublein acquired wines and spirits brands and companies, including Don Q Rum, Jose Cuervo, Black & White, Harvey's Bristol Cream, Bell's whiskey, Lancer's, and United Vintners. Heublein was purchased by R. J. Reynolds Tobacco Company in 1982; five years later, the alcoholic beverages were sold to Grand Metropolitan, which became Diageo in 1997.

You'll make the children happy
with Welch's at the party

Every mother whose child comes to your house for a party will be
glad if she knows you are going to give the children Welch's.

You get Nature's best AT its best in

Welch's
"The National Drink"

This pure unfermented juice of the finest Concords is pressed from the full-ripe grapes and is
hermetically sealed—all by the exact sanitary Welch process. Thus Welch's is a most agreeable and healthful beverage for children and grown-ups.

For a children's party, serve Welch's in the individual 4 oz. bottles, or in this deservedly popular

Welch Punch For a dainty, unfermented punch, take the juice of
three lemons, juice of one orange, one quart of water,
one pint of Welch's and one cup of sugar. If desired, all or part charged
water may be used. Add sliced oranges and pineapple and serve cold.

Do more than ask for "Grape Juice"—say WELCH'S and GET IT

If unable to get Welch's of your dealer we will ship a trial dozen pints for $3.00, express prepaid
east of Omaha. Sample 4-ounce bottle by mail 10 cents.

Book of games
for children's
parties, free
We have compiled a
book of jolly games for
children of all ages
and are glad to send it
to any address free
upon request. It will
make many a happy
day for the youngsters.

The Welch Grape Juice Company, Westfield, New York

Advertisement for Welch's Grape Juice (ca. 1910).
(Courtesy of The Advertising Archives)

9
Unfermented Wine

FRUIT JUICE was so closely associated with alcohol that temperance advocates opposed making and drinking it. This view changed in the mid-nineteenth century for a very unusual reason: some churchgoing Christian temperance advocates were faced with the problem of celebrating communion without using wine. One solution was to reinterpret the New Testament, promoting the view that the passages mentioning wine had been mistranslated and misinterpreted. References to wine, some religious scholars decided, actually referred to *unfermented* wine—that is, grape juice.[1] Other theologians disagreed, concluding that this was a complete misrepresentation of scriptures.[2]

Whatever its religious merits, the idea of "unfermented wine" caught the attention of many temperance advocates, including Dr. Thomas Bramwell Welch, who had been a Methodist minister, a physician, and a dentist in upstate New York. In 1869, Welch—then living in Vineland, New Jersey, where he manufactured dental tools—started a side business producing "unfermented wine for communion purposes" as a service to Methodist ministers who refused to use real wine. Unfermented wine was easy to make, and likely other Methodist ministers did just that. After four years without making much profit, Welch gave up his unfermented wine business.

Enter Thomas Welch's son, Charles E. Welch, who was also a dentist. In 1875, he restarted making nonalcoholic grape juice on a small scale while continuing to practice dentistry and manufacture dental instruments with his father. As the temperance movement picked up steam in the late nineteenth century, Charles Welch changed the name of his product to Welch's Grape Juice, and sales increased. Welch realized that his target market was temperance supporters—a potentially large base, if they could be reached. In 1893, he gave up his other occupations and concentrated on growing his business. He set up displays at medical conventions and fairs, launching a wide-ranging marketing campaign that targeted religious, temperance, and medical publications. In medical journals, the company's advertising emphasized the healthful qualities of the juice; it was recommended for "Typhoid Fever, Pneumonia, Pluritus, Peritonitis, Rheumatism, for Lying-in Patients and for all forms of chronic diseases except Diabetes Melitus."[3] During the following decades, advertising expanded to include ads in national magazines such as *Collier's*, *Red Book*, *Cosmopolitan*, *McClure's*, and *Good Housekeeping*. Other juice makers followed in Welch's footsteps, and the American fruit juice industry was born.

Background

American colonists enjoyed the fruit they found on native trees and bushes, such as cranberries, grapes and persimmons; they also brought favorite fruit varieties over from England and planted them in their new homes. In the northern middle colonies, apples and cherries predominated; pears, peaches, and a variety of other fruit grew farther south. In season, fruit was eaten fresh, cooked into desserts and sauces, and preserved in the form of jams and jellies. Where the humidity was low, fruit could be dried for winter use, while apples could be stored for months in cold cellars. Still, by far the most extensive use of fruit in the colonies was for making juice—which was merely an intermediate step in its conversion to alcohol. At ambient temperatures, fruit juice begins to ferment almost immediately; given the right conditions, it becomes apple cider, for instance, or perry (pear cider) or mobby (peach cider). These ciders can then be distilled to create much more potent fruit brandies. Alcoholic beverages could be preserved for months or even years. In New England, the making, selling, and exporting of hard cider was an important economic resource.

Colonists knew how to stop the fermentation of fruit juice, at least temporarily, if they cared to: they had only to boil it. Most Americans had no interest in unfermented fruit juice, and there was very little market for it.

Religious sects aside, most American preferred their fruit beverages with at least a bit of a "kick" to them. In the 1830s, the Shakers developed a method for boiling juice at low temperatures through the use of a vacuum pan; this technique condensed and preserved the juice so that it could be stored for longer periods.[4] Likewise, the Oneida community (a religious commune in Oneida, New York) bottled and sold condensed fruit juice.[5] However, these were minor operations with limited sales.

Unfermented grape juice was simple enough to make, and recipes for it appeared frequently in nineteenth-century cookbooks. This recipe from the *Centennial Buckeye Cook Book* (1876) uses sugar as a preservative; the result was probably used as a flavoring and not directly as a beverage:

UNFERMENTED WINE FOR COMMUNION

Weigh the grapes, pick from the stems, put in a porcelain kettle, add very little water and cook till stones and pulp separate; press and strain through a thick cloth, return juice to kettle, add three pounds sugar to every ten pounds of grapes; heat to simmering, bottle hot and seal. This makes one gallon, and is good.[6]

In 1893, a breakthrough for unfermented grape juice came when thousands of people sampled Welch's Grape Juice at the World's Columbian Exposition in Chicago. When sales outstripped the supply of Concord grapes available at Welch's company in Vineland, New Jersey, Charles moved his operation to Westfield, New York, in 1897. The business was later incorporated as the Welch's Grape Juice Company.[7]

Welch took the popular temperance slogan, "The lips that touch wine will never touch mine," and gave it a promotional spin: "The lips that touch Welch's are all that touch mine." Welch's Grape Juice received widespread publicity in 1913 when prohibition advocate William Jennings Bryan, then secretary of state under President Woodrow Wilson, served Welch's Grape Juice at a dinner given in honor of the British ambassador, much to the ambassador's dismay. It gained even more visibility in 1914, when Josephus Daniels, the secretary of the navy, banned alcoholic beverages aboard Navy ships and replaced them with Welch's Grape Juice.[8]

When Prohibition went into effect in 1920, Welch's and other fruit juice producers faced major competition with the soft drink business; soda cost just one-quarter as much as fruit juice to manufacture. To distinguish his product from carbonated sugar water, Charles Welch advertised his grape juice as a "therapeutic agent" with significant health benefits. Specifically, the advertisement claimed that treated "constipation, abdominal plethora, in nephritis, renal congestion, edema, cardiac disease and scorbutic conditions in children and infants, hyperacidity, acidemia, anemia and allied conditions."[9] Indeed, many medical professionals endorsed fruit juice as very beneficial. One cited fruit juice's "thinning effect upon the blood, thus diminishing its viscidity, and [it is] consequently an excellent drink for arteriosclerotics." Others reported that juices were good for fever, gout, and diabetes, and had a "stimulating action upon the bowels."[10]

Tomato Cocktail

The Welch's Grape Juice Company branched out in 1923 and began producing tomato juice. But despite the company's success with grape juice, the public just did not take to tomato juice.[11] Tomato juice had been used since the mid-nineteenth century for cooking. Recipes for tomato cocktails appeared in the 1890s. The Manhattan Club in New York made its "cocktail" from oyster juice, Tabasco sauce, chili pepper sauce, ketchup, lemon juice, and tomato juice.[12] Some credit the tomato cocktail to the American-born chef Louis Perrin. In 1917, Perrin served tomato juice to guests at a resort in French Lick Springs, Indiana. Chicago businessmen vacationing there purportedly spread the word about the tomato juice "cocktail," a non-alcoholic beverage that they had enjoyed at the resort in lieu of stronger mixtures. Others credit Chicago's Ernest Byfield, who owned the Ambassador East Hotel and College Inn Food Products Company. He reportedly tasted a tomato cocktail while visiting a friend and put his chefs to work trying to make a commercial product out of it. They added celery and more lemon juice, and sold 60,000 cases in first month.[13] It was praised by temperance advocates and medical professionals alike; when Prohibition arrived, it was also praised by those opposed to Prohibition who used it as a cocktail mixer.

Tomato juice cocktails were heralded during a Tri-State Packers Convention at Philadelphia's Adelphia Hotel in 1922. A can manufacturer served tomato juice to those attending the annual banquet in hopes that they would consider canning the novel beverage. Like grape juice, tomato juice was touted as a health drink and was even served in hospitals. According to Dr.

Hugo Friedstein of Children's Memorial Hospital in Chicago, the vitamin content of tomato juice did "marvelous things in cleansing the system."[14]

Although canned tomato juice was growing more popular by the 1920s, none of the existing commercial products had a consistently appealing color and flavor.[15] Another problem with canned tomato juices was that the solids separated and settled at the bottom of the can or glass when served. In 1924, an Indianapolis pediatrician discussed this problem with his friend Ralph Kemp of Frankfort, Indiana. Kemp had majored in agricultural engineering at the University of Wisconsin, and at the time he worked with his father, John Kemp, operating a canning plant. Intrigued with the challenge, the Kemps began experimenting to find a way to break up the tomato pulp into minute particles that would float in the juice. Their solution was to use a machine called a viscolizer, which was previously employed in the manufacture of ice cream. The device required a great deal of adaptation to process tomato juice successfully, but after four years of work, the Kemps finally succeeded in producing a smooth, pleasingly textured tomato juice that did not separate. In 1928, they initiated the first national advertising campaign for "Kemp's Tomato Juice."[16] This new kind of tomato juice was an instant hit with the American public.

The H. J. Heinz Company and the Campbell Soup Company moved quickly into high gear to produce it. Campbell converted part of its Camden Plant No. 2, built during the 1920s for making tomato soup, into a juice factory. All that remained was to determine which tomato variety was best for making juice. After some experimentation, Campbell's Tomato Juice came on the market in 1931. Until 1932, almost all the tomatoes grown by Campbell were used for making soup, but by 1935 about 30 percent of its tomatoes went into making juice.[17] By the following year, cookbooks began to include recipes naming Campbell's Tomato Juice as an ingredient.[18]

Canned tomato juice received yet a further boost when Prohibition ended in 1933. A cocktail made of tomato juice and vodka was probably first served at Harry's Bar in Paris by a bartender named Ferdinand "Pete" Petiot. Petiot moved to New York City in 1933 and introduced his new creation at the bar of the St. Regis Hotel. Tinkering with his original recipe, he added Worcestershire sauce and called the resulting drink a Bloody Mary. The drink was supposedly named for Queen Mary I of England, who had hundreds of Protestants burned at the stake during her reign in the mid-sixteenth century. Others claimed that the Mary in question was Petiot's girlfriend. Whoever it was named for, it rapidly became a success. American writer Ernest

Hemingway boasted in a 1941 letter that he had personally introduced Petiot's Bloody Mary into bars in Hong Kong.[19]

Shortly after the end of World War II, the Campbell Soup Company purchased V-8 Vegetable Juice from Standard Brands. V-8 was a blend of eight vegetables—particularly tomatoes, but also carrots, celery, beets, parsley, lettuce, watercress, and spinach—along with several flavor enhancers. It had been conceived in 1933 by W. G. Peacock of Evanston, Illinois; several people worked on the formula and Peacock marketed it in 1936 under the name "Veg-min Juice." At the first store that sold it, a clerk suggested that they change its name to V-8. (Later, the hyphen was dropped and the product became V8 Cocktail Vegetable Juice.)

Peacock had produced V-8 entirely by hand; the yield was only twenty-five cases per day, which did not even come close to meeting demand. Peacock lacked the funds to advertise V-8, and he had ideas for other products that he wanted to develop. To raise cash, Peacock sold the V-8 formula to the Loudon Packing Company in 1938; founded by Charles F. Loudon, the firm had manufactured tomato juice for a time in the 1890s. In 1943, the Loudon Packing Company was purchased by Standard Brands. By the time Campbell purchased V8 juice from Standard Brands in 1948, the product's total annual sales generated $5 million.[20]

Liquid Sunshine

Colonial Americans loved the flavor of citrus fruit, particularly oranges, lemons, and limes. In colonial times, the fruit was imported from Bermuda and the Bahamas, so only the well-to-do could afford it. Moreover, citrus fruits were available only during their growing season, which was January through June. As advertised in a 1742 newspaper published in Salem, Massachusetts, "Extraordinary good and very fresh Orange Juice" cost $1 per gallon.[21] The price does not sound like much by today's standards, but it was a small fortune at the time.

When the United States purchased Florida from Spain in 1821, the region's tropical climate made it possible for citrus to be grown domestically. But the fruit still had to be transported north by ship, so prices remained high. Once the United States acquired California during the Mexican-American War, oranges were grown there, too; however, there was no way to ship them back east. Most oranges were eaten fresh, squeezed for flavoring beverages and baked goods, or made into marmalade and other preserves.

When the second transcontinental railroad system was completed in 1883, it became possible to transport oranges from California to the rest of the nation. Technological improvements, such as ventilating and icing, decreased spoilage, and the citrus industry in southern California took off. Rapid expansion, however, generated problems. Orange trees take about seven years to mature, so growers generated little income from their groves during that time. As the market for oranges increased, growers became convinced that the market would continue to rapidly grow. They planted more and more trees until, by the early twentieth century, the market was glutted with oranges during the high season (November to May), and prices decreased.[22] Production greatly exceeded demand, and growers were in financial straits.

The solution was to advertise, but it was almost impossible for individual growers to advertise their product because both retailers and consumers considered fruit to be a generic item rather than a name brand. The solution was grower cooperatives. In 1893, California fruit growers joined together to form a cooperative; they adopted the brand name Sunkist in 1908. Then Sunkist contracted Lord & Thomas, an advertising firm in Chicago, to help increase consumer demand and sell more fruit. A small advertising campaign was conducted in Iowa, and an increase in sales of oranges was promising. This encouraged Sunkist to launch a major national promotional campaign, and sales of oranges rose.[23]

One dimension of this campaign was to increase sales by promoting orange juice. Beginning in 1914, the Sunkist co-op established orange juice stands throughout the country; it also encouraged soda fountains, restaurants, and hotels to put the beverage on their menus.[24] Sunkist even distributed leaflets on how boys could set up orange or lemonade stands.

But extracting the juice from the orange created a mess, and it took too much time. Businesses charged a premium for orange juice and sales were limited because the price of orange juice was much greater than other beverages. So Sunkist worked with manufacturers to make a round, hand-powered glass juice extractor; in 1916, Sunkist launched a major promotional campaign for the affordable 10-cent orange reamer. Advertisements in magazines, such as the *Saturday Evening Post*, were headlined "Drink an Orange." These ads also proclaimed that orange juice was "a delicious beverage" that was "healthfulness itself." Within a short time, 210,000 juice extractors were sold (some estimates run as high as 1 to 3 million).[25] Then in the 1920s, Sunkist produced a heavy-duty electrical juice extractor for soda fountains, cafeterias, and restaurants. Orange sales soared, and this was only the beginning.

Sunkist increased its advertising and sales soared. In 1919, the co-op published full-page magazine advertisements that reached some 62 million readers. Sunkist also supplied grocery stores with 5 million flyers and 4,200 display boxes, and sent out 176,000 promotional recipe books, 100,000 calendars, and 15,000 recipe cards. In 1924, the co-op advertised in 11 national publications, reaching 189 million subscribers, and in 141 newspapers with 109 million readers. The Sunkist co-op placed signs in 40,000 trolley cars and on subway cars in New York, Chicago, and Boston; 2.6 million brochures were distributed to schools and other educational institutions. Sunkist went even further by sponsoring a half-hour program on radio, which was in its infancy; it also produced two films that were shown to 7,000 women's clubs and cooking classes. The co-op distributed 100 million promotional brochures proclaiming that "the juice of oranges has been known for years as one of the most healthful of natural foods. All physicians know it. All dietitians. All food experts. It is not theory. The healthfulness of orange juice is fact. Science has proved it in many ways, by many definite and conclusive tests." More specifically, orange juice was "rich in vitamines particularly Vitamine C. It should be fed to babies," and it made "all other foods more efficient by aiding in releasing the full nourishment of those foods for complete assimilation by the body." In addition, orange juice helped "to effect good digestion and assimilation" and it rendered "one of the most valuable services of any food we know."[26]

The Sunkist cooperative almost doubled its promotions, reaching 311 million magazine subscribers in 1929. Many of these print advertisements promoted orange juice at breakfast and the use of lemon juice and lemonade during the rest of the day. Sunkist also promoted the idea that babies should be consuming fruit juice all day.[27] The co-op had expended almost $12 million in promoting its products, and much of this focused on fruit juices. As a result, Sunkist became one of the country's best-known brand names.[28]

Orange juice continued to be sold in fruit stands across America. One operator was Julius Fried, who sold fresh-squeezed orange juice on the streets of Los Angeles in 1925. Fried wanted to upgrade his operation by opening a store, so he approached Willard Hamlin, a real estate agent. They went into partnership and opened a store in downtown Los Angeles in 1926. Fresh orange juice upset Hamlin's stomach, so he experimented by adding various ingredients, including milk, sugar, crushed ice, vanilla, egg whites, and various powdered mixes. Hamlin finally came up with a special formula that resulted in a frothy, creamy beverage, which they called an Orange Julius. Sales were good. Hamlin gave up his real estate business and focused on franchising their operation. By the time the Depression began in 1929, there were about 100 Orange Julius stores from Los Angeles to Boston. The company contracted during the Depression and World War II, but rapidly expanded during 1950s, targeting especially shopping centers and later malls.[29]

Meanwhile, Florida growers followed Sunkist's lead, forming the Florida Citrus Exchange in 1909 and advertising their products, albeit on a much smaller scale.[30] Their promotion emphasized the therapeutic qualities of lemons and oranges. In addition to the claims made by Sunkist, the Florida Citrus Exchange declared that oranges and grapefruit were "rich in cellulose" and therefore a good laxative. As a rousing conclusion, the advertisement proclaimed that "oranges and grapefruit should never be limited since they are beneficial in all practical amounts."[31]

By the outbreak of World War II, the hundreds of millions of dollars that citrus co-ops had spent on advertising paid off. Largely as a result of such advertising and promotion, millions of Americans became convinced that their health depended on drinking a glass of orange juice at breakfast every day. Citrus consumption increased threefold from 1920 to 1940, and much of this increase was due to orange juice.[32] Commenting on this enthusiasm for orange juice during this period, historian Richard Hooker concluded that "never before had a food habit been adopted so quickly by so many people."[33]

Yet, growers still had a glut of oranges and, unless refrigerated, the oranges turned to mush in a few weeks. They needed to find a way to make orange juice available throughout the year. One possibility was canned orange juice. Growers had canned and bottled juice since the 1880s, but sales of these juices were modest. By the early twentieth century, the annual per capita consumption of bottled and canned orange juice was only about a half a gallon. Growers increased their distribution of canned orange juice through grocery stores and soda fountains, but the product failed to catch on. By the early 1930s, however, new methods of canning orange juice improved its flavor, and by 1935 sales had reached almost 2 million cases. By 1940, annual per capita consumption of canned orange juice in the United States was more than seven gallons per person.[34] This was modestly successful until World War II arrived and the war effort needed metal (such as that used for orange juice cans). Was there some other way to preserve orange juice?

Frozen Juice

Attempts to concentrate orange juice began in 1915,[35] and fruit juices made from concentrate were marketed during the 1920s. The juices were shipped mainly by truck to dairies, where fresh water was added and the reconstituted juice was packaged in cardboard cartons or glass bottles. Dairy companies used their distribution systems to sell the reconstituted juice. By 1925, however, annual consumption of orange juice concentrate was slightly more than three ounces per person. Despite the unprecedented increase in the sale of oranges and canned orange juice during the late 1920s and early 1930s, the sale of frozen orange juice concentrate lagged far behind, although it was produced by a number of companies during the 1930s.[36] Richard M. Nixon, the future American president, invested in one of these companies in 1937. Like many other such frozen juice ventures, the one Nixon invested in failed two years later.[37]

Americans can hardly be blamed for rejecting early forms of frozen orange juice; when reconstituted, its appearance and flavor were not very appealing. There were also several distribution problems. Refrigerated trucks that could carry frozen orange juice to dairies were in short supply. Supermarkets had very limited space in their freezer cases, which were a recent innovation in stores. In addition, consumers did not understand how to handle frozen orange juice, and the iceboxes and refrigerators of the time did a poor job of keeping foods frozen. The concentrate was often thawed and refrozen several times before being reconstituted and poured into a glass, which contributed to the poor quality of frozen orange juice in the era before World War II.

What was the best way to get vitamin C to American armed forces in the thick of war? This was a vital question for the U.S. Army's Quartermaster Corps. Under other circumstances, the answer would have been to dispatch supplies of citrus fruit, but it was not feasible to send vast quantities of oranges, lemons, or grapefruit to millions of soldiers, many fighting thousands of miles from the U.S. mainland. Faced with this problem, scientists developed a process for making powdered orange juice that could be included in a soldier's rations; all the soldier had to do was add water. Like other components of those meals, however, the powdered juice was almost universally detested by the troops. Canned citrus juice was available, but it was bulky and heavy and therefore difficult to transport long distances. But more important, it was wartime, so every possible scrap of metal was needed for the war effort and could not be squandered for making juice cans.

The obvious solution to the military's need for vitamin C was a vitamin pill or tablet, but the Quartermaster Corps determined that the pills would not survive under the diverse conditions where the soldiers were fighting: in jungles, deserts, extreme cold, and high humidity.[38] Some researchers focused their efforts on making a frozen orange juice concentrate. This had been tried and marketed before the war, but with dismal results. When reconstituted, the juice turned an unappetizing ruddy brown. Worse yet, it tasted bitter, with strong off-flavors; it was so awful that some soldiers referred to it as "battery acid," according to citrus historian Thomas B. Mack.[39]

Scientists at the Florida Citrus Commission, working in cooperation with the U.S. Department of Agriculture's Citrus Products Station in Winter Haven, Florida, set to work on a better frozen juice concentrate in 1943. After months of experimentation, they came up with a solution: they mixed the vacuum-evaporated concentrate with freshly extracted juice and then froze it. When reconstituted, the beverage looked and tasted almost like canned orange juice, which, although not great, was certainly better than the alternatives. As a concentrate, it had a smaller volume and weight than did canned juice, making shipping more economical.[40]

Another effort to create fruit concentrate was launched by Dr. Robert James, a former research director for both Parke Davis and DuPont, thought he could solve that problem. After receiving a small grant from the U.S. Department of Agriculture, James set up a modest research facility in Dunedin, Florida. Because it was wartime, he had little equipment, but he cobbled together a few ramshackle buildings and launched Citrus Concentrates, Inc. With three lab assistants, James developed fruit concentrates, which were shipped to England during the war. He also converted the byproducts—the seeds, skin, and pulp—into useful products. By 1944, James had succeeded in making a frozen juice concentrate suitable for commercial use, and he supplied it to a drugstore chain in Washington, D.C. When the frozen concentrate was reconstituted and served at soda fountains, customers reported that it tasted almost like fresh-squeezed juice. Because the concentrate was easier for the chain to handle and could be available all year, the chain sold a lot of frozen orange juice.[41]

The success of this frozen juice concentrate was an eye-opener for Florida orange growers. James's facility burned down in 1945, but his work set off a scramble in the Florida juice industry. Experimenters improved on the process that James developed and patented it.

When the war ended, one company, Vacuum Foods, began producing frozen orange juice concentrate. During the next two years, the company lost

$450,000. In 1948, the company changed its name to the Minute Maid Company, and the brand name for the orange juice concentrate became Minute Maid. This was the right name at the right time: the American economy was booming and so were babies. Busy parents were interested in convenience, and the company felt sure that they would prefer mixing a pitcher of frozen orange juice to squeezing oranges every morning. Minute Maid launched a major advertising campaign, which helped the company earn profits of $179,865 in the first year. Meanwhile, in October 1948, crooner and movie star Bing Crosby signed on to promote Minute Maid frozen orange juice. Crosby also invested in the company and took a seat on its board of directors. Minute Maid sales soared,[42] and the fortunes of other frozen orange juice companies rose as well. By 1950, Americans were drinking 1.2 billion pounds of frozen citrus juice; ten years later, that had more than quadrupled to 4.9 billion pounds.[43]

During the 1945/1946 growing season, 225,000 gallons of frozen concentrate were manufactured. That was not much by any standard, but the frozen juice concentrate earned good reviews from suppliers in some cities. As a result, manufacturers upped production; as the new product became more widely available, more Americans tried it and liked what they tasted. The big news was that it tasted so different from, and so much better than, the frozen juice made before the war. Newspapers such as the *Wall Street Journal* and magazines such as *Reader's Digest* picked up the story. Distributors soon reported that frozen juice concentrate—mainly orange juice—accounted for about 30 percent of their total frozen food sales. By 1949, sales of concentrated fruit juices hit almost 10 million gallons.[44]

Meanwhile, things were changing in the grocery business and in the American home. During the 1930s, the first supermarkets opened, and their low prices quickly crushed many small grocery stores. After the war, large supermarkets were able to invest in capacious frozen food cases that could hold a much wider variety of products. At the same time, refrigerated trucks became common, making it possible to deliver frozen food without having it thaw en route.

Minute Maid had lots of competition in the frozen orange juice business. In 1947, Anthony T. Rossi launched the Manatee River Packing Company in Bradenton, Florida. Rossi began producing frozen fruit juices in 1952 and branded them "Tropicana Pure Premium." The line was so successful that in 1957 Rossi renamed the company Tropicana Products, Inc. Both Tropicana and Minute Maid did so well that they eventually were swallowed up by larger companies. Minute Maid was sold to the Coca-Cola Company in 1960; Tropicana was acquired by PepsiCo in 1998.

Today, an estimated 95 percent of the citrus fruit grown in the United States goes into making juice. The nation also imports a large percentage of juice concentrate from other countries, especially Brazil. In 2010/2011, Americans drank 4.5 gallons of orange juice per capita.[45]

Postscript

⛉ Thomas Welch died in 1903 in Philadelphia. When his son Charles died in 1926, Welch's Grape Juice languished. It was acquired by the National Grape Cooperative Association in 1954. Welch Foods—the manufacturing and marketing arm of the co-op—bottles, cans, and freezes grape juice and related products.

⛉ In 2006, Campbell extended its V8 brand line to create V-Fusion beverages flavored with fruit, such as acai berries, pomegranates, bananas, peaches, and mangos.

⛉ Willard Hamlin bought out Julius Fried and continued to grow his Orange Julius franchise. When he retired in 1967, he sold his 700 franchises to International Industries. Hamlin died in 1987. Today the company is owned by Warren E. Buffett's investment group, Berkshire Hathaway, Inc.

⛉ As a result of the acquisition of both Minute Maid and Tropicana by soft drink giants, with their bottling and distribution practices, single-serving cans of fruit juice are now sold in vending machines and stores alongside bottles and cans of soda.

Soda fountain in a drug store on Staten Island, with
signs advertising Coca-Cola, as seen on a postcard.
(The New York Public Library/Art Resource, NY)

10

The Temperance Beverage

I N 1885, Atlanta druggist John Stith Pemberton needed a new product on his pharmacy shelves. Sales of his popular Pemberton's French Wine Coca, compounded from his own formula consisting mainly of wine and cocaine, were in jeopardy—not because of the cocaine, which was neither illegal nor unusual at the time, but because Atlanta had passed temperance legislation forbidding the manufacture and sale of alcohol (including wine) in the city.[1] Pemberton started experimenting with other mixtures, hoping to formulate a "temperance medicine" using a concoction of coca leaves, kola nut extract, sugar, and flavorings: when he felt he had the right blend, he launched the new syrup called Coca-Cola. Pemberton believed that his concoction was a drug (as indeed it was), and he sold it to other druggists as a "brain tonic" and an "ideal nerve tonic and stimulant;" it cured "neuralgia, hysteria, and melancholy" and "nervous afflictions." Company advertising also proclaimed that it would cure headaches, which it likely did. Ironically, Pemberton also believed it would cure morphine addiction, which it likely did not.[2] Pemberton's new concoction was one of many similar drugstore medicinal products, and like them, it had little chance of survival. But Coca-Cola thrived and so did the soda drink industry. Americans adopted soft drinks as one of their favorite beverages, and they remain so today.

Background

Europeans have long considered mineral waters to be therapeutic, and water containing carbon dioxide was thought to have medicinal attributes. For centuries, European spas and resorts usually have been centered around mineral springs; people drank, and sometimes bathed in, the naturally carbonated waters as part of a health regimen. In the eighteenth century, the chemists Joseph Priestley and Antoine-Laurent Lavoisier were credited with the discovery that carbon dioxide was the source of the bubbles in natural springs, as well as the "fizz" in beer and champagne. By 1800, beverage manufacturers had discovered that they could produce fizzy water by adding a solution of sodium bicarbonate, thus creating carbonated water. However, the carbonation process was more fizzy when made under high pressure using sulfuric acid, and manufacturing carbonated water this way was more difficult and dangerous. Workers could be seriously burned by the acid, and containers of charged soda water sometimes exploded. Nevertheless, bottled sodas were being manufactured in Philadelphia and New York as early as 1807.[3]

It was not until the mid-nineteenth century that safer and easier mechanisms called soda fountains were devised to manufacture carbonated water. Soda fountains were sold throughout the nation by the 1850s.[4] New technology was demonstrated at the 1876 Centennial Exposition in Philadelphia, where soda fountain manufacturers James W. Tufts and Charles Lippincott constructed a building with a thirty-foot-tall soda fountain and dozens of soda dispensers ready to refresh the throngs of fair visitors. Strong alcoholic beverages were banned at the exposition and the summer was extremely hot, so thousands of thirsty fair-goers were treated to their first taste of carbonated beverages. After the exposition closed, Tufts and Lippincott made a fortune selling soda fountains to drugstores around the nation.[5]

One beverage advertised at the Centennial Exposition was Hires Root Beer, created by a Philadelphia drugstore operator named Charles E. Hires. Hires Root Beer became America's first successful national soft drink. Hires sold his root beer concentrate in packages to druggists, who combined it with carbonated water from their own fountains.[6] It was also sold to individuals who could add the package to a gallon of regular water for a "Family Affair," which promised "Health for the Baby, Pleasure for the Parents and New Life for the Old Folks." As the temperance movement picked up steam in the late nineteenth century, Hires began advertising its root beer as "The Great Temperance Drink" and "a temperance drink for temperance people."[7]

At about the same time, drugstore operators and pharmacists around the country began manufacturing and selling carbonated beverages. In Detroit, pharmacist James Vernor introduced ginger ale in the mid-1860s, and the beverage entered into commerce in 1880. In 1896, Vernor established his own soda fountain to dispense it and he began selling ginger ale extract to drugstores in other cities. In New England, an itinerant pharmacist named Augustin Thompson concocted Moxie Nerve Food in Lowell, Massachusetts, in 1876. Seven years later, it was converted into a soft drink that also appealed to the temperance advocates. Its advertisement proclaimed that Moxie was "rapidly crowding liquors out of the barrooms." Quart champagne bottles of Moxie sold for the very pricey 60 cents.[8]

Toward the end of the nineteenth century, a pharmacist named Charles Alderton was employed at Morrison's Old Corner Drug Store in Waco, Texas, which served carbonated beverages at a soda fountain. Alderton experimented with different beverage formulas, many of which became quite popular. The owner of the store, Wade Morrison, is credited with naming one of the soft drinks Dr. Pepper in 1885. One person who liked Dr. Pepper soda was Robert S. Lazenby, the owner of the Circle A Ginger Ale Company in Waco. In 1891, Lazenby went into business with Morrison and formed the Artesian Manufacturing & Bottling Company. One of their products was a black cherry–flavored soft drink that they called Dr. Pepper's Pho-Ferrates, which quickly became a favorite in the Southwest. In 1904, the beverage was marketed at the St. Louis Exposition. The first known advertisement to employ Dr. Pepper's first slogan ("Vim, Vigor, and Vitality") and its mascot (a lion) appeared in Waco in 1906. This beverage became a tremendous success, and the company's name was changed to the Dr. Pepper Company. (Subsequently, the period was removed from the Dr Pepper name.)[9]

A different type of soda company was formed by Roy Allen, who bought a recipe for making root beer; on June 20, 1919, he opened a root beer stand in Lodi, California, offering frosty mugs of root beer for a nickel. He opened more stands in Stockton and Sacramento, one of which may have been a drive-in. In 1920, Frank Wright, an employee at the Stockton stand, became Allen's partner; they combined their surnames and called the company Allen & Wright Root Beer.[10] The partners soon opened additional stands throughout California, Utah, and Texas. Allen bought out Wright in 1924, trademarked the A&W Root Beer logo (a bull's eye and an arrow), and franchised the operation. Franchisees paid a small licensing fee, displayed the A&W logo, and bought root beer syrup from Allen.[11]

Yet another successful soda company was launched by Charles Leiper Grigg of St. Louis, Missouri. Grigg invented an orange-based soft drink called Howdy; in 1920, he created the Howdy Company. Grigg's drink competed with many other sodas, such as Orange Crush, which then dominated the market, so he began experimenting with lemon-lime flavors. After two years of work, he came up with a beverage that blended seven different flavors; he introduced this Bib-Label Lithiated Lemon-Lime Soda in 1929. Shortly thereafter, the name was changed to 7-Up. At the time, Prohibition was still in effect, and 7-Up became a mixer for illegally sold alcoholic drinks. With repeal in 1933, sales were so successful that in 1936 Grigg changed the name of his company to the Seven-Up Company. Within ten years, 7-Up was the third-best-selling soft drink in the world. In 1967, the Seven-Up Company began an advertising campaign positioning the beverage as the "uncola," which greatly increased sales. Later, it launched a campaign stressing the fact that it had no caffeine. This campaign was one reason why other soda companies began manufacturing decaffeinated drinks of their own.[12]

Cola-Based Soft Drinks

Two new soft drink ingredients emerged in the 1880s. The first was the kola nut, which had probably first been imported from Africa and the Caribbean into North America during colonial times. By the late nineteenth century, it was very common for the kola nut to be chewed by laborers, especially African Americans. Although bitter tasting, the nut was loaded with caffeine, and thus it served as a stimulant for exhausted workers.

The second new soft drink ingredient was coca leaves. Imported into America and Europe from South America by the early nineteenth century, the active ingredient in coca leaves—cocaine—became a common ingredient in patent medicines and, like the kola nut, was also used by physical laborers to boost their stamina. In the 1860s, vintners combined cocaine with wine to create Vin Mariani, which became one of the most popular beverages in Europe. In the United States, Henry Downes, a New York syrup manufacturer, produced Imperial Inca Coca in 1881; it was the first known soda drink to include cocaine. Other coca beverages, such as coca coffee and French wine coca, soon followed.[13]

In Atlanta, Georgia, John S. Pemberton had created his own successful mixture of cocaine and wine. When Atlanta went "dry" by banning alcohol in 1885, he returned to the laboratory, seeking to create a new beverage without the wine. During the early months of 1886, Pemberton experimented with a number of different combinations of coca leaves, from which cocaine is extracted, and kola nuts. He sent samples of these mixtures to an associate, Willis Venable, who leased the bottom floor of Jacob's Pharmacy. It was not until May 8, 1886 that Pemberton's experiment paid off. Venable had mixed Pemberton's syrup with soda water, which gave the mixture a sparkling, bubbly effervescence that appealed to many customers.

When Pemberton saw that his latest formula was a success, he trademarked "Coca-Cola Syrup & Extract."[14] He then turned it over to one of his partners, Frank Robinson, to manufacture and sell. Twenty-one days after the drink first appeared at Jacob's Pharmacy, Robinson took out an advertisement in the *Atlanta Journal*, trumpeting Coca-Cola to be "Delicious! Refreshing! Exhilarating! Invigorating! The new and popular soda fountain drink containing the properties of the wonderful Coca plant and the famous Cola nut." When Pemberton's health failed in 1887, he sold a portion of his business to Venable.[15] Pemberton eventually relinquished the recipe for Coca-Cola, which ended up in the hands of a pharmacist and patent medicine manufacturer in Atlanta named Asa Candler. Candler expanded Coca-Cola syrup sales to soda fountain operators, who sold the new beverage for 5 cents a glass. By 1890, Candler was selling almost 9,000 gallons of Coca-Cola syrup annually.[16] He reinvested most of his profits into the business and spent much money on advertising, which paid off handsomely. In 1900, the *National Druggist* magazine announced that Coca-Cola's "commercial history reads like an episode from the Arabian Nights," which "burst on the market some five or six years ago," and its "popularity has increased with every year of its existence." By 1899, almost 281,000 gallons of syrup—the equivalent of 36 million glasses—were being sold, and the following year Coca-Cola's revenues topped $400,000.[17]

The bottling of Coca-Cola in the form of a fizzy beverage first began in 1894, but it was not until 1899 that a company in Chattanooga, Tennessee, was licensed as the exclusive bottler of the beverage. By 1909, there were more than 400 Coca-Cola bottlers in America, and therein lay one reason for the company's early success: franchising the bottling operation made it possible for the company to concentrate on producing the syrup rather than on making or distributing bottled beverages. The syrup for Coca-Cola was easily transported, and there was no need to share the "secret" formula. Local bottlers or soda jerks had only to combine the syrup with soda to create the fizzy form of Coca-Cola. This allowed the company to quickly develop a national distribution system.[18]

The inclusion of coca leaves as an ingredient in Coca-Cola eventually generated problems with temperance movement leaders and medical professionals, who believed that ingesting cocaine was even more harmful than drinking alcohol. As a result, the Coca-Cola Company reduced the amount of cocaine in Coca-Cola in the early twentieth century, but the trademark required it to remain an ingredient. In 1913, the company came up with a compromise: eliminating cocaine and replacing it with "spent coca leaves," which just became a flavoring. It was not until 1929, however, that technological advancements allowed the company to remove all active cocaine from the beverage.[19]

Coca-Cola became enormously popular, and many other druggists strove to match its success. In 1905, a Georgia pharmacist named Claude A. Hatcher began the Union Bottling Works in the basement of his family's grocery store in Columbus, Georgia. Chero-Cola was the first of his Royal Crown line of beverages; this was followed by ginger ale, strawberry, and root beer sodas. In 1912, Hatcher changed the company's name to the Chero-Cola Company. The company struggled through World War I when sugar was scarce, and it continued to have financial difficulties during the early 1920s. By 1924, however, the firm was strong enough to bring out a new line of beverages, called Nehi, with orange-, grape-, and root beer–flavored sodas. When Hatcher died in 1933, his successor—the company's vice president, H. R. Mott— reformulated Chero-Cola and shortened the brand name to RC Cola.[20]

Yet another early cola experimenter was Caleb Bradham, a pharmacist in New Bern, North Carolina, who named one of his kola nut beverages Brad's Drink. The formula for the beverage contained pepsin, a digestive enzyme that helps break down proteins in the stomach for easier digestion. Rechristened as Pepsi-Cola in 1898, the beverage became quite successful, and Bradham incorporated the Pepsi-Cola Company in 1902. Bradham then staked out new territory, and by 1907 the company had forty bottling plants across the United States. By 1910, Bradham had franchised more than 300 bottlers in twenty-four states to produce Pepsi-Cola. Bradham ran into financial problems, however, and the company went into bankruptcy in 1922. It was resurrected by a Wall Street broker named Roy C. Megargel, who controlled the company until 1931. In the midst of the Depression, the company went again into bankruptcy. This time the company was saved by Charles Guth, the president of the Loft Candy Company. The formula for Pepsi-Cola was changed at this time, eliminating pepsin as a major ingredient. By 1934, the Pepsi-Cola Company had turned the corner and started purchasing bottling operations throughout the United States. By 1939, the company's net earnings had risen to over $5.5 million.[21]

The Pepsi-Cola Company was hurt again by World War II. When the U.S. government imposed sugar rationing early in 1942, Pepsi-Cola had to cut back production drastically. The Coca-Cola Company, though, received government contracts to supply America's military with soft drinks, so it was supplied with sugar as needed. After the war, sales of Coca-Cola exploded as soldiers returned home thirsty for Coke. Even after the war, when sugar restrictions were lifted, Pepsi still had difficulty competing with Coke. By 1950, the Pepsi-Cola Company was almost forced to declare bankruptcy for a third time, but a highly successful advertising campaign came to the rescue. Throughout the 1950s, Pepsi expanded aggressively abroad, particularly in Latin America and Europe.

When Pepsi bought Frito-Lay, maker of salty snack foods, in 1965, it renamed the corporation PepsiCo. During the 1970s, PepsiCo acquired several fast food chains, including Pizza Hut, Taco Bell, and Kentucky Fried Chicken (now KFC). PepsiCo considered its fast food chains to be important outlets for its soft drinks, because all the chains sold Pepsi-Cola. However, other fast food chains refused to handle PepsiCo beverages because of competition with Pepsi's own fast food chains. In 1997, PepsiCo divested itself of its restaurant subsidiaries, creating a separate corporate entity now called Yum! Brands. PepsiCo maintains the largest ownership in Yum! Brands, and all these chains continue to sell Pepsi beverages.

Diet Soda

In 1904, a Russian immigrant named Hyman Kirsch founded a soft drink business in Brooklyn. It sold ginger ale and other flavored soda water. In addition to running the soda company, Kirsch served on the board of a sanitarium for chronic diseases, many of whose patients had diabetes. Hyman, his son Morris, and a company chemist named S. S. Epstein began seeking an artificial sweetener that did not taste metallic, and they came up with cyclamate calcium. Their company released the first sugar-free soft drink, called No-Cal, in March 1953. During the following years, Kirsch Beverages aggressively marketed No-Cal ginger ale and root beer. Although its sales were only moderate, the idea encouraged others to produce diet beverages.[22]

The Royal Crown Cola Company introduced a diet beverage called Diet Rite Cola in 1958. Five years later, the Coca-Cola Company introduced Tab, a diet cola drink. The name was a play on words that derived from people "keeping tabs on their weight." It sold well and, in 1967, the company released Fresca, a no-calorie, grapefruit-flavored soda. In 1970, Dr Pepper/ Seven-Up, Inc., released sugar-free 7-Up, which was renamed Diet 7-Up in 1979.

Sales of diet drinks took off in the late 1970s. This increase can be attributed largely to attacks on sugar by nutritionists, who proclaimed that sugar caused many illnesses, including diabetes, heart disease, and obesity—and regular soft drinks were loaded with sugar. By 1980, diet soft drinks claimed about 20 percent of the soda market. In 1982, both Coca-Cola and PepsiCo released diet colas: Diet Coke and Diet Pepsi, respectively. These new products were supported by vast advertising campaigns. Consumers preferred the taste of Diet Coke and Diet Pepsi; their sales skyrocketed while Tab sales plummeted. By the late 1980s, a variety of diet drinks were on the market. Diet Mountain Dew, for instance, made its debut in 1988.

Marketing

Coca-Cola and Pepsi launched sophisticated advertising programs targeting youth. In 1961, Pepsi commercial proclaimed that "Now it's Pepsi, for those who think Young." Pepsi launched a more ambitious promotional effort two years later targeted at the baby boomers, who were now defined as the "Pepsi Generation." In 1984, Pepsi launched another campaign targeting the baby boomers' children: Pepsi was "The Choice of a New Generation." The campaign included asking consumers to try both products in blind taste tests matching Coke and Pepsi. Even confirmed Coke drinkers chose Pepsi in these blind taste tests, and Pepsi inevitably won. The campaign increased sales, and Pepsi narrowed the gap with Coca-Cola. Then Coke made a major blunder: convinced that Americans preferred the taste of Pepsi, the company launched New Coke—a product that promptly failed. However, the company quickly rebounded when it reintroduced Classic Coca-Cola.

The soda advertising campaigns succeeded to such an extent that America's most popular flavored beverage—coffee—was displaced by soda. The president of the National Coffee Roasters bitterly complained that "the Pied Piper" was "one giant cola bottle," which made a lot of noise as he walked "through the marketplace with our youth flocking after him."[23] Soft drink manufacturers spent as much as 18 percent of their entire revenues annually on advertising, much of it targeting young people. Through advertising, soft drinks have not only increased their sales but also have shaped America's self-image. When you quaff a Coke or Pepsi, the idea of quenching your thirst is only part of the picture. If the relentless advertising campaigns for soft drinks are to be believed, drinking the soda will also make you younger, sexier, stronger, smarter, and cooler—in fact, your entire life will be a blast.

Soda Central

Before World War II, hundreds of local soft drink manufacturers dotted the American landscape, but wartime sugar rationing drove many of them out of business. After the war, the surviving companies consolidated. In 1960, the western region soft drink company Shasta was acquired by Consolidated Foods (later renamed Sara Lee), and it was sold to the National Beverage Corporation in 1985. In 1962, Crush International was acquired by the root beer maker Charles E. Hires Company. In 1986, 7-Up and Dr Pepper merged to form the Dr Pepper/Seven-Up Companies, Inc. Schweppes expanded its global operation in 1969 by merging with the English chocolate manufacturer Cadbury to form Cadbury Schweppes. The new partnership then began acquiring other soft drink companies, such as Hires Root Beer in 1989, A&W Beverages in 1993, and Dr Pepper and Seven Up in 1995. In 2000, the RC Cola brand was acquired by Cadbury Schweppes, which, by 2005, had become the world's third largest manufacturer of soft drinks, behind Coca-Cola and PepsiCo. In May 2008, Cadbury and Schweppes demerged. The North American beverages unit became the Dr Pepper Snapple Group, headquartered in Plano, Texas.

Today, the Coca-Cola Company is the most successful of the soft drink manufacturers, and it remains the largest soft drink company in the world. The company's brands account for about 44 percent of the soft drink market in the United States. The company spends about $3 billion annually on advertising, and its annual sales are estimated at 1 billion servings sold in more than 2 million stores, 500,000 restaurants, and 1.4 million vending machines around the world. One of the most widely known brands in the world, Coca-Cola has, for better and worse, become emblematic of the United States of America.

Soda Effects

The cost of producing soft drinks is low because the ingredients—water, carbon dioxide, sweeteners, colorings, and flavorings—are inexpensive. In the 1960s, the sales of soda in the United States surpassed the consumption of coffee, formerly America's number-one beverage. According to the American Beverage Association, soft drink companies now gross almost $93 billion in sales in the United States, and the industry employs some 211,000 people in the United States. Together, Coca-Cola and PepsiCo and their subsidiaries sell more than 70 percent of the carbonated beverages around the world. In 2007, Americans drank 14.7 billion gallons of soda, which almost equaled the combined total sales of bottled water, fruit drinks, sports drinks, and other bottled and canned beverages. The three largest soda companies (Coca-Cola, PepsiCo, and Dr Pepper Snapple Group) account for all ten top-selling beverage trademarks.[24]

By the 1990s, Americans were drinking more than fifty-seven gallons of soda per capita. Although this number declined appreciably in subsequent years, soda remains the most commonly consumed beverage after water in the United States. Although adult consumption has declined over the past three decades, the consumption of soft drinks among American children from six to seventeen years old has tripled. In 2010, Americans bought approximately $18.7 billion of carbonated beverages—$5 billion more than total milk sales. According to Mark Pendergrast, author of *For God, Country, and Coca-Cola* (2000), the Coca-Cola Company alone "sells over 500 brands of 3,300 different drinks in over 200 countries, receiving some 80% of its income from sales outside the United States. Pepsi is still runner-up but a more serious contender."[25]

Postscript

In 1888, three years after his invention of Coca-Cola, John Pemberton died.

Asa Candler, the man who founded the Coca-Cola Company, served as mayor of Atlanta from 1916 to 1919. He suffered a stroke in 1926 and died three years later.

Caleb Bradham, the inventor of Pepsi-Cola who declared bankruptcy in 1922, died in 1934.

🥤 Charles G. Guth, usually considered the founder of the modern Pepsi-Cola Company, died in 1948.

🥤 A&W Root Beer went through many ownership changes beginning in 1960. A&W Beverages, Inc., was formed in 1971; it test-marketed A&W Root Beer in bottles and cans in California and Arizona. The product was well received and subsequently was distributed nationally, along with sugar-free, low-sodium, and caffeine-free versions. Today A&W is part of the Dr Pepper Snapple Group.

🥤 In 1965, Pepsi bought the Frito-Lay company and renamed the combined corporation PepsiCo. PepsiCo is today the largest producer of snack food in the world, but it remains second to the Coca-Cola Company in sales of soft drinks.

🥤 Hyman Kirsch, the maker of the first diet soda, died in 1976 at the age of ninety-nine.

🥤 Environmentalists worry about the amount of garbage produced by soda bottles. Plastic soda bottles produce an enormous amount of waste. Americans trash 40 million soda bottles every day. These bottles produce an estimated 3.2 billion pounds of unrecycled garbage annually.[26]

Deputy Police Commissioner John A. Leach (*right*) watching agents pour liquor into a sewer following a raid in New York at the height of Prohibition (ca. 1921). (The Art Archive at Art Resource, NY)

11

To Root Out a Bad Habit

BEGINNING in the late nineteenth century, prohibition advocates successfully passed legislation at the local and state levels that banned the manufacture and sale of alcoholic beverages. The laws did not make much difference, however; most drinkers just crossed county or state lines and bought liquor where it was legal. Moreover, anti-prohibition forces had a habit of repealing the "dry" laws as soon as they gained the legislative upper hand. As a result, prohibitionists resolved that the only real solution would be an amendment to the U.S. Constitution. Only then would the manufacture and sale of alcohol be illegal in every state, and only then would the alcoholic scourge that afflicted America come to an end. Prohibition amendments had been introduced into Congress repeatedly since 1876, but they had never made it out of congressional committees. In 1913, however, a prohibition amendment finally made it out of committee and reached the House of Representatives—and it seemed to have a chance of passage. Prohibition advocates immediately went to work organizing their constituencies, sending letters, signing petitions, meeting with legislators and their staffs, and publishing articles in newsletters, newspapers, and magazines in support of the amendment.

Despite the optimism of prohibition advocates, it was unlikely that the amendment would pass. At the time, only five amendments to the

Constitution had been ratified since the Bill of Rights was ratified in 1789; the last three of these had been approved immediately after the Civil War. When the House voted on the prohibition amendment in December 1914 it received a majority of the votes, but not the two-thirds majority that was required for passage of an amendment. This failure only encouraged prohibitionists to work harder to elect a more favorable Congress in 1916. Prohibition candidates fared well in the election that year, but still not enough votes were received to pass an amendment.

But then, fate intervened. Europe had been mired in World War I for three horrific years. In hopes of breaking the stalemate and winning a quick victory, Germany began unrestricted submarine warfare against Great Britain in February 1917. Seven American merchant ships were sunk by German subs, and the United States declared war on Germany on April 6, 1917. Patriotic fever swept the nation, and leaders of prohibition organizations made certain that prohibition and patriotism were linked in the public mind. Germans were the enemy overseas, and at home it was the brewers—many of whom were German-born and some of whom had supported Germany before the United States entered the war. Supporters of prohibition exploited anti-German sentiments by publishing posters denouncing the "pro-German brewers and liquor dealers" who were identified as "A Disloyal Combination."[1] Distillers could also be labeled "unpatriotic" for using grain needed for the war effort.

The strategy worked: Congress passed legislation to prevent grain from being distilled into alcohol, and brewing was restricted as well. Finally, in 1917, the U.S. Senate and House of Representatives approved the prohibition amendment with the requisite majorities. All that was needed now was for three-quarters of the states to ratify the amendment, and prohibition would become the law of the land. Prohibition leaders believed this would happen, but that it would take years to achieve. They were wrong. Slightly more than a year later, on January 16, 1919, the Eighteenth Amendment was approved by the final state legislature needed. Congress approved enabling legislation called the National Prohibition Act, popularly called the Volstead Act; this act, passed over President Woodrow Wilson's veto, effectively banned the manufacture, sale, and importation of alcoholic beverages in the United States, making them illegal from January 17, 1920. With the onset of Prohibition, American drinking habits would never be the same.

Background

In colonial New England, drunks were dealt with severely. Sometimes they were put in stocks and ordered to wear the scarlet letter (in this case, "D") to identify themselves as drunks. In 1633, John Winthrop, the governor of the Massachusetts Bay Colony, found one Robert Cole guilty of "having been oft punished for drunkenness." Cole was "ordered to wear a red D about his neck for a year."[2] Increase Mather, the president of Harvard College, noted in 1673 that alcohol was "a good creature of God and to be received with thankfulness, but the abuse of drink is from Satan; the wine is from God, but the Drunkard is from the Devil."[3] By 1686, Mather was focusing his criticism on rum. It was "an unhappy thing," he wrote, "that of later years a kind of *Strong* Drink hath been *common* amongst us, which the poorer sort of people, both in Town & Country, can make themselves drunk with, at cheap & easy rates. They that are poor and wicked too (Ah most miserable creatures), can for a penny or two make themselves *drunk*."[4]

At the urging of local ministers, colonial governments tried to control taverns through licenses and by regulating their opening hours of business. Another way of limiting alcohol was through taxes. But laws need to be enforced, and this proved difficult because the men charged with enforcement were often heavy drinkers themselves, and they preferred to maintain friendly relations with their neighbors. Nevertheless, governments continued to pass ordinances in an attempt to limit drinking. In 1712, the Massachusetts Assembly passed an "Act against Intemperance, Immorality and Profaneness, and for the Reformation of Manners." This law was aimed at tightening licensing procedures and controlling the times and days that taverns could operate, among many other restrictions. But the law—like most passed before and since—proved impossible to enforce, and it was eventually repealed.[5] Still, such failures did not end attempts to control the sale and consumption of alcohol.

When Georgia was established in 1732, its founders banned spirits to "prevent the pernicious effects of drinking Rum" among the settlers. But the law was flouted, and the city of Savannah was soon filled with taverns.[6] Seven years later, the law was repealed. The main reason given for the repeal was that Georgia was at a competitive disadvantage compared with South Carolina when trading with the Indians, who wanted liquor in exchange for furs, food, or land. The amount of alcohol guzzled by Americans worried some of the founding fathers, who certainly drank their share. In 1796, John Adams described a worker on his farm as "a beast associating with the worst beasts in the neighborhood, running to all the shops and private houses, swilling brandy, wine, and cider, in quantities enough to destroy him. If the ancients drank wine as our people drink rum and cider, it is no wonder we read of so many possessed with devils."[7]

Drinking was socially acceptable, even when vast quantities were downed. But as stronger drinks, such as rum and whiskey, became more common and less expensive, concern with drunkenness increased. Religious groups, including the Quakers and Methodists, were particularly opposed to distilled spirits. A Philadelphia Quaker named Anthony Benezet argued in *The Mighty Destroyer Displayed* (1774) against the consumption of any drink that was "liable to steal away a man's senses and render him foolish, irascible, uncontrollable, and dangerous."[8]

Medical professionals had their own concerns about excessive drinking. Benjamin Rush, America's foremost physician in the late eighteenth century, drank mainly coffee and tea, as well as a "glass of or glass and a half of old Madeira wine" after dinner, but he never took "ardent spirits in any way nor at any time." Among the first pamphlets Rush published was *Sermons to Gentlemen on Temperance and Exercise*, which appeared in 1772. Five years later, Rush argued against giving Continental soldiers rum, arguing instead for "plentiful draughts of milk and water."[9] For farm workers, he recommended a number of alternatives to distilled spirits: plain water, hard cider, malt liquors, and wines; water mixed with maple syrup, molasses, or vinegar; buttermilk, coffee, tea, or even water "suffered to stand some time upon parched Indian corn." Rush later estimated that 4,000 people lost their lives every year due to the consumption of hard liquor.[10] The views of Rush and like-minded others, however, did not generate much interest among most Americans, and it would be decades into the nineteenth century before temperance became a major movement in the United States.

After the American Revolution, alcohol consumption rose sharply. The United States had 2,579 registered distilleries in 1792; eighteen years later, this had increased to 14,191, which churned out 25 million gallons of spirits annually.[11] In addition, there were numerous unlicensed commercial stills throughout the country and many Americans operated one in their own homes. As one observer wrote of the period:

Intemperance in liquors had gone to very extraordinary lengths. The practice of dram-drinking had become almost universal. French or Spanish brandy, West India and New England rum, foreign and domestic gin, whisky, apple brandy, and peach brandy, made a variety which recommended itself to individual tastes. But besides this choice, there were numerous artificial compounds, in which fruit of various kinds, eggs, spices, herbs, and sugar, were leading ingredients. Thus, at home, or at the bars of taverns, there was a continual dabbling in spirits, grog, sling, toddy, flip, juleps, elixirs, &c., as if alcohol in one or other of its seductive disguises, had become a necessary of life.[12]

In 1810, Americans drank more than 4.5 gallons of pure alcohol each, and it was also estimated that about 6,000 Americans died each year because of their drinking.[13] As the young country came of age, alcohol use continued to increase. In 1821, the Harvard academic George Ticknor complained to Thomas Jefferson that Americans were "already affected by intemperance; and if the consumption of spirituous liquors should increase for thirty years to come at the rate it has for thirty years back we should be hardly better than a nation of sots."[14] By the mid-1820s, New York State had 1,129 distilleries and New York City alone had more than 1,600 "spirit sellers," who sold whiskey for 38 cents a gallon. According to one British observer, this abundance of sellers and cheap price meant that "the people indulge themselves to excess, and run into all the extravagancies of inebriety."[15] British writer Frances Trollope, who visited America in the late 1820s, reported that in Maryland whiskey flowed at the fatally cheap rate of 20 cents a "gallon, and its hideous effects are visible on the countenance of every man you meet." The price of whiskey soon dropped to a dime.[16] By 1830, alcohol consumption by Americans over the age of fifteen was estimated at seven gallons per capita, most of it in the form of whiskey.

Abetting the rise of the temperance movement was the "Second Great Awakening." This religious revival began in the 1790s when Methodist, Baptist, and (to a lesser extent) Presbyterian preachers rode across America, especially in New England and later the Midwest, espousing a new evangelism. The church and camp meetings led by these men were attended by hundreds of thousands of Americans, particularly in rural areas. The social activism that emerged from this religious fervor eventually launched movements to end slavery, reform prisons and education, promote missionary activities, and encourage women's suffrage—but its first and most glorious cause was temperance.

The Massachusetts Society for the Suppression of Intemperance, founded in 1813, endeavored to persuade people to abstain from alcohol by describing its harmful effects; members of the society tried to convince drinkers that their lives would be far happier and more rewarding without alcohol. They formulated a pledge by which drinkers promised publicly to reform and drink no more.[17] Meanwhile, temperance preachers spoke out against alcohol, and temperance tracts and sermons were widely published and distributed. Lyman Beecher, a Presbyterian minister, gave six sermons on temperance in 1826; they were printed and reprinted for years.[18]

Beecher cofounded the American Society for the Promotion of Temperance (later the American Temperance Society) in Boston. It was intended to be a national umbrella group for temperance organizations, and it succeeded: within five years of its founding, there were 19 affiliated state societies with more than 2,200 chapters and more than 170,000 pledged members.[19] When the French historian and politician Alexis de Tocqueville arrived in America in 1831 and heard that "a hundred thousand men had bound themselves publicly to abstain from spirituous liquors," he thought it was a joke, for he "did not at once perceive why these temperate citizens did not content themselves with drinking water by their own firesides." But when he wrote *Democracy in America* (1835), Tocqueville concluded that "these hundred thousand Americans, alarmed by the progress of drunkenness around them, had made up their minds to patronize temperance."[20]

More than 5,000 temperance societies with a total of 1.25 million members were operating in America by 1833. Two years later, there were 8,000 societies with 1.5 million members.[21] In May 1833, a total of 400 delegates from twenty-one states assembled in Philadelphia for the first national temperance convention. The delegates formed the American Temperance Union, which would help guide the movement until the Civil War.[22]

Despite the growth of temperance organizations, Americans were drinking more than ever. In 1830 it was estimated that 37,000 people died annually because of strong drink. The *Encyclopaedia Americana* reported in 1832 that alcohol "was responsible for three quarters or four fifths of the crimes committed in the country, for at least three quarters of the pauperism existing, and for fully one third of the mental derangement." In addition to the human and family tragedies associated with alcohol, there were other costs as well: the financial cost of housing prisoners who committed crimes while intoxicated, the loss of laborers who were too inebriated to work, and the alcoholic paupers who flooded American communities.[23] It was estimated that in New York City alone, three-quarters of crime and pauperism was related to liquor.[24] None of these statistics was supported by evidence; they were only opinions frequently expressed by temperance advocates.

The New York State temperance convention proposed a very mild resolution supporting total abstinence in 1833, but it was withdrawn due to lack of support. Around that same time, the *Quarterly Temperance Magazine* published several responses by leaders who opposed the resolution. Only two supported complete abstinence, of whom one wrote, "The only means of redemption and preservation for the intemperate is total abstinence from all intoxicating drinks." Some prohibitionists saw no reason to ban wine, beer, or cider. They perceived the resolution as an attempt to dilute the temperance pledge—clearly the real evils were rum, whiskey, and brandy.[25]

Proponents of total prohibition marshaled their arguments. They felt sure that drunkards who had signed the temperance pledge would have a sip of wine or a glass of beer and begin a slow slide back to their old ways. Abstinence backers collected testimonials from medical professionals about the evils of all alcohol. When the New York State temperance convention met the following year, it passed the original resolution, making it the first state temperance society to endorse total prohibition.[26] The following year, the Massachusetts temperance society passed a similar resolution banning all distilled and fermented beverages. In 1836, when the American Temperance Union held its second national convention in Saratoga Springs, New York, it also passed resolutions opposing all alcoholic beverages.

Temperance advocates used sermons, books, tracts, hymns, mass meetings, and cartoons to make life uncomfortable for those who manufactured, sold, and drank alcohol. Temperance orators drew large crowds, and two temperance plays found wide audiences. As the temperance fervor increased, public drinking became less acceptable, and moderate drinkers found themselves in an especially uncomfortable position, despised by both teetotalers and hard drinkers. Because of the efforts of the temperance societies, alcohol consumption dropped sharply, such that by 1845 Americans drank an estimated 75 percent less alcohol than they had in 1830. An estimated 4,000 distilleries closed—although many reopened once temperance advocates moved on to harass other distilleries and the pressure was off.[27]

As temperance leaders continued to press their agenda, several states passed laws that banned or greatly restricted the sale of alcoholic beverages. In 1841, Maine became the first state to pass such a law, and others soon followed. These laws, however, proved impossible to enforce, and the selling and drinking of alcohol simply moved out of the public eye. Over the next decade, most state laws were repealed or annulled by state courts.

The legal setbacks of the 1850s were minor compared with the widespread collapse of temperance movement during the Civil War and the return to hard drinking, especially among soldiers.[28] During and after the war, saloons opened everywhere, and there was no shortage of customers. By 1870, Manhattan had 7,071 licensed suppliers of liquor and probably an even greater number of illegal establishments. A 1897 survey in Manhattan found a ratio of one liquor distributor to every 208 residents.[29] A 1899 police report in Chicago revealed that half the city's population went into a saloon every working day.[30] A major reason for this was the free lunches offered on bar counters—all patrons had to do was buy a drink. This ensured that customers acquired the habit of drinking liquor at noon, and this helped to develop a regular clientele for saloons and bars. Moreover, the food served at saloons was often salty, which increased the desire to drink, and the ingredients served at the free lunches were low cost. In Chicago, the meatpacking plants were said to give bars spoiled salted meat to use in their free lunches.[31]

After the Civil War, new temperance societies emerged to relaunch the crusade against alcohol. Ohio was the birthplace of three most important of these groups: the National Prohibition Party (organized in Cleveland in 1869), the Women's Christian Temperance Union (started in Cleveland in 1874), and the Oberlin Temperance Alliance (also founded in 1874). Of these, the most important was the Oberlin Temperance Alliance, which morphed into the Anti-Saloon League of Ohio in 1893, and Howard Russell, a lawyer and Congregationalist minister, became its general superintendent. The Anti-Saloon League had a single objective: prohibition. No other issue mattered. It organized the evangelical churches, including the Baptists, Congregationalists, Methodists, and Swedish Lutherans. Its local affiliates had at least 75 percent clergymen on their boards; on Sundays, tens of thousands of their parishioners heard the league's message. Just as important, its staff members were paid—not volunteers, as in other organizations—thereby ensuring their dedication and enhancing the effectiveness of the league.

Temperance Beverages

A challenge facing temperance advocates was what to offer the public as a substitute for alcoholic beverages. In the mid-nineteenth century, the increased availability of safe water made it a viable option. Medical authorities had begun to understand the relationship between sanitation and wells. In rural areas, farmers needed to put some distance between their waste pits and their fresh water wells, which also needed to be dug much deeper. In urban areas, authorities modified municipal water systems to include delivery infrastructure that made safe water available throughout the city. Where population outstripped fresh water supplies, cities such as New York embarked on massive projects to bring safe drinking water from surrounding areas. As a result, by the early twentieth century, clean and pure water was available in most American cities. Such improvements in water supplies eliminated one argument offered by those who drank alcohol (that water was unsafe), and drinking water became a reasonable alternative to beer, wine, cider, and spirits. This was especially important in restaurants, where ice water was automatically served, especially to female diners.

Two other alternatives to spirits were coffee and tea. Both had been on American tables since colonial days, but it was not until after the Civil War that affordable coffee became available throughout the United States. Coffeehouses became centers of temperance activities in the United Kingdom, but not in the United States. Tearooms emerged in the United States in the late nineteenth century and became popular, especially with women. At about the same time that water systems were improving, scientific discoveries, technological improvements, and the passage of laws helped create a safe milk supply. Milk became the most important drink for children, who previously would have consumed ciderkin (weak cider) and other mildly alcoholic beverages.

During the mid-nineteenth century, drugstore owners began experimenting with nonalcoholic creations that they promoted as temperance drinks.[32] After the Civil War, such concoctions were marketed locally. Charles E. Hires, a Philadelphia druggist, invented root beer, which he advertised as "The Great Temperance Drink" and "a temperance drink for temperance people."[33] This designation was challenged by temperance leaders, who believed that root beer contained alcohol. But after reputable chemists analyzed the drink and concluded that it contained only water, sugar, and root extracts, the doubters made public apologies.[34] Grape juice, also promoted as a temperance refreshment, became popular during the late nineteenth century. In 1896, a soft drink called Countie's Roma Punch, bottled in Boston, proclaimed itself "The National Temperance Drink."[35] Coca-Cola also was advertised as a temperance beverage, and it flourished under that banner until the temperance movement became concerned about cocaine.[36]

Direct Action

Temperance advocates became impatient with the long, slow grind of lobbying political bodies persuading sinners to renounce alcohol and promoting alternatives to liquor. Some brave souls were willing to take direct action. One such person was six-foot-tall Carrie Amelia More, who lived much of her early life in rural Missouri. Carrie married a doctor named Charles Gloyd, who turned out to be an alcoholic (or so she later claimed). After Gloyd died, Carrie Gloyd married a minister named David A. Nation. The couple eventually moved to Medicine Lodge, Kansas, where Carrie Nation founded a chapter of the Women's Christian Temperance Union. The chapter embarrassed saloon keepers, bartenders and customers to the point that some saloons shut their doors. But they could not keep the locals from patronizing liquor establishments in neighboring Kiowa, Kansas, and these establishments resisted the group's efforts.

Then Carrie Nation had a vision that urged her to take stronger action against the sale of alcohol. In 1899, she went to Kiowa and began throwing rocks at liquor bottles inside saloons. The rocks caused little damage, so in 1901 she upgraded her weaponry to a hatchet and proceeded to perform "hatchetations" by marching into saloons and smashing mirrors, bottles, slot machines, faucets and hoses connected to beer barrels, and anything else that she could before she was arrested. Despite arrests and fines—which she refused to pay—Nation continued to enter and vandalize saloons in Wichita, Kansas City, and elsewhere. Her bold actions generated publicity, and other women jumped on the anti-liquor bandwagon, forcing local bars and saloons to close and supporting efforts to prohibit the sale and distribution of alcohol.[37] Physical attacks could only go so far, however. If prohibition were to succeed, it needed a very different strategy, and Wayne Wheeler was just the man to create it.

Wheeler and the Anti-Saloon League

Wayne B. Wheeler studied at Oberlin College, where he had worked part-time with the Anti-Saloon League. He continued to do so while studying at Western Reserve Law School. Wheeler became an attorney in 1898 and began working full-time for the league. At that time, the Anti-Saloon League was a small group that advocated complete prohibition. Many other organizations, such as the Women's Christian Temperance Union and the National

Prohibition Party, had far larger national memberships. Therefore, it was unlikely that a small state organization, like the Anti-Saloon League, would have much of an influence outside Ohio.

Wheeler absorbed himself in lobbying for prohibition legislation in Ohio. The best way to guarantee appropriate legislation, he thought, was to elect candidates who supported prohibition and defeat those who opposed it. The league soon became a nonpartisan group with but a single issue: prohibition. If a Democratic candidate supported prohibition, he would have the league's support; if a Republican was for prohibition, the league would throw its weight behind his campaign. No other issue mattered. The Anti-Saloon League worked cooperatively with other temperance groups, such as the National Prohibition Party and the Women's Christian Temperance Union, to focus on electing prohibition supporters and passing legislation. The league mobilized its forces for electoral victory; if an elected official later reneged and voted against prohibition legislation, the league did everything possible to defeat him in the next election.

Wheeler's strategy worked: the Anti-Saloon League influenced many local and state elections; as a result, Ohio communities and the state legislature passed laws that restricted or prohibited the sale of alcohol. The league expanded its operations to other states, with similar success. As local and state victories piled up, the league became the leader in the prohibition movement.

As the Anti-Saloon League gained national visibility, funds rolled in; the league used the money to pay its staff, churn out propaganda, and organize campaigns for and against candidates. The league also created a speakers bureau that, at its height, boasted more than 20,000 prohibition advocates, including big names such as the politician William Jennings Bryan, a teetotaler. The groups that hosted the speakers were required to request a hefty contribution from the audience for the league. These tactics worked. Prior to 1900, just five states had adopted prohibition legislation, as had many counties and cities. But then the dominos tumbled. In 1907, Georgia became the first state to enact complete prohibition and five other states followed during the next two years. Five states went dry in 1914, four more in 1915, another nine in 1916, four more in 1917, and an additional eight in 1918.[38]

As successes piled up, the prohibition movement focused on passing a national law prohibiting the sale and distribution of alcohol throughout the nation. In 1895, the Anti-Saloon League had opened an office in Washington, D.C., with a mandate to lobby Congress to pass laws opposing the manufacture and sale of alcohol. Wheeler worked on and off with this lobbying group, applying the same tactics that he had developed at the state level to the national level. The group worked hard to elect representatives who would support their cause.

Eventually, the league and its allies decided that the time had come for Congress to pass prohibition legislation. By 1914, the movement had enough votes in the U.S. House of Representatives to guarantee that the Sheppard-Hobson Joint Resolution for National Prohibition Constitutional Amendment would make it out of committee, and enough power to ensure that it came to a vote. The Women's Christian Temperance Union organized a national petition drive supporting the amendment, and by April 1914 it had collected the endorsements of more than 3 million Americans. When the amendment came up for a vote in the House in December 1914, 197 Congressmen voted in favor, 7 more than voted against it, but it was still far short of the required two-thirds majority.

Rather than give up, the Anti-Saloon League and its allies intensified their efforts, focusing specifically on the next congressional election cycle. Wheeler began working full-time on the national agenda; his first objective was to elect as many congressional supporters as possible in November 1916. Although that election saw victories for many prohibition candidates, there were still not enough to pass an amendment to the Constitution.

As soon as the United States declared war on Germany in April 1917, the Anti-Saloon League began lobbying for laws restricting the production of alcoholic beverages. On August 10, 1917, Congress did pass the Lever Food and Fuel Control Act, which banned the production of distilled spirits for the duration of the war, but this did not satisfy those supporting total prohibition. The U.S. Senate passed a national prohibition amendment—the Eighteenth Amendment—in August 1917, and the House did so in December of that year. Even before the Eighteenth Amendment was ratified by the states, Congress passed the Wartime Prohibition Act, which banned the sale of beverages having alcohol content greater than 2.75 percent. By January 1919, the requisite number of states had finally ratified the Eighteenth Amendment, and national Prohibition became the law of the land a year later.

Success and Failure

It took more than the pressure tactics of the Anti-Saloon League, a barrage of temperance propaganda, and war hysteria and patriotism to get the

Eighteenth Amendment passed. Prohibition was just one measure advocated by a much broader progressive movement, which promoted reforms at the local, state, and federal levels from the 1890s until 1920. National progressive successes included the passage of other constitutional amendments: the income tax (1913), direct election of senators (1913), and women's right to vote (1920).

Another factor that contributed to the success of Prohibition's passage was a lack of cooperation within the alcoholic beverage industry. Brewers would not work with distillers; each viewed the other as competition. Brewers considered beer, which was fairly low in alcohol, to be a temperance beverage; they did not think it would ever be outlawed. There were also divisions within the brewing industry itself. National companies had interests different from those of small brewers serving only a locality or region. Big brewers thus did not oppose local and state bans on brewing because these laws effectively shut down their smaller competitors. Meanwhile, brewers believed that distillers supported closing saloons because distilled spirits could be sold legally in drugstores, whereas druggists did not sell beer.[39]

When the prohibition movement picked up steam in the early twentieth century, brewers, distillers, wholesalers, and retailers never formed a united front to combat its growing opponents, and they never developed much political or public support. Breweries bought or invested in newspapers in several cities and funded editorials in others, but these generated little support. The National Wholesale Liquor Dealers Association of America, which represented only a fraction of the nation's distillers, wineries, and wholesalers, issued four anti-prohibition manuals beginning in 1915. Other anti-prohibition propaganda presented the liquor industry as a friend of the workingman—a characterization that Americans just did not buy.[40] These efforts were too little, too ineffective, and too late.

Societal shifts that took place after the Civil War also contributed to the success of Prohibition. Prior to the war, the temperance movement was strongest in New England, followed by the Midwest. Southerners did not support the temperance bandwagon, partly because New Englanders supported the abolition of slavery. After the Civil War, however, the temperance movement took off in the South, in large part as a means of keeping alcohol out of the hands of African Americans.[41] The southern temperance movement affiliated with the Ku Klux Klan, which was reinvigorated in 1915 after the release of the film *Birth of a Nation* and the proliferation of books and articles portraying blacks as aggressive drunks and merciless rapists. The

Klan went after not just African Americans but also immigrants, such as the Irish, Italians, Germans, and Jews—many of whom were leaders in the distilling industry.[42] Throughout Prohibition, the Klan supported enforcement efforts against minorities and immigrants. Where law enforcement was lax, the Klan was willing to take up the slack, especially in the rural South.[43]

Another factor in Prohibition's success was the rapid industrialization that took place in the post–Civil War period, which required sober workers for the nation's factories. The nation's industrial elite, such as oil magnate John D. Rockefeller and automobile manufacturer Henry Ford, supported Prohibition as a means of guaranteeing a sober workforce. Rockefeller, a life-long nondrinker and America's wealthiest Baptist, strongly supported Prohibition; he donated 10 percent of the Anti-Saloon League's total budget. Ford required that all his workers be teetotalers, and he hired undercover agents to make sure they stayed that way. Ford workers caught buying liquor a second time were fired. Other companies followed similar rules, and many refused to hire anyone who was known to drink. Industrialists also blamed alcohol for the worker unrest sweeping America in the early twentieth century, and they thus supported and financed prohibition groups, especially the Anti-Saloon League. Industrialists became even more interested in supporting prohibition when states passed workmen's compensation laws, which required employers to pay workers for on-the-job accidents, even if the injuries were the fault of inebriated workers.[44]

The prohibition movement had figured out how to pressure legislators and had succeeded in the most difficult task of passing an amendment to the Constitution, but they had not bothered to gain support from mainstream Americans. Many Americans were moderately swayed by the propaganda machines of the temperance societies, but were not deeply committed to the cause. Others were upset by the tactics that had been used by the prohibition movement. Some believed that the majority of Americans would not have voted for prohibition had they been given the opportunity.

Even before Prohibition went into effect, organized opposition emerged. The Association Against Prohibition was organized in 1918, and it quickly picked up members as the economic costs became evident: hundreds of thousands of Americans were put out of work when breweries, wineries, distilleries, cider mills, and retail outlets closed. The officers of the brewer's union wrote in 1920 that there was no analogy in the history of any nation "in which hundreds of thousands of men were deliberately deprived by the state and the nation of their employment and business, without a semblance of consideration of the wishes of the people." Neither the prohibition movement nor the legislation they supported included provisions for unemployment insurance or compensation for the stockholders.[45] Then there were the millions of Americans who liked to drink: when opportunities presented themselves, they were willing to violate the law.

But public opposition was minimal at first, and most Americans seemed resigned to not drinking when the law went into effect in January 1920. Americans did cut down on their drinking. Prohibition advocates claimed that workers were using the money they saved on alcohol to buy more food for their families, and grocery store sales did in fact increase during the early 1920s. One businessman reported that before Prohibition, absenteeism on the day after payday had been about 10 percent, but this dropped to just 3 percent after Prohibition took effect. Death rates associated with alcohol also dropped precipitously. Moreover, diseases connected with alcohol, such as cirrhosis of the liver, had declined in dry states before Prohibition, and they continued to decline during the years of national Prohibition. Hospitals treated fewer patients. Violent crime was down. Drunkenness was less common.[46] It looked as if Prohibition would be a great success.

The major flaw in prohibition legislation was enforcement. The Eighteenth Amendment had given concurrent enforcement power to the federal and state governments; however, the federal government hired only 1,500 enforcement agents, and it was impossible for them to enforce the law throughout the United States. Meanwhile, local and state law enforcement officials were not always supportive of Prohibition, and many state and local agencies lacked the trained manpower to enforce it or to deal with the organized crime that emerged.

The Anti-Saloon League and other prohibition organizations had been very effective in passing the Eighteenth Amendment and accompanying legislation, but they had not been effective in mobilizing public support for it. Lack of widespread support outside of particular religious groups contributed to the willingness of many Americans to violate the law. Twenty months after Prohibition took effect, the Bureau of Internal Revenue estimated that Americans drank 25 million gallons of illegal liquor, and that bootlegging was already a $1 billion business—and this was before bootlegging began in earnest. Speakeasies (illegal establishments that served alcohol) soon replaced saloons. By 1922, there were an estimated 5,000 speakeasies in New York City alone. An extensive underground economy developed around illegal alcohol; rural moonshiners flourished, as did the urban makers of "bathtub gin."

Gin was the easiest alcoholic beverage to make; its harsh taste could be masked by juniper oil, which also increased volume and diluted the alcohol. When organized crime began centralizing the manufacture, distribution, and retail sales of liquor, wealth and power flowed to the crime syndicates. In addition, as Americans increasingly flouted Prohibition, a generation came of age with little respect for the law.[47]

Violation of Prohibition became more common. Advocates were convinced that most violators were foreigners, especially immigrants from Italy and Mexico. A bill was introduced into the House of Representatives that would deport violators of the Volstead Act who were not citizens. It passed with a wide margin in the House but was ignored by the Senate.[48]

Meanwhile, wealthier Americans never felt that Prohibition was intended for them, and members of the upper class never had a problem securing whatever beverages they wanted throughout the Prohibition era. Over time, the urban middle class also gained access to alcohol through speakeasies and other channels. It was only the working class that suffered the most during Prohibition. The main drink of working-class Americans—beer—was almost completely unobtainable: it was too difficult to brew, transport, and sell. Distilled spirits were more readily available in most cities and the business was more lucrative, but they were much more costly than pre-Prohibition prices and unaffordable for the working class.[49]

The liquor served in speakeasies was notorious. Prior to Prohibition, saloons, bars, and other drinking establishments served beer, wine, and whiskey purchased from commercial breweries, distilleries, and vintners, whose practices were regulated. The alcohol served in speakeasies, however, was usually made by amateurs: it occasionally contained poisons and frequently tasted terrible. Imported alcohol was available, but only at extremely high prices—and much of what was sold as imports was actually domestic bootleg liquor poured into fancy bottles with fake labels. Customers never knew where their drinks came from or what they were made from.

The Volstead Act permitted the production of industrial alcohol for various purposes, such as making antifreezes or lacquers, but required that such alcohol be "denatured" through the addition of a noxious substance, such as wood alcohol (methanol), benzene, formaldehyde, or sulfuric acid, to make it unpalatable or toxic. It was relatively easy to remove these substances, however. As soon as Prohibition went into effect, illegal operations popped up around the country to purchase industrial alcohol, convert it into drinkable form, and distribute it to speakeasies. The problem was that many engaged in this were not scientists, the process was not always successful, and people who drank the alcohol sometimes died or went blind. A report by the Bureau of Prohibition showed that 98 percent of the alcohol it confiscated contained poisons. Another report claimed that downing just three drinks made with improperly converted industrial alcohol could be fatal. In New York alone, an estimated 700 people died in a single year during Prohibition because of poisonous spirits. When Wayne Wheeler was asked about these deaths, he responded unsympathetically, "The person who drinks this industrial alcohol is a deliberate suicide." He concluded that "to root out a bad habit costs many lives and long years of effort."[50]

As violent crime increased, newspapers, magazines, radio programs, and newsreels in movie theaters kept Americans, even in rural areas, abreast of the latest murders, violence, arrests, and corruption associated with illegal alcohol. Partly as a result, Prohibition lost support, especially among America's elite. Industrialists who had once supported Prohibition now opposed it, as did many political leaders. Without the financial support of the well-to-do, organizations such as the Anti-Saloon League had difficulty staying afloat. In addition, states and local communities slackened their enforcement efforts.

By 1930, authorities that estimated 250,000 speakeasies operated in the United States. The New York City police commissioner estimated that there were 32,000 speakeasies in that city alone—more than twice the number of legal bars and saloons that existed prior to Prohibition. Others said that the commissioner's estimate was actually way too low—that there were at least 100,000 speakeasies in the city. Mabel Willebrandt, the U.S. assistant attorney general responsible for prosecuting violations of the Volstead Act, commented on the lawlessness in New York's speakeasies: "It can not truthfully be said that prohibition enforcement has failed in New York. It has not yet been *attempted*."[51] As enforcement failed, Congress stepped in and passed the Jones Act, which greatly increased the penalties for violating the Volstead Act. The first conviction was a felony, with the maximum penalty increased to five years of imprisonment and a fine of $10,000. Even with harsh provisions, enforcement did not work.

The Jones Act alienated many prominent Americans, including William Randolph Hearst, owner of one of America's largest newspaper chains. Opposition to Prohibition strengthened. In 1927, membership in the Association Against Prohibition had more than 750,000 members. Two years later Pauline Sabin, a wealthy and politically well-connected New York socialite, formed the Women's Organization for National Prohibition Reform. In less than a year, it had more than 100,000 members; by 1931, its membership had reached 300,000; by November 1932, membership was more than 1.1 million.[52]

Despite growing opposition to the Volstead Act, the widespread disregard for its provisions, and the associated violent crime and corruption, the Eighteenth Amendment might not have been repealed had it not been for the Depression. Republicans had strongly associated themselves with Prohibition, whereas many Democrats—especially those who were Irish, Italian, Jewish, Catholic, and German—strongly opposed it. When the stock market crashed in 1929 and the economic system collapsed, the Republicans, who had controlled Congress since 1919 and the presidency since 1921, were blamed. In November 1932, President Herbert Hoover lost his reelection bid and the Democrats swept into power with large majorities in both houses of Congress. President Franklin Roosevelt pledged to get the economy moving again.

At the time, federal coffers were empty. With almost 25 percent of the American workforce unemployed, income tax revenue was down. Roosevelt and his allies presented repeal as a means of generating revenue. Reinstating the excise tax on the sale of liquor was thus one argument for ending Prohibition. Others argued that repeal would relaunch industries that had once employed hundreds of thousands of Americans. Still others believed that repeal would help put an end to the burgeoning crime generated by the illegal production and sale of alcohol. On February 20, 1933, the U.S. Congress proposed and approved the Twenty-First Amendment to the Constitution, which repealed Prohibition. The amendment was ratified by the last of the required number of states on December 5, 1933. The "noble experiment," as it was called, was over. Throughout the country, countless toasts were raised to repeal.

Prohibitory Effects

Prohibition had lasting effects on what Americans drank. The sale of nonalcoholic beverages rose during Prohibition. Fruit juices (such as grape, orange, and lemon) were advertised as healthful, and their sales accelerated. The sale of fizzy soft drinks also increased, partly because sodas—such as ginger ale and Coca-Cola—became mixers for cocktails made with unpalatable bootleg hooch.[53] When Prohibition ended, Americans continued to use sodas in many cocktails. Soda companies also introduced new products during Prohibition. The Chero-Cola Company, for instance, introduced its Nehi beverage line, with orange, grape, and root beer flavors. The product that would eventually become 7-Up was first marketed in 1929.

Most complicated prohibition cocktails devised to mask the taste of the alcohol disappeared after repeal. The bartender Patrick Gavin Duffy included formulas for Prohibition cocktails in his *Official Mixer's Manual* (1934), but noted that he did so that future Americans could see "the follies which the enactment of the Eighteenth Amendment produced." Dr. Charles Browne, a former member of Congress and author of *The Gun Club Drink Book* (1939), praised the cocktail's "general return to reason."[54]

A number of new and novel beverages appeared on the market during Prohibition, and many survived after repeal. Edwin Perkins, head of the Perkins Products Company of Hastings, Nebraska, marketed a bottled soft drink concentrate called Fruit Smack, which was intended to be combined with water and sugar. Fruit Smack was popular, but the heavy bottles were expensive to ship. Perkins tried a second idea—a powdered concentrate that could be sold in paper packets. Customers just had to dissolve the powder in water and add sugar. Perkins called his product Kool-Ade (later renamed Kool-Aid). This helped to create a new category of beverages—children's drinks—that still flourishes.

Prohibition wrought changes in alcohol consumption as well. Hard cider, which had been in decline for decades before Prohibition, never recovered its popularity, although sales of nonalcoholic apple juice were strong during and after Prohibition. Prior to Prohibition, beer had been America's second most popular beverage after water; before Prohibition, Americans drank an estimated 20.2 gallons per person annually. Beer consumption declined precipitously during Prohibition; it was difficult to brew beer undetected, and its low alcohol content made it less profitable than distilled spirits. Prohibition had converted many drinkers from beer to spirits. Following repeal, beer consumption dipped to 10.9 gallons per person, almost half what it had been before Prohibition.

Conversely, wine consumption skyrocketed during Prohibition. It was legal to make wine at home, and many Americans took up winemaking. Homemade wine filled a void, but with repeal, wine consumption plummeted as other alcoholic beverages became available again. To survive, many wineries produced the cheapest wines possible, which drove well-to-do Americans to seek out better-quality European imports.

The most important change wrought by Prohibition, however, was related to alcohol production. Many breweries, wineries, and distilleries did not survive the Prohibition era, and many of those that reopened in 1933 had a tough time regaining their footing because of the Depression. The brewing, distilling, and winemaking industries consolidated, and today a small number of corporations control a large percentage of their respective markets.

Prior to Prohibition, high-end restaurants made much of their profits from the sale of liquor that preceded, accompanied, and followed a meal. Prohibition sounded the death knell for most big-name restaurants, although a few—such as New York's Twenty-One Club—hung on by selling good food and illegal alcohol and paying bribes to the police and city officials. However, soda fountains thrived during Prohibition, but disappeared shortly after repeal. By this time, the country was in the depths of the Depression, and soon restaurants would experience the rationing that took effect during World War II. It was not until after the war that high-end restaurants reemerged.

Postscript

Wayne B. Wheeler steadfastly supported Prohibition until his death in 1927, five years before repeal.

Despite the problems with the Eighteenth Amendment, Americans consumed less alcohol after Prohibition than they had before. Per capita consumption of alcohol would not return to pre-Prohibition levels until 1965.[55]

The Twenty-First Amendment repealed national Prohibition, but it did not contravene state or local temperance laws. Mississippi was the last state to repeal its prohibition law, in 1966.

While Prohibition ended eight decades ago, concern with alcoholic consumption has remained part of American life. Groups such as Alcoholics Anonymous, Mothers Against Drunk Driving, and Students Against Drunk Driving, and stricter enforcement of driving while under the influence of alcoholic beverages, have emerged to deal with some problems that caused Prohibition.

Advertisement for Kool-Aid (ca. 1950s). (Courtesy
of The Advertising Archives)

12
Youth Beverages

I N 1920, Edwin Perkins—head of the Perkins Products Company of Hastings, Nebraska—marketed a new drink mix called Fruit Smack—a bottled syrup to be combined with water and sugar. The product did fairly well, but the heavy bottles were expensive to mail and they often broke in transit, dismaying customers and costing Perkins money to replace. In 1927, he came up with the ideal alternative: inspired by the tremendous success of Jell-O dessert powder, Perkins devised a powdered concentrate to be sold in paper packets. Customers still just had to add water and sugar, but with paper packets instead of bottles, they were much less likely to receive a soggy, drippy package when they ordered the product by mail. Perkins created six flavors— cherry, grape, lemon-lime, orange, raspberry, and strawberry—and sold the packets by mail for 10 cents apiece. He called the product Kool-Ade, which he trademarked in February 1928.

Not content to sell his product by mail, Perkins soon began a campaign to distribute Kool-Ade through grocery stores. It was promoted in newspapers, magazines, and on the radio—a very novel way to promote products at the time. The campaign brought Kool-Ade to the attention of the U.S. Food and Drug Administration (FDA), which claimed that "-ade" meant "a drink made from." Because most Kool-Ades were named after fruit, such as oranges, grapes, and lemons, this implied (according to the FDA) that it should be composed of fruit juice; however, Kool-Ade was artificially flavored and colored. The company renamed its product to Kool-Aid in 1934.

During the Depression, Perkins lowered the price of Kool-Aid to a nickel per packet and launched a national advertising campaign aimed at children. The company placed advertisements in children's magazines; like promotions for other children's products, Kool-Aid ads promised readers a gift, such as a pilot's cap, in exchange for empty Kool-Aid packages.[1]

Kool-Aid dominated the children's beverage market throughout the Depression. It was priced low for consumers and cost little to make, and the Kool-Aid flavors were loved by many children. During World War II, sugar was rationed, so Kool-Aid sales lagged; after the war, however, the product took off. By 1950, Perkins Products was cranking out 1 million packets of Kool-Aid a day. In 1953, Edwin Perkins sold the company to General Foods Corporation, which introduced the famous "Smiling Face Pitcher" advertising campaign for Kool-Aid in 1954.

Kool-Aid sales skyrocketed, which encouraged researchers at General Foods to experiment with variations on Kool-Aid. In 1957, they came up with an orange-flavored, powdered breakfast-drink mix fortified with vitamins. Sold in jars, the new product was released in 1959 under the brand name Tang. The mix might have disappeared quietly from the market if the National Aeronautic and Space Administration had not sent Tang on its Gemini space flights in 1962. Inextricably linked to the glamour of astronauts and space flight, Tang's popularity soared. Kool-Aid and Tang are just two of thousands of beverages targeted at children, adolescents, and those younger than thirty years.

Background

Throughout much of early American history, children drank pretty much the same beverages as did their parents; alcoholic beverages served to children were sometimes, but not always, diluted. In New Orleans, for example, children were given watered-down wine. Ciderkin was a drink made specifically for children. It was made by adding water to pomace—the compressed apple mush left over from making cider—and then pressing it again.[2] The problem with fruit juice was that it started fermenting as soon as it was made. The temperance movement encouraged the development of unfermented juices, and the scientific discoveries of Louis Pasteur helped juice makers produce nonalcoholic fruit beverages. Sales of nonalcoholic fruit beverages were limited until Prohibition took effect in 1920. Fruit juice producers—such as those making grape, grapefruit, lemon, and orange juice—launched advertising campaigns that touted the healthful effects of consuming juices, especially for children.

Other companies, such as the makers of Hi-C, Hawaiian Punch, and Delaware Punch, developed fruit-flavored drinks. Delaware Punch consisted of a variety of ingredients, prominently grape. It originated with Thomas E. Lyons in 1913. To market his noncarbonated beverage, he created the Delaware Punch Company of America in San Antonio, Texas. By 1925, the company was selling 172 million bottles per year, which was more than Coca-Cola at the time. The company's early advertising targeted families, as well as "schools, on athletic fields and at social gatherings," among other demographics.[3]

Beverages targeting youth increased after World War II as the so-called baby boom generation emerged. Hawaiian Punch originated in Fullerton, California, as an ice cream topping. A. W. Leo, Tom Yates, and Ralph Harrison converted it into a concentrate that was sold to local soda fountains. In 1946, the company was purchased by Reuben P. Hughes and others, who renamed it the Pacific Hawaiian Products Company. Hughes shifted from selling concentrate to soda fountains to selling concentrate to grocery stores. In 1950, Highs expanded a ready-to-serve red Hawaiian Punch in large forty-six-ounce cans.[4] The company used cartoon characters, Punchy and his frequent target Opie, to advertise its fruit-flavored juice to children.[5]

Hi-C Enriched Orangeade—a fruit-flavored drink with 10 percent orange juice, sugar, and flavorings—originated with Niles Foster, a bottling plant owner, in 1946. It was marketed in 1948 through a massive promotional effort targeting children. One 1949 advertisement proclaimed that it was a "healthful drink the children begged for." It quickly became the leading fruit drink in the children's market.[6] In 1954, Hi-C was sold to Minute Maid, a subsidiary of the Coca-Cola Company. They extended the product line to include other fruit juices, such as apple and grape. Two years later, Minute Maid began advertising Hi-C on television. One advertisement espoused that Hi-C was "made from fresh fruit and naturally sweetened" and "was good for children." In 1971, the Federal Trade Commission brought suit against the company for allegedly misleading advertisements. The lawsuit dragged on for two years, and finally Coca-Cola won the argument.[7]

Fruit juice had been bottled since the late nineteenth century, but usually in large family-size bottles for purchase in grocery stores. In 1972, three

New York entrepreneurs launched a very small company called Unadulterated Food Products, Inc., in Brooklyn. It produced ready-to-drink fruit juices, sodas, and seltzers in wide-mouth bottles. The company sold its products to health-food stores, using a slogan of "made from the best stuff on earth." It was so successful in its "new-age" marketing approach that sales surged. The company marketed other beverages, such as lemonade; in 1988, it launched flavored tea. In 1993, the company changed its name to the Snapple Beverage Company. It had fifty-five different products and sales were accelerating.

Snapple was so successful that it attracted competition. Pepsi created a partnership with Lipton to launch Pepsi Lipton Teas in 1991. The Coca-Cola Company jumped in as well: in 1994, it launched a line of fruit drinks called Fruitopia. Coca-Cola's first juices were Born Raspberry, Peaceable Peach, Lemon Berry Intuition, and Curious Mango. It targeted teens and young adults. Fruitopia sales increased initially but then declined, and Fruitopia was discontinued.[8]

Snapple was purchased by the Quaker Oats Company for $1.7 billion in 1994. Quaker also owned Gatorade, and the company concluded that it could sell both products to youth in a similar manner. Quaker quickly found that Snapple could not be sold in the same way as Gatorade: although they were both targeted at youth, one was a sports drink and the other was a health drink. At the same time, new competing products came on the market—AriZona Iced Tea, Nantucket Nectars, and Mystic—and Snapple sales declined. Quaker sold Snapple twenty-nine months after acquiring it for $700 million to Triarc.[9] Snapple recovered, and Triarc sold the division to Cadbury Schweppes in 2000. Cadbury and Schweppes demerged in 2008, and a new beverage company, Dr Pepper Snapple Group, was formed in North America.

Snapple consistently marketed its beverages as healthy alternatives to soft drinks. In September 2003, New York banned the sale of candy, soft drinks, and other sugary snacks at its schools. City officials selected Snapple as the official beverage of the city. As part of the $166 million agreement, Snapple acquired exclusive rights to sell its beverages in the city's 1,225 public schools. Critics pointed out that many Snapple beverages contained more calories than soft drinks. Michael Jacobson, executive director of the Center for Science in the Public Interest, complained that "the new Snapple drinks are a little better than vitamin-fortified sugar water because the juices may provide low levels of some additional nutrients."[10]

Flavored Milk

By far the most important children's beverage was—and continues to be—milk. During the nineteenth century, breastfeeding declined in America. Despite concerns about the safety of milk, it was a necessary beverage for children. By the early twentieth century, the dairy industry problems declined and nutritionists praised milk as the "perfect food," especially for children. The dairy industry saw this as an opportunity to promote the health benefits of milk, and advertisements pictured robust, happy children thriving on pure, nutritious milk.[11] The ads emphasized milk's fortification with vitamin D (that began in the 1930s)—something that made it even more important for children.

As milk sales soared, entrepreneurs started to develop products that could flavor milk in ways that appealed more to children. In 1926, Hershey's Chocolate Syrup was introduced at soda fountains for use on ice cream as well as an additive to beverages; two years later, the retail version of the syrup went on sale. Meanwhile, the William S. Scull Company of Camden, New Jersey, which specialized in coffee and tea, introduced a product in 1928 called Bosco Chocolate Syrup. It was marketed as a sauce for ice cream and cake, as well as a "milk amplifier." During the early 1930s, the company promoted Bosco as a milk amplifier and thus a health-giving children's beverage. Bosco was soon enriched with iron, which was another important promotional point. The syrup's advertisements proclaimed that "Dr. Philip B. Hawk has proved the unique bodybuilding qualities of Bosco."[12] Other companies began producing similar products. In 1939, the Taylor-Reed Corporation of Mamaroneck, New York, began manufacturing Cocoa-Marsh, a "milk amplifier" that was advertised as a chocolate syrup that made "milk haters, milk lovers."[13]

Milk "modifiers" also came in powdered form, like the malt powder used at soda fountains. Ovaltine, a Swiss product created by a physician in 1904 to nourish seriously ill patients, was first marketed in the United States in 1905. A sweetened, malted chocolate powder to be mixed with milk and drunk hot or cold, Ovaltine sponsored some of the most popular American radio shows of the 1930s and 1940s; its healthful qualities, particularly five vitamins (protein, iron, niacin, calcium, and phosphorus) were always touted in its advertising. Nestlé Quik (now called Nesquik) was another chocolate drink powder; introduced in 1948, its long sponsorship of children's television programming ensured its lasting popularity.

Yet another milk-related beverage that appealed to young people was the milkshake. By the late nineteenth century, soda fountains offered a drink concocted from milk, flavorings, and ice cream that were shaken up vigorously to make a thick, smooth mixture. With the invention of a practical electric blender by Hamilton Beach in 1910, milkshakes became popular, particularly during Prohibition.[14] The malt shop became a feature of small-town Main Streets throughout America. Fast food restaurants put milkshakes on their menus in the 1930s, although some chains discontinued them after discovering that the shakes took too long to make and ruined customers' appetites for hamburgers.

The invention of the Multimixer by Earl Prince in 1936 permitted several milkshakes to be made simultaneously. Salesman Ray Kroc was so impressed with the invention that he purchased the rights to the machine in 1939. After World War II, the Multimixer was sold to ice cream chains such as Tastee-Freez and Dairy Queen. Because of stiff competition, sales of Multimixers declined in the early 1950s. At that time, Kroc noted that two West Coast entrepreneurs, Richard and Maurice McDonald, had purchased eight Multimixers. Kroc visited the McDonalds' new hamburger stand, which was located in San Bernardino, California, and discovered that every morning the staff prepared 80 milkshakes and stored them in the freezer, ready to serve. If the supply ran out during the day, the staff made more shakes. The McDonald brothers were selling an astounding 20,000 milkshakes per month. The visit ended with Ray Kroc acquiring the rights to franchise McDonald's nationwide.[15]

Since the 1950s, shakes have been offered regularly at most fast food operations; some chains have created their own versions, such as Wendy's Frosty, made with milk, sugar, cream, and flavorings. Today, the thickness of a fast food milkshake is likely created by ingredients such as microcrystalline cellulose rather than rich ice cream; moreover, shakes and similar treats have received considerable criticism because of their high calorie and fat content.

Smoothies are blended drinks inspired by milkshakes, but sometimes they contain no dairy products. These nonalcoholic cold beverages include a mixture of healthful (or purportedly healthful) ingredients, such as fruit, fruit juice, ice, yogurt, milk, and occasionally ice cream. When smoothies first appeared in the 1960s, they were usually blends of fresh fruit and yogurt, typically dispensed in health-food stores. Composed of fresh ingredients, smoothies are usually made to order. They began to be sold outside of health-food stores in the early 1970s.

In the 1960s, a Louisiana teenager named Steve Kuhnau worked as a soda jerk, mixing up malts, shakes, and sodas. Ironically, Kuhnau suffered from lactose intolerance and was unable to sample many of his creations. He began experimenting at home with nutritional drinks, blending fruit, nutrients, vitamins, minerals, and protein powders. In 1973, Kuhnau opened a health-food store in Kenner, Louisiana, where he began selling the beverages, which he called smoothies. The drinks proved popular, so Kuhnau perfected the recipes and, in 1989, franchised the operation as Smoothie King. The company now has more than 550 locations in the United States, with a menu offering dozens of different combinations of smoothies and snacks.

Once Kuhnau's success became evident, various competitors surfaced. Kirk Perron opened his first smoothie store, called the Juice Club, in San Luis Obispo, California, in 1990. Five years later, the company changed its name to Jamba Juice. It featured all-natural foods, such as made-to-order fruit smoothies, fresh-squeezed juices, healthy soups, and baked goods. Jamba Juice expanded by acquiring a smaller chain, Zuka Juice, in 1999.[16]

As of 2010, an estimated 3,000 juice bars throughout the United States sold smoothies, as did tens of thousands of smoothie outlets, including Dairy Queen, Froots, and Tropical Smoothie Café. In 2010, McDonald's also began selling smoothies, much to the consternation of the more specialized drink chains.

Sports and Energy Drinks

Sports drinks are designed to enhance athletic performance by fostering endurance and recovery. The first such beverage was Gatorade, which was formulated in 1965 by Robert Cade and Dana Shires of the University of Florida to solve rehydration problems faced by the school's football team, called the Gators. Gatorade is a noncarbonated drink that consists of water, carbohydrates (in this case, sugar), and electrolytes (sodium and other minerals vital for muscle function and fluid balance). Gatorade was used by the team in 1967, when the Gators won the Orange Bowl. This gave the drink extensive national visibility, and Gatorade soon commercialized.[17]

Intended for athletes participating in serious competition or intense exercise, sports drinks promote rehydration (the sweetness makes it easy to drink lots of liquid), replace electrolytes, and increase energy levels (as would any sugar-sweetened drink). Most people, however, do not work up enough of a sweat to need electrolyte replenishment, and chugging a sports drink while exercising can cause cramps.

Gatorade launched the sports beverage industry. Coca-Cola introduced Powerade in 1990, and since then the company has introduced various new flavors and formulas. In 1992, PepsiCo created the All Sport athletic drinks, promoted as the "Official Sport Drink" of the top soccer leagues. However, neither Powerade nor All Sport was able to challenge the success of Gatorade, which has remained the dominant sports drink on the market. In 1967, Stokely-Van Camp of Indianapolis secured the rights to Gatorade and marketed it nationally. Thirteen years later, Stokely-Van Camp was acquired by Quaker Oats, which was acquired by PepsiCo in 2003.[18]

The success of sports drinks encouraged the introduction of energy drinks, such as the ones developed by an Austrian named Dietrich Mateschitz, as a salesman for Blendax, a cosmetic firm. The company was acquired by Procter & Gamble, and Mateschitz's job focused on selling the company's toothpaste in other countries. His travels took him to Thailand, where he noticed that pharmacists sold low-cost energy tonics, such as *Krating Daeng* (Thai for "red water buffalo"), to factory workers who wanted to work a second shift and drivers who stopped at service stations. He tasted a variety of energy drinks in Asia, and he liked what he tasted. He also believed there was a market for these beverages in Europe. He resigned from Blendax, formed his own company in Austria, and with a partner introduced a nonalcoholic carbonated energy drink called Red Bull to Europe in 1987.[19]

Mateschitz was not the first to market energy drinks in Europe. An English pharmaceutical company developed the first energy drink, called Glucozade, in 1927. It was a fizzy liquid filled with sugar, mainly used to help children recover from illness. A British pharmaceutical picked up the formula, renamed it Lucozade, and promoted it with the slogan "Lucozade aids recovery." In 1983, the company decided to reposition the product as an energy drink using the slogan, "Lucozade replaces lost energy." It was rebranded as an energy drink for those engaged in sports, and Olympic athletes were hired to promote the product. Within five years, sales tripled.

A Japanese company, Tashio Pharmaceuticals, popularized an energy drink called Lipovitan in 1962. The drink was so successful that the company was one of Japan's top corporations within twenty years. It is likely that Mateschitz was aware of these successes before he launched his own business with Red Bull.[20]

Red Bull was introduced into the United States in 1997; it became America's first popular energy drink. Each 8.3-ounce can supplied 80 milligrams of caffeine—about the same as a strong cup of coffee—as well as taurine (an amino acid) and glucuronolactone, a chemical that supposedly detoxifies the body. Red Bull started a frenzy of copycat beverages, such as Jolt, Monster Energy, No Fear, Rockstar, Full Throttle, and myriad other brands. Large companies jumped in, with Anheuser-Busch's 180, Coca-Cola's KMX, Del Monte Foods's Bloom Energy, and PepsiCo's Adrenaline Rush, SoBe, and Amp brands. These drinks boast caffeine levels up to 500 mg per 16 ounces, and they are often loaded with various forms of sugar. By the early twenty-first century, there were more than 300 energy drinks on the American market. Many include caffeine combined with other substances such as guarana, ginseng, and ginkgo biloba.[21] Unlike sports drinks, which hydrate the body to replace fluid lost during exercise, the caffeine in energy drinks dehydrate the body.

Red Bull's prime consumers were young adults (eighteen to thirty-four years old), particularly college students and young men who considered it to be a performance enhancer.[22] Red Bull controls about 40 percent of the energy beverage market in the United States. In 2004, the most important energy drinks in the United States were Rockstar International and Coca-Cola Full Throttle and Tab brands. Energy drink consumption increased at an annual rate of 55 percent per year, according to Packaged Facts. They estimated that, in 2006, the U.S. market for energy drinks totaled $5.4 billion. Americans drink 3.8 quarts per person annually, according to Zenith International.[23]

The percentage of adolescents and young adults who consume energy drinks increased markedly between 2001 and 2008. The effects of these drinks on children and teens have not been well studied, but some health professionals cite a number of potential dangers, including heart palpitations, seizures, and cardiac arrest, among others.[24]

Red Bull and other energy drinks were often used as mixers for alcoholic beverages. Then, in 2000, Agwa, a beverage made from spent coca leaves that combined caffeine and alcohol, was introduced into America. Other companies began producing caffeinated alcoholic beverages. Within two years, the two leading brands of caffeinated alcoholic beverages sold 337,500 gallons. By 2008, sales reached 22,905,000 gallons, and they continued to increase ever since.[25] A major reason for their success has been their heavy marketing to youth.[26] Warnings about the consumption of alcohol and caffeine have proliferated and some countries have banned caffeinated alcoholic beverages. Today, more than 25 brands of caffeinated alcoholic beverages are sold in a variety of U.S. retail alcohol outlets, including many convenience stores.[27]

Today, beverages that particularly target teenagers and young adults are rapidly expanding. Supermarkets, grocery stores, convenience stores, and fast-food chains sell thousands of beverages that cater to these demographics. The diversity of these beverages has been rapidly increasing along with sales, and they likely will continue to increase in the future.

Postscript

◕ The Hastings Museum of Natural and Cultural History has a permanent exhibit on Kool-Aid and its inventor, Edwin Perkins, who died in 1961.

◕ Thomas E. Lyons, the founder of Delaware Punch, died in 1951. His company was acquired by the Coca-Cola Company.

◕ Dietrich Mateschitz remains as the chief operating officer of the company that manufactures Red Bull. He is a multibillionaire.

◕ As of 2010, Jamba Juice had about 800 outlets in thirty states and was the leading chain in the field. Jamba Juice is headquartered in Emeryville, California.

CHATEAU
MONTELENA

ESTABLISHED 1882

NAPA & ALEXANDER VALLEYS

CHARDONNAY

1973

Produced and Bottled by
Chateau Montelena~Calistoga, Napa Valley, California

Alcohol 13.2% by Volume

Label of a 1973 chardonnay from Chateau Montelena, the top wine in a blind taste test held on May 24,
1976, between French and California wines.

13
Judgment of Paris

A YOUNG ENGLISHMAN named Steven Spurrier bought a Parisian wine shop called Les Caves de la Madeleine. He startled the French wine world in 1973 when, with an American partner named Patricia Gallagher, he launched a wine school, l'Académie du vin. What could two foreigners know about wine, the French wondered. Spurrier became something of a celebrity, and California wine producers began visiting his shop, sometimes bringing samples of their best wines.

At the time, California vineyards mainly produced inexpensive jug wines, but for a few years some wineries had also been producing premium wines. Les Caves de la Madeline carried only French wines (in 1975, no California wines were sold anywhere in Paris), but Spurrier liked some of the California wines he tried. In several tastings held in the United States at which French and American wines were compared, the domestic products had done quite well—but all the judges were American, and their rankings received little notice outside the United States.

As the United States Bicentennial approached in 1976, Spurrier came up with the idea of celebrating it in Paris with a tasting comparing French and California wines—this time with a panel of French judges. Spurrier talked with Gallagher about the possibility. She was scheduled to visit her sister in California in the summer of 1975, so Spurrier asked her to visit some California wineries. She called Robert Finigan, an American wine and food critic who published a wine newsletter in San Francisco, and he made recommendations. She returned to Paris with the startling news that there were, indeed, some very good California wines. Spurrier invited eleven top French wine judges to a blind tasting to be held on May 24, 1976, and they all accepted. In March 1976, Spurrier visited California to make the final selections of the wine.[1] He selected a few comparable bottles of French and California chardonnays and cabernet sauvignons.

Spurrier also invited the press to his tasting, which was held at the Intercontinental Hotel in Paris, but only one bothered to show up—George M. Taber from *Time* magazine. To the surprise of both the judges and Stephen Spurrier himself, California wines scored highest in both categories. Taber wrote up the shocking results for the following week's issue of *Time*.[2] Other American magazines and newspapers jumped on the story, and the American wine world would never be the same.

Background

Grapes thrive in many parts of the world. In Europe, *Vitis vinifera* has been grown and made into wine for 8,000 years.[3] Under the proper conditions, *V. vinifera* produces grapes with a high sugar content, thin skins, and delicate flavors. For the best wines, these grapes must be grown in a certain climate— warm enough in summer so that the grapes mature and cold enough in winter so that the vines go dormant. In western Europe, these conditions existed in only a few areas, so winemaking developed in parts of Germany, France, Italy, Spain, and Portugal—but not in Great Britain. Although winemaking did not develop in Great Britain, the English upper classes developed a taste for wine and imported it from many countries; sweet wines—port, Madeira, and canary—were particularly popular in England. These wines traveled well because they were fortified, and they more easily withstood temperature shifts on voyages to America.

Early European explorers found an abundance of grapevines along the eastern coast of North America, and in some areas the climate seemed right for growing grapes that make good wine. The English were particularly excited about this discovery; if they established settlements in North America, they could produce their own wine, making it unnecessary for them to import wine from other countries. Expectations for viticulture were extravagant, and this led to determined efforts that lasted decades. John Smith reported that the colonists at Jamestown had made twenty gallons of wine from wild grapes they found, but he did not say whether the wine was palatable. Thomas West, Earl De La Warr, the governor of Virginia, also tried making wine. Governor John Winthrop of Massachusetts tried to start a vineyard, but it was unsuccessful. Thomas Jefferson learned to love wine in Paris while serving as American ambassador there in the 1780s. When he became president in 1801, he served good wines—imported from France, of course—in the White House. Jefferson experimented with making wine from native American grapes, but he could not make a go of it. Elsewhere in the country, others tried to make wine; although some had brief success, most eventually failed.[4]

The early American winemakers faced an almost insurmountable obstacle: the native North American grapes were mainly small, thick-skinned, and sour. The vines were hardy and the fruits fragrant, but the grapes were deficient in sugar and abundant in acid. These wild "fox grapes" (in the northern colonies, *Vitis labrusca*) were later cultivated and hybridized to produce the familiar Concord, Catawba, and Niagara varieties of grapes, which were used mainly for juice and jelly. Some were also used to make wine, but their flavor was off-putting to colonists familiar with wine made from European grapes.

Some Old World grapevines were imported to the colonies, but they did not survive, mainly due to diseases and insect pests. New World varieties were largely immune to these pests, but *Vitis vinifera* was defenseless against them. Another obstacle to the establishment of a New World winemaking tradition was that it was simply easier and less expensive to produce other alcoholic beverages, such as cider and rum, and there was much more profit in growing other crops, such as tobacco and grain, or raising cattle. Ultimately, demand for the low-quality wine made from native grapes was just too small to make economic sense.

Those who really craved wine could easily secure imported wines and brandies from Spain, Portugal, and their island possessions in the Atlantic. Fortified wines were preferred in America, as they were in England. The most inexpensive imported wines came from the Azores and the Canary Islands. Because these wines did not come directly from European nations but from their colonial possessions, the wines could be shipped directly to the North American colonies without violating the Navigation Acts or incurring import duties, thereby keeping their prices down. A Virginia minister reported that these wines were the "fittest to cheer the fainting Spirits in the Heat of Summer, and to warm the chilled Blood in the bitter Colds of Winter, and [seem] most peculiarly adapted for this Climate."[5]

Other wines also were imported to North America. Foremost on the colonial wine list were canary, port, sherry, and muscadine. Sack (fortified white wines from Spain and the Canary Islands) and hock or Hockheimer (German white wines) were also common by the late eighteenth century. Frequent hostilities between England and France made it difficult for colonists to import French wines, but after the French alliance with the colonies in 1778, the colonists began consuming more French wine. A particular favorite was claret, a dark French Bordeaux; other favorites were Burgundy and Champagne.[6]

For the most part, wines were enjoyed by the wealthy and the middle class, who frequently added sugar and diluted them with water. Wine was also mixed with other beverages to make punches. Wine was also an ingredient in a negus, a popular colonial hot drink consisting of sweet wine and water with lemon and spices. Another popular drink, morning bitters or wine bitters, consisted of Madeira flavored with bitter barks.[7] Sangaree (sangria) consisted of spiced red wine, water, sugar, and fruit juices. For dessert, the colonists drank syllabubs, made with cream or milk flavored with wine and spices.

Not everyone was happy with the quantity of wine and brandy some colonists enjoyed. William Bradford, the governor of Plymouth Plantation, asserted in 1646 that wine was "plentifull" and the best came "from Malago, the Cannaries, and other places." So much wine was available that colonists were drinking an excessive amount "even to drunkennes." The colony exerted a tight control over wine sellers.[8] In 1638, Virginia's governor asserted that half of the colony's income from the sale of tobacco was wasted on wines and "strong waters."[9] In 1679, a European visitor in Maryland reported that arriving ships with wine and brandy attracted everyone's attention. Colonists drank "so abominably" that they expended all their money, which created a hardship for their households.[10]

Nineteenth Century

Despite early winemaking failures, attempts continued well into the nineteenth century. The first two American books written specifically on viticulture were John Adlum's *A Memoir on the Cultivation of the Vine in America* (1823) and John James Dufour's *The American Vine-Dresser's Guide* (1826). The authors represent two different philosophies: Dufour, a Swiss native who emigrated to America in 1796, believed that the New World grape was not worthy of commercial production, and turned to Old World grapes for his winemaking; Adlum, a native-born Pennsylvanian, favored the New World grape varieties and explored what Catawba grapes had to offer. These and other similar attempts at viticulture were not particularly successful. Well-to-do Americans continued to drink imported wine; in addition, whiskey and rum, America's national beverages, were much less expensive. Some groups drank wine only on special occasions, but not when dining at home.[11]

A Swiss-born sea captain named Giovanni Del-Monico would change American views toward wine—at least among the wealthy. In 1824, Del-Monico sold his ship and used the proceeds from the sale to open a wine shop in New York City. At the time, most Americans did not drink wine, so his customers were mostly Frenchmen and other European immigrants or foreign visitors. To maximize profits, Del-Monico imported casks of wine from Europe and did the bottling himself. He was not satisfied with the business, however, and decided to try his hand at something new. He sold his wine shop in 1826 and convinced his brother Pietro, a pastry chef, to help him launch a café and pastry shop in New York. In December 1827, under their Americanized names, John and Peter Delmonico, the brothers opened their little café.[12] A few years later, in March 1830, they expanded the café into a fine dining establishment, soon to be called Delmonico's Restaurant Français. Delmonico's veneration of French haute cuisine and good wine presaged American restaurant menus and wine lists, but all the wine was imported.[13] All other high-end restaurants soon would also serve a wide variety of imported wines.

As East Coast restaurants began offering more sophisticated wine lists, events were fermenting on the West Coast that would also change the American wine world. In 1845, the United States annexed Texas, then an independent country that had broken away from Mexico. The border between Texas and Mexico, however, was disputed. President James K. Polk, a southerner interested in extending slavery westward, authorized the U.S. Army to occupy the disputed territory, an action that initiated war between Mexico and the United States. The military engagements of the war ended in September 1847, with an American victory. According to the provisions of the Treaty of Guadalupe Hidalgo, the peace treaty with Mexico signed in February 1848, the United States gained the former Mexican territories in California and the Southwest.

These newly acquired territories already had a modest wine industry. Franciscan missionaries had established vineyards in California as early as 1779.

Their interest in winemaking was religious—they needed wine to celebrate Mass. Rather than work with native grapes, however, the Franciscans had imported European grape vines. Because California had a Mediterranean-like climate, Old World grapes thrived there. Although California winemaking received a setback when the missions were secularized in 1833, some vineyards survived, as did some winemaking. The gold rush, which began in 1848, brought new wine drinkers and winemakers to California, and the wine industry soon prospered as new vineyards were planted and wine production increased. One California vineyard worker, Hungarian-born Agoston Haraszthy, published his experiences in *Grape Culture, Wines and Wine-Making* (1862), which was the first book to discuss California wine production. Thomas Hart Hyatt's *Hand-Book of Grape Culture* (1867) was the first wine book actually published in California.

With the completion of the transcontinental railroad in 1869, California wines could be shipped eastward more easily, but their "quality was usually poor and they were often sold under foreign labels to gain a market."[14] Nevertheless, wine sales did lead to increased production, and by the end of the nineteenth century California wineries were producing 30 million gallons annually of all kinds of wine. Thanks to programs on viticulture and enology begun at the University of California at Davis in 1880, wine production in California improved. In 1889, California wines were displayed at the Paris Exposition; twenty-seven received awards, but a special award was given to the wine from Inglenook winery in Napa Valley for its "excellence and purity." At the 1893 World's Columbian Exposition in Chicago, fifty-three California vintners presented samples of their wines and brandies, many of which received awards.[15] This was the first time that California wines received national visibility.

Despite the increased visibility of California wines, most Americans who drank wine still preferred imported vintages. However, due to high duties and taxes, imported wines were expensive when compared with other available beverages, such as domestic wine and whiskey. Wines soon disappeared from many middle-class homes, mainly due to the cost. The exception was New Orleans with its Creole traditions, where wine was served daily—even to children, who drank it with water.[16] Elsewhere, the temperance movement did have an effect on wine consumption. While Ulysses Grant was president, his wife forbade the drinking of wine at the family dinner table, although she permitted wine for state dinners. In 1877, incoming first lady Lucy Hayes banned the serving of any wine at the White House, earning her the nickname Lemonade Lucy.

In 1878, an English visitor to the United States, George Towle, reported that "wine is very expensive, and it is only once in a while that it appears on the tables even of the rich—so seldom that it cannot be called a custom. Sherry, port, claret, madeira, and champagne are rare luxuries, and only appear on festive occasions, or in the houses of epicures and wealthy foreigners."[17] Five years later another British visitor, George Sala, was assured by Americans that "the custom of wine drinking would speedily fade out altogether from good society in America" due to the temperance movement.[18] Sala noted, however, that "an immense quantity of champagne is consumed in Chicago, and the very best brands are to be found at no very extortionate rates at the hotels; but the claret leaves a great deal to be desired."[19]

Dago Red

Fewer than 4,000 people of Italian heritage lived in the United States in 1850. Beginning in 1876, however, large numbers of Italians started to immigrate to America, and by 1880 the total number of Italian Americans reached 44,000. By 1920, more than 4 million Italians had arrived in the United States. This influx of Italian immigrants was good news for the American wine industry, for Italians drank an estimated twenty gallons of wine per capita annually; other Americans averaged less than one-third of a gallon per year.[20] Many Italian immigrants also were skilled in viticulture and winemaking.

Most Italian immigrants ended up in cities, but some launched agricultural colonies. In 1878, Secchi de Casale, a political refugee from Italy, helped found an agricultural colony in Vineland, New Jersey. The members of the colony planted grape vines and produced their first wine in 1881. They concluded, however, that it would be more economical to grow fruits and vegetables for the fresh market, so wine production waned.[21]

The most successful agricultural colony—at Asti in Sonoma County, California—was founded in 1881 by Andrea Sbarboro, an immigrant from Genoa, Italy. Along with other Italian and Swiss-Italian immigrants, Sbarboro created an agricultural cooperative called Italian Swiss Colony. The intent of the members of the Italian Swiss Colony was to sell fresh grapes in bulk, but they soon found that the cost of growing grapes was greater than the price they could get for selling them. Because one of the leaders of the cooperative, Pietro C. Rossi, was an experienced winemaker from Asti,

Italy, the co-op members decided to try to make wine. It was difficult to sell wine in San Francisco, however, so the co-op shipped its wine to Chicago, New York, New Orleans, and many other cities with large Italian immigrant populations.

Among the wines made and sold by Italian Swiss Colony were "Chianti, Barolo, Barbera, Grignolino, and Marsala of Italy, and also the red and white wines of France and Germany, such as Burgundy, Zinfandel, Carigan, Cabernet, Medoc, Hock, Chasselas, Riesling, Chablis, Sauterne. and Johannisberger, besides all the sweet wines, such as sherry, port, Muscat, Angelica, Madeira, Malaga, Tokay, together with the sparkling Moscato and extra dry Monte Cristo champagnes." By 1895, Italian Swiss Colony was producing 1 million gallons of wine annually; seven years later, it was producing 10 million gallons per year. By 1900, the wines made at Italian Swiss Colony were being sold to countries in Central and South America, Asia, and Europe. Italian Swiss Colony wines even received gold awards at exhibitions in Italy.[22]

Italian immigrants and their interest in drinking wine encouraged some winemakers throughout America to produce a low-cost red table wine, which was sold in jugs. By 1899, this wine had become known as "Dago Red." For those immigrants who could afford something better, good-quality wines from Italy were imported into the United States. Although immigrants were the major consumers of wine mainstream Americans also became exposed to yet another culinary tradition. By 1900, the average per capita consumption of wine in the United States had reached 0.4 gallon a year—only a slight increase from 1870, and still very low when compared to the consumption of other alcoholic beverages. What was more important, however, was that per capita wine consumption continued to increase for the next three decades.[23]

Threats

Despite increasing sales, the American wine industry faced serious challenges. One serious threat was phylloxera (*Daktulosphaira vitifoliae*), an aphid-like parasite native to eastern North America that lives on the roots and sometimes the leaves of grape vines. The native American grape vines east of the Rocky Mountains are generally immune to the disease. Sometime between 1858 and 1863, American grape vines were sent to France, where the *vinifera* grape was very susceptible to the disease. Virtually all European vineyards were affected, and the vast majority of native grape vines were destroyed over the next few decades, threatening the centuries-old tradition of European winemaking. The solution was to graft European *vinifera* onto the roots of American grapes, a technique that is still employed. Phylloxera first appeared in California sometime before 1870, but it was not until the following decades that the disease decimated California vineyards. As a result, by the 1880s the number of grapes under cultivation in California had decreased substantially. California winemakers used the same techniques of grafting that the Europeans had used, and within a decade California vineyards were back on line.[24]

Phylloxera was not the only threat to American viticulture. An even more serious threat was the temperance movement, which eventually morphed into Prohibition. In the late nineteenth century, cities and states began passing laws restricting the sale of alcohol, including wine; eventually, many banned the sale of any alcohol. Early temperance advocates had excluded beer and wine from their main targets, which were rum and whiskey. Subsequent advocates, however, wanted to prohibit the making and sale of all spirituous beverages. In 1880, Kansas became the first state to amend its state constitution to outlaw the manufacturing, transporting, or selling of any alcoholic beverages.[25]

The National Prohibition Act, commonly known as the Volstead Act, defined "intoxicating" as any beverage containing more than 0.5 percent alcohol, which eliminated the manufacturing of wine. Its passage devastated many wineries. Unlike breweries, which could produce near beer and meet the alcohol content requirements of the law, wineries could not produce wine at 0.5 percent alcohol. Not all wine production was illegal, however. Sacramental wine was permitted under the law, so some wineries survived by producing wine for religious use; in 1922, the demand for sacramental wine had increased by 800,000 gallons, and it continued to increase in subsequent years.[26]

Wine could also be made for medical purposes for the infirm and convalescent. Such medicinal wines and wine tonics were filled with bad-tasting medicaments to make them less appealing to anyone who might want the wine and not the medications. (Sales shot up after consumers found that refrigerating the medicinal wines and tonics caused the horrible-tasting stuff to settle to the bottom of the bottle, leaving a palatable wine.) Some wineries produced vinegar and flavorings for food; others tried to make grape juice and concentrate, but this market was controlled largely by the East Coast growers of Concord grapes. There were 919 bonded wineries in 1922 and only 268 in 1933, and 135 million gallons of wine were produced by bonded wineries during Prohibition.[27]

One unusual provision of the Volstead Act was that "the manufacture of liquor without permit shall not apply to a person manufacturing nonintoxicating cider and fruit juice exclusively for use in his home." The meaning of "nonintoxicating" was unclear from the legislation, however. Vineyard owners had urged Congress to include this provision. It was interpreted to mean that home winemaking was legal. As a result, vineyards not only survived during Prohibition, but thrived. The price of fresh grapes shot up as demand for grapes that could make wine increased. The higher prices encouraged growers to increase the size of their vineyards. As a result, the acreage of grapes grown in California almost doubled during Prohibition, and the grape crop outside California doubled as well. Most grapes went to manufacturers that produced juice and grape concentrate that could be used more readily by home winemakers.[28]

Vine-Glo was one such concentrate. It was made by a grape-marketing cooperative, Fruit Industries. With only water added to the concentrate, home winemakers had wine in two months. In 1929, the co-op hired Mabel Willebrandt, who had just resigned after serving for eight years as the U.S. assistant attorney general, the position responsible for prosecuting violations of the Volstead Act. Willebrandt was able to secure a $27 million loan from the Federal Farm Board for the co-op, which used the funds to build its home-winemaking business. Advertisements for Vine-Glo noted that it came in nine varieties, including claret, muscatel, port, riesling, sauterne, and tokay. Advertisements also proclaimed that it was "entirely legal in your home, but it must not be transported."[29]

Homemade wine, however, was not particularly enjoyable. As one writer noted in *Harper's* magazine, although Americans made lots of homemade wine, "most of it is terrible. There are probably few Italian-American families that do not make their own wine; but the wine they make, as a rule, can be endured only by stomachs toughened by a racial experience of hardship."[30]

Nevertheless, by 1930 more than 100 million gallons of wine were produced in homes, according to the Bureau of Prohibition, the federal enforcement agency. Wine consumption in the United States had increased by 66 percent above pre-Prohibition levels, thanks to home winemaking.[31]

Unfortunately, the wine bubble burst when the Eighteenth Amendment was repealed in December 1933. Then, California vineyards produced a very poor quality of wine in 1934. When other alcoholic beverages rebounded, home winemaking almost ceased. Americans drank about one gallon of wine per person annually before Prohibition. After repeal, this figure dropped to 0.5 gallon a person—mostly low-quality jug wine, which was often the beverage of choice for the less affluent, and sweet wines, which were often drunk by alcoholics. Wine consumption rates did not rise to pre-Prohibition levels until 1975.[32]

Despite difficulties, many new wineries were started after Prohibition and changes were under way in the American wine industry. In 1933, Ernest and Julio Gallo, who for years had grown and sold grapes, launched the E. & J. Gallo Winery in Modesto, California. The Gallo winery initially specialized in making inexpensive blended jug wines, but when the Gallo brothers saw that the market was moving away from inexpensive wines to varietal wines, they acquired vineyards in Sonoma, California, that could produce premium wines. Ernest and Julio Gallo were among the first American vintners to advertise their wines, and this paid off well. The Gallo Winery quickly became one of the largest wine companies in America.[33]

Frank Schoonmaker, an American wine writer and merchant, urged California vintners to stop using French names on their wine bottles and to call each wine after the grape variety used to make it. This system of labeling made it possible to judge each wine on its merits. Schoonmaker publicized the best California wines through his numerous books and articles. Louis M. Martini founded a winery in Napa Valley in California and became among the first American vintners to release vintage dated varietal wines.

Another reason for the eventual success of the California wine industry was the re-creation in 1935 of the Department of Viticulture and Enology at the University of California, Davis. It had been discontinued during Prohibition, but from the 1930s on, it would engage in research and extension activities to assist vineyards and wineries. During the following decades, this would greatly improve the quality of California wines.[34]

Post–World War II

World War II had several positive impacts on the American wine industry. For one thing, the war cut off the importation of European wines to the United States, and American vintners filled the void. Perhaps even more important was the fact that many American servicemen had been in Europe during the war; after the war, American tourists, businessmen, and government officials flooded Europe. Many Americans were exposed to good wine, and they wanted access to it on their return to the United States.

After the war, a number of new wineries were established in different parts of the United States. In 1945, Marvin Sands established the Canandaigua Industries Company in the Finger Lakes region of New York. This winery produced mainly bulk wine and fortified wines, especially dessert wines. It grew rapidly by acquiring other wineries and soon began marketing a wide number of brands, including Paul Masson, Manischewitz, Wild Irish Rose, and Inglenook.

The quality of American wines improved significantly in the 1960s. At the same time, Americans became more interested in wine. In the United States, wine tastings multiplied in number, and literature on the subject of wine grew. Other new wineries also were opened during that time, and their goal was to create the best wines possible. Robert Mondavi, whose father had immigrated from Italy in 1906, was a winemaker at the Charles Krug winery in northern California; he established his own winery in Oakville in Napa County, California, in 1966. Warren Winiarski, who had worked at a winery, established Stag's Leap Wine Cellars in Napa Valley, California, in 1970. The Chateau Montelena winery, in Napa Valley, was established in 1968 by Lee and Helen Paschich, dedicated home winemakers, and James L. Barrett, a southern California attorney. They had purchased an existing winery, but they installed the latest winemaking equipment and techniques. Chateau Montelena began producing wine in 1972.

Judgment of Paris

The French have been producing wine for a couple of thousand years, and French wine has been recognized among the best in the world. In contrast, Stag's Leap Wine Cellars and the Chateau Montelena winery were very new at winemaking, and the wineries and their wines were practically unknown. American wine critics had claimed that California wines were underrated and that some were as good as French wines, but few Europeans had even tasted California wines.[35]

When Steven Spurrier began selecting California wines for his blind wine tasting in 1976, he selected comparable French and California wines. The results of Spurrier's wine tasting were surprising: the California chardonnays took four of the top five slots at the first wine tasting, with California's Chateau Montelena in first place. In the second tasting, French Grand Cru

Bordeaux were compared with California cabernets. California's Stag's Leap Wine Cellars cabernet took the top spot.

Spurrier, whose business in Paris was devoted to selling French wines, never thought the California wines would score well in the tastings; neither did the French judges or the makers of the wines that had been tasted. Normally, the event would have been just one of hundreds of wine tastings held that year—except that the results were so contrary to expectations, and, just as important, there was a reporter present who wrote about the tasting results in *Time* magazine. The story subsequently was picked up by many American newspapers and magazines. California wines had "achieved recognition at the highest level of competition," as Thomas Pinney wrote in his history of American wine.[36]

The story about Spurrier's wine tastings was largely ignored by French news media; if mentioned, reporters played down the significance of the tastings and complained about the procedures employed by Spurrier. However, subsequent tastings using the same wine produced similar results. Within a few years, the wine world had been globalized to include not only American wines, but also wines from a number of other countries, including Chile, Australia, and South Africa. American wines have consistently scored well in tastings and wine judgings around the world.

The most important effect of the "Judgment of Paris"—as Spurrier's tasting was inevitably called—was the confidence that it gave American vintners to continue on the path of producing higher-quality wines. American wine gained new respect. It now was possible for California vintners to increase their prices and make premium wine profitable. In the years since, the production of jug wine has declined while the number of premium wines has escalated.

Another effect of the Judgment of Paris was that it convinced investors to jump into the wine business and launch their own wineries. It was not just the California wineries that gained from the Paris tasting—new wineries were established throughout the United States in the years that followed. In 1975, there were 578 wineries in the United States. By 2004, this number had increased to 3,726.[37] Six years later, in 2010, there were 6,223 wineries. Wineries can now be found in all states, but California has regularly topped the list with 49 percent of the total.[38] Wine store managers and customers have thousands of selections from which to choose. The number of new wines on the market "has seen a doubling in wine label applications over the past ten years to over 130,000 last year," reports Tyler Colman, author of *Wine*

Politics: How Governments, Environmentalists, Mobsters, and Critics Influence the Wines We Drink (2008).[39]

It was not just the number of wineries or the number of wines that have increased in the United States over the past several decades. American consumption of wine has increased as well. In 1935, Americans drank about 0.33 gallon of wine per person annually. In 1973, this figure had increased sixfold.[40] Since Spurrier's wine tasting in Paris in 1976, American annual wine consumption has increased to 2.8 gallons per person.

Postscript

♀ Frank Schoonmaker wrote the *Complete Wine Book* in 1934 and *Frank Schoonmaker's Encyclopedia of Wine* in 1975. He died the following year.

♀ Robert Mondavi sold his winery to Constellation Brands in 2004; he died in 2008 at the age of ninety-four.

♀ In the 1930s, Italian Swiss Colony was America's third largest winemaker. It was purchased by National Distillers in 1942 and resold to United Vintners eleven years later. Heublein, a food importer and distributor, acquired United Vintners in 1968 and transformed Italian Swiss Colony wines; it also shortened the name to just Colony.

♀ In 2002, the California winery founded by Louis M. Martini was acquired by E. & J. Gallo. Julio Gallo died in an auto accident in 1993; the brothers' autobiography was published the following year. Ernest Gallo died in 2007. The business that the Gallos created is now the second largest wine company in America.[41]

♀ The Canandaigua Industries Company began acquiring a wide range of wine and nonwine brands. In 2002, its name was changed to Constellation Brands. It is the world's largest wine company.

♀ Steven Spurrier sold Les Caves de la Madeleine and l'Académie du vin in 1989. He returned to the United Kingdom, where he is a wine consultant and journalist.

♀ Patricia Gallagher became the academic director and director of the wine department of Le Cordon Bleu in Paris and coauthored *Le Cordon Bleu Wine Essentials: Professional Secrets to Buying, Storing, Serving, and Drinking Wine.*

♀ George M. Taber, the *Time* reporter who covered the Judgment of Paris, wrote the book, *Judgment of Paris: California vs. France and the Historic 1976 Paris Tasting That Revolutionized Wine* (2005). *Bottle Shock*, an American comedy released in 2008, was loosely based on the 1976 tasting. A second film is in production based on Taber's book.

From the people
who brought you food.

What the French don't know about eating probably isn't worth eating, and that includes what they drink when they eat.

And they drink Perrier. They say the natural, sparkling spring water refreshes the palate, separates the flavours, and brings out the true taste of the food.

They drink a million bottles every day, and if you think that's extravagant, remember one thing. On the subject of food, they've never ever been wrong.

With added je ne sais quoi.

Advertisement for Perrier (ca. 1970s). (Courtesy of The Advertising Archives)

14

The Only Proper Drink for Man

BRUCE NEVINS was a veteran advertising executive. After graduating from the Stanford Business School, he worked in advertising at Benton & Bowles in Manhattan before moving on to Levi Strauss to become merchandising manager for international operations, where he spearheaded the advertising campaign that propelled Levi's jeans from $10 million operation to a $400 million operation in 1973. He left Levi Strauss and began consulting with small companies. In February 1976, while acting as a consultant for Pony Sporting Goods, a small Canadian firm, Nevins visited Paris to meet with one of the company's investors, Gustave Leven. Leven also happened to be the chairman of Source Perrier, a French company that sold bottled water throughout the world.[1]

Bottled Perrier water had been sold in the United States since the early twentieth century, but the Depression had pretty much killed the market for imported water. Even by the 1970s, few Americans were willing to pay high prices for imported sparkling water, especially when it tasted pretty much like club soda. Consumers also resisted paying for bottles of uncarbonated Poland Spring because it tasted about the same as tap water. There were many other bottled waters on the market and none sold very well in the United States, especially when compared to the wildly successful Coca-Cola and Pepsi-Cola soft drinks.

In the course of their conversation, Gustave Leven asked Bruce Nevins what he thought could be done to increase Perrier's sales in the United States. At the time, Perrier was sold in some restaurants but few stores. Distributors were unwilling to tie up funds in a product that just did not sell. Therefore, a small advertising campaign would just not work because there were few places where consumers could buy Perrier. Nevins had a ready answer: Perrier needed to be repositioned as a health and fitness drink. A massive marketing and public relations campaign could simultaneously promote Perrier to the public and to distributors. Impressed with Nevins's concept, Leven invited him to become president and part owner of Perrier's U.S. distribution company.

In his new capacity with Perrier, Nevins launched an advertising campaign in the spring of 1977 with a hefty television budget. The legendary actor and director Orson Welles was hired to do the voice-overs for the television commercials, in which he announced in his inimitable baritone: "There is a place in the south of France where there is a spring, and its name is Perrier."[2] The Perrier logo was splashed on the sides of distributors' trucks and café umbrellas. Customers were served chilled Perrier water in stores. Perrier sponsored fitness programs and running events in many cities, such as the New York Marathon; the company gave a substantial sum to the organizers of the marathon and supplied 7,500 bottles of Perrier for the runners, along with shorts and shirts bearing the Perrier logo.[3] This was just the beginning of a promotional effort that soon changed the entire bottled water industry and created a new product category. Within a decade, Americans everywhere—at work, play, home, or on the road—could be seen clutching their ever-present plastic bottles of brand-name water.

Background

Colonial Americans were not keen on drinking water, and for good reason: there was a constant fear about the quality and purity of water. This was particularly true in the southern colonies. Because the principles of sanitation were only dimly understood, colonists polluted their rivers; moreover, the colonists' wells were too shallow and too close to their outhouses. Water supplies, particularly in cities, often were contaminated with various disease-causing organisms, and epidemics of typhoid and other waterborne diseases were fairly common occurrences. Constantin-François de Volney, a

Frenchman who lived in the United States for three years beginning in 1795, wrote with disgust of Philadelphia's water, which received "filtrations from the cemeteries and privies" and, if kept for a few days, "acquired a cadaverous stench."[4]

There were solutions—effective and otherwise—for the problem of bad water. It could be boiled, for instance, or filtered. Catching and storing rainwater or getting water from a spring were other possibilities. Some people also believed that adding alcohol to water would purify it. That said, even water acknowledged as pure was considered second best to alcoholic beverages because water had no nutritional value. There was also a class stigma associated with drinking water—after all, even the poorest Americans had access to it.

As the temperance movement gained adherents during the early nineteenth century, water came to the fore as the answer to the evils of alcohol. William Alcott, an early-nineteenth-century physician, believed that water was "the only proper drink for man." In his writings, he bolstered this view with quotes from European medical authorities, one of whom proclaimed that "water drinkers are in general long livers, are less subject to decay of the faculties, have better teeth, more regular appetites, and less acrid evacuations, than those who indulge in a more stimulating diluent for their common drink." Alcott opposed the consumption of any alcohol, coffee, or tea.[5] Health reformer Sylvester Graham strongly concurred: "Pure water is, as a general rule, the most salutary liquid that can be used."[6]

Alcott's and Graham's successors became interested in hydropathy, an idea imported from Germany around 1840. Hydropathists believed in the "water cure," a therapeutic system for improving health that emphasized frequent bathing in and consumption of mineral waters. One hydropath, a doctor named Joel Shew, began publishing the *Water Cure Journal* in 1845.[7] Another leading hydropath, James Caleb Jackson, had been a farmer and then a newspaperman; throughout his early life, he had been plagued with ill health. In 1847, Jackson visited a spa and took the water cure. To his amazement, the water cure helped relieve his ailments. That same year, Jackson opened a hydropathic institute in Cortland County, New York; when it burned down eleven years later, he reopened the institute in Dansville, New York. Like Graham and Alcott, Jackson also banned the use of alcoholic beverages and such stimulants as tea and coffee.[8] His spa, like others that focused on hydropathy, was always all about the water.

Spas and Bottled Water

In Europe, spas had been frequented by the infirm (and the wealthy) since the sixteenth century. Cities like Bath, in England, and Baden Baden, in Germany, grew up around the reputation of their healing waters. It was believed that European spa water—which bubbled up in springs or was drawn from wells, steaming hot or icy cold, crystal clear or cloudy with minerals—had curative power and even, in some cases, spiritual powers.

In the nineteenth century, European health spas became increasingly popular with the general public, especially in France. One of the most famous healing springs is at Lourdes, in the Pyrenees; since the mid-nineteenth century, the sick and lame have drunk and bathed in the spring water at Lourdes, hoping for a miraculous cure. By the end of the nineteenth century, an estimated 300,000 French men and women visited spas annually. But the spas fell out of fashion in the early twentieth century, and their owners bottled water as a supplement to their income. In France alone, there were more than 1,100 registered springs. By the end of the century, a single small spa at Val-les-Bains exported several million bottles of Vals water annually.[9] Among the venerable European spa waters still bottled today are Apollinaris, Evian, Perrier, San Pellegrino, Vichy, and Vittel.

Although there are millions of natural springs in the United States, successful spas and bottling operations were established at only a few. Saratoga Springs, in upstate New York, had attracted the well-to-do well since well before the American Revolution, and it remained popular throughout the nineteenth and early twentieth centuries. In 1820, Dr. Darius Griswold began bottling water at Saratoga's Congress Springs. He stuck with the business for just a few years before leasing the bottling rights to the springs to Dr. John Clarke and Thomas Lynch in 1823. Clarke and Lynch promoted Saratoga Mineral Water, the first commercially successful bottled water in the United States. Their water was first distributed to New York City and then shipped to other eastern cities. By 1830, Dr. Clarke was shipping 1,200 bottles of water a day. By 1856, the company was distributing more than 11 million bottles annually throughout the United States and to foreign countries.[10]

As the nineteenth century progressed, more Americans ventured into the bottled water business. One of the most successful entrepreneurs was Hiram Ricker of Poland Spring, Maine. His father founded a spa there in the late eighteenth century, but it was not until 1845 that Hiram began bottling water in three-gallon clay jugs, which he sold for 15 cents each. Ricker's Poland

Spring water was sold in Boston, New York, and Philadelphia. When submitted to judges at Chicago's World's Columbian Exposition in 1893, Poland Spring water was awarded a Medal of Excellence for its "purity" and "natural medicinal properties." The company was so delighted with the award that it purchased the Maine State Building from the exposition and moved it to Poland Spring. In 1903, Poland Spring water won another award at the St. Louis World's Fair; this buoyed sales so much that by 1907 the company built a new bottling facility that incorporated all the latest technology.[11]

The secret to Poland Spring's success was its advertising, which claimed that it could cure "dyspepsia, liver and kidney complaint" and that it "purifies the blood." Virtually all spring water bottlers claimed similar health benefits for their products. Baldwin Cayuga Mineral Water, from upstate New York, was touted as a cure for "Bright's disease, diabetes, kidney afflictions, liver complaints, dyspepsia, all affections of the bladder, all forms of rheumatism, all skin diseases" and was a "wonderful tonic for general debility." The bottlers of Middletown Healing Spring Water, in Middletown Springs, Vermont, claimed that their product was "nature's remedy. Drink it. It will cure your ills. Cures kidney diseases, scrofula, salt rheum, erysipelas, dyspepsia, general debility, chronic consumption, catarrh, bronchitis, constipation, tumors, piles and cancerous affections." Drinking Chippewa Natural Spring Water, from Chippewa Falls, Wisconsin, was supposed to be "beneficial and remedial in cases of Typhoid Fever, Kidney Diseases, Rheumatism, Gout, Constipation, Indigestion, Headache, etc."[12]

With the passage of the Food and Drug Act by the U.S. Congress in 1906, transporting products with such extravagant medical claims across state lines became illegal. The U.S. Food and Drug Administration (FDA) took legal action against many companies for making such claims, including a number of bottled water companies. Partly as a result of such increased scrutiny, many spas and spring water bottlers shut down over the years. Several thrived, however, and their brand names, at least, have survived: Deer Park, founded in 1873 in western Maryland; Shasta Water, founded in 1889 at Shasta Springs, California; Arrowhead, founded in 1892 near San Bernardino, California; Sparkletts, founded in Los Angeles in 1925; Ozarka, founded in Texas in 1905; and Calistoga Mineral Water, founded in Napa, California, in 1924. These and other small regional companies mainly distributed five-gallon bottles of water, which were used for office and home water coolers. As bottling technology became more efficient, smaller bottles of water for table use became available and affordable for most Americans.[13]

In the early twentieth century, Americans also began taking an interest in bottled water from other countries. One early favorite was Perrier, which came from springs at Les Bouillens, a spa in the town of Vergèze in southern France. Les Bouillens was a fashionable nineteenth-century resort for both the French and English upper classes. For those unable to visit, the owners had been bottling and selling its carbonated water since 1863. In 1898, an entrepreneur and physician named Louis-Eugène Perrier, along with some financial backers, bought the spa. For five years, Perrier tried to sell the bottled water for health purposes, since it reputedly cured all sorts of illnesses. The business did not do as well as he had hoped, however, so he sold it to a British visitor named John Harmsworth, the younger brother of the founder of the London *Daily Mail*. Harmsworth, no doubt thinking that "Frenchness" would enhance its appeal to British consumers, renamed the water after Perrier. He designed a chubby twelve-ounce bottle of green glass and coined the slogan "The Champagne of Bottled Waters." In 1904, Harmsworth launched a massive advertising campaign in England, promoting Perrier as a good mixer for whiskey (for teetotalers, the ads pointed out, it was just as good with a slice of lemon). The ad campaign included huge front-page advertisements in the *Daily Mail*.[14] Medical professionals endorsed Perrier, calling it "the most perfect table water" that was "absolutely perfect in organic purity, while its very light mineralization makes it safe for table use."[15] Promotion and testimonials paid off, and sales of bottled Perrier skyrocketed.

Harmsworth distributed and promoted Perrier throughout the British Empire; sales outside England surged in such diverse places as India, Uganda, and Jamaica.[16] His next target was the United States. Even before Perrier was imported into the United States, the American medical profession had been alerted to its purported healing qualities.[17] In 1907, Harmsworth established an American subsidiary, Great Waters of France, to distribute Perrier, and it began a massive marketing campaign in the United States. Perrier water was identified as a "luxury from France" and as "the chosen table water of Europe." To distinguish Perrier from other sparkling waters, advertisements stressed that Perrier's carbonation contained "only natural gas," while other sparkling waters were charged "with artificial carbonic acid gas," which was condemned in Europe. Perrier was promoted as a health beverage, and advertisements carried endorsements from various sports figures. Jay Gould, who had recently won an international tennis match, was quoted as saying, "When taking violent exercise, I always drink Perrier, and I always find it most beneficial." And, he added, "Ladies greatly appreciate [it]."

Advertisements advised readers to "drink Perrier with your meals at your home, restaurant or club."[18] Perrier advertisements that appeared in 1909 proclaimed that France possessed "the finest table water in the world" and warned Americans of "imitations in similar shaped bottles."[19]

By 1914, Harmsworth was selling 2 million bottles of Perrier annually. Although World War I disrupted sales, after the war ended in November 1918 sales rebounded. When Prohibition took effect in 1920, Perrier's sales in America skyrocketed. Presumably, it was in demand as an alternative to alcoholic beverages or for use as a mixer with bootleg hooch.[20] Another downturn came when Prohibition was repealed during the depths of the Depression; few Americans could afford water imported from France, especially when bottled soft drinks sold for a nickel at the time.[21]

At the time of Harmsworth's death in 1933, production of Perrier water was at 19 million bottles per year.[22] A group of British shareholders took over the company, which thrived until World War II broke out in 1939. The German occupation of France disrupted the production of Perrier, and this time the war's end did not bring a resurgence of sales. Imports into the United States were limited, and the price of Perrier remained high because bottling the water at the spring and then shipping the heavy, bulky glass bottles was expensive.

In 1947 the British investors sold the Perrier company to Gustave Leven, an energetic businessman. Leven rebuilt the company through mergers and acquisitions of other spring water companies. He modernized the company's bottling plants and streamlined operations. He also engaged in massive promotional campaigns using endorsements from sports stars. By the early 1960s, Perrier was the largest advertiser in France. The effort paid off, and Perrier soon caught up with its two major competitors, Evian and Vittel.

Having reestablished his European operations, Leven was ready to tackle sales in the United States; the company's American subsidiary launched a major advertising campaign in 1963. Sales soon reached 500,000 bottles, but this was disappointing when compared with pre–World War II sales figures.[23] It seemed that Americans were just not ready to buy imported water, especially since most tap water in the United States was basically free, more or less palatable, and safe—or so most Americans believed.

Water Controversies

As American cities rapidly expanded in the nineteenth century, problems with municipal water supplies were almost inevitable. In 1832, more than 3,500 people in New York City died of cholera, a waterborne disease. Beginning in the late 1830s, city planners improved their water delivery systems and made other changes to guarantee an adequate and safe water supply. Water contamination, however, continued to be a problem in many cities. In 1900, about 200 of every 100,000 deaths in America were caused by waterborne diseases. By the beginning of the twentieth century, microbiologists had identified the waterborne bacteria—such as *Salmonella typhi, Shigella,* and *Vibrio cholerae*—that caused diseases. They also found that these bacteria could easily be killed by exposure to chlorine. In 1909, the city of Philadelphia added small amounts of compressed liquefied chlorine gas to its public water supply in order to eliminate bacteria, and many other municipal water systems followed suit. Safe tap water, of course, contributed to a decline in the consumption of bottled water.[24]

Chlorination was so effective in combating waterborne disease that scientists explored other ways of using drinking water to improve public health. During the 1930s, scientists working at the U.S. National Institutes of Health (NIH) found widely divergent rates of dental cavities in different communities in the United States. They hypothesized that higher levels of natural fluoride in the water were helping protect teeth against decay. To test their theory, NIH scientists fluoridated the water in Grand Rapids, Michigan, for five years (1945–1950). The experiment demonstrated a significant reduction of cavities among those living in Grand Rapids. As a result of this experiment, water fluoridation became an official policy of the U.S. Public Health Service, and, within a decade, fluoridation was widely used throughout the United States. Wherever fluoridation has been instituted, the incidence of tooth decay has dropped dramatically. Fluoridation was not without its critics, however. Citing various reasons, some dental and medical professionals, health-food advocates, religious groups, environmentalists, and libertarian groups opposed—and continue to oppose—fluoridation.

Simultaneously with the concern about fluoridated water came an increased interest in the environment. For decades, industrial waste and untreated sewage had been dumped into the nation's rivers and lakes—the water sources for many municipalities. The publication of the book *Silent Spring* by American biologist Rachel Carson in 1962 opened the eyes of many Americans to the dangers of pesticides and their impact on the environment. During the late 1960s and early 1970s, a large and vocal environmental movement emerged, leading to the passage of the Clean Water Act in 1972 and the Safe Drinking Water Act two years later. Although this legislation would greatly improve the quality of municipal water systems and other laws would outlaw dumping sewage and industrial contaminants into the nation's water system, many Americans remained concerned about drinking water that came out of a tap.

Promoting Bottled Water

Bottled water companies perceived an opportunity as the environmental controversies swirled around tap water. In 1971, Schweppes introduced its "pure drinking water" in hopes of cashing in on tap water concerns. Poland Spring promoted its bottled water with the slogan "City water . . . is enough to drive you to drink." Such ads did not endear the bottled water companies to city water planners, who protested that American tap water was perfectly safe.[25] Meanwhile, bottled water companies and manufacturers of home water filters continued to attack tap water, generating serious doubt about its quality in the minds of many Americans.[26] Bottled water sales continued to increase, and, in addition to the delivery of water-cooler-size quantities, bottled water subsequently was sold in more manageable one-gallon and smaller sizes at grocery stores and supermarkets.

The promotional campaign that Bruce Nevins conceived for Perrier in 1977 meshed perfectly with the rise of anti-tap-water sentiment. To distinguish Perrier from cheaper brands of seltzer and soda water, it was described as "naturally carbonated" by unique processes that took place deep underground within the Perrier spring. Nevins targeted the campaign at college students and young professionals who, he thought, would be susceptible to the dual message that Perrier was not just healthful (free of impurities, sodium, and caffeine) but also a chic drink without calories.[27]

Another message in Nevins's promotional campaign was that Perrier took "time to make" (by Mother Nature, of course) and was therefore in limited supply.[28] Retailers that ordered ten cases received only one, intensifying the demand for Perrier while enhancing its mystique. For many baby boomers, the cost of bottled water meant nothing, but drinking water imported from France had definite cachet. Before the ad campaign was launched, Perrier sales generated $500,000 annually; three years later, sales exceeded $5 million.[29]

Once the success of the Perrier model became apparent, other bottled water companies instituted aggressive advertising campaigns to increase their name recognition and sales. Evian, another French bottled water, was introduced in the United States in 1978. Despite such emerging competition, Perrier continued to dominate the industry until 1990.

Bottled Water Crises

The bottled water industry made a significant shift in 1989 when the polyethylene terephthalate (PET) plastic bottle was first used for Nestlé's bottled water.[30] The PET half-liter bottle was lightweight and recyclable. PET bottles had been used for soft drinks since 1977; after its introduction in the bottled water industry, it quickly became the industry standard for bottled water as well. However, PET bottles became a target for environmentalists, who pointed out that making and recycling plastic bottles consumes a disproportionate amount of energy. The recycling potential of the bottles was not a selling point for environmentalists because most PET bottles—an estimated 75 percent of the single-serve size—ended up in landfills (and in 2006 Americans bought and tossed out an estimated 50 billion bottles).[31] The proliferation of such bottles as waste is thus another environmental issue. The bottled water industry has been attacked by many environmental and other groups, such as the National Resource Defense Council, Corporate Accountability International, and the Center for Science in the Public Interest.

Despite issues raised by environmentalists, bottled water sales continued to increase and Perrier dominated the bottled water industry; by 1990, it produced 1.2 billion bottles annually, controlling almost 45 percent of the entire global bottled water market. In the United States, Perrier accounted for 80 percent of the imported water sold, but this was all to change in a matter of months.

Researchers at the Mecklenberg County Environmental Protection Department in Charlotte, North Carolina, were investigating industrial pollution; one of their assays required an absolutely pure solvent. For this solvent they selected Perrier water, long touted as the product of a pristine natural spring. When test results in January 1991 showed the presence of minute quantities of benzene, a known industrial pollutant and carcinogen, the investigators identified the source of the chemical as the Perrier spring water. The quantities found did not justify a recall, but investigators issued a health advisory warning consumers not to drink Perrier until more tests had been conducted.[32]

On February 9, 1990, Perrier management announced that the benzene contamination had been caused by a cleaning fluid mistakenly used on a machine that bottled water only for the North American market. Perrier's American subsidiary recalled all 72 million bottles in the United States.

Then, three days later, other scientists reported finding benzene in samples of Perrier water sold in their countries as well. Gustave Leven, the company's seventy-five-year-old chairman, immediately issued a worldwide recall.

Three months after the benzene crisis, Perrier relaunched its product, but now both the water and its reputation were held up to further scrutiny. An investigation by the New York State attorney general's office subsequently found that

> Perrier has not bubbled up to the ground surface to be collected and bottled without processing since at least 1956, but rather is pumped from the ground through a pipe, the natural gas is removed, and then recombined with the natural and processed gas. A significant portion of Perrier came from recent rainwater and was not of "ancient" origin. In addition, Perrier sometimes contained more than 5 milligrams of sodium per eight-ounce serving.

Perrier settled out of court without admitting guilt.[33] Thanks to another highly effective promotional campaign, sales of Perrier did eventually rebound, but it never again dominated the American bottled water industry the way it had before the benzene crisis.[34]

Despite these problems, the bottled water industry in America continued to grow exponentially. When Perrier fell from grace, other brands readily took up the slack. Evian, for instance, began a major marketing campaign in 1992, quickly becoming America's most purchased imported bottled water. Despite ongoing concerns about the purity and authenticity of bottled water, such concerns were just a minor blip on the road to stardom: sales of bottled water jumped from $115 million in 1990 to $4 billion just seven years later.[35]

As the bottled water industry expanded, a number of labeling problems have also emerged. Many consumers, understandably, believe that the water actually comes from a spring at the location named on the label. In many cases, however, production has expanded far beyond the capacity of the original springs. Today, for instance, Poland Spring water comes from an estimated 400 wells in Maine, and many other "spring waters" named for specific places have simply become brand names; the water is no longer sourced at a single location.

Expansion and Consolidation

Perrier began acquiring other water companies, starting with Calistoga Mineral Water in Napa, California, in 1980, followed by Arrowhead Spring Water in 1987. In 1992, Perrier was itself acquired by Nestlé, a Swiss corporation that is the world's largest food conglomerate. Nestlé had first entered the bottled water industry in 1969 by acquiring the French company that bottled Vittel water. A decade later, Nestlé began gobbling up American water bottlers: Poland Spring in 1980, Ozarka and Zephyrhills in 1987, and Deer Park in 1993. By 2006, Nestlé's bottled water brands controlled 32 percent of the U.S. market. Its largest brand is Poland Spring, which generated $600 million in sales annually by the early twenty-first century.[36]

A number of other corporations became involved in the bottled water industry. For example, the European food company Danone, best known in the United States for Dannon yogurt, acquired Evian in 1970. It was Danone that established a significant place for Evian in the U.S. market when the American bottled water industry took off in the 1970s.

As the bottled water industry revved up, various soft drink bottlers, notably PepsiCo and the Coca-Cola Company, also became interested in the field. With their existing facilities, these companies already had what they needed to bottle water easily, as well as experience in producing, distributing, promoting and selling bottled beverages. Both PepsiCo and Coca-Cola introduced bottled water products in the 1990s." PepsiCo introduced Aquafina in 1994, and Coca-Cola followed suit in 1999 with Dasani. Unlike spring waters, both Dasani and Aquafina are purified products that originate as city water, with the minerals, salts, bacteria, and pollutants filtered out. Dasani is simply filtered water, while PepsiCo adds minerals and other components to its Aquafina. Aquafina quickly became the largest-selling bottled water brand in the United States, followed by Dasani.

Bottled water was sold just about everywhere in the United States—at grocery stores, supermarkets, and bodegas; from street vendors; at sporting events; and from vending machines in schools, offices, gyms, and public buildings. In many restaurants, waiters were instructed to encourage customers to order bottled water, eventually generating an estimated $200 to $450 million annually in bottled water orders at American restaurants.[37]

Enhanced Water

Not content with selling simply spring or mineral water, bottlers eventually introduced enhancements to their products. Perrier, for instance, added lemon and lime flavors to its line of bottled water products back in the 1960s.[38] Inevitably, as the bottled water market grew, more and more unusual products appeared. There was glacial water from Iceland, artesian well water from Fiji, and spring water from a dormant French volcano. Bottled waters are also flavored with a wide variety of substances, such as cucumbers, fruit essences, and even black truffles—substances that supposedly add vitamins and minerals and improve the taste of the water. As one bottler admitted, "You might think that pure H_2O would taste the best." Jim Shepherd, Dasani's group director of research and development, said that pure water "tastes flat. All wrong. Water is not supposed to be that pure." Waters made in America add magnesium sulfate, potassium chloride, and sodium chloride, which give the water a "crispness" that Americans love. Europeans, however, want the chalky flavor and smooth feel given by calcium carbonate, noted Shepard.[39]

Enhancing or fortifying water to make it more "healthful" is now a huge industry worldwide. You can buy bottled water pepped up with caffeine, ginseng, vitamins, and "superoxygen," to name a few additives. Other companies jumped on the enriched-water wagon. One was Fuze Beverage, which was formed in 2000 in Englewood Cliffs, New Jersey. The company makes energy drinks and vitamin-enriched beverages. It was purchased for $250 million by the Coca-Cola Company in 2007.

Yet another company producing enriched water was Energy Brands, headquartered in Whitestone, New York, which operates under the name of Glaçeau. Founded in 1996, the company was acquired by the Coca-Cola Company in 2007 for $4.1 billion. Its calorie-free Smartwater was enhanced with electrolytes and marketed as a sports drink. Energy Brands also produces Fruitwater, a fructose-sweetened version of Smartwater that comes in raspberry, peach, grape, and lime flavors. Another of the company's products is Vitaminwater, which contains minute amounts of added vitamins but has sugar as its main ingredient (33 grams per 20-ounce bottle). The ad campaign for Vitaminwater said that it would keep the consumer "healthy as a horse" and bring about a "healthy state of physical and mental well-being." Advertisements also claimed that Vitaminwater "may reduce the risk of age-related eye disease."[40] The Center for Science in the Public Interest (CSPI) filed a class action lawsuit against Coca-Cola, claiming that Vitaminwater's marketing claims were likely to mislead consumers. CSPI's lead litigator described Vitaminwater as "no more than non-carbonated soda, providing unnecessary added sugar and contributing to weight gain, obesity, diabetes, and other diseases." In July 2010, a federal judge ruled against the Coca-Cola Company, stating that its advertising violated FDA regulations. Vitaminwater, as well as the similar PepsiCo product SoBe Lifewater, and many others—artificially colored and flavored, heavily sweetened, and "enhanced" with additives— have brought bottled water a long, long way from its origins as the purest, most natural beverage for humankind.

Bottled Water Today

Today, millions of Americans pay anywhere from 240 to 10,000 times more per gallon for bottled water than for tap water,[41] partly because they believe that bottled water is purer and safer than tap water. But the fact is that an estimated 90 percent of tap water in the United States meets or exceeds federal health and safety standards, while some bottled waters have been shown to be contaminated.[42]

Some people choose bottled water for its taste—or so they think. Whether bottled waters really taste different has been questioned. In the 1970s, during a radio interview with Perrier executive Bruce Nevins, Michael Jackson of KABC in Los Angeles presented Nevins with six unmarked samples of club soda and one of Perrier and asked him to pick out the Perrier. Nevins got it right—on the fifth try. In the years since then, many more formal blind taste tests have proved that most Americans are unable to distinguish carbonated bottled water from club soda or mineral water from tap water.[43]

Largely because of the economic downturn that began in late 2007, bottled water consumption in the United States dropped off in 2008 and 2009 for the first time in three decades. Even so, Americans still consume about 27.6 gallons of bottled water per person—more than any other beverage category except soft drinks. By 2010, bottled water accounted for an estimated 29 percent of total beverage consumption in the United States[44] and total annual revenues equaled almost $11 billion. As with many American products, the main reason for the success of bottled water was, and continues to be, promotion through advertising and marketing.[45]

Elizabeth Royte, author of *Bottlemania: How Water Went on Sale and Why We Bought It* (2008), summed up Americans' interest in bottled water:

> Over the last fifty years, bottled water went from a specialty item—for snobs and aesthetes—to a commodity widely available to anyone with a little cash and a desire to set him or herself apart from the tap-drinking masses. Molded by hundreds of millions of dollars' worth of advertisements, many of which traded on the sex appeal of supermodels, athletes,

and Hollywood celebrities, we started to think that bottled water was healthier and tastier than tap, and that it would somehow make us more attractive to the opposite sex.[46]

Postscript

Nevins left Perrier in October 1980 and has worked with a number of smaller companies since then, including the Adams Natural Beverage Company, which produced carbonated Napa Natural with 67 percent fruit juice and no preservatives. When the product was rolled out in March 1984, it had to be recalled as the high sugar content of the juice encouraged fermentation and the cans bulged and some exploded. It was reformulated—this time with 30 percent fruit juice—and rolled out again the following year with O. J. Simpson was selected as the company's spokesperson. The venture might have succeeded; however, at the same time PepsiCo came out with Slice—a 10 percent fruit juice—and its sales swamped those of Natural Napa, which promptly disappeared.[47] None of Nevins's other efforts have been as successful as his promotional campaign with Perrier.

Caramel Macchiato
A DELICIOUS BLEND OF CARAMEL, VANILLA, MILK AND COFFEE.

The Caramel Macchiato may be the trendiest thing to be seen with this winter. But if you're riding one of those funny little kiddie scooters at the same time, it doesn't count.

Advertisement for the Caramel Macchiato from Starbucks (ca. 2000s). (Courtesy of The Advertising Archives)

15

The Coffee Experience

A XEROX SALESMAN named Howard Schultz was offered a job with Perstorp, a Swedish company just starting up an American operation to sell housewares and building supplies in 1979. After a stint as a salesman with the company, Schultz was placed in charge of the firm's twenty American sales representatives. He soon noticed an anomaly in the sales figures: a very small chain of stores in Seattle was ordering an awful lot of Hammarplast plastic drip coffeemakers. In 1981, Schultz traveled to Seattle to find out more about the small chain called Starbucks Coffee, Tea and Spice.

Starbucks had only four outlets—all in Seattle—but Schultz liked what he saw. The stores were filled with the aroma of roasting coffee beans from around the world—Costa Rica, Sumatra, Kenya, and Ethiopia—and each outlet featured an array of red, yellow, and black Hammarplast coffeemakers. Each store served coffee, but primarily as samples intended to educate customers about the various beans and coffee blends.

Schultz met with Starbucks's owners, Jerry Baldwin and Gordon Bowker, and stayed in touch with them during the following year. In September 1982, Schultz proposed that Baldwin and Bowker hire him to help grow the company. This was a leap of faith by Schultz, who already had a great job with Perstorp; the small Seattle-based chain could not match the salary or benefits he enjoyed with the Swedish firm. But Baldwin and Bowker offered equity in a company that Schultz thought had great potential, and that was good enough for him.[1]

Over the next two years, Schultz learned the coffee business from the bottom up. In the spring of 1983, he attended a conference in Italy, where he fell in love with the ubiquitous Italian espresso bars. It was not just the coffee that impressed him, but the convivial, customer-friendly coffee experience. On his return to Seattle, Schultz urged Starbucks's owners to install espresso bars in their stores. Baldwin and Bowker, however, were absorbed with purchasing Peet's Coffee & Tea chain in San Francisco, and they did not pursue the concept.

Schultz, however, was able to test his idea in a new Starbucks—the chain's sixth store—which opened in Seattle in April 1984. The concept proved a success, but Jerry Baldwin and Gordon Bowker had no interest in such a business. They were willing, however, to help Schultz launch such a chain. In 1985, Schultz left Starbucks and, with about forty investors (including Jerry Baldwin from Starbucks), launched an espresso bar chain called Il Giornale (Italian for "the daily").

The first Il Giornale store, which debuted in April 1986, was a success from day one. The following year, Baldwin and Bowker decided to sell their business—consisting of six stores plus a roasting plant—to Il Giornale for $3.8 million. Schultz and his investors jumped at the offer, and the combined company was named Starbucks Corporation. With the formation of Starbucks Corporation, American coffee, which had long been simply a cheap shot of caffeine, would soon evolve into a rich, aromatic premium beverage going for several dollars per cup.

Background

The coffee plant (*Coffea arabica*) likely originated in Ethiopia, but early on it spread to the Arabian Peninsula. Beginning around 1500, coffee cast its spell throughout the Middle East, where it became a favored beverage in the Ottoman Empire. During the seventeenth century, coffee drinking caught on in Europe. Coffeehouses had opened in England by 1634, and coffee arrived in the British North American colonies shortly thereafter. Directions for preparing and serving coffee appeared in British cookbooks by the mid-seventeenth century; this 1662 recipe was likely followed in North America as well:

TO MAKE THE DRINK THAT IS NOW MUCH USED
CALLED COFFEE

The coffee-berries are to be bought at any Druggist, about three shillings the pound; take what quantity you please, and over a charcoal fire, in an old pudding-pan or frying-pan, keep them always stirring until they be quite black, and when you crack one with your teeth that it is black within as it is without; yet if you exceed, then do you waste the Oyl, which only makes the drink; and if less, then will it not deliver its Oyl, which must make the drink; and if you should continue fire till it be white, it will then make no coffee, but only give you its salt. The Berry prepared as above, beaten and forced through a Lawn Sive, is then fit for use.

Take clean water, and boil one-third of it away what quantity soever it be, and it is fit for use. Take one quart of this prepared Water, put in it one ounce of your prepared coffee, and boil it gently one-quarter of an hour, and it is fit for your use; drink one-quarter of a pint as hot as you can sip it.[2]

Coffee was not a particularly important beverage in colonial America, but for many patriotic Americans, it displaced tea as the beverage of choice during the American War of Independence. Still, by the war's end in 1783, Americans consumed, on average, less than an ounce of coffee beans per person per year. In the years after the war, however, coffee consumption increased. In 1791, Americans imported less than 1 million pounds of coffee annually; five years later, imports hit 62 million pounds.[3]

During the early nineteenth century, Americans craved coffee in ever-increasing quantities, and supply could not keep up with demand. At the time, coffee was mainly grown in Arabia and the Caribbean islands. Because of the increased demand, coffee prices jumped from 42 cents per pound in 1810 to $1.08 in 1812. As fortunes were made in the coffee trade, more coffee plantations were established in Brazil and the Dutch colonies of Java and Sumatra. As these plantations came online, coffee prices started to fall—to 30 cents per pound in 1823 and bottoming out at 8 cents seven years later. While this decline in price hurt coffee producers, it was a boon to U.S. consumers. Many Americans became hooked on coffee drinking when the federal government abolished import taxes on coffee; in 1832, U.S. consumption jumped even more.[4] Americans drank three pounds of coffee in 1830. By 1840, this number reached more than five pounds; nine years later, it topped eight pounds.[5]

By the 1830s, coffee surpassed tea as America's hot beverage of choice. Tea was more expensive; after all, it was associated with the old colonial power, Great Britain, whereas coffee was identified as a purely American beverage. Coffee also had a greater caffeine payload, making it better suited to a new country undergoing rapid growth. In addition, tea had a lingering feminine association, whereas coffee quickly became the more "manly" choice. In the mid-nineteenth century, immigrants to the United States from Germany, Scandinavia, and other countries already had established coffee traditions at home, which further upped the demand for coffee.

Total coffee consumption declined during the Civil War, largely due to the blockade that prevented Southerners from consuming much coffee. However, Union soldiers were given 0.1 pound of coffee as part of their daily rations; even men who had not been coffee drinkers soon took a liking to the bracing beverage. As one soldier later wrote, "It was coffee *at* meals and *between* meals; and the men going on guard or coming off guard drank it at all hours of the night." After the war, coffee consumption revived and continued to accelerate, hitting nine pounds per person in 1882.[6] The problem was, at least according to *Good Housekeeping*, "that nine-tenths of that decoction which passes under the name of coffee, is unworthy to be so called."[7]

Anti-Coffee

Some members of the medical establishment strongly endorsed the drinking of coffee. A 1835 article on coffee's virtues, published in the *North American Archives of Medical and Surgical Science*, proclaimed that "coffee is our gold, and in the place of its libations we are in the enjoyment of the best and noblest society."[8] This view, however, was not universal. The medical doctor William Alcott in Massachusetts proclaimed that the effects of coffee resembled those produced by drinking "moderate quantities of spirits, and by many narcotic or poisonous medicines." Coffee sipped in small quantities reduced "slight nervous headaches and other nervous affections," but if drunk "very strong, and in large quantity, all admit that it is powerfully sedative."[9]

Sylvester Graham, a vegetarian health reformer from New England, believed that coffee was "among the most powerful poisons of the vegetable kingdom."[10] Graham's works were studied by a young medical doctor named John Harvey Kellogg, who would eventually become the director of the famous Battle Creek Sanitarium in Battle Creek, Michigan. Kellogg identified coffee drinking as a "grave menace to the health of the American people."[11] He refused to serve coffee at the sanitarium; instead, he developed a number of coffee substitutes, including a caffeine-free bran-and-molasses beverage he called caramel coffee.

One visitor to the Battle Creek Sanitarium, Charles W. Post, particularly liked the coffee substitutes served there, and he decided to formulate his own version.[12] In 1894, Post perfected a cereal-based beverage made from wheat berries, glutinous bran, and New Orleans molasses. He called it Postum and began manufacturing the beverage in his barn in Battle Creek, Michigan.

Post advertised his product in the local Battle Creek newspaper and also visited local grocers and offered them a deal: they did not have to pay for the new product until they sold it. He followed up with another unusual offer: he would supply free sample cups of Postum in hopes that customers would buy some on the spot. The "free sample" ploy, unusual at the time, brought in droves of customers; frantic grocers had to reorder more Postum just a week later. In its first year, the product generated an unprecedented profit of $174,000. In 1896, Post incorporated the Postum Cereal Company to manufacture and sell his grain-based coffee substitute, which he marketed as just the thing for "jangled nerves." He also used scare tactics against coffee, stating that coffee was "an alkaloid poison and a certain disintegrator of brain tissues."[13] Particularly helpful to the product's success was the Postum Cereal Company's Battle Creek address, which misleadingly suggested a connection with Kellogg's sanitarium. From his initial success with Postum, Post went on to create a cereal empire—and so, of course, did the Kellogg Company, under the leadership of John Harvey Kellogg's brother, Will.

Ground Coffee

Compared with making tea by pouring water over tea leaves, brewing coffee is a complicated process. This is one reason why it took a while for coffee to catch on in America. At first, unbranded green coffee beans were sold from open barrels, scooped out by the customer or grocer, and then weighed and priced. Exposed to air, odors, and dust, the beans, "from long transit and resting in the small stores, became tough and tasted as much of codfish and oil as [they] did of coffee," as one observer reported.[14]

People roasted the coffee beans at home and ground them as needed. Coffee roasting is an art, and roasting beans in a nineteenth-century oven was unpredictable. Beans that scorched were ruined, whereas underroasted beans did not develop their full flavor. Home roasting of the beans often produced an acrid brew that had to be camouflaged with milk, cream, or sugar. Roasted coffee was available commercially in big cities, but if it sat in a store for very long it lost its flavor.

In the mid-nineteenth century, a Pittsburgh grocery wholesaler named John Arbuckle thought that there must be a better way to roast coffee. His family had emigrated from Scotland to Allegheny, Pennsylvania (now part of Pittsburgh), where Arbuckle was born in 1839. At age twenty, he formed a wholesale grocery business with his uncle; when his uncle retired and his younger brother joined the firm, the business was renamed Arbuckles & Company. Two events in the early 1860s enabled Arbuckle to build the nation's largest coffee company: the invention of the first efficient industrial coffee roaster and the mechanization of paper bag manufacturing.

Inventor and manufacturer Jabez Burns addressed a key problem in coffee roasting—the fact that the beans rested directly on a hot surface, where they could quickly scorch. In 1864, Burns devised a screw-like device that pushed beans out when the door was open. The equipment was too bulky and expensive for home use, but it was ideal for large-scale coffee-roasting operations.

The manufacture of paper bags also underwent a change. They had been sold commercially in Great Britain since the 1840s, but the machinery for making them left much to be desired. Several new inventions in the 1850s, however, made the manufacturing of paper bags more efficient. In 1862, America's first paper bag factory opened in New York City.

John Arbuckle began using the new technologies for coffee roasting and paper bag manufacturing to bring consumers consistently tastier coffee. Arbuckle carefully packed roasted beans by the pound in paper bags and distributed them through his firm's wholesale operation.[15] This made things easier for the grocer, who did not have to scoop out the beans from barrels and weigh and price them. It also proved to be a boon to coffee drinkers, who would no longer have to fuss with hit-or-miss home roasting. Three years later, in 1868, Arbuckle claimed to have found another way to preserve the freshness of roasted beans. After experimenting with various substances such as gelatin, isinglass, and Irish moss, he began glazing the beans with a mixture of egg whites and sugar, which helped keep the beans fresh longer.[16]

Packing the roasted beans in paper bags also allowed the name of Arbuckle's company, and the coffee's brand name, to be printed on it. As a result, coffee beans were no longer a cheap generic commodity; they became an upscale brand-name item. There were already some other branded coffees on the market, but Arbuckle's Ariosa, which debuted in 1873, quickly became the most popular brand in America.

The Arbuckle brothers also pioneered in the use of advertising gimmicks, including the trade card—a colorful, collectible token tucked into each bag of coffee. One Ariosa series consisted of fifty cards, one for each U.S. state and territory; other series had scenes from foreign cities and countries. Children collected the cards, trading them and pasting them into albums, and the Arbuckle brothers knew that the young collectors would beg their parents to buy more Ariosa coffee until the set was complete. The state maps that originally appeared on Ariosa cards were later reprinted as an atlas and distributed to schools.[17]

Adulteration

Processed and manufactured foods proliferated in the late nineteenth century, and with them came adulteration practices, such as adding copper to canned peas to intensify their color. Coffee was easy to adulterate with cheaper (if not unhealthful) ingredients, such as roasted peas, beans, or grains, which were almost undetectable once ground with the coffee. Some grocers sold "coffee" made entirely from legumes or grains and completely free of any actual coffee.[18]

Counterfeit and adulterated coffee was a common problem throughout the nineteenth century. In an 1881 study, Francis Thurber, a New York City grocery distributor, deplored "the adulteration of coffee and the vast scale on which it is practiced" and noted that despite what was being sold in many grocery stores, "a primary requisite for making a good cup of coffee is, of course coffee."[19] Thurber's efforts and those of others enticed newspapers to examine coffee adulteration; newspapers, such as the *New York Times*, alerted readers to these problems by publishing articles with headlines, such as "Poison in Every Cup of Coffee." Beginning in 1879, Thurber pushed for a national pure food law; he sponsored a national contest for a model pure food statute and, once it was selected, he promoted it throughout the country. Versions of the model statue eventually were enacted in New York, Massachusetts, and New Jersey.[20] These early laws contributed to the passage of the Pure Food and Drug Act by U.S. Congress in 1906.

Proliferation and Consolidation

Although some medical professionals continued to speak out against coffee, sales continued to increase. The temperance movement played a role in encouraging coffee consumption. Despite initial concerns with the stimulating qualities of coffee and tea, temperance advocates eventually concluded that these beverages were good alternatives to alcohol. Temperance coffeehouses, or "temperance drinking saloons," were launched in various cities to counter the ubiquitous bars and taverns. Coffeehouses offered a place where people could socialize without being tempted by strong drink. As one observer commented, "A coffee-house is a liquor saloon without liquor. It is a place where a workingman can get a well-cooked meal at a cheap rate, where he can read his newspaper and enjoy his game of chess or draughts without being preached at. It is the saloon, less the saloon's evil concomitants."[21]

Another reason for the increase in coffee consumption was the introduction of canned coffee by Chase & Sanborn. In 1864, Caleb Chase had gone into the coffee-roasting business in 1864; three years later, James Sanborn moved from Maine to Boston and eventually also began roasting coffee. Chase and Sanborn formed a partnership in 1878, and subsequently they sealed ground coffee in cans to prevent staling from air. The cans were easy to distribute, and they were more protected than the paper bags championed by Arbuckle.

The problem was that air was sealed into the can along with the ground coffee, and staling continued to be a problem. The process would not be perfected until 1900 when vacuum seal canning technology was first used by Hills Brothers. Austin Hills and Reuben Hills launched a coffee business in San Francisco in 1878. They claimed that their vacuumed sealed coffee would "keep fresh forever" if the seal was unbroken.[22]

The Hills brothers were not the only coffee roasters in San Francisco. James Folger had arrived in the city in 1850. After trying to make money by prospecting, he began working at a coffee company, which was a success among miners. Folger went into partnerships with others; finally in 1881, he formed J. A. Folger & Company. Yet another coffee roaster was formed in San Francisco by a German immigrant named Max J. Brandenstein in 1881. The company he created would later be named MJB Company.[23]

Coffee roasters were launched in other American cities. In Nashville, Joel Cheek launched Maxwell House. In New York, the A&P grocery store chain, originally just a tea importer and distributor, began selling other products, including coffee, after the Civil War. Its model was to import products itself and sell them cheaper than other companies, which had to pay middlemen. The company entered the coffee-roasting business by launching a wholly owned subsidiary, the American Coffee Corporation, which purchased coffee directly from growers in other countries. It marketed its coffee under its brand name Eight O'Clock Coffee.

By the 1920s, coffee had become ubiquitous in American homes, luncheonettes, diners, cafeterias, cafés, coffee shops, restaurants, and emerging fast food chains. Coffeehouses provided a place where Americans could socialize legally, and many were opened during Prohibition. Coffee consumption increased by about two pounds a person. During the Depression, coffee consumption accelerated up to almost fifteen pounds a person.[24]

During the mid-twentieth century, the coffee roaster industry consolidated. In 1929, Chase & Sanborn was acquired by Royal Baking Powder Company, which renamed itself Standard Brands. Postum bought Maxwell House Coffee and renamed the company General Foods, which also owned Yuban and Sanka, a decaffeinated coffee released in 1932. General Foods was acquired by the tobacco company Phillip Morris in 1985 and later was merged with Kraft Foods. Procter & Gamble acquired Folgers coffee in 1963.

Instant coffee had been around since 1901, but it was not a commercial success until 1938, when Nestlé, the Swiss food multinational, released its coffee, Nescafé. It was used extensively by American armed forces during World War II, and it became popular in America after the war. Nestlé acquired Hills Brothers Coffee, MJB, Chase & Sanborn, and Chock Full o' Nuts. In 1999, Nestlé sold many of these brands to Sara Lee Corporation, which in turn sold them in 2005 to Massimo Zanetti Beverage Group, headquartered in Bologna, Italy.

For years, American coffee was primarily a cheap generic beverage of widely varying quality—gulped down at breakfast, lunch, dinner, and as a pick-me-up throughout the day. One of the more successful coffee-dispensing operations was founded by William Rosenberg in 1946 in suburban Boston, where he began selling coffee, sandwiches, and baked goods from trucks. Within three years, his company was operating 140 trucks. In 1948, he saw that doughnuts were in high demand, and he opened a small doughnut shop called the Open Kettle in Quincy, Massachusetts. Two years later, he renamed it Dunkin' Donuts. In 1955, he sold his first franchise, and the franchise operations quickly expanded. In 1966, he opened the Dunkin' Donuts University to help franchisors run their shops. In 1968, there were 334 outlets; by 1986, there were 6,900. Fresh-brewed coffee was an important part of the success of Dunkin' Donuts.

Premium Coffee

As middle-class Americans began traveling abroad after World War II—most commonly to Italy or France—they discovered specially blended, dark-roasted, carefully brewed European-style coffee. Not just espresso and cappuccino, but even an "everyday" cup of coffee in Europe was a surprising new experience. Beginning in the 1960s, some specialty stores in the United States began selling "premium" coffee beans with full flavor and exotic names from unusual places. Along with the beans came home roasters, coffee grinders, brewing systems, and a panoply of coffee-making accessories.

Dutch immigrant Alfred Peet was at the forefront of the shift toward better coffee. Peet had learned about coffee while working for his father, who was a coffee trader in the Netherlands. In 1948, Peet struck out on his own and moved from the Netherlands to Indonesia, then a Dutch colony, where he was employed by the government as a tea taster. He also tasted the rich coffees available on the island of Java. When Indonesia gained its independence in 1950, Peet immigrated to New Zealand; five years later, he moved to San Francisco and took a job with an American coffee importer.

In the San Francisco beatnik culture of the 1950s and early 1960s, coffeehouses were the meeting places of choice, but the coffee served along with poetry and folk music at these venues was mediocre at best. Alfred Peet concluded that America was ready for strong roasted premium coffee. In 1966, he opened Peet's Coffee & Tea in Berkeley, near the University of California campus. The shop sold whole coffee beans and coffeemaking equipment; in order to win customers over to his pricier beans, Peet set up a coffee bar to introduce and explain high-quality dark-roasted coffee blends. There was no sign out front, but the business took off, and soon customers were queuing up for a taste of Peet's strong, dark coffees.

Two of Peet's customers—Jerry Baldwin and Gordon Bowker, who were roommates at the University of San Francisco—were reluctant to leave that memorable brew behind after graduation when they both relocated to Seattle, Bowker's hometown. The two men ordered coffee beans by mail from Peet's until Bowker found an alternative—Murchie's Tea & Coffee in Vancouver, Canada. While returning from a cross-border coffee pickup, Bowker had an idea: Why not open a premium coffee store in Seattle? After discussing this idea with Jerry Baldwin and a neighbor, Zev Siegl, the three men agreed that it was a viable concept. Each contributed $1,500 of their own money and borrowed an additional $5,000 for their startup. They rented space in Pike Place Market, near the Seattle waterfront, and opened a store they called Starbucks Coffee, Tea and Spice. (The store was named after the first mate in Herman Melville's *Moby-Dick*.) The three partners initially bought coffee beans from Peet's and sold them along with associated coffee equipment, such as a drip coffeemaker manufactured by the Swedish firm Hammarplast.

When Howard Schultz took over Starbucks in 1987, it was still a local chain with just seventeen stores; premium coffee beans and equipment for roasting, grinding, and brewing were Starbucks's stock-in-trade. Schultz added coffee bars to the stores, offering a variety of premium brewed coffee beverages. Then he started opening outlets outside Seattle; by 1992, Starbucks had 165 stores. By 1999, there were 1,900 Starbucks stores; three years later, the number had more than tripled, to 6,400 worldwide.

In addition to opening stores in the United States, Starbucks expanded abroad to Canada (1987), Japan (1996), the United Kingdom (1998), and then to Continental Europe and the Middle East. Starbucks opened its first store in China in 1999. By 2010, the company had 400 stores in China and 400 more in Hong Kong, Macao, and Taiwan. By 2011, Starbucks had 16,858 company-owned and franchised outlets in more than fifty countries and territories, and Starbucks had become the largest coffee store chain in the world.

It was not just premium coffee that Starbucks sold: it sold an *experience*, a customer-friendly place where patrons could sit over a cup (or more) of coffee for hours, chatting with friends, reading, or, at a later time, surfing the Web with free wireless Internet access. Coffee consumption became an act of connoisseurship, and Starbucks regulars became educated about coffee varieties and sources—Kenya, Guatemala, Sumatra, or Java—and about concepts such as fair trade (which guarantees customers that the workers on coffee plantations operate under decent conditions and that the coffee is grown in an environmentally responsible manner.) Starbucks patrons did not just ask for "a cup of coffee," but they learned to specify the size, bean, drink, and dairy (or nondairy) additive that they wanted. The era of the "half double decaffeinated half-caff with a twist of lemon," as parodied by Steve Martin in *L.A. Story*, had dawned. Company-trained baristas custom-crafted each customer's order and served it at exactly the right temperature. Although coffee was its raison d'être, Starbucks was more about the whole package: the music, lights, design, ambiance, and service.[25]

Coffee Wars

The success of Starbucks set off a chain reaction in the coffee industry. In 1971, Kraft, the owner of Maxwell House, purchased a Swedish company that marketed Gevalia Kaffe in Scandinavia. A little more than a decade later, in 1983, Kraft began low-key mail-order marketing of Gevalia in the United States. When Starbucks went national in the 1990s, Kraft began mass marketing Gevalia as a premium coffee. It also offered a variety of other premium brands, including Italian Espresso Roast, Irish Cream, Rich French Roast, Master Blend, and Colombian Supreme. Other companies also began developing their own specialty coffees. In 2003, Procter & Gamble began advertising Millstone Coffee's Mountain Moonlight, an organic Fair Trade–certified coffee, for purchase online at a price of $8.99 for a ten-ounce bag. Starbucks, which still retailed coffee beans and ground premium coffees in its stores, responded to the competition by moving into the mass market in 2009 with Via, an instant coffee, which was sold in both Starbucks outlets and supermarkets.

Fresh-brewed coffee had long been an important part of the success of America's fast food chains. Dunkin' Donuts, which claimed to serve "America's favorite coffee," sold its 8 billionth cup of coffee in 1999. Despite this success, the company viewed Starbucks as a threat—and an opportunity. In 2002, the company launched a new line of its own premium coffees and coffee products, including espressos, lattes, and cappuccinos. Sales were phenomenal.

Starbucks struck back by moving into the mass market in 2003, when it acquired Seattle's Best Coffee and began selling this lower-priced product in places like J. C. Penny's department stores, movie theaters, Taco Bell, Subway, Borders, and Barnes & Noble. By 2011, Seattle's Best Coffee was being distributed in more than 40,000 locations, including convenience stores and vending machines.

McDonald's entered the competition by expanding its McCafé, a concept that had been developed in Australia in 1993. The McCafé is a separate area within McDonald's restaurants that has its own counters and sells pastries, premium coffee, mocha frappés, and cappuccinos. The intent of McDonald's move was to compete with the wildly successful Starbucks franchises, but the McCafé offerings are notably cheaper. McDonald's set up McCafés in its outlets in Canada and Europe, and also introduced premium coffee in most of its U.S. stores. With the addition of McCafe, McDonald's revenues jumped an estimated 20 to 25 percent, and high-end coffee now accounts for an estimated 6 percent of McDonald's total sales. Burger King responded to McDonald's success by introducing Seattle's Best Coffee in more than 7,000 of its establishments.

Responding to such changes at competitors, Dunkin' Donuts again raised the ante by creating partnerships with other companies—including Jet-Blue, Procter & Gamble, and the Hess Corporation—to distribute Dunkin' Donuts coffee at retail outlets, such as supermarkets and service stations, and on airlines. Like Starbucks, the company also rapidly expanded its coffee outlets abroad.

The success of coffee sales at Starbucks, Dunkin' Donuts, and McDonald's encouraged other chains to develop brands of their own. Tim Horton's, a Canadian sandwich chain with 600 outlets in the United States, spiced up its coffee offerings to include specialty blends and a variety of hot beverages (Caramel Café Mocha, Flavored Cappuccino) and iced beverages (Iced Mocha, Mocha Iced Cap, Iced Cappuccino). The Boston Market fast food chain, which originally specialized in rotisserie chicken but now offers a broader menu, began using Green Mountain Coffee Roasters' Keurig single-cup coffeemakers. The coffee wars continue as companies try to outdo their competitors and increase their market share.

Today, coffee remains one of America's most consumed beverages. According to Mark Pendergrast, author of *Uncommon Grounds: The History of Coffee and How It Transformed Our World* (2010),

> Today, high-quality all-Arabica beans are widely available through local roasters, the Internet, or in one-way valve bags in supermarkets. Single origins are popular from all over the world. Even canned mass-produced coffee has improved, as has instant coffee. The beverage is usually brewed with a drip-over method or press-pot infusion. Per capita consumption has stabilized. Coffee has also become the avatar for Fair Trade and other certifications.[26]

Starbucked

The "Starbucks effect" has been praised—and criticized—by journalists and academics alike. Starbucks did not invent premium coffee, nor did it invent the convivial coffeehouse experience. Yet the company weaned many Americans away from mediocre generic coffee and instilled a craving for high-end coffee and specialty coffee drinks. Coffee drinking became an "experience" with caffè lattés, espressos, and a wide variety of other premium beverages. Starbucks also changed American cities with its proliferation of outlets—there is likely one within five miles of most Americans—and it created both a challenge and an opportunity for fast food chains to improve the quality of their beverages. As Joseph Michelli, author of *The Starbucks Experience*

(2007), concluded, "Not only has Starbucks changed American business, but it has also changed American culture and affected culture worldwide."[27]

Although Starbucks has no close national competitors, the company created a climate conducive to the establishment of independent coffee outlets and regional chains, such as Caribou Coffee and New England Coffee. During a twenty-five-year period beginning in 1982, specialty coffees jumped from 2 percent of the coffee market in the United States to slightly more than 20 percent. By 2007, 63 percent of adults reported drinking premium coffees.[28] Starbucks and its competitors also moved into the cold-beverage field, and these icy coffee drinks have challenged the soda industry. As a result of Starbucks's efforts to promote its coffee, the entire category reaped higher prices and profits.[29] Starbucks not only has captivated Americans with the Starbucks experience, but has expanded aggressively abroad, and today it is the largest coffee chain in the world.

Postscript

Charles Post's coffee substitute, Postum, was withdrawn from the market in 2007.

When John Arbuckle died in 1912, his estate was valued at $33 million. The company he founded survived his death. In 1914, it launched Yuban coffee—supposedly John Arbuckle's private blend, which he had served only on special occasions. But soon after Yuban's introduction, the company declined. It sold most of its coffee brands, with the exception of Yuban, to General Foods in 1933. Today, Yuban is owned by Kraft Foods.

Alfred Peet died at age eighty-seven in 2007. The company he founded, Peet's Coffee & Tea, has flourished, and today has more than 200 outlets, mainly in California and four other states. Peet's coffee is also sold in 250 supermarkets nationwide.

Jerry Baldwin, one of the founders of Starbucks, became the chairman of Peet's, a position he held until 2001 when Peet's went public. Baldwin remains a director of the company.

Howard Schultz remains the chairman, president, and chief executive officer of Starbucks. According to *Forbes*, he is among America's wealthiest men, and *Time* has recognized him as one of the most influential people in the world.

Epilogue

IF THE FIFTEEN TURNING POINTS presented in this book tell us anything about American beverage history, it is that change is endemic. The most significant turning point was the first: colonial diversity. None of the beverages drunk by Native Americans prior to the colonial period—water excluded—were adopted by European settlers.

The colonists, coming from different countries and cultures, brought their own beverage preferences and traditions with them, so no one drink predominated. Of course, as settlers in a new world, the colonists had to adapt their beverage recipes and formulas, as well as their drinking habits. The barley that grew in America was not the same variety that grew in Europe, so neither American ale nor beer nor whiskey was quite the same. The grape varieties used for winemaking in the Old World did not grow in North America, so colonial winemakers had to adapt to new varieties of grape. Moreover, new political enmities and alliances sometimes made supplies of certain beverages unavailable, as was evident from the Boston Tea Party.

Resourceful colonists used what was available in America. Beer was made from molasses or persimmons, and wild North American grapes became the basis for a very different style of wine. A serviceable tea could be brewed from the leaves of wild plants. Over the succeeding centuries, as new immigrant groups arrived in America, they too contributed to this diversity. Of necessity, they also adapted their favorite drinks to American ingredients and customs. Today, the United States boasts a unique variety of liquid options—hot or cold, alcoholic or nonalcoholic, simply refreshing or completely nourishing.

Although diversity is perhaps the most significant single attribute of American beverage history, another important aspect of that history is the often surprising changes that took place with different groups of beverages.

Cider and rum were the most important alcoholic beverages in America until the early nineteenth century. It would have seemed laughable at the time to predict that both beverages would virtually disappear by the middle of the century, but beer and whiskey did replace them. Likewise, tea was the colonists' foremost and favorite hot drink, yet it too would decline in importance by mid-century, when coffee became affordable for the masses.

The story of rum is an incredible one, from its creation in the mid-seventeenth century to its near-universal consumption in North America by the eighteenth century. The tale also includes the history of how rum became so important that it contributed to a political divide between a mighty empire and a small clutch of colonies. Rum's later decline in popularity was partly attributable to the rise of cheap whiskey—and who would have ever predicted that whiskey would inspire a rebellion?

Beer drinking underwent change in America as well. Many colonial Americans drank English-style beer, particularly in New England and the middle colonies, but it declined in importance during the early nineteenth century. No one could have known that lager beer would rise to favor, thanks to an influx of German immigrants in the 1840s and 1850s.

Less surprising was America's love affair with milk, which was long seen as vital nourishment for children. European colonists brought cows to North America during the earliest period of colonization, and adults drank milk too, especially in New England and the Middle Colonies. Later, however, tainted, adulterated milk became reviled as a source of disease and death until concerns raised by temperance advocates resurrected it as a healthy beverage. As a result, most Americans—children and adults—consumed even more milk.

The temperance movement also contributed to the rise of fruit juices—fresh, canned, and bottled—at first for religious reasons, and later because of the promotion of juice's health benefits. The temperance movement also helped jump-start the rise of soda to the apex of the beverage world. Soft drinks, originally formulated by a handful of druggists for medicinal purposes, sparked the imagination of entrepreneurs and took America by storm in the late nineteenth century, becoming America's most consumed beverage category by the mid-twentieth century.

The temperance movement was the forerunner of national Prohibition, but it is unlikely that many Americans, even temperance advocates, believed that the United States would pass a constitutional amendment banning the manufacture, sale, and consumption of all intoxicating beverages. Neither did those who celebrated the passage of the Eighteenth Amendment anticipate that Prohibition would foster a new criminal culture and, in the end, be overturned. Yet even the repeal of Prohibition affected what Americans drank, particularly soda, fruit juices, and children's drinks such as Kool-Aid and milk additives.

Beer and spirits rebounded quickly after Prohibition's repeal, but the wine industry had been devastated during Prohibition. It took more than forty years for the industry to recover. When it did, American wines would be judged favorably against the best wines that the Old World had to offer.

Among all the changes in American drinking habits over the centuries, perhaps the most unusual were the astounding growth of the bottled water market and today's ubiquitous "gourmet" coffee outlets. Americans have always drunk more water than any other beverage, and the safety of the public water supply improved tremendously during the twentieth century. Yet the producers of spring water (from actual springs or elsewhere), mineral water, and purified bottled water have managed to convince Americans that it is a better idea to drink from a plastic bottle than to fill a glass from the tap.

Just as surprising has been the rise of franchised coffee stores. Coffee was America's second-most-popular beverage until the 1950s, when it was overtaken by soft drinks. Still, an inexpensive cup of coffee (if not necessarily a good one) was available virtually everywhere—in restaurants, coffee shops, fast food establishments, bodegas, and grocery stores. This makes it even more surprising that a coffee chain could emerge to dominate America's (and the world's) coffee industry—but that is precisely what Starbucks did.

The Foreseeable Future

It is always easier to impose an explanation on past occurrences and discuss their influence upon the present than it is to predict future events with any degree of accuracy. Yet some near-term projections about American food and drink are relatively easy to make. A number of trends from the past are likely to continue:

⊟ Lacking a dominant beverage tradition, Americans have developed a taste for diversity and experimentation.

⊟ Experimentation has led to a large number of small beverage producers, but the past century has seen consolidation of some industries, such as soft drinks, brewing, coffee roasting, water bottling, winemaking, and distilling. In each of these fields, just a few corporations now control most of the market.

⊟ At the opposite end of the spectrum, a backlash against food industry giants has spawned a large number of smaller, often artisanal, competitors. Microbreweries, local wineries, and small coffee roasters, for instance, offer a wide variety of alternatives.

⊟ The American beverage titans, including the Coca-Cola Company, PepsiCo, and Starbucks, have gone global; simultaneously, foreign firms have acquired large segments of some traditional American industries, such as beer. Even some "all-American" beverages, such as orange juice, now originate in other countries (in the case of orange juice, in Brazil). Other beverages, such as sake from Japan and wine from Australia, are now available in the United States, and the availability of beverages from other countries will continue to proliferate.

⊟ For the past decade, per-capita soda consumption has been decreasing as other beverages have emerged. With health authorities campaigning against sugar-sweetened sodas as a major factor in America's obesity epidemic, it is likely that soda consumption will continue to decrease.

⊟ It is unlikely that Prohibition will ever return; nevertheless, Americans have cut down on alcohol consumption during the past three decades, largely due to stricter enforcement of drunk-driving laws. Alcohol consumption may not drop further, but neither is it likely to rise.

And what of the long-term future for American beverages? With our well-known national thirst for the new and the novel, it is likely that the future will be as full of surprises as the past.

Notes

Prologue

1. Michael N. Sawka, Samuel N. Cheuvront, and Robert Carter III, "Human Water Needs," *Nutrition Reviews* 63 (2005): S30.
2. Some historians estimate that humans arrived in America as early as 40,000 to 50,000 years ago.
3. John G. Bourke, "Distillation by Early American Indians," *American Anthropologist* 7 (1894): 34; V. Havard, "Drink Plants of the North American Indians," *Bulletin of the Torrey Botanical Club* 23 (1896): 34, 35, 37.
4. Havard, "Drink Plants of the North American Indians," 45; Alice Ross, interview with author, April 28, 2011.
5. George H. Loskiel, *History of Missions of the United Brethren* (London: Brethren's Society for the Furtherance of the Gospel, 1794), 70, 74.
6. Charles H. Fairbanks, "The Function of Black Drink Among the Creeks," in *Black Drink: A Native American Tea*, ed. Charles M. Hudson (Athens: University of Georgia Press, 1979), 123.
7. Charles M. Hudson, "Introduction," in Hudson, *Black Drink*, 2–4.
8. Fairbanks, "Function of Black Drink Among the Creeks," 142.
9. Virgil Vogel, *American Indian Medicine* (Norman: University of Oklahoma Press, 1970), 42, 48, 73.
10. Hector St. John de Crèvecoeur, "Customs," in *Sketches of Eighteenth Century America*, ed. Henri L. Bourdin, Ralph H. Gabriel, and Stanley T. Williams (New Haven, Conn.: Yale University Press, 1925), 123;

John Bartlett, "Remarks of the Toxic Qualities of Sassafras," *Virginia Medical Monthly* 12 (1886): 693; "Editorial," *Medical and Surgical Reporter* 7 (1854): 534; John Urt Lloyd, "An Historical Study of Sassafras," *American Druggist* 33 (1898): 195–196; Stanley Baron, *Brewed in America* (Boston: Little, Brown, 1962), 19; Harriott Pinckney Horry, *A Colonial Plantation Cookbook: The Receipt Book of Harriott Pinckney Horry, 1770,* ed. Richard J. Hooker (Columbia: University of South Carolina Press, 1984), 134.

11. George C. Deikman, "The Pharmacy of Sassafras," *Bulletin of Pharmacy* (1898): 540–541.

12. In 1960, the U.S. Food and Drug Administration banned the use of safrole (an ingredient in sassafras root, bark, and oil) as a known precarcinogen.

13. Richard J. Hooker, *A History of Food and Drink in America* (Indianapolis: Bobbs-Merrill, 1981), 131.

14. Horry, *Colonial Plantation Cookbook*; Amelia Simmons, *American Cookery: A Facsimile of the First Edition with an Essay by Mary Tolford Wilson* (New York: Oxford University Press, 1958), 64.

15. Melvin R. Gilmore, "Some Chippewa Uses of Plants," in *An Ethnobiology Source Book: The Uses of Plants and Animals by American Indians*, ed. Richard I. Ford (New York: Garland, 1986), 128.

1. Colonial Diversity

1. George Percy, "Observations by Master George Percy," in *Narratives of Early Virginia, 1606–1625,* ed. Lyon Gardiner Tyler (New York: Scribner, 1907), 9–10.

2. Ibid.

3. George Percy, "A Discourse on the Plantation of the Southern Colony in Virginia by the English, 1606," in *Hakluytus Posthumus, Or, Purchas His Pilgrimes,* comp. Samuel Purchas (Glasgow: MacLehose, 1906), 18:418.

4. Don Diego Sarmiento de Acuña to H. M., London, October 5, 1613, in *The Genesis of the United States*, ed. Alexander Brown (Boston: Houghton Mifflin, 1891), 2:660.

5. Thomas Harriot, *A Briefe and True Report of the New Found Land of Virginia* (Frankfurt: De Bry, 1590), 13.

6. James E. Thorold Rogers, *A History of Agriculture and Prices in England: From the Year After the Oxford Parliament (1259) to the Commencement of the Continental War (1793),* 7 vols. (Oxford: Clarendon Press, 1866–1902).

7. *A Relation or Iournall of the Beginning and Proceeding of the English Plantation Settled at Plimoth in New England* (London: Iohn Bellamie, 1622), quoted in *Collections of the Massachusetts Historical Society for 1802* (Boston: Munroe and Francis, 1802), 8:208.

8. Edward Johnson, *A History of New-England* (London: Nath. Brooke, 1654), 48–49.

9. William Bradford, *Of Plymouth Plantation, 1620–1647* (New York: Modern Library, 1981), 143.

10. William Wood, *New-Englands Prospect* (London: Tho. Cotes for Iohn Bellamie, 1634), 15.

11. Hugh Jones, "Of the Habits, Customs, Parts, Employment, Trade," in *The Present State of Virginia*, ed. Richard L. Morton (Chapel Hill: University of North Carolina Press, 1956), 86.

12. Gottlieb Mittelberger, "Description of the Land," in *Gottlieb Mittelberger's Journey*, ed. Karl Theodor Eben (Philadelphia: John Jos. McVey, 1898), 67.

13. Douglas Southall Freeman, *George Washington* (New York: Scribner, 1948), 1:105.

14. *A Short Description of the Province of South Carolina: With an Account of the Air, Weather, and Diseases, at Charlestown, Written in the Year 1763*, in *Historical Collections of South Carolina*, comp. B. R. Carroll (New York: Harper, 1836), 2:496, 508, 510.

15. Ibid., 2:482.

16. Peter Kalm, *Travels into North America*, trans. John Reinhold Goresterm (Barre, Mass.: Imprint Society, 1972), 328.

17. Ibid., 131.

18. Keith Thomas, *Religion and the Decline of Magic* (London: Weidenfeld & Nicolson, 1971), 17, 19.

19. David W. Conroy, *In Public Houses: Drink and the Revolution of Authority in Colonial Massachusetts* (Chapel Hill: University of North Carolina Press, 1995), 19–20, 24–25, 39.

20. Jack S. Blocker, *American Temperance Movements: Cycles of Reform* (Boston: Twayne, 1989), 3.

21. Hector St. John de Crèvecoeur, *Sketches of Eighteenth Century America*, ed. Henri L. Bourdin, Ralph H. Gabriel, and Stanley T. Williams (New Haven, Conn.: Yale University Press, 1925), 123.

22. Samuel Morewood, *An Essay on the Inventions and Customs of Ancient and Modern Nations in the Manufacture and Use of Inebriating Liquors* (London: Longman, Hurst, Rees, Orme, Brown and Green, 1824), 182.

23. William Penn, "The Beginnings of the City," in *Memorial History of the City of Philadelphia*, ed. John Russell Young (New York: New-York History, 1895), 1:72.

24. John Josselyn, *New-England Rarities Discovered* (Boston: William Veazie, 1865), 90, 112.

25. Robert Beverley, "Edibles, Potables, and Fuel in Virginia," in *The History and Present State of Virginia*, ed. Louis Booker Wright (Chapel Hill: University of North Carolina Press, 1947), 293.

26. George Washington, "To Make Small Beer," in *Washington's Notebook as a Virginia Colonel, 1757*, New York Public Library, Manuscripts and Archives Division, http://exhibitions.nypl.org/treasures/items/show/130 (accessed May 6, 2011).

27. Stanley Baron, *Brewed in America* (Boston: Little, Brown, 1962), 19–30, 43–51, 75–79.

28. "1648, March 10th. An Ordinance Against Drinking to Excess, Sabbath Breaking, for Regulating Taverns and to Prevent Frauds Upon the Excise," quoted in *First Report of the State Commissioner of Excise, Documents of the Assembly of the State of New York* (Albany, N.Y.: Wynkoop Hallenbeck Crawford, 1897), 1:279.

29. Robert Beverley, "Of the Natural Products of Virginia," in *The History of Virginia*, ed. Charles Campbell (Richmond, Va.: J. W. Randolph, 1855), 259; Jean Anthelme Brillat-Savarin, *The Physiology of Taste* (Mineola, N.Y.: Dover, 2002), 58.

30. Beverley, "Of the Natural Products of Virginia," 259; Tench Coxe, *A View of the United States* (Philadelphia: William Hall, 1794), 209.

31. Morewood, *Essay on the Inventions and Customs of Ancient and Modern Nations in the Manufacture and Use of Inebriating Liquors*, 182.

32. Jones, "Of the Habits, Customs, Parts, Employment, Trade," 86.

33. Walt Winthrop, "Winthrop Papers," in *Collections of the Massachusetts Historical Society*, 6th ser. (Boston: Massachusetts Historical Society, 1892), 5:11, 107, 169, 311, 352.

34. Samuel Sewall, "Diary of Samuel Sewall: 1699–1714," in *Collections of the Massachusetts Society*, 5th ser. (Boston: Massachusetts Historical Society, 1879), 6:15, 18, 34, 36, 116, 187, 203, 222, 253, 265, 282, 440.

35. Peter C. Mancall, *Deadly Medicine: Indians and Alcohol in Early America* (Ithaca, N.Y.: Cornell University Press, 1995), xi.

36. Mittelberger, "Description of the Land," 66.

37. Celia D. Shapiro, "Nation of Nowhere: Jewish Role in Colonial American Chocolate History," in *Chocolate: History, Culture, and Heritage,* ed. Louis E. Grivetti (Hoboken, N.J.: Wiley, 2009), 54–60.

38. William H. Ukers, *All About Coffee* (New York: Tea and Coffee Trade Journal, 1935), 111–112.

39. Richard J. Hooker, *A History of Food and Drink in America* (Indianapolis: Bobbs-Merrill, 1981), 93.

40. Jones, "Of the Habits, Customs, Parts, Employment, Trade," 86.

41. *Pennsylvania Gazette*, March 3, 1765, and August 1, 1865, as located by Clarissa Dillon, letter to author, January 14, 2012.

42. Mittelberger, "Description of the Land," 66.

43. "A Receipt for All Young Ladies That Are Going to Be Married, to Make a Sack Posset," *New York Gazette*, February 13, 1744, in "Extracts from the Earliest Newspapers of the City," in D. T. Valentine, *Manual of the Corporation of the City of New York* (New York: Edmund Jones, 1862), 720.

44. Henry G. Crowgey, *Kentucky Bourbon: The Early Years of Whiskeymaking* (Lexington: University Press of Kentucky, 2008), 9–12.

45. "Mr. Rantoul's Establishment in Business—Intemperance and Pauperism," in *Historical Collections of the Essex Institute* (Salem, Mass.: Essex Institute, 1863), 5:247.

46. Médéric Moreau de Saint-Méry, "Sojourn in Philadelphia," in *Moreau de St. Méry's American Journey*, trans. and ed. Kenneth Roberts and Anna M. Roberts (Garden City, N.Y.: Doubleday, 1947), 265–266.

47. John James McCusker, "The Rum Trade and the Balance of Payments of the Thirteen Continental Colonies, 1650–1775" (Ph.D. diss., University of Pittsburgh, 1970), 476–477; W. J. Rorabaugh, *The Alcoholic Republic: An American Tradition* (Oxford: Oxford University Press, 1979), 232.

48. Merton M. Hyman, Marilyn A. Zimmermann, Carol Gurioli, and Alice Helrich, *Drinkers, Drinking, and Alcohol-Related Mortality and Hospitalizations: A Statistical Compendium* (New Brunswick, N.J.: Publications Division, Center of Alcohol Studies, Rutgers University, 1980), 3.

49. Blocker, *American Temperance Movements*, 4.

50. *Journal of Jasper Danckaerts, 1679–1680*, ed. Bartlett B. James and J. Franklin Jameson (New York: Scribner, 1913), 135.

51. Conroy, *In Public Houses*, 12–16, 75–77.

52. Daniel Webster, *A Discourse, Delivered at Plymouth, December 22, 1820* (Boston: Wells and Lilley, 1821), 20; Sidney Morse, *Freemasonry in the American Revolution* (Washington, D.C.: Masonic Service Association of the United States, 1924), 37.

2. An Essential Ingredient in American Independence

1. Raymond McFarland, *A History of the New England Fisheries* (Philadelphia: University of Pennsylvania, 1911), 103; Allen S. Johnson, "The Passage of the Sugar Act," *William and Mary Quarterly*, 3rd ser., 16 (1959): 507.

2. "The Sugar Act," Yale Law School, The Avalon Project, http://avalon.law.yale.edu/18th_century/sugar_act_1764.asp (accessed August 17, 2010).

3. Arthur Meier Schlesinger, *The Colonial Merchants and the American Revolution, 1763–1776* (New York: Columbia University, 1918), 43.

4. Frederick Bernays Wiener, "The Rhode Island Merchants and the Sugar Act," *New England Quarterly* 3 (1930): 465–466.

5. Yale Law School, "Sugar Act."

6. John Adams, "To William Tudor, August 11, 1818," in *The Works of John Adams*, ed. Charles Francis Adams (Boston: Little, Brown, 1856), 10:345.

7. Wiener, "Rhode Island Merchants and the Sugar Act," 464.

8. Adam Smith, *An Inquiry into the Nature and Causes of Wealth of Nations* (Nashville, Tenn.: Plain Label Books, 1963), 118, 659–660.

9. Gilman M. Ostrander, "The Colonial Molasses Trade," *Agricultural History* 30 (1956): 77, 82.

10. Robert Beverley, "Of Edibles, Potables, and Fuel in Virginia," in *The History and Present State of Virginia*, ed. Louis Booker Wright (Chapel Hill: University of North Carolina Press, 1947), 238.

11. Increase Mather, *A Sermon Occasioned by the Execution of a Man Found Guilty of Murder* (Boston: Printed by R. P., 1687), 25; Thomas James Holmes, *Cotton Mather: A Bibliography of His Works* (Cambridge, Mass.: Harvard University Press, 1940), 992.

12. David W. Conroy, *In Public Houses: Drink and the Revolution of Authority in Colonial Massachusetts* (Chapel Hill: University of North Carolina Press, 1995), 9.

13. Richard J. Hooker, *A History of Food and Drink in America* (Indianapolis: Bobbs-Merrill, 1981), 85–86.

14. W. J. Rorabaugh, *The Alcoholic Republic: An American Tradition* (Oxford: Oxford University Press, 1979), 29.

15. Daniel K. Richter, *Ordeal of the Longhouse: The Peoples of the Iroquois League in the Era of European Colonization* (Chapel Hill: University of North Carolina Press, 1993), 266.

16. Benjamin Franklin, *Memoirs of the Life and Writings of Benjamin Franklin*, 2nd ed. (London: Henry Colburn, 1818), 1:188.

17. Stanley B. Alpern, "What Africans Got for Their Slaves: A Master List of European Trade Goods," *History in Africa* 22 (1995): 25.

18. Gilman M. Ostrander, "The Making of the Triangular Trade Myth," *William and Mary Quarterly*, 3rd. ser., 30 (1973): 642; Charles Coulombe, *Rum: The Epic Story of the Drink That Conquered the World* (New York: Citadel Press, 2004), 61.

19. Alpern, "What Africans Got for Their Slaves," 25.

20. William Byrd, "Progress to the Mines in the Year 1732," in *Prose Works: Narratives of a Colonial Virginian*, ed. Louis B. Wright (Cambridge, Mass.: Belknap Press of Harvard University Press, 1966), 374.

21. Israel Acrelius, *A History of New Sweden*, trans. William M. Reynolds (Ann Arbor, Mich.: Readex Microprint, 1966), 162; William Penn, "A Further Account of the Province of Pennsylvania," in *Narratives of Early Pennsylvania, West New Jersey, Delaware*, ed. Albert Cook Myers (New York: Scribner, 1912), 267; Benjamin Rush, *An Inquiry into the Effects of Ardent Spirits upon the Human Body and Mind*, 8th ed. (Boston: James Loring, 1823), 25; Eric Burns, *The Spirits of America: A Social History of Alcohol* (Philadelphia: Temple University Press, 2004), 12–13; Dudley C. Gould, *Times of Brother Jonathan: What He Ate, Wore, Believed In and Used for Medicine During the War of Independence* (Middletown, Conn.: Southfarm Press, 2001), 14; Edward Emerson, *Beverages, Past and Present: An Historical Sketch of Their Production, Together with a Study of the Customs Connected with Their Use* (New York: Putnam, 1908), 2:462, 465; Hooker, *History of Food and Drink in America*, 86, 135.

22. Johann David Schöpf, "Return from Pittsburg," in *Travels in the Confederation, 1783–1784*, trans. and ed. Alfred James Morrison (Philadelphia: Campbell, 1911), 362–363.

23. Richard B. Sheridan, "The Molasses Act and the Market Strategy of the British Sugar Planters," *Journal of Economic History* 17 (1957): 62–63; Albert B. Southwick, "The Molasses Act—Source of Precedents," *William and Mary Quarterly*, 3rd ser., 8 (1951): 390; Coulombe, *Rum*, 59.

24. Frank Wesley Pitman, *The Development of the British West Indies, 1700–1763* (New Haven, Conn.: Yale University Press, 1918), 214.

25. Coulombe, *Rum*, 59.

26. Schlesinger, *Colonial Merchants and the American Revolution*, 44.

27. "Answer: November 3, 1764," in *Speeches of the Governors of Massachusetts, from 1765–1775; and the Answers of the House of Representatives to the Same; With Their Resolutions and Addresses for That Period and Other Public Papers Relating to the Dispute Between This Country and Great Britain Which Led to the Independence of the United States*, ed. Alden Bradford (Boston: Russell and Gardner, 1818), 19.

28. Johnson, "Passage of the Sugar Act," 508.

29. "The Stamp Act," March 22, 1765, in *Journals of the House of Burgesses of Virginia, 1761–1765*, ed. John Pendleton Kennedy (Richmond, Va.: Colonial Press, 1907), lxxv.

30. George Washington, "To Captain Josiah Thompson, July 2, 1766," in *The Writings of George Washington*, ed. Worthington Chauncey Ford (New York: Putnam, 1889), 2:212.

31. Peter Thompson, *Rum Punch and Revolution: Taverngoing and Public Life in Eighteenth-Century Philadelphia* (Philadelphia: University of Pennsylvania Press, 1999), 20.

32. Alpern, "What Africans Got for Their Slaves," 25.

33. Samuel Morewood, *An Essay on the Inventions and Customs of Ancient and Modern Nations in the Manufacture and Use of Inebriating Liquors* (London: Longman, Hurst, Rees, Orme, Brown and Green, 1824), 184.

34. Benjamin Rush, "A Moral and Physical Thermometer, or, a Scale of the Progress of Temperance and Intemperance. Liquors, with Effects in Their Usual Order," in *An Inquiry into the Effects of Spiritous Liquors on the Human Body* (Boston: Thomas and Andrews, 1790), 16.

35. Benjamin Rush, in *Massachusetts Spy*, July 31, 1788, quoted in Richard Hopwood Thornton, *An American Glossary: Being an Attempt to Illustrate Certain Americanisms* (Philadelphia: Lippincott, 1922), 2:811.

36. Horace Greeley, *The Autobiography of Horace Greeley* (New York: Treat, 1872), 100.

37. Mark Wahlgren Summers, *Rum, Romanism, and Rebellion: The Making of a President, 1884* (Chapel Hill: University of North Carolina Press, 2000), 282.

38. Ian Williams, *Rum: A Social and Sociable History of the Real Spirit of 1776* (New York: Nation Books, 2005); Ian Williams, e-mail to author, July 14, 2011.

3. Tea Parties

1. William Tudor, *Life of James Otis of Massachusetts* (Boston: Wells & Lilly, 1823), 118.
2. Quoted by Francis Roth, in Bernhard Knollenberg, *Origin of the American Revolution, 1759–1766* (New York: Macmillan, 1960), 100.
3. Quoted in Benjamin Bussey Thatcher, *Traits of the Tea Party: Being a Memoir of George R. T. Hewes, One of the Last of Its Survivors* (New York: Harper, 1835), 178.
4. This composite version was taken from several sources, the most important being ibid., 165–178; Henry Clay Watson, *The Yankee Tea-Party; or, Boston in 1773* (Philadelphia: Lindsay and Blackiston, 1852), 17–23; Francis Samuel Drake, *Tea Leaves: Being a Collection of Letters and Documents Relating to the Shipment of Tea to the American Colonies in the Year 1773, by the East India Tea Company* (Boston: A. O. Crane, 1884).
5. John Adams, "Diary, December 17, 1773," in *The Works of John Adams, Second President of the United States*, comp. and ed. Charles Francis Adams (Boston: Little, Brown, 1865), 2:324.
6. Alonzo Lewis, *The History of Lynn*, 2nd ed. (Boston: Samuel M. Dickenson, 1844), 194.
7. George Wingate Chase, *The History of Haverhill, Massachusetts: From Its First Settlement, in 1640 to the Year 1860* (Haverhill: Printed by author, 1861), 258.
8. Peter Kalm, *Travels into North America,* trans. John Reinhold Foresterm (Barre, Mass.: Imprint Society, 1972), 185.
9. Chase, *History of Haverhill, Massachusetts,* 258.
10. John E. Wright and Doris S. Corbett, *Pioneer Life in Western Pennsylvania* (Pittsburgh: University of Pittsburgh Press, 1940), 60–61.
11. Edward Eggleston, "The Colonists at Home," *The Century* 29 (1885): 886.
12. Henry Parsons Hedges, *A History of the Town of East-Hampton, N.Y.* (Sag Harbor, N.Y.: J. H. Hunt, 1897), 142.
13. Esther Singleton, *Social New York Under the Georges, 1714–1776: Houses, Streets, and Country Homes, with Chapters on Fashions, Furniture, China, Plate, and Manners* (New York: Appleton, 1902), 375.
14. Benjamin Franklin, in *Pennsylvania Gazette*, March 1742, quoted in Jerry Weinberger, *Benjamin Franklin Unmasked: On the Unity of His Moral, Religious, and Political Thought* (Lawrence: University Press of Kansas, 2005), 70; William Burling, "Early Anti-Slavery Advocates," *The Friend* 29 (1856): 220; Andreas Mielke, "An Inquiry Concerning Sarah and Benjamin Lay, Abolitionists," *Quaker History* 86 (1997): 41–43.
15. William Smith, "The History of the Late Province of New-York," *New-York Historical Society Collections* 1 (1830): 333.

16. Richard J. Hooker, *A History of Food and Drink in America* (Indianapolis: Bobbs-Merrill, 1981), 91.

17. Charles W. Elliott, *The New England History, from the Discovery of the Continent by the Northmen, A.D. 986, to the Period When the Colonies Declared Their Independence, A.D. 1776* (New York: Scribner, 1857), 149.

18. *Boston Gazette*, November 21, 1768, quoted in John James Currier, *History of Newbury Port, Mass.: 1764–1905* (Newbury Port, Mass: Author, 1906), 1:48.

19. Hoh-Cheung and Lorna H. Mui, "Smuggling and the British Tea Trade Before 1784," *American Historical Review* 74 (1968): 44.

20. James Spear Loring, *The Hundred Boston Orators Appointed by the Municipal Authorities*, 3rd ed. (Boston: John P. Jewett, 1854), 77.

21. *Boston Gazette*, April 1770, quoted in Drake, *Tea Leaves*, x.

22. Thatcher, *Traits of the Tea Party*, 145–146, 148–149.

23. *Works of John Adams*, 2:255.

24. Benjamin Woods Labaree, *The Boston Tea Party* (Boston: Northeastern University Press, 1979), ix.

25. George C. Rogers, Jr., "The Charleston Tea Party: The Significance of December 3, 1773," *South Carolina Historical Magazine* 75 (1974): 158.

26. "An Account of the Proceedings of the Inhabitants of Philadelphia," December 27, 1773, quoted in Drake, *Tea Leaves*, 361–366; William Ukers, *The Romance of Tea* (New York: Knopf, 1936), 89.

27. Drake, *Tea Leaves*, lxxxiv.

28. Emma Willard, *History of the United States: Or, Republic of America*, 4th ed. (New York: White, Gallaher & White, 1831), 155.

29. Henry White to Captain Benjamin Lockyer, April 20, 1774, quoted in Drake, *Tea Leaves*, lxxxiii.

30. Ibid., 360.

31. James McSherry, "The Days Before the Revolution," in *History of Maryland*, ed. Bartlett Burleigh James (Baltimore: John Murphy, 1852), 173.

32. "Account of the Destruction of the Brig 'Peggy Stewart,' at Annapolis, 1774," *Pennsylvania Magazine of History and Biography* 25 (1901): 248–250.

33. John Adams, "John Adams to Abigail Adams, July 6, 1774," in *Familiar Letters of John Adams and His Wife Abigail Adams*, comp. and ed. Charles Francis Adams (New York: Hurd and Houghton, 1876), 18.

34. Benjamin W. Labaree, *The Boston Tea Party, 1773: Catalyst for Revolution* (Boston: Massachusetts Bicentennial Commission, 1973), 164.

35. *Journals of the Continental Congress, 1774–1789* (Washington, D.C.: Government Printing Office, 1906), 4:277–279.

36. Quoted in Charles H. Sherrill, *French Memories of Eighteenth-Century America* (New York: Scribner, 1915), 316.

37. "The Narrative of Prince de Broglie," trans. E. W. Balch, *Magazine of American History* 1 (1877): 233.

38. Abbé Claude C. Robin, *New Travels Through North-America* (Philadelphia: Robert Bell, 1783), 251.
39. Sherrill, *French Memories of Eighteenth-Century America*, 78.
40. J.-P. Brissot de Warville, *New Travels in the United States of America* (London: J. S. Jordan, 1784), 2:71–72.
41. *Nancy Shippen: Her Journal Book*, ed. Ethel Armes (Philadelphia: Lippincott, 1935), 248.
42. Dietrich Heinrich and Freiherr Von Bülow, *Der Freistaat von Nordamerika in seinem neusten zustand* (Berlin: J. H. Unger, 1797), cited in Ellis Paxson Oberholtzer, *Philadelphia: A History of the City and Its People, a Record of 225 Years* (Philadelphia: J. S. Clarke, 1912), 1:387.
43. Médéric Moreau de Saint-Méry, "Sojourn in Philadelphia," in *Moreau de St. Méry's American Journey*, trans. and ed. Kenneth Roberts and Anna M. Roberts (Garden City, N.Y.: Doubleday, 1947), 6, 256.
44. Timothy Pitkin, *A Statistical View of the Commerce of the United States of America* (New York: James Eastburn, 1817), 246–247; William H. Ukers, *All About Tea* (New York: Tea and Coffee Trade Journal, 1935), 2:247.
45. Ukers, *All About Tea*, 2:250–251; Axel Madsen, *John Jacob Astor: America's First Multimillionaire* (New York: Wiley, 2001), 53.
46. Thomas Beddoes, *Hygëia, or, Essays Moral and Medical* (London: R. Phillips, 1802), 35–38; Eggleston, "Colonists at Home," 886; Kalm, *Travels into North America*, 185.
47. William Alcott, "Tea Drinking, Again," *Moral Reformer and Teacher on the Human Constitution* 1 (1835): 301.
48. Dio Lewis, *Weak Lungs, and How to Make Them Strong* (Boston: Ticknor and Fields, 1863), 135.
49. Fanny Trollope, *Domestic Manners of the Americans* (New York: Reprinted for the Bookseller, 1832), 43–44, 107, 111, 132, 272, 297.
50. Ibid., 38, 245; Frederick Marryat, *A Diary in America: With Remarks on Its Institutions* (Paris: Baudry's European Library, 1839), 44, 164.
51. Solon Robinson, *How to Live: Saving and Wasting* (New York: Fowler and Wells, 1860), 157; Marion Harland, *Breakfast, Luncheon and Tea* (New York: Scribner, 1875), 360–361; D. A. Lincoln, *Boston Cook Book* (Boston: Roberts, 1884), 112; Robert Somers, *The Southern States Since the War* (New York: Macmillan, 1871), 235; Hooker, *History of Food and Drink in America*, 276.
52. Marc Levinson, *The Great A&P and the Struggle for Small Business in America* (New York: Hill and Wang, 2011), 16.
53. *New York Journal of Commerce*, March 21, 1902, 1, cited in John Peter Nichols, *The Chain Store Tells its Story* (New York: Institute of Distribution, 1942), 57.
54. "Holiday Goods, the Great American Tea Company," *New York Times*, December 24, 1872; William I. Walsh, *The Rise and Decline of the Great Atlantic & Pacific Tea Company* (Secaucus, N.J.: Lyle Stuart, 1986), 20–32.

55. "India," in *The Official Directory of the World's Columbian Exposition*, ed. Moses P. Handy and Richard Blechynden (Chicago: Conkey, 1893), 128; "Wonderful Foreign Exhibits," *Dun's Review* 4 (1904): 56; Pamela J. Vaccaro, *Beyond the Ice Cream Cone: The Whole Scoop on Food at the 1904 World's Fair* (St. Louis: Enid Press, 2004), 108–111.

56. Levinson, *Great A&P and the Struggle for Small Business in America*, 52.

57. Jan Whitaker, *Tea at the Blue Lantern Inn: A Social History of the Tea Room Craze in America* (New York: St. Martin's Press, 2002), 10–11.

58. Many secondary sources claim that Thomas Sullivan, a New York tea distributor, invented the tea bag in 1904 or 1908; if so, no primary source evidence for this has surfaced, and Sullivan's obituaries make no mention of it; neither does Ukers in *All About Tea*. The Sullivan story appears to be a late-twentieth-century invention.

59. Ukers, *All About Tea*, 2:79–81, 422–424, 443.

60. Laura C. Martin, *Tea: The Drink That Changed the World* (Rutland, Vt.: Tuttle, 2007), 190.

4. Tarantula Juice

1. Henry G. Crowgey, *Kentucky Bourbon: The Early Years of Whiskeymaking* (Lexington: University Press of Kentucky, 2008), 19.

2. Johann David Schöpf, *Travels in the Confederation*, trans. and ed. Alfred James Morrison (Philadelphia: Campbell, 1911), 2:183–184; Crowgey, *Kentucky Bourbon*, 9–12.

3. Charles Woodmason, "The Journal of C. W. Clerk: Itinerant Minister in South Carolina, 1766, 1767, 1768," in *The Carolina Backcountry on the Eve of the Revolution*, ed. Richard J. Hooker (Chapel Hill: University of North Carolina Press, 1953), 30, 53, and "A Report on Religion in the South: The New Lights Now Infest the Whole Backcountry," in Hooker, *Carolina Backcountry*, 78; Berton Roueche, *The Neutral Spirit* (Boston: Little, Brown, 1960), 39–40.

4. Israel Acrelius, "Drinks Used in North America," in *A History of New Sweden*, ed. William M. Reynolds (Ann Arbor, Mich.: Readex Microprint, 1966), 161, 163; John E. Wright and Doris S. Corbett, *Pioneer Life in Western Pennsylvania* (Pittsburgh: University of Pittsburgh Press, 1940), 60–61; Woodmason, "Journal of C. W. Clerk," 30, 53.

5. Israel Daniel Rupp, *Early History of Western Pennsylvania, and of the West* (Pittsburgh: D. W. Kauffman, 1846), 272.

6. William Hogeland, *The Whiskey Rebellion: George Washington, Alexander Hamilton, and the Frontier* (New York: Scribner, 2006), 67.

7. Thomas P. Slaughter, *The Whiskey Rebellion: Frontier Epilogue to the American Revolution* (New York: Oxford University Press, 1986), 64.

8. Hogeland, *Whiskey Rebellion*, 66.

9. Harry M. Ward, *George Washington's Enforcers: Policing the Continental Army* (Carbondale: Southern Illinois University Press, 2006), 23.

10. Benjamin Rush to John Adams, October 31, 1777, quoted in Alyn Brodsky, *Benjamin Rush: Patriot and Physician* (New York: Truman Talley Books, 2004), 191.

11. L. H. Butterfield, "Dr. Benjamin Rush's Journal of a Trip to Carlisle in 1784," *Pennsylvania Magazine of History and Biography* 74 (1950): 456.

12. Benjamin Rush, *An Enquiry into the Effects of Spirituous Liquors upon the Human Body, and Their Influence upon the Happiness of Society* (Philadelphia: Thomas Bradford, 1784); Brian S. Katcher, "Benjamin Rush's Educational Campaign Against Hard Drinking," *American Journal of Public Health* 83 (1993): 273–276; Carl Alfred Lanning Binger, *Revolutionary Doctor: Benjamin Rush, 1746–1813* (New York: Norton, 1966), 199.

13. College of Physicians of Philadelphia, "Memorial on Temperance, Addressed to the Congress of the United States," in *Transactions of the College of Physicians of Philadelphia*, 3rd ser. (Philadelphia: College of Physicians, 1887), 9:ccxv.

14. Alexander Hamilton, "Report on Public Credit," in *Reports of the Secretary of the Treasury of the United States* (Washington, D.C.: Blair & Reves, 1837), 1:23.

15. Leland D. Baldwin, *Whiskey Rebels: The Story of a Frontier Uprising* (Pittsburgh: University of Pittsburgh Press, 1939), 56.

16. "The Petition of the Inhabitants of Westmoreland County, 1790," in *Pennsylvania Archives* (Philadelphia: Joseph Severns, 1854), 11:671.

17. *Register of Debates in Congress* (Washington, D.C.: Gales & Seaton, 1825), 2:1692–1693.

18. College of Physicians of Philadelphia, "Memorial on Temperance," 9:ccxvii; "The Humble Address of Ten Thousand Federal Maids," *Gazette of the United States,* January 26, 1791, in *Public Women, Public Words: A Documentary History of American Feminism*, ed. Dawn Keetley and John Pettegrew (Madison, Wis.: Madison House, 1997), 46–47; *Gazette of the United States,* February 12, 1791, cited in Slaughter, *Whiskey Rebellion*, 100, 252.

19. Kevin T. Barksdale, "Our Rebellious Neighbors: Virginia's Border Counties During Pennsylvania's Whiskey Rebellion," *Virginia Magazine of History and Biography* 111 (2003): 10.

20. Ron Chernow, *Alexander Hamilton* (New York: Penguin Press, 2004), 342; Hogeland, *Whiskey Rebellion*, 62.

21. Alexander Hamilton, "Report on the Difficulties in the Execution of the Act Laying Duties on Distilled Spirits," in *The Papers of Alexander Hamilton*, ed. Harold C. Syrett (New York: Columbia University Press, 1962), 11:96.

22. Ibid., 11:78–102.

23. George Washington, *The Writings of George Washington* (Boston: Russell, Shattuck, and Williams, 1836), 10:532.

24. Crowgey, *Kentucky Bourbon*, 96.

25. Peter S. Onuf, *Establishing the New Regime: The Washington Administration* (New York: Garland, 1991), 281.

26. Mary K. Bonsteel Tachau, "A New Look at the Whiskey Rebellion," in *The Whiskey Rebellion: Past and Present Perspectives*, ed. Steven Boyd (Westport, Conn.: Greenwood Press, 1985), 97–118; Roland M. Baumann, "Philadelphia's Manufacturers and the Excise Tax of 1794: The Forging of the Jeffersonian Coalition," in Boyd, *Whiskey Rebellion*, 135–164; David W. Maurer, *Kentucky Moonshine* (Lexington: University Press of Kentucky, 2003), 19–20.

27. Crowgey, *Kentucky Bourbon*, 92–93.

28. Barksdale, "Our Rebellious Neighbors," 16–18; Onuf, *Establishing the New Regime*, 281.

29. F. A. Michaux, quoted in "Review," *Literary Miscellany* 2 (1806): 388.

30. Slaughter, *Whiskey Rebellion*, 223.

31. John Melish, *Travels Through the United States of America, in the Years 1806 & 1807, and 1809, 1810, and 1811* (Philadelphia: Palmer, 1812), 312.

32. Richard F. Burton, *The City of the Saints, and Across the Rocky Mountains to California* (New York: Harper, 1862), 24; Robert Brown, *The Countries of the World* (New York: Cassell, Petter & Gilpin, 1876), 2:27; Thomas Augustus Bland, *Life of Alfred B. Meacham* (Washington, D.C.: Bland, 1883), 17; Hooker, *History of Food and Drink in America*, 200.

33. William F. Shughart, *Taxing Choice: The Predatory Politics of Fiscal Discrimination* (New Brunswick, N.J.: Transaction, 1997), 182.

34. David O. Whitten, "An Economic Inquiry into the Whiskey Rebellion of 1794," *Agricultural History* 49 (1975): 491.

35. Crowgey, *Kentucky Bourbon*, xi.

5. Cider's Last Hurrah

1. *Baltimore Republican*, December 11, 1839, quoted in Robert Gray Gunderson, *The Log-Cabin Campaign* (Lexington: University of Kentucky Press, 1957), 74.

2. Isaac Rand Jackson, *A Sketch of the Life and Public Services of General William Henry Harrison* (St. Louis: Churchill & Harris, 1840), 40; Richard Smith Elliott, *Notes Taken in Sixty Years* (St. Louis: Studley, 1883), 120–121.

3. Ephraim Hubbard Foster, *Hard Cider: A Poem, Descriptive of the Nashville Convention* (Louisville, Ky., 1840).

4. A. B. Norton, *The Great Revolution of 1840: Reminiscences of the Log Cabin and Hard Cider Campaign* (Mount Vernon, Ohio: Norton, 1888), 52.

5. *Hard Cider and Log Cabin Almanac for 1841* (New York: Turner & Fisher, 1840); *The People's Line—Take Care of the Locomotive* (1840), Library of Congress, http://loc.gov/pictures/resource/ppmsca.15770 (accessed May 18, 2010).

6. *Federal-Abolition-Whig Trap, to Catch Voters in* (New Orleans, 1840); "Harrison & Tyler," campaign emblem, Library of Congress, http://loc.gov/pictures/resource/cph.3a32036 (accessed May 18, 2010).

7. Norton, *Great Revolution of 1840*, 213.

8. Richard Carwardine, "Evangelicals, Whigs and the Election of William Henry Harrison," *Journal of American Studies* 17 (1983): 47–75.

9. Norton, *Great Revolution of 1840*, 287.

10. Elliott, *Notes Taken in Sixty Years*, 126.

11. John Winthrop, *The History of New England from 1630 to 1649* (Boston: Little, Brown, 1853), 2:417.

12. "Chap. XXI of the Suddain and Unexpected Fall of Cattel," in *Johnson's Wonder-Working Providence, 1628–1651*, ed. J. Franklin Jameson (New York: Scribner, 1910), 210.

13. Sarah F. McMahon, "A Comfortable Subsistence: The Changing Composition of Diet in Rural New England, 1620–1840," *William and Mary Quarterly*, 3rd ser., 42 (1985): 42–43.

14. Israel Acrelius, *History of New Sweden*, trans. William M. Reynolds (Philadelphia: Historical Society of Pennsylvania, 1874), 161; Alice Morse Earle, *Home Life in Colonial Days* (New York: Macmillan, 1898), 162.

15. *New England Farmer*, quoted in *The Balance and Columbian Repository*, September 6, 1803, 284; Alice Morse Earle, *Stage-coach and Tavern Days* (New York: Macmillan, 1900), 130–131.

16. John T. Krumpelmann, "Timothy Flint, Contributor of Americanisms, 1826," *American Speech* 44 (1969): 138.

17. John Josselyn, *An Account of Two Voyages to New-England*, 2nd ed. (London: G. Widdowes, 1675), 190–191.

18. Richard J. Hooker, *A History of Food and Drink in America* (Indianapolis: Bobbs-Merrill, 1981), 36.

19. Acrelius, *History of New Sweden*, 161; Oscar Kuhns, *The German and Swiss Settlements of Colonial Pennsylvania* (New York: Abingdon Press, 1914), 110; Susan M. Burke and Matthew H. Hill, *From Pennsylvania to Waterloo: Pennsylvania-German Folk Culture in Transition* (Kitchener, Ont.: J. Schneider Haus, 1991), 97.

20. Acrelius, *History of New Sweden*, 161.

21. Burke and Hill, *From Pennsylvania to Waterloo*, 97.

22. William Alexander Alcott, *The Young House-keeper: Or, Thoughts on Food and Cookery*, 5th ed. (Boston: George W. Light, 1842), 281.

23. Ibid., 281.

24. *The American Cook Book: One Thousand Recipes* (New York: Hearst, 1901), 78–79, 358; *A Book of Beverages* (Worcester, Mass.: Colonel Timothy Bigelow Chapter of Daughters of the American Revolution, 1904), 1, 5, 7, 22, 25; Hooker, *History of Food and Drink in America*, 85.

25. Acrelius, *History of New Sweden*, 161.

26. Alice Felt Tyler, *Freedom's Ferment: Phases of American Social History to 1860* (Minneapolis: University of Minnesota Press, 1944), 310.

27. Edward Field, The *Colonial Tavern* (Providence, R.I.: Preston and Rounds, 1897), 138–141; Jean-Anthelme Brillat-Savarin, *Physiology of Taste*, trans. Anne Drayton (Harmondsworth: Penguin Books, 1994), 78.

28. Ulysses Prentiss Hedrick, *A History of Agriculture in the State of New York* (New York: Hill and Wang, 1966), 226; Hooker, *History of Food and Drink in America*, 131.

29. Axel Klinkowström, *Baron Klinkowström's America, 1818–1820* (Evanston, Ill.: Northwestern University Press, 1952), 69.

30. Alice Morse Earle, *Customs and Fashions in Old New England* (New York: Scribner, 1893), 173.

31. Newton D. Mereness, *Travels in the American Colonies* (New York: Macmillan, 1916), 406.

32. Acrelius, *History of New Sweden*, 161.

33. Médéric Moreau de Saint-Méry, "Route Between Philadelphia and New York," in *Moreau de St. Méry's American Journey*, trans. and ed. Kenneth Roberts and Anna M. Roberts (Garden City, N.Y.: Doubleday, 1947), 114.

34. Douglas Freeman, *George Washington: A Biography* (New York: Scribner, 1951), 3:72.

35. War Department, Surgeon General's Office, *A Report on the Hygiene of the United States Army*, Circular 8 (Washington, D.C.: Government Printing Office, 1875), xix.

36. John Adams, "Introspections July 28, 1796," in *The Wisdom of John Adams*, ed. Kees De Mooy (New York: Citadel Press, 2003), 82.

37. Thomas Jefferson, "To Ellen W. Coolidge, March 19, 1826," in *The Writings of Thomas Jefferson*, ed. Albert Ellery Bergh (Washington, D.C.: Thomas Jefferson Memoir Association, 1907), 18: 353.

38. J. P. Brissot de Warville, "Letters," in *New Travels in the United States of America, 1788*, ed. Durand Echeverria (Cambridge, Mass.: Belknap Press of Harvard University, 1964), 91.

39. Howard Means, *Johnny Appleseed: The Man, the Myth, the American Story* (New York: Simon & Schuster, 2011), 54, 61–65.

40. Ibid., 8–9; W. D. Haley, "Johnny Appleseed, a Pioneer Hero," *Harper's New Monthly Magazine*, November 1871, 830–837.

41. Benjamin Rush, "A Moral and Physical Thermometer, Or, a Scale of the Progress of Temperance and Intemperance. Liquors, with Effects in Their Usual Order," in *An Inquiry into the Effects of Spiritous Liquors on the Human Body* (Boston: Thomas and Andrews, 1790), 16.

42. H. K. Carroll, "Total Abstinence Through the Century," in *One Hundred Years of Temperance: A Memorial Volume of the Centennial Temperance Conference Held*

in Philadelphia, Pa., September, 1885 (New York: National Temperance Society and Publication House, 1886), 137.

43. Ibid., 138.

44. Alcott, *Young House-keeper*, 281.

45. William Alcott, "Record of Reform," *Moral Reformer and Teacher on the Human Constitution* 1 (1835): 380.

46. Carwardine, "Evangelicals, Whigs and the Election of William Henry Harrison," 59.

47. Carroll, "Total Abstinence Through the Century," 137–141.

48. Ellen G. White, *Christian Temperance and Bible Hygiene* (Battle Creek, Mich.: Good Health Publishing, 1890), 33.

49. "Condensed Apple Juice," *American Agriculturalist* 23 (1864): 79.

50. R. T. Trall, "Sweet Cider," *Herald of Health* 2 (1863): 181.

51. "Manufacturers Win a Victory in Contest over Provisions of the Volstead Prohibition Enforcement Act," *American Food Journal* 17 (1922): 52.

52. Erika Janik, *Apples: A Global History* (London: Reaktion Books, 2011).

53. Michael Pollan, *The Botany of Desire: A Plant's-Eye View of the World* (New York: Random House, 2001).

6. The Most Popular Drink of the Day

1. The first located reference to Johann Wagner's brewing lager beer appeared in Edwin Troxell Freedley, *Philadelphia and Its Manufactures: A Hand-book Exhibiting the Development, Variety and Statistics of Manufacturing Industry in Philadelphia in 1857* (Philadelphia: Edward Young, 1858), 196; John Leander Bishop, Edwin Troxell Freedley, and Edward Young, *A History of American Manufactures from 1608 to 1860*, 3rd ed. (Philadelphia: Edward Young, 1868), 3:81; Hermann Schlüter, *The Brewing Industry and the Brewery Workers' Movement in America* (Cincinnati: International Union of United Brewery Workmen of America, 1910), 52. After he left Philadelphia, Wagner may have migrated west, ending up in St. Louis. There is a John Wagner who sold lager beer in St. Louis during the 1850s.

2. Laurel Thatcher Ulrich, *Good Wives: Image and Reality in the Lives of Women in Northern New England, 1650–1750* (New York: Vintage, 1991), 23.

3. Israel Acrelius, *A History of New Sweden*, trans. William M. Reynolds (Philadelphia: Historical Society of Pennsylvania, 1874), 163.

4. W. J. Rorabaugh, *The Alcoholic Republic: An American Tradition* (Oxford: Oxford University Press, 1979), 108–109.

5. Tench Coxe, *A Statement of the Arts and Manufactures of the United States of America, for the Year 1810* (Philadelphia: Cornman, 1814), xl.

6. Gallus Thomann, *Liquor Laws of the United States: Their Spirit and Effect* (New York: United States Brewers' Association, 1885), 124.

7. Rorabaugh, *Alcoholic Republic*, 232.

8. Joel Munsell, *Reminiscences of Men and Things in Northfield as I Knew Them from 1812 to 1825* (Albany, N.Y.: Munsell, 1876), 6.

9. Coxe, *Statement of the Arts and Manufactures of the United States of America*, 22; Thomann, *Liquor Laws of the United States*, 123–124.

10. Bishop, Freedley, and Young, *History of American Manufactures from 1608 to 1860*, 3:81.

11. Mark A. Noon, *Yuengling: A History of America's Oldest Brewery* (Jefferson, N.C.: McFarland, 2005), 9.

12. Richard W. Unger, *Beer in the Middle Ages and the Renaissance* (Philadelphia: University of Pennsylvania Press, 2004), 149, 153.

13. "Lager Beer: Its History Manufacture and Consumption in the United States," *New York Tribune*, October 3, 1854, 5.

14. Kim Carpenter, "'We Demand Good and Healthy Beer: The Nutritional and Social Significance of Beer for the Lower Classes in Mid-Nineteenth-Century Munich," in *The City and the Senses: Urban Culture Since 1500*, ed. Alexander Cowan and Jill Steward (Aldershot, Eng.: Ashgate, 2007), 140–141.

15. "Lager Beer," *New York Tribune*, 5.

16. Jeffrey S. Gaab, *Munich: Hofbräuhaus and History: Beer, Culture, and Politics* (New York: Lang, 2006), 29.

17. Maldwyn Allen Jones, *American Immigration* (Chicago: University of Chicago Press, 1960), 93.

18. Ibid., 93–94.

19. Hasia R. Diner, *Hungering for America: Italian, Irish, and Jewish Foodways in the Age of Migration* (Cambridge, Mass.: Harvard University Press, 2001), 140.

20. "Lager Beer," *Ledger*, December 1, 1849, 2; "Lager Beer," *Public Ledger*, December 4, 1849, 3; "Our Philadelphia Correspondence," *New York Herald*, August 16, 1850, 3; "Lager Beer," *Trenton State Gazette*, March 7, 1850, 4; "Our German Population," *Boston Evening Transcript*, August 11, 1851, 2; "Baltimore Correspondence," *Times Picayune*, January 9, 1852, 1; "Lager Beer," *New York Tribune*, 5; "Lager Beer," *Mountain Democrat* (Placerville, Calif.), September 15, 1855, 4; Freedley, *Philadelphia and Its Manufactures*, 196; J. Burnitz Bacon, "Lager Beer in America: How It Came Here, What It Should Be, What It Is," *Frank Leslie's Popular Monthly*, August 1882, 215; "Manufacturing Interests of Albany," in *Bi-Centennial History of Albany: History of the County of Albany*, ed. George Rogers Howell and Jonathan Tenney (New York: Munsell, 1886), 557; *One Hundred Years of Brewing: A Supplement to the Western Brewer, 1903* (Chicago: Rich, 1903), 203; Schlüter, *Brewing Industry and the Brewery Workers' Movement in America*, 52.

21. "Lager Beer," *New York Tribune*, 5.

22. *One Hundred Years of Brewing*, 207.

23. John Thomas Scharf and Thompson Westcott, *History of Philadelphia, 1609–1884* (Philadelphia: L. H. Evertts, 1884), 2:2281.

24. Freedley, *Philadelphia and Its Manufactures*, 197.

25. Scharf and Westcott, *History of Philadelphia*, 2281.

26. Noon, *Yuengling*, 25.

27. "Our German Population," 2.

28. Bishop, Freedley, and Young, *History of American Manufactures from 1608 to 1860*, 3:81; George Ehret, *Twenty-five Years of Brewing: With an Illustrated History of American Beer* (New York: Gast Lithograph & Engraving, 1891), 40.

29. "Lager Beer," *Trenton State Gazette*, 4.

30. Ibid., 4.

31. William Vollmer, *The United States Cook Book*, trans. J. C. Oehlschlager (Philadelphia: John Weik, 1856), 24.

32. Georg von Skal, *History of German Immigration in the United States* (New York, 1908), 193; Schlüter, *Brewing Industry and the Brewery Workers' Movement in America*, 52.

33. "Lager Beer," *New York Tribune*, 5; "Breweries and Lager Bier," *Bankers Magazine*, February 1857, 600–602.

34. "Lager Bier—Changes in the Beverages of the City," *New York Times*, September 17, 1855.

35. Junius Henri Browne, *The Great Metropolis: A Mirror of New York* (Hartford, Conn.: American Publishing, 1869), 160; "The Home Field," *Christian World*, August 1864, 247.

36. Kenneth G. Elzinga, "Beer," in *The Structure of American Industry*, 9th ed., ed. Walter Adams and James W. Brock (Englewood Cliffs, N.J.: Prentice-Hall, 1995), 120–121.

37. Lewis Feuchtwanger, *Fermented Liquors* (New York: Feuchtwanger, 1858), 28–29.

38. *Yankee Notions*, November 1852, 344; *Swilly Willy Wink, or the Lager Bier Song* (Philadelphia: John H. Johnson, 1858); "Lager Beer," *Mountain Democrat*; "A Tale of Lager Bier," *Emerson's Magazine and Putnam's Monthly*, October 1957, 469–470; Hans Punder, "A Little More LA," *The Agitator*, April 26, 1860, 4.

39. George Henry Thurston, *Pittsburgh as It Is: Or, Facts and Figures, Exhibiting the Past and Present* (Pittsburgh: W. S. Haven, 1857), 151.

40. Charles Cist, *Sketches and Statistics of Cincinnati in 1859* (Cincinnati, 1859), 246.

41. *Weekly Vincennes (Ind.) Western Sun*, April 3, 1858.

42. Thomas C. Cochran, *The Pabst Brewing Company* (New York: New York University Press, 1948), 22, 56, 70.

43. *The New World in 1859: Being the United States and Canada* (New York: Bailliere, 1859), 98; Allan Nevins, *The Emergence of Modern America, 1865–1878* (New York: Macmillan, 1927), 46.

44. "Lager Beer Trade at St. Louis," *St. Louis Intelligencer*, quoted in *Hunt's Merchants' Magazine and Commercial Review*, November 1854, 606–607.

45. "German Almanacks for 1860," *Bentley's Miscellany* 46 (1859): 568.

46. Joseph A. Dacus and James William Buel, *A Tour of St. Louis: Or, the Inside Life of a Great City* (St. Louis: Western Publishing, 1878), 478.

47. Ronald Plavchan, "A History of Anheuser-Busch, 1852–1933" (Ph.D. diss., St. Louis University, 1960), 26–27.

48. Harry Dwight Nims, *The Law of Unfair Competition and Trademarks*, 2nd ed. (New York: Baker, Voorhis, 1921), 219; Plavchan, "History of Anheuser-Busch," 37; Eoghan P. Miller, "St. Louis's German Brewing Industry: Its Rise and Fall" (Ph.D. diss., University of Missouri, 2008), 7–8, 13–32.

49. Isaac D. Guyer, *History of Chicago: Its Commercial and Manufacturing Interests and Industry* (Chicago: Church, Goodman & Cushing, 1862), 42–43.

50. "New Liquor Law," *National Era*, October 12, 1854.

51. Richard Willson Renner, "In a Perfect Ferment: Chicago, the Know-Nothings and the Riot for Lager Beer," *Chicago History* 5 (1976): 161–170.

52. "Germany in New York," *Atlantic Monthly*, May 1867, 560, 564.

53. Francis Wyatt, "The Influence of Science in Modern Brewing," *Journal of the Franklin Institute* 150 (1900): 194.

54. Henry Anders, "An Analysis of Lagerbier: As Medicinal and Dietetic Qualities," *American Homoeopathic Review* 1 (1858): 129–131.

55. "Lager Beer," *New York Herald*, in the *Weekly Vincennes Western Sun*, June 25, 1859.

56. *Journal of Proceedings of the Grand Division of the Sons of Temperance of the State of Pennsylvania* (Philadelphia: Wm. F. Geddes, 1850), 54–58.

57. Bell Irvin Wiley, *The Life of Billy Yank: The Common Soldier of the Union* (Baton Rouge: Louisiana State University Press, 2008), 252.

58. Cochran, *Pabst Brewing Company*, 177.

59. J. S. Ingram, *The Centennial Exposition* (Philadelphia: Hubbard, 1876), 450–451; *A Memorial of the International Temperance Conference, Held in Philadelphia, June, 1876* (New York: National Temperance Society and Publication House, 1877), 307, 532–533.

60. James Dabney McCabe, *The Illustrated History of the Centennial Exhibition, Held in Commemoration of the One Hundredth* (Philadelphia: National Publishing, 1876), 62; "Centennial Fair," *New York Tribune*, May 17, 1876, 1; Donald G. Mitchell, "In and About the Fair," *Scribner's Monthly*, November 1876, 116; Julia Coleman, "Beer and Bread," *Phrenological Journal and Science of Health* 71 (1880): 230.

61. Eugene F. Weigel, "Beer: History and Advancement of the Art of Brewing," in *Report of the Committee on Awards of the World's Columbian Commission: 1893*

Special Reports upon Special Subjects or Groups in Two Volumes (Washington, D.C.: Government Printing Office, 1901), 2:990.

62. Bishop, Freedley, and Young, *History of American Manufactures from 1608 to 1860*, 3:81; Ehret, *Twenty-five Years of Brewing*, 40.

63. Audrey L. Olson, *St. Louis Germans, 1850–1920: The Nature of an Immigrant Community* (New York: Arno Press, 1980), 214; Clifford Neal Smith, *Early Nineteenth-Century German Settlers in Ohio* (McNeal, Ariz.: Westland, 1984), 43.

64. "Germany in New York," 560.

65. *Sunday Milwaukee Telegram*, April 16, 1922, in William George Bruce, *History of Milwaukee, City and County* (Chicago: Clarke, 1922), 1:782–783; H. Russell Austin, *The Milwaukee Story: The Making of an American City* (Milwaukee: Milwaukee Journal, 1946), 143.

66. Browne, *Great Metropolis*, 159–166.

67. James Dabney McCabe, *Lights and Shadows of New York Life* (Philadelphia: National Publishing, 1872), 550; Charles Haynes Haswell, *Reminiscences of New York by an Octogenarian* (New York: Harper, 1896), 360; Robert Ernst, *Immigrant Life in New York City, 1825–1863* (New York: King's Crown Press, 1949), 125.

68. Frederick W. Hackwood, *Inns, Ales, and Drinking Customs of Old England* (London: Unwin, 1909), 59–79.

69. George Ade, *The Old-Time Saloon* (New York: Long & Smith, 1931), 26–28, 86; Madelon Powers, *Faces Along the Bar: Lore and Order in the Workingman's Saloon, 1870–1920* (Chicago: University of Chicago Press, 1998), 89.

70. John Marshall Barker, *The Saloon Problem and Social Reform* (Boston: Everett Press, 1905), v, 49–50.

71. Plavchan, "History of Anheuser-Busch," 93–94, 114; Cochran, *Pabst Brewing Company*, 221.

72. Plavchan, "History of Anheuser-Busch," 114; Cochran, *Pabst Brewing Company*, 145; Powers, *Faces Along the Bar*, 242–243.

73. Raymond Calkins, *Substitutes for the Saloon* (Boston: Houghton Mifflin, 1901), 25; Plavchan, "History of Anheuser-Busch," 94–95.

74. Luc Sante, *Low Life: Lures and Snares of Old New York* (New York: Farrar, Straus & Giroux, 1991), 105; Rorabaugh, *Alcoholic Republic*, 232.

75. Rorabaugh, *Alcoholic Republic*, 232.

76. Ibid., 232.

77. Joint Committee on Taxation, "Excise Tax on Certain Trucks; Home Production of Beer and Wine; Fuels Tax Refund to Aerial Applicators; Rollovers of Lump Sum Distributions," 95th Cong., 1979, H.R. 1337 (P.L. 95–458), 3; Hayagreeva Rao, *Market Rebels: How Activists Make or Break Radical Innovations* (Princeton, N.J.: Princeton University Press, 2009), 52–53.

78. Rao, *Market Rebels*, 42.

79. Ibid., 44.

80. Bishop, Freedley, and Young, *History of American Manufactures from 1608 to 1860*, 3:81; Ehret, *Twenty-five Years of Brewing*, 40.

7. Nature's Perfect Food

1. Robert M. Hartley, *An Historical, Scientific, and Practical Essay on Milk, as an Article of Human Sustenance: With a Consideration of the Effects Consequent upon the Present Unnatural Methods of Producing It for the Supply of Large Cities* (New York: Leavitt, 1842), 220; Edward K. Spann, *The New Metropolis: New York City, 1840–1857* (New York: Columbia University Press, 1981), 123.

2. Hartley, *Historical, Scientific, and Practical Essay on Milk*, 34; E. Melanie DuPuis, "The Body and the Country: A Political Ecology of Consumption," in *New Forms of Consumption: Consumers, Culture, and Commodification*, ed. Mark Gottdiener (Lanham, Md.: Rowman & Littlefield, 2000), 138.

3. "The Relation of Lord De-La-Ware, 1611," in *Narratives of Early Virginia, 1606–1625*, ed. Lyon Gardiner Tyler (New York: Scribner, 1907), 213.

4. "Extract of a Letter of Captain Thomas Yong to Sir Toby Matthew, 1634," in *Narratives of Early Maryland, 1633–1684*, ed. Clayton Colman Hall (New York: Scribner, 1910), 60.

5. Jack P. Greene, *Landon Carter: An Inquiry into the Personal Values and Social Imperatives of the Eighteenth-Century Virginia Gentry* (Charlottesville: University Press of Virginia, 1965), 1:211.

6. *The Secret Diary of William Byrd of Westover, 1709–1712*, ed. Louis B. Wright and Marion Tinling (Richmond: Dietz Press, 1941), 3, 7, 8, 11, 32, 41, 57, 122, 298, 299, 300, 301, 302, 303, 354, 404.

7. Richard J. Hooker, *A History of Food and Drink in America* (Indianapolis: Bobbs-Merrill, 1981), 21.

8. George Francis Dow, *Every Day Life in the Massachusetts Bay Colony* (Boston: Society for the Preservation of New England Antiquities, 1935), 98.

9. T. R. Pirtle, *History of the Dairy Industry* (Chicago: Mojonnier, 1926), 17; Mary Caroline Crawford, *Social Life in Old New England* (Boston: Little, Brown, 1914), 249; Dow, *Every Day Life in the Massachusetts Bay Colony*, 98; Bayrd Still, *Mirror for Gotham: New York as Seen by Contemporaries from Dutch Days to the Present* (New York: New York University Press, 1956), 25–26; Hooker, *History of Food and Drink in America*, 32–33.

10. Crawford, *Social Life in Old New England*, 249.

11. Reverend Jonas Michaëlius, "Letter, 1628," in *Narratives of New Netherland, 1609–1664*, ed. J. Franklin Jameson (New York: Scribner, 1909), 132.

12. Pehr Kalm, *Travels into North America* (London: Longman, Hurst, Rees, Orme and Brown, 1812), 346–347.

13. Israel Acrelius, *A History of New Sweden*, trans. William M. Reynolds (Philadelphia: Historical Society of Pennsylvania, 1874), 158, 162, 163, 164, 381, 415.

14. Fredrika Bremer and Mary Botham Howitt, *The Homes of the New World: Impressions of America* (New York: Harper, 1853), 1:63, 280, 281, 521.

15. Edwin James, *Account of an Expedition from Pittsburgh to the Rocky Mountains Performed in the Years 1819, 1820* (London: Longman, Hurst, Rees, Orme and Brown, 1823), 1:77.

16. Sarah Kemble Knight, *The Private Journal of a Journey from Boston to New York in the Year 1704 Kept by Madam Knight* (Albany, N.Y.: F. H. Little, 1865), 33; Hooker, *History of Food and Drink in America*, 58, 66, 86, 92, 124.

17. John J. Dillon, *Seven Decades of Milk: A History of New York's Dairy Industry* (New York: Orange Judd, 1941), 1.

18. Esther Singleton, *Social New York Under the Georges, 1714–1776* (New York: Appleton, 1902), 358.

19. Dillon, *Seven Decades of Milk*, 1.

20. Ibid., 2.

21. Ibid.; Charles E. Rosenberg, *No Other Gods: On Science and American Social Thought*, 2nd ed. (Baltimore: Johns Hopkins University Press, 1997), 118; Richard A. Meckel, *Save the Babies: American Public Health Reform and the Prevention of Infant Mortality* (Ann Arbor: University of Michigan Press, 1998), 64; E. Melanie DuPuis, *Nature's Perfect Food: How Milk Became America's Drink* (New York: New York University Press, 2002), 21–35.

22. Hartley, *Historical, Scientific, and Practical Essay on Milk*, 198–200; Isaac Smithson Hartley, *Memorial of Robert Milham Hartley* (Utica, N.Y.: Curtiss & Childs, 1882), 156–165.

23. Hartley, *Memorial of Robert Milham Hartley*, 168.

24. "Diseased Milk and Meat," *New York Tribune*, June 6, 1849; "Milk in Cities," *New York Tribune*, January 18, 1853; Mitchel Okun, *Fair Play in the Market Place: The First Battle for Pure Food and Drugs* (Dekalb: Northern Illinois University Press, 1986), 9–10; Meckel, *Save the Babies*, 64.

25. John Mullaly, *The Milk Trade of New York and Vicinity, Giving an Account of the Sale of Pure and Adulterated Milk* (New York: Fowlers and Wells, 1853).

26. "New York City: Adjourned Meeting of the Board of Health Committee. The Swill Milk Nuisance," *New York Times*, August 23, 1854, 6; "New York City: Adulterations of Food at Home and Abroad," *New York Times*, June 12, 1855, 1; "Hard Times in the City: A Dull Season for Distillers" *New York Times*, October 28, 1857, 1; "More Arrests of Milk Wagons," *New York Times*, May 14, 1858, 4.

27. "Startling Exposure of the Milk Trade of New York and Brooklyn," *Frank Leslie's Illustrated Newspaper*, May 8, 1858, 353–354, 359.

28. David Marshall Owen, "Four Hundred Years of Milk in America," *New York History* 31 (1950): 452.

29. "Swill Milk: History of the Agitation of the Subject—The Recent Report of the Committee of the New York Academy of Medicine," *New York Times,* January 27, 1860, 2.
30. Meckel, *Save the Babies,* 65.
31. X. A. Willard, *Willard's Practical Dairy Husbandry* (New York: American News, 1872), 214.
32. Dillon, *Seven Decades of Milk,* 4.
33. DuPuis, *Nature's Perfect Food,* 35.
34. Dillon, *Seven Decades of Milk,* 2–3.
35. Willard, *Willard's Practical Dairy Husbandry,* 247.
36. Austin Flint, *A Treatise on the Principles and Practices of Medicine,* cited in Meckel, *Save the Babies,* 68. For a summary of the research on milk adulterations at the time, see "Distillery Milk Report," *Science,* July 1, 1887, 4–7.
37. Arthur M. Schlesinger, *Paths to the Present,* rev. ed. (Boston: Houghton Mifflin, 1964), 233.
38. Meckel, *Save the Babies,* 68–69.
39. Ibid., 72–73.
40. Owen, "Four Hundred Years of Milk in America," 460.
41. DuPuis, *Nature's Perfect Food,* 39, 72.
42. Pauline Arnold and Percival White, *Food: America's Biggest Business* (New York: Holiday House, 1959), 176.
43. Henry Alvord, "Dairy Development in the United States," in U.S. Department of Agriculture, *Yearbook of Agriculture, 1899* (Washington, D.C.: Government Printing Office, 1900), 381.
44. Mary Ronald, *The Century Cook Book* (New York: Century, 1897), 257.
45. W. G. Marshall, *Through America: Or, Nine Months in the United States,* 2nd ed. (New York: Arno Press, 1974), 98.
46. Henry A. Alford, "The Milk Question," in *Annual Report of the Secretary of the Board of Agriculture for 1882* (Boston: Wright & Potter, 1883), 49.
47. M. P. Catherwood, *Statistical Study of Milk Production for the New York Market,* cited in DuPuis, *Nature's Perfect Food,* 41.
48. DuPuis, "Body and the Country," 148–150.
49. William H. Allen, *Civics and Health* (Boston: Ginn, 1909), 260; DuPuis, *Nature's Perfect Food,* 72–73, 109.
50. DuPuis, *Nature's Perfect Food,* 72–73.
51. DuPuis, "Body and the Country," 148; Hooker, *History of Food and Drink in America,* 341.
52. Lisa Nicole Mills, *Science and Social Context: The Regulation of Recombinant Bovine Growth Hormone in North America* (Montreal: McGill-Queen's University Press, 2002); Nina Redman, *Food Safety: A Reference Handbook* (Santa Barbara, Calif.: ABC-CLIO, 2007), 57–58.
53. Anne Mendelson, e-mail to author, July 25, 2011.

54. DuPuis, *Nature's Perfect Food*, 210.

55. Rosenberg, *No Other Gods*, 109; DuPuis, *Nature's Perfect Food*, 21.

8. The Most Delightful and Insinuating Potations

1. "List of New Works," *American Publishers' Circular and Literary Gazette*, June 4, 1859, 271; David Wondrich, *Imbibe: From Absinthe Cocktail to Whiskey Smash, a Salute in Stories and Drinks to "Professor" Jerry Thomas, Pioneer of the American Bar* (New York: Perigee, 2007), 285.

2. Elizabeth Moxon, *English Housewifry: Exemplified in Above Four Hundred and Fifty Receipts* (Leeds: Griffin Wright, 1763), 145.

3. Isaac Weld, *Travels Through the States of North America, 1795, 1796 & 1797* (London: J. Stockdale, 1799), 81.

4. Israel Acrelius, *A History of New Sweden*, trans. William M. Reynolds (Philadelphia: Historical Society of Pennsylvania, 1874), 162.

5. C. Anne Wilson, *Food and Drink in Britain* (London: Constable, 1973), 403.

6. Weld, *Travels Through the States of North America*, 360; John E. Wright and Doris S. Corbett, *Pioneer Life in Western Pennsylvania* (Pittsburgh: University of Pittsburgh Press, 1940), 60.

7. Constantin-François de Volney, *View of the Climate and Soil of the United States of America* (London: Johnson, 1804), 288.

8. Isaac Holmes, *An Account of the United States of America* (London: Caxton Press, 1823), 352; William Howard Russell, *My Diary North and South* (Boston: Burnham, 1863), 210; Richard J. Hooker, *A History of Food and Drink in America* (Indianapolis: Bobbs-Merrill, 1981), 138.

9. Holmes, *Account of the United States of America*, 352.

10. Captain J. E. Alexander, *Transatlantic Sketches* (Philadelphia: Key and Biddle, 1833), 368.

11. Ibid., 368.

12. Eliza Leslie, *Miss Leslie's New Cookery Book* (Philadelphia: R. B. Peterson, 1857), 610; John Russell Bartlett, *Bartlett's Dictionary of Americanisms*, 2nd ed. (Boston: Little, Brown, 1859), 90.

13. Frederick Marryat, *A Diary in America: With Remarks on Its Institutions* (Paris: Baudry's European Library, 1839), 38.

14. Ibid., 44, 164.

15. Charles F. Hoffman, *Wild Scenes in the Forest and Prairie: With Sketches of American Life* (New York: William H. Colyer, 1843), 1:144; Bartlett, *Bartlett's Dictionary of Americanisms*, 90, 223, 273.

16. Washington Irving, *A History of New York*, in *The Works of Washington Irving* (New York: Putnam, 1809), 1:395.

17. James Fenimore Cooper, *The Spy*, rev. ed. (London: Henry Colburn, 1831), 185.

18. "To the Editor of *The Balance*," *Balance, and Columbian Repository*, May 13, 1806, 146.

19. "Journal of a Tour Through the Eastern States," *St. Tammany's Magazine*, December 17, 1821, 72; Alexander, *Transatlantic Sketches*, 368; Edward Henry Durell, *New Orleans as I Found It* (New York: Harper, 1845), 25.

20. Elliot West, *Saloon on Rocky Mountain Mining Frontier* (Lincoln: University of Nebraska Press, 1979), 34–35, 91; Hooker, *History of Food and Drink in America*, 139.

21. Christine Sismondo, *America Walks into a Bar: A Spirited History of Taverns and Saloons, Speakeasies and Grog Shops* (New York: Oxford University Press, 2011), 109; Wondrich, *Imbibe*, 9.

22. Marryat, *Diary in America*, 46.

23. William Henry Milburn, *Ten Years of Preacher-Life* (New York: Derby & Jackson, 1859), 236–237.

24. Thomas L. Nichols, *Forty Years of American Life* (London: J. Maxwell, 1864), 1:191, 195–196.

25. Alexander, *Transatlantic Sketches*, 368; Charles H. Haswell, *Reminiscences of an Octogenarian of the City of New York* (New York: Harper, 1897), 379; Luc Sante, *Low Life: Lures and Snares of Old New York* (New York: Farrar, Straus & Giroux, 1991), 104–105; Sismondo, *America Walks into a Bar*, 104–105; Madelon Powers, *Faces Along the Bar: Lore and Order in the Workingman's Saloon, 1870–192* (Chicago: University of Chicago Press, 1998), 17, 242–243.

26. John Frederick Fitzgerald De Ros, *Personal Narrative of Travels in the United States and Canada in 1826* (London: William Harrison Ainsworth, 1827), 5.

27. Alexander, *Transatlantic Sketches*, 368; "The Mint Julep," *The Corsair*, August 31, 1839, 395.

28. Wondrich, *Imbibe*, 13–35.

29. Edward Peron Hingston, *The Genial Showman, Reminiscences of the Life of "Artemus Ward"* (London: John Camden Hotten, 1870), 361.

30. *The American Bar-Tender, Or, the Art and Mystery of Mixing Drinks* (New York: Hurst, 1874); Harry Johnson, *The New and Improved Illustrated Bartenders' Manual; Or: How to Mix Drinks* (New York: Johnson, 1882); O. H. Byron, *The Modern Bartenders' Guide* (New York: Excelsior, 1884); Albert Barnes, *The Complete Bartender* (Philadelphia: Crawford, 1884); Naber, Alfs and Brune, *Catalogue and Bartenders' Guide: How to Mix Drinks* (San Francisco: Schmidt, 1884); William T. Boothby, *Cocktail Boothby's American Bartender: The Only Practical Treatise on the Art of Mixology* (San Francisco: H. S. Crocker, 1891); Henry J. Wehman, *Wehman's Bartender's Guide, Or, the Art of Preparing All Kinds of Plain and Fancy Drinks Both Native and Foreign* (New York: Wehman, 1891); Chris F. Lawlor, *The Mixicologist* (Cincinnati: Lawlor, 1895); *Haney's Steward & Barkeeper's Manual* (New York: Haney, 1896); Harry Lamore, *The Bartender: Or, How to Mix Drinks, etc.* (New York: R. K. Fox, 1896); *Cocktails: How to Make*

Them (Providence: Livermore & Knight, 1898); J. Henry Schell, *Mixed Drinks Up-to-Date* (New York: Schell, 1900); John Applegreen, *Applegreen's Bartenders' Guide, or How to Mix Drinks* (Chicago: Hotel Monthly, 1901); Charles S. Mahoney and Harry Montague, *New Bartender's Guide: Telling How to Mix All the Standard and Popular Drinks Called for Everyday* (New York: Royal, 1914); Tom Bullock, *The Ideal Bartender* (St. Louis: Buxton & Skinner, 1917).

31. Jerry Thomas, *Bartender's Guide: Or How to Mix Drinks* (New York: Dick & Fitzgerald, 1862), 49–52, 106, 110, 114, 115.

32. Perry Duis, *The Saloon: Public Drinking in Chicago and Boston, 1880–1920* (Urbana: University of Illinois Press, 1999), 295.

33. Jerry Thomas, *Jerry Thomas' Bar-Tender's Guide of How to Mix Drinks* (New York: Dick & Fitzgerald, 1887), 24; William Grimes, *Straight Up or On the Rocks: The Story of the American Cocktail* (New York: North Point Press, 2001), 84–85; Wondrich, *Imbibe*, 236–240.

34. Thomas, *Jerry Thomas' Bar-Tender's Guide*, 25; Johnson, *New and Improved Illustrated Bartenders' Manual*, 39–40; Barnaby Conrad III, *The Martini: An Illustrated History of an American Classic* (San Francisco: Chronicle Books, 1995); Grimes, *Straight Up or On the Rocks*, 27–29; Wondrich, *Imbibe*, 243–244, 295–300.

35. George Edwin Roberts, *Cups and Their Customs* (London: John van Voorst, 1863), 30.

36. Thomas Colley Grattan, *Civilized America* (London: Bradbury and Evans, 1859), 1:62.

37. George Sala, *Notes and Sketches of the Paris Exhibition* (London: Tinsley Brothers, 1868), 374.

38. William Terrington, *Cooling Cups and Dainty Drinks* (London: Routledge, 1869), v.

39. Andrew Barr, *Drink: A Social History of America* (New York: Carroll & Graf, 1999), 51.

40. Harry MacElhone, *Harry's ABC of Mixing Cocktails: More Than 300 Famous Cocktails* (London: Dean, 1919).

41. E. Ricket and C. Thomas, *The Gentleman's Table Guide: Being Practical Recipes for Wine Cups, American Drinks, Punches, Cordials, Summer and Winter Beverages* (London: H. Born, 1871), 37–53.

42. George Ade, *The Old-Time Saloon* (New York: Long & Smith, 1931), 26–27.

43. Ibid., 26–28, 86; Powers, *Faces Along the Bar*, 89.

44. Stephen Birmingham, *The Right People: A Portrait of the American Social Establishment* (Boston: Little, Brown, 1968), 241–242; Barr, *Drink*, 49, 106–108.

45. Lucius Beebe and Charles Clegg, *Narrow Gauge in the Rockies* (Berkeley, Calif.: Howell-North, 1958), 30; Birmingham, *Right People*, 242–243, 246.

46. Norman Anthony, *Noble Experiments* (New York: Day, 1930); Johnny Brooks, *My Thirty-five Years Behind Bars* (New York: Exposition Press, 1954).

47. Victor J. Bergeron, *Trader Vic's Pacific Island Cookbook with Side Trips to Hong Kong, Southeast Asia, Mexico, and Texas* (Garden City, N.Y.: Doubleday, 1968), 184.

48. Marion Gorman and Felipe de Alba, *The Tequila Book* (Chicago: Contemporary Books, 1978), 78–80; John F. Mariani, *America Eats Out: An Illustrated History of Restaurants, Taverns, Coffee Shops, Speakeasies, and Other Establishments That Have Fed Us for 350 Years* (New York: Morrow, 1991), 81, and *The Dictionary of American Food and Drink* (New York: Hearst Books, 1994), 194; James Trager, *The Food Chronology: A Food Lover's Compendium of Events and Anecdotes, from Prehistory to the Present* (New York: Holt, 1995), 467.

49. Advertisement, *Puck*, December 25, 1901.

50. Linda Himelstein, *The King of Vodka: The Story of Pyotr Smirnov and the Upheaval of an Empire* (New York: Harper, 2009), 320–324, 327–330.

51. *The Club Cocktail Party Book* (Hartford, Conn.: Heublein, 1941).

52. Bill Ryan, "Smirnoff Vodka: No Taste, No Smell," *New York Times*, February 19, 1995.

53. Harry Craddock, comp., *The Savoy Cocktail Book* (London: Constable, 1930); Victor Bergeron, *Trader Vic's Bartender's Guide* (Garden City, N.Y.: Doubleday, 1947).

54. H. L. Mencken, "The Vocabulary of the Drinking Chamber," *New Yorker*, November 5, 1948, 108–109.

55. "Joseph Carlin," interview with author, July 18, 2011.

56. David Wondrich, "Paying Homage, a Bit Belatedly, to a Mix Master of Renown," *New York Times*, October 10, 2004.

9. Unfermented Wine

1. M. Stewart, *Scriptural View of the Wine: Question, in a Letter to the Rev. Dr. Nott, President of Union College* (New York: Leavitt Trow, 1848), 53; Frederic Richard Lees, *The Temperance Bible Commentary: Giving at One View, Version, Criticism, and Exposition, in Regard to All Passages of Holy Writ Bearing on "Wine" and "Strong Drink"* (New York: Sheldon, 1870), 431; Frederick Powell, *Bacchus Dethroned: Prize Essay* (New York: National Temperance Society and Publication House, 1873), 211.

2. "The Wine Question," *Christian Review*, March 1836, 139; Lewis Mayer, "Is It Morally Wrong to Drink Wine or Strong Drink, Which When Taken in Excess Produces Intoxication?" *American Biblical Repository*, 2nd ser., 2 (1839):421; "Nephalism," *Medical Times and Gazette*, February 9, 1861, 147.

3. William Chazanof, *Welch's Grape Juice: From Corporation to Co-operative* (Syracuse, N.Y.: Syracuse University Press, 1977), 78.

4. Edward Deming Andrews and Faith Andrews, *Work and Worship Among the Shakers* (New York: Dover, 1982), 67.

5. *Oneida Community Limited, Packers of Choice Fruits, Vegetables, Jellies, Fruit Juices, Poultry & Soups* (Oneida, N.Y.: Oneida Community, 1885).

6. Estelle Woods Wilcox, comp., *Centennial Buckeye Cook Book* (Marysville, Ohio: J. H. Shearer, 1876), 303.

7. "Welch," in *Genealogical and Family History of Western New York*, ed. William Richard Cutter (New York: Lewis Historical Publishing, 1912), 2:545; Chazanof, *Welch's Grape Juice*, 57–58.

8. Chazanof, *Welch's Grape Juice*, 81–82.

9. *Grape Juice as a Therapeutic Agent* (Westfield, N.Y.: Welch Grape Juice Company, 1921), 17.

10. Arnold Lorand, *Health Through Rational Diet* (Philadelphia: Davis, 1912), 90; House of Representatives, *Unfermented Fruit Juices: Hearing Before a Subcommittee on H.R. 7840, March 30, 1920* (Washington, D.C.: Government Printing Office, 1920), 103.

11. Chazanof, *Welch's Grape Juice*, 96.

12. "A Recipe Returned from Over Sea," *Medical Record* 41 (1892): 308.

13. Earl Chapin May, *The Canning Clan: A Pageant of Pioneering Americans* (New York: Macmillan, 1937), 304; George Ephraim Sokolsky, *The American Way of Life* (New York: Farrar & Rinehart, 1939), 35; "The Exclusive Story of Tomato Juice," *Indianapolis Star Magazine*, July 19, 1959, 26, 28; Anistatia Miller and Jared Brown, *Spirituous Journey: A History of Drink*, book 2, *From Publicans to Master Mixologists* (London: Mixellany, 2009), 163.

14. Florence M. Albright, "Eat Tomatoes," *Indiana Farmer's Guide*, October 14, 1922, 1078; "Advertise Tomatoes as Food and Medicine," *Market Growers Journal*, August 15, 1923, 118.

15. Ingrid Nelson Waller, *Where There Is Vision: The New Jersey Agricultural Experiment Station 1880–1955* (New Brunswick, N.J.: Rutgers University Press, 1955), 53.

16. May, *Canning Clan*, 304–306; Walter J. Kemp, US Patent 1,746,657; May, *Canning Clan*, 306.

17. "Campbell Soup Company Historical Synopsis," 11, undated mimeographed paper, Campbell Soup Company Archives, Camden, N.J.; "Campbell's Soup," *Fortune*, November 1935, 68; Belle Terre Garden Club, *Belle Terre Favorites* (New York: Stewart, Warren & Benson, 1936), 13.

18. *Annual Report of the General Manager of the California Fruit Growers* (Los Angeles: California Fruit Growers Exchange, 1933), 25.

19. John Ayto, *Food and Drink from A to Z: A Gourmet's Guide*, 2nd ed. (Oxford: Oxford University Press, 1993), 34; John F. Mariani, *The Dictionary of Italian Food and Drink* (New York: Broadway Books, 1998), 32–33.

20. A. W. Carswell, "V-8 Cocktail Vegetable Juices–History," memorandum, December 18, 1953, Campbell Soup Company Archives.

21. Alice Morse Earle, "Old Colonial Drinks and Drinkers," *National Magazine*, June 1892, 156.

22. Paul Sayres, *Food Marketing: Twenty-two Leaders of the Food Industry Tell How the Nation's Biggest and Most Complex Business Works, and Why* (New York: McGraw-Hill, 1950), 4.

23. Jeffrey L. Cruikshank and Arthur W. Schultz, *The Man Who Sold America: The Amazing (But True!) Story of Albert D. Lasker and the Creation of the Advertising Century* (Boston: Harvard Business Review Press, 2010), 117–119.

24. *Annual Report of the General Manager of the California Fruit Growers* (Los Angeles: California Fruit Growers Exchange, 1916), 7; *Annual Report of the General Manager of the California Fruit Growers* (Los Angeles: California Fruit Growers Exchange, 1918), 12; *Annual Report of the General Manager of the California Fruit Growers* (Los Angeles: California Fruit Growers Exchange, 1919), 15.

25. Cruikshank and Schultz, *Man Who Sold America*, 119–121; "Drink and Orange," *Simmons' Spice Mill*, January 1916, 74; Eric Clark, *The Want Makers: The World of Advertising: How They Make You Buy* (New York: Viking, 1989), 54.

26. *Pure Concentrated Orange Juice; What It Is, How to Use It* (San Dimas, Calif.: Exchange Orange Products, ca. 1920s).

27. *Annual Report of the General Manager of the California Fruit Growers* (Los Angeles: California Fruit Growers Exchange, 1924), 20; *Annual Report of the General Manager of the California Fruit Growers* (Los Angeles: California Fruit Growers Exchange, 1929), 18–19.

28. *Annual Report of the General Manager of the California Fruit Growers* (1929), 18.

29. "Willard Hamlin, 90, Creator of Orange Julius Fruit Drink," *New York Times*, June 8, 1987, http://www.nytimes.com/1987/06/08/obituaries/willard-hamlin-90-creator-of-orange-julius-fruit-drink.html (accessed July 17, 2011).

30. James T. Hopkins, *Fifty Years of Citrus: The Florida Citrus Exchange, 1909–1959* (Gainesville: University of Florida Press, 1960), 9.

31. M. G. Frank, *Keeping Well with Oranges and Grapefruit* (Tampa: Florida Citrus Exchange, 1931), 7, 9.

32. James Rorty and N. Philip Nonnan, *Tomorrow's Food* (New York: Devin-Adair, 1956), 121.

33. Richard J. Hooker, *A History of Food and Drink in America* (Indianapolis: Bobbs-Merrill, 1981), 317.

34. A. W. Bitting, *Appertizing or the Art of Canning* (San Francisco: Trade Pressroom, 1937), 265; *Historical Statistics of the United States: Colonial Times to 1970* (Washington, D.C.: U.S. Department of Commerce; Bureau of the Census, 1975), 1:330.

35. *Annual Report of the General Manager of the California Fruit Growers* (Los Angeles: California Fruit Growers Exchange, 1923), 20.

36. *Annual Report of the General Manager of the California Fruit Growers* (Los Angeles: California Fruit Growers Exchange, 1930), 26; *Annual Report of the General Manager of the California Fruit Growers* (Los Angeles: California Fruit Growers Exchange, 1931), 28; Hopkins, *Fifty Years of Citrus*, 121–122.

37. Elizabeth Drew, *Richard M. Nixon* (New York: Times Books, 2007), 7.

38. V. O. Wodicka, "Preservation of Foodstuffs," in *Development of Special Rations for the Army*, ed. Harold W. Thatcher (Washington, D.C.: Office of the Quartermaster General, General Administrative Services Division, Historical Section, 1944), 107, cited in Alissa Hamilton, *Squeezed: What You Don't Know About Orange Juice* (New Haven, Conn.: Yale University Press, 2009), 16.

39. Quoted in Hamilton, *Squeezed*, 18.

40. F. W. Wenzel, C. D. Atkins, and Edwin L. More, "Frozen Concentrated Orange Juice—Past, Present and Future," *Florida State Horticultural Society Proceedings* 62 (1949): 180.

41. *Annual Report* (Tampa: Florida Citrus Exchange, 1945), 66; Alistair Cooke, *The American Home Front, 1941–1942* (New York: Atlantic Monthly Press, 2006), 78–79; Hopkins, *Fifty Years of Citrus*, 196.

42. Donald K. Tressler and Clifford F. Evers, *The Freezing Preservation of Foods* (New York: Avi, 1943), 311; "Corporations: Minute Maid's Man," *Time*, October 18, 1948, http://www.time.com/time/magazine/article/0,9171,799353,00.html (accessed April 18, 2012); C. Lester Walker, "What's in the Deep Freeze?" *Harper's Magazine*, June 1949, 46–47; Edwin W. Williams, *Frozen Food: Biography of an Industry* (Boston: Cahners, 1963), 10–11, 58–60, 85–86; Harvey Levenstein, *Paradox of Plenty: A Social History of Eating in Modern America* (New York: Oxford University Press, 1993), 107; Sidney Mintz, "Frozen in Time: The Other Orangemen," *Wall Street Journal*, June 23, 2000, 13.

43. *Statistical Abstract of the United States* (Washington, D.C.: Superintendent of Documents, 1963), 83:791.

44. Wenzel, Atkins, and More, "Frozen Concentrated Orange Juice," 179.

45. Susan Pollack and Agnes Perez, *Fruit and Tree Outlook* (Washington, D.C.: Economic Research Service, U.S. Department of Agriculture, 2009), http://www.ers.usda.gov/publications/fts/2009/11Nov/FTS340.pdf (accessed April 18, 2012).

10. The Temperance Beverage

1. Mark Pendergrast, *For God, Country, and Coca-Cola: The Definitive History of the Great American Soft Drink and the Company That Makes It* (New York: Scribner, 1993), 24–29.

2. *Atlanta Evening Journal*, June 30, 1887, 1; "The Full Text of the Koke Co.–Coca-Cola Co. Case," *Simmons' Spice Mill*, September 1919, 1220; David Gerard Hogan, *Selling 'Em by the Sack: White Castle and the Creation of American Food* (New York: New York University Press, 1997), 18.

3. John J. Riley, *A History of the American Soft Drink Industry: Bottled Carbonated Beverages, 1807–1957* (Washington, D.C.: American Bottlers of Carbonated Beverages, 1958), 56.

4. Everett Dick, *The Sod House Frontier, 1854–1890* (Lincoln: University of Nebraska Press, 1979), 63.

5. Riley, *History of the American Soft Drink Industry*, 66–67.

6. "History of Root Beer," in *American Stone Ginger Beer and Root Beer Heritage, 1790 to 1920*, ed. Donald Yates and Elizabeth Yates (Homerville, Ohio: Yates, 2003).

7. "A Family Affair," *New York Times*, April 8, 1892, 2; "Said the Owl," *New York Times*, May 8, 1893, 2; "Nervous," *New York Times*, May 5, 1894, 3.

8. "A Great Substitute," *Cosmopolitan*, August 1886, 8.

9. Harry E. Ellis, *Dr Pepper: King of Beverages, Centennial Edition* (Dallas: Dr Pepper Company, 1986).

10. *Sacramento City Directory* (Sacramento: Sacramento Directory, 1921).

11. John A. Jakle and Keith A. Sculle, *Fast Food: Roadside Restaurants in the Automobile Age* (Baltimore: Johns Hopkins University Press, 1999), 165–166.

12. Jeffrey L. Rodengen, *The Legend of Dr Pepper/Seven-Up* (Fort Lauderdale, Fla.: Write Stuff Syndicate, 1995).

13. Baron W. Stone, "Opiates and Ethics," in *Transactions of the Kentucky State Medical Society Forty-fifth Annual Session* (Georgetown: Kentucky State Medical Society, 1900), 8:180; Milward W. Martin, *Twelve Full Ounces*, 2nd ed. (New York: Holt, Rinehart and Winston, 1969), 12–14; Richard J. Hooker, *A History of Food and Drink in America* (Indianapolis: Bobbs-Merrill,1981), 274.

14. "Coca-Cola Syrup and Extract," *Official Gazette of the U. S. Patent Office*, June 28, 1887, 430.

15. Pendergrast, *For God, Country, and Coca-Cola*, 27–31, 40.

16. Ibid., 57.

17. "Coca-Cola's Continuous Conquests," *National Druggist* 30 (1900): 108; Pendergrast, *For God, Country, and Coca-Cola*, 74.

18. For more on the history of soda fountains, see Anne Cooper Funderburg, *Sundae Best: A History of Soda Fountains* (Bowling Green, Ohio: Bowling Green State University Popular Press, 2002).

19. Frederick Allen, *Secret Formula: How Brilliant Marketing and Relentless Salesmanship Made Coca-Cola the Best-Known Product in the World* (New York: HarperBusiness, 1994), 41–42, 142–143.

20. Riley, *History of the American Soft Drink Industry*, 136.

21. E. J. Kahn, Jr., *The Big Drink: The Story of Coca-Cola* (New York: Random House, 1960), 55–56; Martin, *Twelve Full Ounces*, 11–12, 19; Riley, *History of the American Soft Drink Industry*, 117–118.

22. "Hyman Kirsch, 99, Made Diet Sodas; Originator of No-Cal Dies Brooklyn Philanthropist," *New York Times*, May 13, 1976; Wolfgang Saxon, "Morris Kirsch Is Dead at 79; Headed No-Cal Soft Drinks," *New York Times*, June 25, 1986.

23. Mark Pendergrast, *Uncommon Grounds: The History of Coffee and How It Transformed Our World*, 2nd ed. (New York: Basic Books, 2010), 248.

24. Gary A. Hemphill, "Led by Energy Drinks, Teas and Bottled Water, the U.S. Liquid Refreshment Beverage Market Grew by 1.3% in 2007, Beverage Marketing Corporation Reports," press release, Beverage Marketing Corporation, March 12, 2008.

25. Mark Pendergrast, e-mail to author, July 25, 2011.

26. Elizabeth Royte, *Garbage Land: On the Secret Trail of Trash* (New York: Little, Brown, 2005), 176, and *Bottlemania: How Water Went on Sale and Why We Bought It* (New York: Bloomsbury, 2008), 5.

11. To Root Out a Bad Habit

1. Ronald Plavchan, "A History of Anheuser-Busch, 1852–1933" (Ph.D. diss., St. Louis University, 1960), 139–140; Hayagreeva Rao, *Market Rebels: How Activists Make or Break Radical Innovations* (Princeton, N.J.: Princeton University Press, 2009), 49.

2. John Winthrop, *The History of New England from 1630 to 1649* (Boston: Phelps and Farnham, 1825), 1:125.

3. Increase Mather, *Wo to Drunkards: Two Sermons Testifying Against the Sin of Drunkenness* (Cambridge, Mass.: Marmaduke Johnson, 1673), 4.

4. Increase Mather, *A Sermon Occasioned by the Execution of a Man Found Guilty of Murder* (Boston: Printed by R.P., 1687), 25.

5. David W. Conroy, *In Public Houses: Drink and the Revolution of Authority in Colonial Massachusetts* (Chapel Hill: University of North Carolina Press, 1995), 62–63, 66–72, 78–81.

6. J. C. Furnas, *The Life and Times of the Late Demon Rum* (New York: Putnam, 1965), 65.

7. John Adams, "Diary, 1796," in *The Works of John Adams, Second President of the United States*, comp. and ed. Charles Francis Adams (Cambridge, Mass.: Little, Brown, 1851), 3:418.

8. Anthony Benezet, *The Mighty Destroyer Displayed, in Some Account of the Dreadful Havock Made by the Mistaken Use as Well as Abuse of Distilled Spirituous Liquors* (Philadelphia: Joseph Crukshank, 1774), quoted in "Dr. Benjamin Rush and Anthony Benezet," *The Friend*, October 7, 1885, 92.

9. Benjamin Rush, *Sermons to Gentlemen on Temperance and Exercise*, cited and quoted in Alyn Brodsky, *Benjamin Rush: Patriot and Physician* (New York: St. Martin's Press, 2004), 39, 95–96.

10. Benjamin Rush, *Letters, 1761–1792* (Princeton, N.J.: Princeton University Press, 1951), 272; Benjamin Rush, "An Inquiry into the Effects of Ardent Spirits upon the Human Body and Mind," in *Medical Inquiries and Observations*, 2nd ed. (Philadelphia: Conrad, 1805), 1:369.

11. Charles A. Lee, "History of Intoxicating Liquors in the United States," cited in Ralph Barnes Grindrod, *Bacchus: An Essay on the Nature, Causes, Effects, and*

Cure of Intemperance (New York: Langley, 1840), 462; Henry William Blair, *The Temperance Movement: Or, the Conflict Between Man and Alcohol* (Boston: Smythe, 1888), 424.

12. "The Temperance Movement," in *Chambers's Miscellany of Useful and Entertaining Tracts* (Edinburgh: William and Robert Chambers, 1845), 23.

13. Francis Lieber and others, *Encyclopaedia Americana* (Philadelphia: Carey and Lea, 1832), 12:175–176.

14. "George Ticknor to Thomas Jefferson, December 2, 1821," in *The Jefferson Papers, 1770–1826*, 7th ser. (Boston: Massachusetts Historical Society, 1900), 1:310.

15. Samuel Morewood, *An Essay on the Inventions and Customs of Ancient and Modern Nations in the Manufacture and Use of Inebriating Liquors* (London: Longman, Hurst, Rees, Orme, Brown and Green, 1824), 187.

16. Fanny Trollope, *Domestic Manners of the Americans* (New York: Reprinted for the Bookseller, 1832), 41; W. J. Rorabaugh, "Alcohol in America," *OAH Magazine of History* 6, no. 2 (1991):17.

17. Perry Duis, *The Saloon: Public Drinking in Chicago and Boston, 1880–1920* (Urbana: University of Illinois Press, 1999), 10–11.

18. Lyman Beecher, *Six Sermons on the Nature, Occasions, Signs, Evils, and Remedy of Intemperance* (New York: American Tract Society, 1827).

19. *The American Cyclopaedia: A Popular Dictionary of General Knowledge* (New York: Appleton, 1876), 15:816.

20. Alexis de Tocqueville, *Democracy in America* (New York: Edwin Walker, 1847), 118.

21. Earnest H. Cherrington, *The Evolution of Prohibition in the United States of America* (Westerville, Ohio: American Issue Press, 1920), 93.

22. Ibid., 93.

23. Lieber and others, *Encyclopaedia Americana*, 176.

24. John Granville Woolley and William Eugene Johnson, *Temperance Progress in the Century* (Philadelphia: Bradley-Garretson, 1903), 115.

25. *The Temperance Textbook: A Collection of Facts and Interesting Anecdotes Illustrating the Evils of Intoxicating Drinks* (Philadelphia: Carey and Hart, 1837), 108–109.

26. H. K. Carroll, "Total Abstinence Through the Century," in *One Hundred Years of Temperance* (New York: National Temperance Society and Publication House, 1886), 131.

27. W. J. Rorabaugh, *The Alcoholic Republic: An American Tradition* (Oxford: Oxford University Press, 1979), 232.

28. Woolley and Johnson, *Temperance Progress in the Century*, 142.

29. Luc Sante, *Low Life: Lures and Snares of Old New York* (New York: Farrar, Straus & Giroux, 1991), 105.

30. Raymond Calkins, *Substitutes for the Saloon* (Boston: Houghton Mifflin, 1901), 353.

31. Christopher Corkscrew, *Hardscrabble or Ballad of the Free Lunch Bar* (New York: W. I. Whiting, 1894); Madelon Powers, *Faces Along the Bar: Lore and Order in the Workingman's Saloon, 1870–1920* (Chicago: University of Chicago Press, 1998), 224.

32. "Jefferson Drug & Variety Store," *Wisconsin Weekly Jeffersonian*, August 6, 1857, 3.

33. "A Family Affair," *New York Times*, April 8, 1892, 2; "Said the Owl," *New York Times*, May 8, 1893, 2; "Nervous," *New York Times*, May 5, 1894, p. 3.

34. *American Druggist and Pharmaceutical Record*, August 17, 1894, 126.

35. *The Spatula* 2 (1896): 424.

36. Martha Meir Allen, *Alcohol: A Dangerous and Unnecessary Medicine* (Marcellus, N.Y.: Department of Medical Temperance of the National Woman's Christian Temperance Union, 1900), 427; "Coca-Cola," *National Magazine*, March 1906, 720.

37. Dee Brown, *The Gentle Tamers: Women of the Old West* (New York: Putnam, 1973), 272–277.

38. Jack S. Blocker, *American Temperance Movements: Cycles of Reform* (Boston: Twayne, 1989), 114.

39. Amy Mittelman, *Brewing Battles: A History of American Beer* (New York: Algora, 2008), 76.

40. *The Anti-Prohibition Manual: A Summary of Facts and Figures Dealing with Prohibition* (Cincinnati: National Wholesale Liquor Dealers Association of American, 1918), 1–128.

41. Will Irwin, "The American Saloon," *Collier's Weekly*, May 16, 1908, 10, and "More About 'Nigger Gin,'" *Collier's Weekly*, August 15, 1908, 28, 30.

42. Daniel Okrent, *Last Call: The Rise and Fall of Prohibition* (New York: Scribner, 2010), 33–36.

43. Fabian Franklin, *What Prohibition Has Done to America* (New York: Harcourt, Brace, 1922), 73; Kathleen Morgan Drowne, *Spirits of Defiance: National Prohibition and Jazz Age Literature* (Columbus: Ohio State University Press, 2005), 21–23; Rory McVeigh, *The Rise of the Ku Klux Klan: Right-Wing Movements and National Politics* (Minneapolis: University of Minnesota Press, 2009), 134–138; Christine Sismondo, *America Walks into a Bar: A Spirited History of Taverns and Saloons, Speakeasies and Grog Shops* (New York: Oxford University Press, 2011), 227–228.

44. Robert Eadie and Andrew S. Eadie, *Physiology and Hygiene for Children* (New York: University Publishing, 1904), 56–59; Sean Dennis Cashman, *Prohibition, the Lie of the Land* (New York: Free Press, 1981), 6; Edward Behr, *Prohibition: Thirteen Years That Changed America* (New York: Arcade, 1996), 59, 149; Okrent, *Last Call*, 51.

45. Thomas C. Cochran, *The Pabst Brewing Company* (New York: New York University Press, 1948), 302.

46. Behr, *Prohibition*, 148.

47. Richard J. Hooker, *A History of Food and Drink in America* (Indianapolis: Bobbs-Merrill, 1981), 342; Behr, *Prohibition*, 147.

48. "Hearings Before the Committee on Immigration and Naturalization," in *Deportation of Aliens Convicted of Violation of Narcotic and Prohibition* (Washington, D.C.: Government Printing Office, 1922), 545.

49. David W. Maurer, *Kentucky Moonshine* (Lexington: University Press of Kentucky, 2003), 85.

50. Louise Chipley Slavicek, *The Prohibition Era: Temperance in the United States* (New York: Chealsea House, 2009), 75; Behr, *Prohibition*, 222; "National Affairs: Poison," *Time*, January 10, 1926, http://www.time.com/time/magazine/article/0, 9171,881577,00.html (accessed July 10, 2011).

51. John Kobler, *Arden Spirits: The Rise and Fall of Prohibition* (Boston: Da Capo Press, 1993), 224; Behr, *Prohibition*, 87; Mabel Walker Willebrandt, *The Inside of Prohibition* (Indianapolis: Bobbs-Merrill, 1929), 170.

52. David E. Kyvig, "Women Against Prohibition," *American Quarterly* 28 (1976): 465–482.

53. John J. Riley, *A History of the American Soft Drink Industry: Bottled Carbonated Beverages, 1807–1957* (Washington, D.C.: American Bottlers of Carbonated Beverages, 1958), 139.

54. Harry Craddock, comp., *The Savoy Cocktail Book* (London: Constable, 1930); Patrick Gavin Duffy, *The Official Mixer's Manual* (New York: Long & Smith, 1934); Charles Browne, *The Gun Club Drink Book, Being a More or Less Discursive Account of Alcoholic Beverages, Their Formulae and Uses, Together with Some Observations on the Mixing of Drinks* (New York: Scribner, 1939).

55. Rorabaugh, *Alcoholic Republic*, 232.

12. Youth Beverages

1. "Keep Kool with Kool-Aid," *Boys' Life*, August 1939, 39.

2. Richard J. Hooker, *A History of Food and Drink in America* (Indianapolis, Bobbs-Merrill, 1981), 84, 179; Lyle Saxon and others, comps., *Gumbo Ya-Ya* (Boston: Houghton Mifflin, 1945), 172.

3. "New Beverage Advertised," *Printer's Ink*, April 15, 1915, 75; "Story of Delaware Punch Is More Than a Business Romance," *Lloyd's Magazine*, 1923, 9–12, http://www.delawarepunch.org (accessed July 27, 2011); Brooks Parker (grandson of Thomas E. Lyons), interview with author, July 28, 2011.

4. Hawaiian Punch, "History," http://www.hawaiianpunch.com/history.php (accessed June 10, 2012).

5. Dr Pepper Snapple Group, "Hawaiian Punch," http://www.drpeppersnapplegroup.com/brands/hawaiian-punch (accessed July 27, 2011).

6. "The New Drink Sensation," *Life*, November 7, 1949, 93; "Hi-C," *Life*, February 20, 1950, 119.

7. Mark Pendergrast, *For God, Country, and Coca-Cola: The Definitive History of the Great American Soft Drink and the Company That Makes It* (New York: Scribner, 1993), 297.

8. Ibid., 402; Gabriel Stricker, *Mao in the Boardroom: Marketing Genius from the Mind of the Master Guerrilla* (New York: St. Martin's Griffin, 2003), 47–51.

9. Sydney Finkelstein, *Why Smart Executives Fail: And What You Can Learn from Their Mistakes* (New York: Portfolio, 2003), 79–83; Robert F. Bruner and Arthur Levitt Jr., *Deals from Hell: M&A Lessons That Rise Above the Ashes* (Hoboken, N.J.: Wiley, 2009), 228–245.

10. Quoted in Marian Burros, "The Snapple Deal: How Sweet It Is," *New York Times*, September 17, 2003, http://www.nytimes.com/2003/09/17/dining/the-snapple-deal-how-sweet-it-is.html; Marion Nestle, *What to Eat: An Aisle-by-Aisle Guide to Savvy Food Choices and Good Eating* (New York: North Point Press, 2006), 326–327.

11. E. Melanie DuPuis, "The Body and the Country: A Political Ecology of Consumption," in *New Forms of Consumption: Consumers, Culture, and Commodification*, ed. Mark Gottdiener (Lanham, Md.: Rowman & Littlefield, 2000), 148–150.

12. *Ladies Home Journal*, October 1933, 58; "Where There's Pep, There's Iron," *Life*, November 3, 1941, 8.

13. "How 10 Seconds Changed Billy's Mind About Milk," *Life*, June 24, 1946, 123.

14. Anne Cooper Funderburg, *Chocolate, Strawberry, and Vanilla: A History of American Ice Cream* (Bowling Green, Ohio: Bowling Green State University Popular Press, 1995), 106–107.

15. Ray Kroc and Robert Anderson, *Grinding It Out: The Making of McDonald's* (Chicago: Regnery, 1977), 54–55, 63; Adam Ried and André Baranowski, *Thoroughly Modern Milkshakes* (New York: Norton, 2009), 15–16.

16. Kirk Perron and Stan Dembecki, *Jamba Juice Power: Smoothies and Juices for Mind, Body, and Spirit* (New York: Avery, 2004).

17. Darren Rovell, *First in Thirst: How Gatorade Turned the Science of Sweat into a Cultural Phenomenon* (New York: American Management Association, 2006), 17–21.

18. Ibid., 193–196.

19. David Noonan and Kevin Peraino, "Red Bull's Good Buzz," *Newsweek*, May 14, 2001, 39.

20. Barry D. Smith, *Caffeine and Activation Theory: Effects on Health and Behavior* (Boca Raton, Fla.: CRC Press, 2007), 32–33.

21. Ryan Corazza, "Energy Drinks the New Coffee?" *Weekend*, February 24, 2005, http://www.idsnews.com/news/weekend/Story.aspx?id=39803 (accessed July 20, 2011).

22. N. Pennington and others, "Energy Drinks: A New Health Hazard for Adolescents," *Journal of School Nursing* 26 (2010): 352–359.

23. Elizabeth Weise, "Petition Calls for FDA to Regulate Energy Drinks," *USA Today*, October 22, 2008, http://www.usatoday.com/news/health/2008-10-21-energy-drinks_ N.htm (accessed July 25, 2011).

24. N. Ranjit and others, "Dietary and Activity Correlates of Sugar-Sweetened Beverage Consumption Among Adolescents," *Pediatrics* 126 (2010): e754–e761; Sarah M. Seifert and others, "Health Effects of Energy Drinks on Children, Adolescents, and Young Adults," *Pediatrics* 127 (2011): 511–528; Committee on Nutrition and the Council on Sports Medicine and Fitness, "Sports Drinks and Energy Drinks for Children and Adolescents: Are They Appropriate?" *Pediatrics* 127 (2011): 1182–1189.

25. *The U.S. Beer Market: Impact Databank Review and Forecast* (New York: M. Shanken Communications, 2009), 533.

26. Michele Simon and James Mosher, *Alcohol, Energy Drinks, and Youth: A Dangerous Mix* (San Rafael, Calif.: Marin Institute; 2007), 6–8.

27. California Department of Alcohol and Drug Programs, "Alcoholic Energy Drinks," http://www.adp.ca.gov/youth/aed_index.shtml (accessed April 20, 2012).

13. Judgment of Paris

1. George M. Taber, *Judgment in Paris: California vs. France and the Historic 1976 Paris Tasting That Revolutionized Wine* (New York: Scribner, 2005), 155–158; Robert Finigan, *Corks and Forks: Thirty Years of Wine and Food* (Emeryville, Calif.: Shoemaker & Hoard, 2006), 120–125.

2. George M. Taber, "Modern Living: Judgment of Paris," *Time*, June 7, 1976, http://www.time.com/time/magazine/article/0,9171,947719,00.html (accessed June 10, 2012), and *Judgment of Paris*, 213.

3. Patrick E. McGovern, *Ancient Wine: The Search for the Origins of Viniculture* (Princeton, N.J.: Princeton University Press, 2003), 15.

4. Robert Beverley, "Of Edibles, Potables, and Fuel in Virginia," in *The History and Present State of Virginia,* ed. Louis Booker Wright (Chapel Hill: University of North Carolina Press, 1947), 133–136; Liberty Hyde Bailey, *Sketch of the Evolution of Our Native Fruits* (New York: Macmillan, 1898), 3, 12–13; Thomas Pinney, *A History of Wine in America*, vol. 2, *From Prohibition to the Present* (Berkeley: University of California Press, 1989), 14–24; John Hailman, *Thomas Jefferson on Wine* (Jackson: University Press of Mississippi, 2009).

5. Hugh Jones, "Of the Habits, Customs, Parts, Imployments, Trade," in *The Present State of Virginia*, ed. Richard L. Morton (Chapel Hill: University of North Carolina Press, 1956), 86.

6. Ibid.; *The Secret Diary of William Byrd of Westover, 1709–1712*, ed. Louis B. Wright and Marion Tinling (Richmond: Dietz Press, 1941), 188, 230, 359; J. P. Brissot de

Warville, "Letter XLI," in *New Travels in the United States of America, 1788*, ed. Durand Echeverria (Cambridge, Mass.: Belknap Press of Harvard University, 1964), 91.

7. John E. Wright and Doris S. Corbett, *Pioneer Life in Western Pennsylvania* (Pittsburgh: University of Pittsburgh Press, 1940), 60–61; Constantin-François de Volney, *View of the Climate and Soil of the United States of America* (London: Johnson, 1804), 288, 307.

8. William Bradford, footnote in response to letter written by Robert Cushman to Bradford, January 24, 1623, in *Bradford's History of Plymouth Plantation, 1606–1646*, ed. William T. Davis (New York: Scribner, 1908), 168.

9. Philip Alexander Bruce, *Economic History of Virginia in the Seventeenth Century* (New York: Macmillan, 1895), 2:221.

10. *Journal of Jasper Danckaerts, 1679–1680*, ed. Bartlett B. James and J. Franklin Jameson (New York: Scribner, 1913), 135.

11. E. C. Wines, *A Trip to Boston* (Boston: Little, Brown, 1838), 23; Harriet Martineau, *Society in America* (London: Saunders and Otley, 1836), 186.

12. Joe O'Connell, "History of Delmonico's Restaurant and Business Operations in New York," http://www.steakperfection.com/delmonico/history.html.

13. *Carte de Restaurant Français des Freres Delmonico* (New York: Wood, 1838), in Lately Thomas, *Delmonico's: A Century of Splendor* (Boston: Houghton Mifflin, 1967).

14. "California Wines," *Grape Culturist*, July 1870, 177–178; J. H. Beadle, *The Undeveloped West: Or, Five Years in the Territories* (Philadelphia: National, 1873), 270, 486, 660–661, 747; Vincent P. Carosso, *The California Wine Industry* (Berkeley: University of California Press, 1951), 76, 78, 87–89, 96; James Fullarton Muirhead, *The Land of Contrasts: A Briton's View of His American Kin* (London: Lane, 1902), 270–271; Richard J. Hooker, *A History of Food and Drink in America* (Indianapolis: Bobbs-Merrill, 1981), 279.

15. K. Dubois, "Wines and Brandies of California," *Report of the Committee on Awards of the World's Columbian Commission* (Washington, D.C.: Government Printing Office, 1901), 2:1043–1048.

16. Lyle Saxon and others, comps., *Gumbo Ya-Ya* (Boston: Houghton Mifflin, 1945), 172.

17. Joseph A. Dacus and James William Buel, *A Tour of St. Louis: Or, the Inside Life of a Great City* (St. Louis: Western Publishing, 1878), 478.

18. George Sala, *America Revisited: From the Bay of New York to the Gulf of Mexico, and from Lake Michigan to the Pacific* (London: Vizetelly, 1882), 1:100.

19. Ibid., 2:122.

20. "Consumption of Spirituous Beverages," *Medical Record* 58 (1900): 678; W. J. Rorabaugh, *The Alcoholic Republic: An American Tradition* (Oxford: Oxford University Press, 1979), 232.

21. United States Industrial Commission, *Report of the Industrial Commission on Immigration* (Washington, D.C.: Government Printing Office, 1901), 15:499.

22. Ibid., 15:xlix, 500–503; Thomas Pinney, *A History of Wine in America*, vol. 1, *From the Beginnings to Prohibition* (Berkeley: University of California Press, 2007), 327–331; Jack Florence, *Legacy of a Village: The Italian Swiss Colony Winery and People of Asti, California* (Phoenix, Ariz.: Raymond Court Press, 1999).

23. "Supplementary Brief of Italian Chamber of Commerce, New York, Relative to Duties on Wines and Spirits," in *Tariff Hearings Before the Committee on Ways and Means of the House of Representatives, December 10, 1908* (Washington, D.C.: Government Printing Office, 1908), 6207–6208; Rorabaugh, *Alcoholic Republic*, 232.

24. Carosso, *California Wine Industry*, 109–119; Christy Campbell, *Phylloxera: How Wine Was Saved for the World* (London: HarperCollins, 2004), xxxvi, 187–189, 261.

25. Andrew J. Jutkins, *Hand-book of Prohibition* (Chicago: McCabe, 1884), 137; Robert Smith Bader, *Prohibition in Kansas: A History* (Lawrence: University Press of Kansas, 1986), 1.

26. Norman H. Clark, *Deliver Us from Evil: An Interpretation of American Prohibition* (New York: Norton, 1976), 159.

27. "Threat to Increase Medicinal Contents of Preparations," *National Druggist* 50 (1920): 414; Leon D. Adams, *The Wines of America* (Boston: Houghton Mifflin, 1973), 24; Pinney, *History of Wine in America*, 2:10; Richard Mendelson, *From Demon to Darling: A Legal History of Wine in America* (Berkeley: University of California Press, 2009), 66–71.

28. Pinney, *History of Wine in America*, 2:18–20.

29. Ibid., 28–29; Iain Gately, *Drink: A Cultural History of Alcohol* (New York: Gotham Books, 2008), 282–283; Daniel Okrent, *Last Call: The Rise and Fall of Prohibition* (New York: Scribner, 2010), 346–347.

30. Elmer Holmes Davis, "What Can We Do About It? The Candid Misgivings of a Wet," *Harper's*, December 1928, 7.

31. *Report on the Enforcement of the Prohibition Laws of the United States* (Washington, D.C.: National Commission on Law Observance and Enforcement, 1931), 1:132; Clark Warburton, "Prohibition and Economic Welfare," *Annals of the American Academy of Political and Social Science* 163 (1932): 90; Andrew Sinclair, *Era of Excess: A Social History of the Prohibition Movement* (New York: Harper & Row, 1964), 206–208.

32. Rorabaugh, *Alcoholic Republic*, 232; Charles Lewis Sullivan, *A Companion to California Wine: An Encyclopedia of Wine and Winemaking* (Berkeley: University of California Press, 1998), 283.

33. Amy B. Trubek, *The Taste of Place: A Cultural Journey into Terroir* (Berkeley: University of California Press, 2008), 112.

34. Pinney, *History of Wine in America*, 2:99–105.

35. James Conaway, *Napa: The Story of an American Eden* (Boston: Houghton Mifflin, 1990), 191.

36. Pinney, *History of Wine in America*, 2:240.

37. Taber, *Judgment in Paris*, 213–224; Thane Peterson, "Moveable Feast," *Business Week*, May 8, 2001, http://www.businessweek.com/bwdaily/dnflash/may2001/nf20010058_228.htm.

38. Cathy Fisher, "Number of U.S. Wineries Reaches 6,223," *Wine Business Monthly*, February 15, 2010, http://www.winebusiness.com/wbm/?go=getArticle&dataId=72744 (accessed May 29, 2011).

39. Tyler Colman, e-mail to author, July 14, 2011.

40. Frank J. Prial, "Wine Talk, Italy Ranks First in Wine Drinking," *New York Times*, January 7, 1976, 44; Rorabaugh, *Alcoholic Republic*, 232.

41. Ernest Gallo and Julio Gallo, *Ernest and Julio: Our Story* (New York: Random House, 1994); Frank J. Prial, "Ernest Gallo, 97, Founder of Winery, Dies," *New York Times*, March 7, 2007.

14. The Only Proper Drink for Man

1. Bruce G. Posner, "Once Is Not Enough," in *The Best of Inc. Guide to Marketing and Selling* (New York: Prentice-Hall, 1988), 246–247.

2. Julia Moskin, "Must Be Something in the Water," *New York Times*, February 15, 2006, http://www.container-recycling.org/media/newsarticles/plastic/2006/2-16-NYT-MustBeSomething.htm.

3. "Talk of the Town," *New Yorker*, November 7, 1977, 46; Bernice Kanter, "A Run for the Money," *New York Magazine*, October 25, 1982, 22; Posner, "Once Is Not Enough," 247.

4. Constantin-François de Volney, *View of the Climate and Soil of the United States of America* (Philadelphia: Conrad, 1804), 323.

5. William Alcott, "Coffee," *Moral Reformer and Teacher on the Human Constitution* 1 (1835): 346.

6. Sylvester Graham, *Lectures of the Science of Human Life* (London: Horsell, Aldine Chambers, 1849), 274.

7. Richard W. Schwarz, *John Harvey Kellogg, M.D.* (Nashville, Tenn.: Southern Publication Association, 1970), 23.

8. Richard H. Shryock, "Sylvester Graham and the Popular Health Movement, 1830–1870," *Mississippi Valley Historical Review* 18 (1931): 180; William B. Walker, "The Health Reform Movement in the United States, 1830–1870," (Ph.D. diss., Johns Hopkins University, 1955), 198–202; Ronald L. Numbers, *Prophetess of Health: Ellen G. White and the Origins of Seventh-Day Adventist Health Reform* (Knoxville: University of Tennessee Press, 1992), 72–76.

9. Eugen Weber, *France; Fin de Siècle* (Cambridge, Mass.: Belknap Press of Harvard University Press, 1986), 183; George Weisz, *The Medical Mandarins: The French Academy of Medicine in the Nineteenth and Early Twentieth Century* (New York: Oxford University Press, 1995), 139.

10. William Leete Stone, *Reminiscences of Saratoga and Ballston* (New York: Virtue & Yorston, 1875), 296–297; Edmund Huling, "Saratoga in 1831," in *Huling's Saratoga Springs, Ballston Spa and Schuylerville Directory for 1882–83* (Saratoga Springs, N.Y., 1883), 32–33; Thomas A. Chambers, *Drinking the Waters: Creating an American Leisure Class at Nineteenth-Century Mineral Springs* (Washington, D.C.: Smithsonian Institution Press, 2002), 19; Francis H. Chapple, *Wellsprings: A Natural History of Bottled Spring Waters* (New Brunswick, N.J.: Rutgers University Press, 2005), 74.

11. George Jones Varney, *A Gazetteer of the State of Maine* (Boston: Russell, 1881), 453; "Poland Water," *Journal of Medicine and Science* 2 (1896): 695.

12. *Meyer Brothers Druggist*, May 1906, 4; "Mineral Waters," in *Nostrums and Quackery: Articles on the Nostrum Evil, and Quackery* (Chicago: Press of American Medical Association, 1911), 1:462–468; Don Fritschel, "Mineral Waters of the Green Mountain State," *Antique Bottle and Glass Collector*, http://www.glswrk-auction.com/contest-4.htm (accessed June 12, 2011).

13. Chapple, *Wellsprings*, 4.

14. *The Spectator* 93 (1904): 607; "French Natural Sparkling Table Water, Perrier," *Daily Mail*, June 12, 1905, 1.

15. "Perrier," *British Homoeopathic Review* 48 (1904): 510.

16. "Received Ex Recent Arrivals," *Daily Gleaner* (Jamaica), October 19, 1906, 8; "Random Jottings," *The Bystander* 19 (1908): 388; Eustace Alfred Reynolds-Ball, *The Tourist's India* (London: S. Sonnenschein, 1907), 322.

17. "Laboratory Notes," *Medical Press and Circular* 128 (1904) 680–681.

18. "American Athletes in England," *New York Times*, October 17, 1907, 10; "A Luxury from France," *New York Times*, October 22, 1907, 3; "The Chosen Table Water of Europe," *New York Times*, October 22, 1907, 6; "The Chosen Table Water of Europe," *New York Times*, November 21, 1907, 5.

19. *New York Times*, October 23, 1908, 6; *Life*, April 1, 1909, 415.

20. "France: Business Is Bubbling," *Time*, June 3, 1964, http://www.time.com/time/magazine/article/0,9171,940816,00.html (accessed April 20, 2012).

21. May Company advertisement, *Los Angeles Times*, December 15, 1929, 33.

22. Milton Moskowitz, *The Global Marketplace: 102 of the Most Influential Companies Outside America* (New York: Macmillan, 1987), 465.

23. "France: Business Is Bubbling."

24. Chapple, *Wellsprings*, 3–5, 15–16; Peter H. Gleick, *Bottled and Sold: The Story Behind Our Obsession with Bottled Water* (Washington, D.C.: Island Press, 2010), 28–29.

25. *CSA Super Markets*, July–September 1971, 258.

26. Gleick, *Bottled and Sold*, 1–13.

27. Hale N. Tongren, *Cases in Consumer Behavior*, 2nd ed. (Englewood Cliffs, N.J.: Prentice-Hall, 1992), 42.

28. Robert Tyrrell Davis, Harper W. Boyd, Jr., and Frederick E. Webster, Jr., *Marketing Management Casebook*, 3rd ed. (Homewood, Ill.: Irwin, 1980), 218.

29. Aljean Harmetz, "Bottled Water Battle Beginning on Coast: Change in Drinking Habits Poland Water's Lineage Snob Appeal vs. Price," *New York Times*, July 17, 1978, D4; John Sutton, *Sunk Costs and Market Structure: Price Competition, Advertising, and the Evolution of Concentration* (Cambridge, Mass.: MIT Press, 1991), 463–464; Tongren, *Cases in Consumer Behavior*, 42.

30. Elizabeth Royte, *Bottlemania: How Water Went on Sale and Why We Bought It* (New York: Bloomsbury, 2008), 33.

31. National Defense Resource Council, *Public Water Supply Distribution Systems* (New York: National Defense Resource Council, 2005); Royte, *Bottlemania*, 42.

32. "When the Bubble Burst," *Economist*, August 1991, 67–68.

33. "Perrier Pays New York $40,000 in Labeling Inquiry," *New York Times*, August 21, 1991, http://www.nytimes.com/1991/08/21/garden/perrier-pays-new-york-40000-in-labeling-inquiry.html (accessed June 10, 2011).

34. Bernice Kanner, *The 100 Best TV Commercials—and Why They Worked* (New York: Times Business, 1999), 65.

35. Royte, *Bottlemania*, 33.

36. Ibid., 86; Gleick, *Bottled and Sold*, 52.

37. Gleick, *Bottled and Sold*, 9.

38. "France: Business Is Bubbling."

39. Moskin, "Must Be Something in the Water."

40. Michael Blanding, *The Coke Machine: The Dirty Truth Behind the World's Favorite Soft Drink* (New York: Avery, 2010), 140–142.

41. David Schardt, "Water, Water Everywhere," *Nutrition Action*, June 2000, http://www.cspinet.org/nah/water/index.html (accessed June 13, 2011); National Defense Resource Council, *Public Water Supply Distribution Systems*; Royte, *Bottlemania*, 42.

42. Gleick, *Bottled and Sold*, 46–48.

43. Posner, "Once Is Not Enough," 25–26; Gleick, *Bottled and Sold*, 81.

44. John G. Rodwan, Jr., "Challenging Circumstances Persist: Future Growth Anticipated," at http://www.bottledwater.org/files/2009BWstats.pdf (accessed June 11, 2011).

45. Royte, *Bottlemania*, 39.

46. Elizabeth Royte, e-mail to author, July 16, 2011.

47. Posner, "Once Is Not Enough," 252; Kathryn Petras and Ross Petras, *Unusually Stupid Americans: A Compendium of All-American Stupidity* (New York: Villard, 2003), 195.

15. The Coffee Experience

1. Howard Schultz and Dori Jones Yang, *Pour Your Heart into It: How Starbucks Built a Company One Cup at a Time* (New York: Hyperion, 1997), 22–24.

2. Richard Mathews, *The Unlearned Alchymist His Antidote* (London: Printed for Ioseph Leigh, 1662).

3. Timothy Pitkin, *A Statistical View of the Commerce of the United States of America* (New York: James Eastburn, 1817), 167.

4. Steven Topik, "Coffee as a Social Drug," *Cultural Critique* 71 (2009): 95–96; Francis B. Thurber, *Coffee from Plantation to Cup*, 9th ed. (New York: American Grocer Publishing Association, 1884), 183–184.

5. J. D. B. De Bow, *The Industrial Resources, etc., of the Southern and Western States* (New Orleans: Debow's Review, 1853), 1:278–288; Thurber, *Coffee from Plantation to Cup*, 247.

6. John B. Billings, *Hard Tack and Coffee* (Boston: Smith, 1889), 130; Thurber, *Coffee from Plantation to Cup*, 247.

7. Maria Parloa and others, *Six Cups of Coffee* (Springfield, Mass.: Good Housekeeping Press, 1887).

8. "Virtues of Coffee," *North American Archives of Medical and Surgical Science* 2 (1835): 353.

9. William Alcott, "Coffee," *Moral Reformer and Teacher on the Human Constitution* 1 (1835): 344.

10. Sylvester Graham, *Lectures of the Science of Human Life* (London: Horsell, Aldine Chambers, 1849), 274.

11. John Harvey Kellogg, *The New Dietetics, What to Eat and How* (Battle Creek, Mich.: Modern Medicine, 1921), 451.

12. Nettie Leitch Major, *C. W. Post—The Hour and the Man: A Biography with Genealogical Supplement* (Washington, D.C.: Judd & Detweiller, 1963), 32.

13. Quoted in Mark Pendergrast, *Uncommon Grounds: The History of Coffee and How It Transformed Our World*, 2nd ed. (New York: Basic Books, 2010), 96.

14. Abram Wakeman, *History and Reminiscences of Lower Wall Street and Vicinity* (New York: Spice Mill, 1914), 89.

15. Arbuckle was not the first to package coffee in bags. That honor goes to Lewis A. Osborn and Thomas Reid, who marketed Osborn's Celebrated Prepared Java Coffee in the early 1860s. See "Mr. Lewis A. Osborn," *New York Times*, November 11, 1863.

16. John Arbuckle, US Patent 73,486, in *Annual Report of the Commissioner of Patents for the Year 1868* (Washington, D.C.: Government Printing Office, 1869), 1:520.

17. Francis L Fugate, *Arbuckles: The Coffee That Won the West* (El Paso: University of Texas at El Paso, 1994); Margaret E. Hale, "The Nineteenth-Century American Trade Card," *Business History Review* 74 (2000): 686.

18. Frederick Accum, *A Treatise on Adulterations of Food* (Philadelphia: Ab'm Small, 1820), 238–248.

19. Thurber, *Coffee from Plantation to Cup*, 162.

20. "Poison in Every Cup of Coffee," *New York Times*, May 3, 1884, 8; Marc T. Law, "The Origins of State Pure Food Regulation," *Journal of Economic History* 63 (2003): 1122.

21. I. W. Howerth, "The Coffee-house as a Rival of the Saloon," *American Magazine of Civics* 6 (1895): 590.

22. William H. Ukers, *All About Coffee*, 2nd ed. (New York: Tea and Coffee Trade Journal, 1935), 441; Pendergrast, *Uncommon Grounds*, 118.

23. Ukers, *All About Coffee*, 441.

24. *Consumption of Food in the United States, 1909–1952*, Handbook no. 62 (Washington, D.C.: U.S. Department of Agriculture, 1953), 241.

25. Peter Romeo, "The $6 Billion Gorilla: The Influence of the Seattle-based Coffeehouse Giant Is Evident in the Upgraded Decor, Beverages and Business Practices of Its Rivals," *Nations Restaurant News*, http://findarticles.com/p/articles/mi_m3190/is_5_41/ai_n27135985/?tag=mantle_skin;content (accessed April 22, 2011).

26. Mark Pendergrast, e-mail to author, July 25, 2011.

27. Joseph Michelli, *The Starbucks Experience: 5 Principles for Turning Ordinary Into Extraordinary* (New York: McGraw-Hill, 2007), 4.

28. Ted R. Lingle, "State of the Specialty Coffee Industry," *Tea and Coffee Trade Journal*, July 1, 2007, http://www.allbusiness.com/manufacturing/food-manufacturing-food-coffee-tea/4510403-1.html (accessed April 22, 2011).

29. V. Vishwanath and others, "The Starbucks Effect," *Harvard Business Review*, March–April 2000, 17–18.

Bibliography

General

Amerine, Maynard A., and Axel E. Borg. *A Bibliography on Grapes, Wines, Other Alcoholic Beverages, and Temperance: Works Published in the United States Before 1901*. Berkeley: University of California Press, 1996.

Amerine, Maynard A., and Herman Phaff, comps. *Bibliography of Publications by the Faculty, Staff, and Students, of the University of California, 1876–1980, on Grapes, Wines, and Related Subjects*. Berkeley: University of California Press, 1986.

Barr, Andrew. *Drink: A Social History of America*. New York: Carroll & Graf, 1999.

Burns, Eric. *The Spirits of America: A Social History of Alcohol*. Philadelphia: Temple University Press, 2004.

Emerson, Edward. *Beverages, Past and Present: An Historical Sketch of Their Production, Together with a Study of the Customs Connected with Their Use*. New York: Putnam, 1908.

Etkin, Nina L. *Foods of Association: Biocultural Perspectives on Foods and Beverages that Mediate Sociability*. Tucson: University of Arizona Press, 2009.

Hooker, Richard J. *A History of Food and Drink in America*. Indianapolis: Bobbs-Merrill, 1981.

Lender, Mark Edward, and James Kirby Martin. *Drinking in America: A History*. Rev. ed. New York: Free Press, 1987.

Murdock, Catherine Gilbert. *Domesticating Drink: Women, Men, and Alcohol in America, 1870–1940*. Baltimore: Johns Hopkins University Press, 1998.

Noling, A. W., comp. *Beverage Literature: A Bibliography.* Metuchen, N.J.: Scarecrow Press, 1971.

Pittman, David Joshua, and Charles R. Snyder, eds. *Society, Culture, and Drinking Patterns.* New York: Wiley, 1962.

Rumbarger, John J. *Profits, Power, and Prohibition: Alcohol Reform and the Industrializing of America, 1800–1930.* Albany: State University of New York Press, 1989.

Schlink. F. J. *Eat, Drink and Be Wary.* New York: Covici Friede, 1935.

Sismondo, Christine. *America Walks into a Bar: A Spirited History of Taverns and Saloons, Speakeasies and Grog Shops.* New York: Oxford University Press, 2011.

Standage, Tom. *A History of the World in Six Glasses.* New York: Walker, 2005.

Wilson, Ted, and Norman J. Temple, eds. *Beverages in Nutrition and Health.* Totowa, N.J.: Humana Press, 2004.

Prologue

Havard, V. "Drink Plants of the North American Indians." *Bulletin of the Torrey Botanical Club* 23 (1896): 33–46.

Hudson, Charles M., ed. *Black Drink: A Native American Tea.* Athens: University of Georgia Press, 1979.

Mancall, Peter C. *Deadly Medicine: Indians and Alcohol in Early America.* Ithaca, N.Y.: Cornell University Press, 1995.

Unrau, William E. *White Man's Wicked Water: The Alcohol Trade and Prohibition in Indian Country, 1802–1892.* Lawrence: University Press of Kansas, 1996.

Vogel, Virgil. *American Indian Medicine.* Norman: University of Oklahoma Press, 1970.

1. Colonial Diversity

Conroy, David W. *In Public Houses: Drink and the Revolution of Authority in Colonial Massachusetts.* Chapel Hill: University of North Carolina Press, 1995.

Grivetti, Louis E. *Chocolate: History, Culture, and Heritage.* Hoboken, N.J.: Wiley, 2009.

McCusker, John James. "The Rum Trade and the Balance of Payments of the Thirteen Continental Colonies, 1650–1775." Ph.D. diss., University of Pittsburgh, 1970.

McWilliams, James E. *A Revolution in Eating: How the Quest for Food Shaped America.* New York: Columbia University Press, 2005.

Meacham, Sarah Hand. *Every Home a Distillery: Alcohol, Gender, and Technology in the Colonial Chesapeake.* Baltimore: Johns Hopkins University Press, 2009.

Miller, John C. *The First Frontier: Life in Colonial America.* Lanham, Md.: University Press of America, 1966.

Ulrich, Laurel Thatcher. *Good Wives: Image and Reality in the Lives of Women in Northern New England, 1650–1750.* New York: Vintage Books, 1991.

Woolsey, David Alan. *Libations of the Eighteenth Century: A Concise Manual for the Brewing of Authentic Beverages from the Colonial Era of America and Times Past.* Boca Raton, Fla.: Universal, 2002.

2. An Essential Ingredient in American Independence

Bergeron, Victor J. *Trader Vic's Rum Cookery and Drinkery.* Garden City, N.Y.: Doubleday, 1974.

Coulombe, Charles. *Rum: The Epic Story of the Drink That Conquered the World.* New York: Citadel Press, 2004.

Curtis, Wayne. *And a Bottle of Rum: A History of the New World in Ten Cocktails.* New York: Crown, 2006.

Foss, Richard. *Rum: A Global History.* London: Reaktion Books, 2012.

Furnas, J. C. *The Life and Times of the Late Demon Rum.* London: Allen, 1965.

Hawkes, Alex D. *The Rum Cookbook.* New York: Drake, 1972.

McCusker, John James. "The Rum Trade and the Balance of Payments of the Thirteen Continental Colonies, 1650–1775." Ph.D. diss., University of Pittsburgh, 1970.

Ostrander, Gilman M. "The Making of the Triangular Trade Myth." *William and Mary Quarterly,* 3rd ser., 30 (1973): 635–644.

Smith, Frederick H. *Caribbean Rum: A Social and Economic History.* Gainesville: University Press of Florida, 2008.

Stephen, John. *A Treatise on the Manufacture, Imitation, Adulteration, and Reduction of Foreign Wines, Brandies, Gins, Rums, etc. etc.* Philadelphia: Published for the Author, 1860.

Thompson, Peter. *Rum Punch and Revolution: Taverngoing and Public Life in Eighteenth-Century Philadelphia.* Philadelphia: University of Pennsylvania Press, 1999.

Williams, Ian. *Rum: A Social and Sociable History of the Real Spirit of 1776.* New York: Nation Books, 2005.

3. Tea Parties

Alcott, William A. *Tea and Coffee.* Boston: Light, 1839.

Anderson, Avis H. *A&P: The Story of the Great Atlantic & Pacific Tea Company.* Charleston, S.C.: Arcadia, 2002.

Carp, Benjamin L. *Defiance of the Patriots: The Boston Tea Party and the Making of America.* New Haven, Conn.: Yale University Press, 2010.

Drake, Francis Samuel. *Tea Leaves: Being a Collection of Letters and Documents Relating to the Shipment of Tea to the American Colonies in the Year 1773, by the East India Tea Company.* Detroit: Singing Tree Press, 1970.

Levinson, Marc. *The Great A&P and the Struggle for Small Business in America.* New York: Hill and Wang, 2011.

Martin, Laura C. *Tea: The Drink That Changed the World.* Rutland, Vt.: Tuttle, 2007.

Ukers, William H. *All About Tea.* New York: Tea and Coffee Trade Journal, 1935.

Unger, Harlow Giles. *American Tempest: How the Boston Tea Party Sparked a Revolution.* Cambridge, Mass.: Da Capo Press, 2011.

Vaccaro, Pamela J. *Beyond the Ice Cream Cone: The Whole Scoop on Food at the 1904 World's Fair.* St. Louis: Enid Press, 2004.

Whitaker, Jan. *Tea at the Blue Lantern Inn: A Social History of the Tea Room Craze in America.* New York: St. Martin's Press, 2002.

4. Tarantula Juice

Carson, Gerald. *The Social History of Bourbon: An Unhurried Account of Our Star-Spangled American Drink.* New York: Dodd, Mead, 1963.

Crowgey, Henry G. *Kentucky Bourbon: The Early Years of Whiskeymaking.* Lexington: University of Kentucky Press, 2008.

Hogeland, William. *The Whiskey Rebellion: George Washington, Alexander Hamilton, and the Frontier.* New York: Scribner, 2006.

Hopkins, Kate. *99 Drams of Whiskey: The Accidental Hedonist's Quest for the Perfect Shot and the History of the Drink.* New York: St. Martin's Press, 2009.

Kosar, Kevin. *Whiskey: A Global History.* London: Reaktion Books, 2010.

Richards, Leonard L. *Shay's Rebellion; The American Revolution's Final Battle.* Philadelphia: University of Pennsylvania Press, 2002.

Slaughter, Thomas P. *The Whiskey Rebellion: Frontier Epilogue to the American Revolution.* New York: Oxford University Press, 1986.

5. Cider's Last Hurrah

Chapman, Thomas. *The Cyder-maker's Instructor, Sweet-maker's Assistant, and Victualler's and Housekeeper's Director.* Boston: Green & Russell, 1762.

French, R. K. *The History and Virtues of Cyder.* New York: St. Martin's Press, 1982.

Means, Howard. *Johnny Appleseed: The Man, the Myth, the American Story.* New York: Simon & Schuster, 2011.

Weiss, Harry B. *The History of Applejack or Apple Brandy in New Jersey from Colonial Times to the Present.* Trenton: New Jersey Agricultural Society, 1954.

6. The Most Popular Drink of the Day

Ade, George. *The Old-Time Saloon.* New York: Long & Smith, 1931.

Baron, Stanley. *Brewed in America: A History of Beer and Ale in the United States.* Boston: Little, Brown, 1962.

Baum, Dan. *Citizen Coors: A Grand Family Saga of Business, Politics, and Beer*. New York: Morrow, 2000.

Cochran, Thomas C. *The Pabst Brewing Company*. New York: New York University Press, 1948.

Duis, Perry. *The Saloon: Public Drinking in Chicago and Boston, 1880–1920*. Urbana: University of Illinois Press, 1999.

Herbst, Henry, Don Roussin, and Kevin Kious. *St. Louis Brews: 200 Years of Brewing in St. Louis, 1809–2009*. St. Louis: Reedy Press, 2009.

Hernon, Peter. *Under the Influence: The Unauthorized Story of the Anheuser-Busch Dynasty*. New York: Simon & Schuster, 1991.

Holian, Timothy J. *Over the Barrel: The Brewing History and Beer Culture of Cincinnati, 1800 to the Present*. St. Joseph, Mo.: Sudhaus Press, 2000.

MacIntosh, Julie. *Dethroning the King: The Hostile Takeover of Anheuser-Busch, an American Icon*. Hoboken, N.J.: Wiley, 2011.

Miller, Eoghan P. "St. Louis's German Brewing Industry: Its Rise and Fall." Ph.D. diss., University of Missouri, Columbia, 2008.

Mittelman, Amy. *Brewing Battles: The History of American Beer*. New York: Algora, 2007.

Noon, Mark A. *Yuengling: A History of America's Oldest Brewery*. Jefferson, N.C.: McFarland, 2005.

Ogle, Maureen. *Ambitious Brew: The Story of American Beer*. Orlando, Fla.: Harcourt, 2006.

Plavchan, Ronald. "A History of Anheuser-Busch." Ph.D. diss., St. Louis University 1960.

Powers, Madelon. *Faces Along the Bar: Lore and Order in the Workingman's Saloon, 1870–1920*. Chicago: University of Chicago Press, 1998.

Rose, Bob, and Jean Buchanan. *Anheuser-Busch, the King's Reign: The History of the Brewery in St. Louis*. St. Louis: St. Louis Post-Dispatch Books, 2008.

Salem, Frederick William. *Beer, Its History and Its Economic Value as a National Beverage*. Hartford, Conn.: Salem, 1880.

Skilnik, Bob. *The History of Beer and Brewing in Chicago, 1833–1978*. St. Paul, Minn.: Pogo Press, 1999.

Smith, Gregg. *Beer in America: The Early Years, 1587–1840: Beer's Role in the Settling of America and the Birth of a Nation*. Boulder, Colo.: Siris Books, 1998.

West, Elliot. *Saloon on Rocky Mountain Mining Frontier*. Lincoln: University of Nebraska Press, 1979.

Yenne, Bill. *American Brewery: From Colonial Evolution to Microbrew Revolution*. St. Paul, Minn.: MBI, 2003.

7. Nature's Perfect Food

Catherwood, M. P. *A Statistical Study of Milk Production for the New York Market*. Ithaca, N.Y.: Cornell University Agricultural Experiment Station, 1931.

Cohen, Robert. *Milk: The Deadly Poison*. Englewood Cliffs, N.J.: Argus, 1998.

Dillon, John J. *Seven Decades of Milk: A History of New York's Dairy Industry*. New York: Orange Judd, 1941.

DuPuis, E. Melanie. *Nature's Perfect Food: How Milk Became America's Drink*. New York: New York University Press, 2002.

Engs, Ruth Clifford. *Clean Living Movements: American Cycles of Health Reform*. Westport, Conn.: Praeger, 2001.

Freidberg, Susanne. *Fresh: A Perishable History*. Cambridge, Mass.: Belknap Press of Harvard University Press, 2009.

Gottdiener, Mark. *New Forms of Consumption: Consumers, Culture, and Commodification*. Lanham, Md.: Rowman & Littlefield, 2000.

Hartley, Robert Milham. *An Historical, Scientific, and Practical Essay on Milk, as an Article of Human Sustenance: With a Consideration of the Effects Consequent Upon the Present Unnatural Methods of Producing It for the Supply of Large Cities*. New York: Leavitt, 1842.

Mendelson, Anne. *Milk: The Surprising Story of Milk Through the Ages*. New York: Knopf, 2008.

Meckel, Richard A. *Save the Babies: American Public Health Reform and the Prevention of Infant Mortality*. Ann Arbor: University of Michigan Press, 1998.

Mullaly, John. *The Milk Trade of New York and Vicinity Giving an Account of the Sale of Pure and Adulterated Milk*. New York: Fowlers and Wells, 1853.

Parker, Horatio Newton. *City Milk Supply*. New York: McGraw-Hill, 1917.

Patton, Stuart. *Milk: Its Remarkable Contribution to Human Health and Well-being*. New Brunswick, N.J.: Transaction, 2004.

Pirtle, T. R. *History of the Dairy Industry*. Chicago: Mojonnier, 1926.

Rimas, Andrew, and Evan D. G. Fraser. *Beef: The Untold Story of How Milk, Meat, and Muscle Shaped the World*. New York: Morrow, 2008.

Roadhouse, Chester Linwood, and James L. Henderson. *The Market-Milk Industry*, 2nd ed. New York: McGraw-Hill, 1950.

Spencer, Leland, and Charles J. Blanford. *An Economic History of Milk Marketing and Pricing: A Classified Bibliography with Reviews of Listed Publications, 1840–1970*. Columbus, Ohio: Grid, 1973.

Walker, Harlan, ed. *Milk: Beyond the Dairy: Proceedings of the Oxford Symposium on Food and Cookery, 1999*. Totnes, Eng.: Prospect Books, 2000.

Walker, William B. "The Health Reform Movement in the United States, 1830–1870." Ph.D. diss., Johns Hopkins University, 1955.

8. The Most Delightful and Insinuating Potations

Boothby, William T. *Cocktail Boothby's American Bartender: The New Anchor Distilling Edition*. San Francisco: Anchor Distilling, 2009.

Carlin, Joseph. *Cocktail: A Global History*. London: Reaktion Books, 2012.

Conrad, Barnaby. *The Martini: An Illustrated History of an American Classic*. San Francisco: Chronicle Books, 1995.

Curtis, Wayne. *And a Bottle of Rum: A History of the New World in Ten Cocktails*. New York: Crown, 2006.

DeGroff, Dale. *The Craft of the Cocktail*. New York: Clarkson Potter, 2002.

Grimes, William. *Straight Up or On the Rocks: The Story of the American Cocktail*. New York: North Point Press, 2001.

Hamilton, Carl. *Absolut: Biography of a Bottle*. New York: Texere, 2000.

Himelstein, Linda. *The King of Vodka: The Story of Pyotr Smirnov and the Upheaval of an Empire*. New York: Harper, 2009.

Marlowe, Tommy. *"The Repeal": A Cocktail Guide: Formulas for Preparation of Cocktails, Fizzes and Punches*. San Francisco: Marlowe, 1933.

Miller, Anistatia, and Jared Brown. *Spirituous Journey: A History of Drink*. Book 2, *From Publicans to Master Mixologists*. London: Mixellany, 2009.

Parsons, Brad Thomas. *Bitters: A Spirited History of a Classic Cure-All, with Cocktails, Recipes, and Formulas*. Berkeley: Ten Speed Press, 2011.

Solmonson, Lesley Jacobs. *Gin: A Global History*. London: Reaktion Books, 2012.

Wondrich, David. *Imbibe! From Absinthe Cocktail to Whiskey Smash, a Salute in Stories and Drinks to "Professor" Jerry Thomas, Pioneer of the American Bar*. New York: Perigee, 2007.

Wondrich, David. *Punch: The Delights (and Dangers) of the Flowing Bowl*. New York: Penguin, 2010.

9. Unfermented Wine

Alamillo, José M. *Making Lemonade Out of Lemons: Mexican American Labor and Leisure in a California Town, 1880–1960*. Urbana: University of Illinois Press, 2006.

Carpenter, Kenneth J. *The History of Scurvy and Vitamin C*. New York: Cambridge University Press, 1986.

Chazanof, William. *Welch's Grape Juice: From Corporation to Co-operative*. Syracuse, N.Y.: Syracuse University Press, 1977.

Hamilton, Alissa. *Squeezed: What You Don't Know About Orange Juice*. New Haven, Conn.: Yale University Press, 2009.

Hopkins, James T. *Fifty Years of Citrus: The Florida Citrus Exchange, 1909–1959*. Gainesville: University of Florida Press, 1960.

Kirkman, C. H., Jr. *The Sunkist Adventure*. Washington, D.C.: Farmer Cooperative Service, U.S. Department of Agriculture, 1975.

Merlo, Catherine. *Heritage of Gold: The First 100 Years of the Sunkist Growers, Inc., 1893–1993*. Los Angeles: Sunkist Growers, 1993.

Moses, H. Vincent. "G. Harold Powell and the Corporate Consolidation of the Modern Citrus Enterprise, 1904–1922." *Business History Review* 69 (1995): 119–155.

Sackman, Douglas Cazaux. *Orange Empire: California and the Fruits of Eden*. Berkeley: University of California Press, 2005.

10. The Temperance Beverage

Allen, Frederick. *Secret Formula: How Brilliant Marketing and Relentless Salesmanship Made Coca-Cola the Best-Known Product in the World*. New York: HarperBusiness, 1994.

Blanding, Michael. *The Coke Machine: The Dirty Truth Behind the World's Favorite Soft Drink*. New York: Avery, 2010.

Dubelle, G. H., ed. *Soda Fountain Beverages: A Practical Receipt Book for Druggists, Chemists, Confectioners and Venders of Soda Water*. 2nd ed. New York: Spon & Chamberlain, 1901.

Hays, Constance L. *The Real Thing: Truth and Power at the Coca-Cola Company*. New York: Random House, 2005.

Kahn, E. J., Jr. *The Big Drink: The Story of Coca-Cola*. New York: Random House, 1960.

Louis, J. C., and Harvey Yazijian. *The Cola Wars: The Story of the Global Corporate Battle Between the Coca-Cola Company and PepsiCo*. New York: Everest House, 1980.

MacMahon, Albert C. *MacMahon's Latest Recipes and American Soda Water Dispenser's Guide: A Complete Compilation*. Chicago: Goodall & Loveless, 1893.

Merlo, Catherine. "The Beverage Battle." *Dairy Today*, June 7, 2005.

Pendergrast, Mark. *For God, Country, and Coca-Cola: The Definitive History of the Great American Soft Drink and the Company That Makes It*. New York: Scribner, 2000.

Riley, John J. *A History of the American Soft Drink Industry. Bottled Carbonated Beverages, 1807–1957*. Washington, D.C.: American Bottlers of Carbonated Beverages, 1958.

Rodengen, Jeffrey L. *The Legend of Dr. Pepper/Seven-up*. Fort Lauderdale, Fla.: Write Stuff Syndicate, 1995.

Siler, Julia Flynn. *The House of Mondavi: The Rise and Fall of an American Wine Dynasty*. New York: Gotham Books, 2007.

Witzel, Michael Karl, and Gyvel Young-Witzel. *Soda Pop: From Miracle Medicine to Pop Culture*. Stillwater, Minn.: Town Square Books, 1998.

11. To Root Out a Bad Habit

Asbury, Herbert. *The Great Illusion: An Informal History of Prohibition*. Garden City, N.Y.: Doubleday, 1950.

Behr, Edward. *Prohibition: Thirteen Years That Changed America*. New York: Arcade, 1996.

Beyer, Mark. *Temperance and Prohibition: The Movement to Pass Anti-liquor Laws in America*. New York: Rosen, 2006.

Blocker, Jack S. *American Temperance Movements: Cycles of Reform*. Boston: Twayne, 1989.

Gusfield, Joseph R. *Symbolic Crusade: Status Politics and the American Temperance Movement*. 2nd ed. Urbana: University of Illinois Press, 1986.

Haworth, Alan, and Ronald Simpson, eds. *Moonshine Markets: Issues in Unrecorded Alcohol Beverage Production and Consumption*. New York: Brunner-Routledge, 2004.

Hendricks, Edwin. *Liquor and Anti-Liquor in Virginia*. Durham, N.C.: Duke University Press, 1967.

Hirschfeld, Al. *The Speakeasies of 1932*. Milwaukee: Young, 2003.

Hogan, Charles Marshall. "Wayne B. Wheeler: Single Issue Exponent (Prohibition, Anti-Saloon League, Ohio, Pressure Groups)." Ph.D. diss., University of Cincinnati, 1986.

Kerr, K. Austin. *Organized for Prohibition: A New History of the Anti-Saloon League*. New Haven, Conn.: Yale University Press, 1985.

Kobler, John. *Arden Spirits: The Rise and Fall of Prohibition*. Boston: Da Capo Press, 1993.

Maurer, David W. *Kentucky Moonshine*. Lexington: University Press of Kentucky, 2003.

Odegard, Peter H. *Pressure Politics: The Story of The Anti-Saloon League*. New York: Columbia University Press, 1928.

Okrent, Daniel. *Last Call: The Rise and Fall of Prohibition*. New York: Scribner, 2010.

Rowley, Matthew B. *The Joy of Moonshine!* New York: Lark Books, 2007.

Sinclair, Andrew. *Era of Excess: A Social History of the Prohibition Movement*. New York: Harper & Row, 1964.

Slavicek, Louise Chipley. *The Prohibition Era: Temperance in the United States*. New York: Chelsea House, 2008.

Worth, Richard. *Teetotalers and Saloon Smashers: The Temperance Movement and Prohibition*. Berkeley Heights, N.J.: Enslow, 2009.

Unrau, William E. *White Man's Wicked Water: The Alcohol Trade and Prohibition in Indian Country, 1802–1892*. Lawrence: University Press of Kansas, 1996.

12. Youth Beverages

Peters, Tyler. *Energy Drinks, the New Age Beverage*. Monroe, Wis.: Mountain Crest, 2009.

Rovell, Darren. *First in Thirst: How Gatorade Turned the Science of Sweat into a Cultural Phenomenon*. New York: American Management Association, 2006.

The 2009–2014 World Outlook for Sports and Energy Drinks. San Diego: ICON Group International, 2008.

13. Judgment of Paris

Amerine, Maynard A., and Axel E. Borg. *A Bibliography on Grapes, Wines, Other Alcoholic Beverages, and Temperance: Works Published in the United States Before 1901.* Berkeley: University of California Press, 1996.

Amerine, Maynard A., and Vernon L. Singleton. *A List of Bibliographies and a Selected List of Publications That Contain Bibliographies on Grapes, Wines, and Related Subjects.* Oakland: Agricultural Experiment Station, University of California, 1923.

Amerine, Maynard A., and Louise B. Wheeler. *A Checklist of Books and Pamphlets on Grapes and Wine and Related Subjects, 1938–1948.* Berkeley: University of California Press, 1951.

Beyer, Mark. *Temperance and Prohibition: The Movement to Pass Anti-liquor Laws in America.* New York: Rosen, 2006.

Buchanan, Robert. *The Culture of the Grape and Wine-Making.* 5th ed. Cincinnati: Moore Anderson, 1854.

Campbell, Christy. *Phylloxera: How Wine Was Saved for the World.* London: HarperCollins, 2004.

Cass, Bruce, ed. *The Oxford Companion to the Wines of North America.* New York: Oxford University Press, 2000.

Conaway, James. *Napa: The Story of an American Eden.* Boston: Houghton Mifflin, 1990.

Fuller, Robert C. *Religion and Wine: A Cultural History of Wine Drinking in the United States.* Knoxville: University of Tennessee Press, 1996.

Haraszthy, Arpad. *Wine-Making in California.* San Francisco: Book Club of California, 1978.

McCoy, Elin. *The Emperor of Wine: The Rise of Robert M. Parker, Jr., and the Reign of American Taste.* New York: Ecco, 2005.

Mendelson, Richard. *From Demon to Darling: A Legal History of Wine in America.* Berkeley: University of California Press, 2009.

Pinney, Thomas. *A History of Wine in America.* Vol. 1, *From the Beginnings to Prohibition.* Berkeley: University of California Press, 2007.

Pinney, Thomas. *A History of Wine in America.* Vol. 2, *From Prohibition to the Present.* Berkeley: University of California Press, 1989.

Sullivan, Charles L. *Napa Wine: A History.* San Francisco: Wine Appreciation Guild, 1994.

Taber, George M. *Judgment of Paris: California vs. France and the Historic 1976 Paris Tasting That Revolutionized Wine.* New York: Scribner, 2005.

14. The Only Proper Drink for Man

Chambers, Thomas A. *Drinking the Waters: Creating an American Leisure Class at Nineteenth-Century Mineral Springs.* Washington, D.C.: Smithsonian Institution Press, 2002.

Chapple, Francis H. *Wellsprings: A Natural History of Bottled Spring Waters.* New Brunswick, N.J.: Rutgers University Press, 2005.

Clarke, Tony. *Inside the Bottle: An Exposé of the Bottled Water Industry.* 2nd ed. Ottawa: Canadian Centre for Policy Alternatives, 2007.

Corbett, Theodore. *The Making of American Resorts: Saratoga Springs, Ballston Spa, and Lake George.* New Brunswick, N.J.: Rutgers University Press, 2001.

Gleick, Peter H. *Bottled and Sold: The Story Behind Our Obsession with Bottled Water.* Washington, D.C.: Island Press, 2010.

Royte, Elizabeth. *Bottlemania: How Water Went on Sale and Why We Bought It.* New York: Bloomsbury, 2008.

15. The Coffee Experience

Alcott, William A. *Tea and Coffee.* Boston: Light, 1839.

Cheney, Ralph Holt. *Coffee: A Monograph of the Economic Species of the Genus Coffea L.* New York: New York University Press, 1925.

Conroy, David. *In Public Houses: Drink and the Revolution of Authority in Colonial Massachusetts.* Chapel Hill: University of North Carolina Press, 1995.

Parloa, Maria, and others. *Six Cups of Coffee.* Springfield, Mass.: Good Housekeeping Press, 1887.

Pendergrast, Mark. *Uncommon Grounds: The History of Coffee and How It Transformed Our World.* New York: Basic Books, 2010.

Schultz, Howard, and Dori Jones Yang. *Pour Your Heart into It: How Starbucks Built a Company One Cup at a Time.* New York: Hyperion, 1997.

Schultz, Howard, with Joanne Gordon. *Onward: How Starbucks Fought for Its Life Without Losing Its Soul.* New York: Rodale, 2011.

Ukers, William H. *All About Coffee.* 2nd ed. New York: Tea and Coffee Trade Journal, 1935.

Ukers, William H. *Coffee Facts.* New York: Tea and Coffee Trade Journal, 1954.

Index

Arts and Traditions of the Table: Perspectives on Culinary History

ALBERT SONNENFELD, SERIES EDITOR